MW01037336

AMERICAN DIPLOMATS

"William Morgan and Charles Stuart Kennedy provide a comprehensive look into the professional lives of America's diplomats. Their insights and the wide range of venues and experiences they cover will enlighten anyone, veteran or newcomer, with an interest in diplomacy."

—Ambassador Ruth A. Davis, former Director General of the U.S. Foreign Service and U.S. Ambassador to Benin

"The authors of *American Diplomats*, both veteran Foreign Service officers, have drawn expertly on the oral history collection of the Association for Diplomatic Studies and Training to produce an outstanding introduction to America's diplomacy and to the extraordinarily varied roles our diplomats play in defending American interests around the globe."

—Ambassador Samuel W. Lewis, past president of the U.S. Institute of Peace and former U.S. Ambassador to Israel

AMERICAN DIPLOMATS

❖

The Foreign Service at Work

Edited by
William D. Morgan
and
Charles Stuart Kennedy

Memoirs and Occasional Papers
Association for Diplomatic Studies and Training

iUniverse, Inc.
New York Lincoln Shanghai

AMERICAN DIPLOMATS
The Foreign Service at Work

iUniverse, Inc.

For information address:
iUniverse, Inc.
2021 Pine Lake Road, Suite 100
Lincoln, NE 68512
www.iuniverse.com

Cover photo: Entrance gate to U.S. Embassy, Jakarta, Indonesia, 1959. Department of State photo.

ISBN: 0-595-32974-8

Printed in the United States of America

Contents

Foreword

Diplomats provide the first line of America's defense as they help formulate and implement our country's foreign policy. Too often, the stories of their experiences and insights remain untold. In 2003, the Association for Diplomatic Studies and Training (ADST) created the Memoirs and Occasional Papers Series to preserve such firsthand accounts and other informed observations on foreign affairs for both the scholar and the general reader.

Sponsoring publication of the series is one of numerous ways in which ADST, a nonprofit organization founded in 1986, seeks to promote understanding of American diplomacy. Along with its activities in support of training foreign affairs personnel at the State Department's Foreign Service Institute, these efforts constitute the fundamental purposes of ADST.

American Diplomats is the second book in this new series. Editors WILLIAM D. MORGAN and CHARLES STUART KENNEDY have selected forty accounts of the experiences of American diplomats during the period 1920–1997. The editors, both former senior Foreign Service officers, also set the stories in their historical context.

Drawn from some 1400 recorded oral histories, these first-person accounts convey the wide array of situations—including incidents of terror—with which diplomats are faced and to which they must react. They also demonstrate the important proactive role American diplomats play in influencing the course of events in the world.

ADST is pleased to make *American Diplomats* available through its Memoirs and Occasional Papers Series.

Kenneth L. Brown
President
Association for Diplomatic Studies and Training
Arlington, Virginia
August 2004

Preface

What do American diplomats and consuls, also called Foreign Service officers (FSOs), do for a living? What are their professional responsibilities? How do they carry them out? Who instructs them?

Drawing on their personal recollections and experiences given mostly in oral history interviews, retired FSOs describe their lives, work, ideas, and accomplishments. This book is based on excerpts from interviews. It is an informal, "how it was done" history of the United States' human activities in foreign affairs, told from the vantage point of those who served the nation as a profession. These stories are limited to the period since the early 1920s, around the time (1924) when the United States Foreign Service was created out of the diplomatic and consular services.

The editors provide brief, italicized background remarks before each oral history extract. Chapter One's introductory pages lay out an historical context, which outlines serious institutional fractures and inefficiencies in the first one hundred fifty years of American diplomatic and consular services. They describe the establishment of the Foreign Service of the United States. Throughout the chapters, the editors have also, in italics, added background texts of historical and institutional material applicable to subsequent periods.

The oral history interviews were conducted under the auspices of the not-for-profit Association for Diplomatic Studies and Training. The full texts of these interviews can be read at the Lauinger Library of Georgetown University, Washington, DC, or on a CD-ROM, which can be purchased through ADST at the Web site: www.ADST.org.

William D. Morgan and Charles Stuart Kennedy
August 2004

Acknowledgments

The authors wish to thank the following people who helped in bringing this book together through their reading and editing of the manuscript. In alphabetical order: Matthew Bandyk, Ambassador Kenneth L. Brown, Ann Calanni, Dr. Stephen Grant, Stacey Hohl, Dr. Donald Hook, Isabelle Levy, Consul General Michael M. Mahoney, Jessica D. Puglisi, Ambassador William E. Ryerson, Nina Robbins, and Margery Thompson. Also, the authors are extremely grateful for the support given them by the Association for Diplomatic Studies and Training.

1

The Beginning Years

✦

Historical Setting

To understand better and more fully the experiences of the Foreign Service Officers interviewed in this account, it is worth knowing the realities of the pre-1924 years of American foreign affairs. The years since then have brought significant improvements, but old and new issues still overlap. No profession, including the Foreign Service, is ever legally or administratively fully set right. Some of the issues still relevant to the Foreign Service institution can be read in the remarks of the FSOs interviewed.

The creation of the Foreign Service in 1924, with the enactment of the Rogers Act, was part of a gradual evolution in the United States of taking public service out of the political process and making government service more efficient and rewarding. Though both the Diplomatic and Consular Services were entered by a degree of competitive examinations beginning in 1906, they had developed quite independently and unequally.

The demands on the Consular Service principally involved regulating and promoting trade and protecting American citizens abroad. It had a strong and independent structure in the Department of State, run for years by Wilbur J. Carr (1870–1942), who had excellent connections with Congress. From the beginning of the twentieth century, there was an established consular promotion system as well as a corps of roving inspectors to monitor the quality of service.

The Diplomatic Service, on the other hand, did not have such cohesiveness or structure. Rather, each geographic bureau in the Department of State—Europe, Latin America, the Near East, and Asia—was responsible for the assignment of and direction to its diplomatic officers. There were not enough independent countries to warrant a bureau for Africa. Colonies were dealt with through U.S. consulates.

1

Since the Wilson Administration in 1913, ambassadors were almost exclusively political appointees of varying competence. Prior to that, there had been ambassadors, appointed and re-appointed by administrations in power, who had various degrees of experience. Diplomatic officers had no well-defined promotion system and were dependent on the goodwill of their politically appointed ambassadors or ministers to move ahead. There was no inspection system.

Duplication in services and resources existed between the two corps. Often each would have separate buildings and offices in foreign capitals. Out-of-capital consulate establishments were solely consular-service run, and there was little, if any, coordination with the Embassy. When assigned in capitals, the two staffs did not necessarily work together, share their contacts or experiences, or mix socially. The American public was not well served by this fractured and often demoralizing system which existed prior to the Rogers Act.

In the America of the first quarter of the twentieth century, social distinctions carried far greater weight than they would in later years. Congress was well aware of this reality at posts abroad, and was not sympathetic to such social distinctions. The author of the Rogers Act, John Jacob Rogers, was clear about this:

> One of the most intolerable things that I have come across in connection with inquiries into the foreign service is the fact that some of the little secretaries who have the background of a social position and money have the effrontery to look down upon the Consular Service and on the big men who have grown distinguished and experienced in the work. [Mr. Carr of State, p. 250]

In his book *A Pretty Good Club: The Founding Fathers of the U.S. Foreign Service*, Martin Weil describes life in the American diplomatic service prior to the Rogers Act as a pleasant one for the sons of the wealthy, or socially well placed:

> The actual business of diplomacy often seemed merely an agreeable accompaniment to the pleasures of membership in an international society of elegance and sophistication. The genteel and leisurely life of an international elite laced with the agreeable obligations of negotiation, representation, and reporting, made a very pleasant life.... The disdain for business never left those who had consciously rejected it for public calling. [p.21]

The need to have more efficient and responsive American representation abroad, balanced with the anti-aristocratic impulses in Congress, resulted in the Rogers Act. There was a further fine tuning of the process in the Moses-Linthicum Act of 1931. This provided a career status for Foreign Service clerks, and established a fairer promotion service for all Foreign Service members. This history and this legal evolution come to life with accounts from Foreign Service employees of the time.

LIFE AS A CONSUL IN THE 1920S

Richard Butrick's work as a vice consul in unhealthy ports in Latin America, just prior to the creation of the Foreign Service in 1924, rebuts the common perception of how American representatives abroad lived. Like his other consular colleagues, Butrick was helping American business in Latin America and did everything possible to assist Americans in trouble.

Richard Butrick
Vice Consul, American Consulates, Valparaiso, Chile and Guayaquil, Ecuador, 1921–1926

I took courses at the beginning of the Foreign Service School in Georgetown. I more or less self-educated myself in Spanish until I became fluent enough to pass the consular examination in Spanish, which was a two-day and rather stiff examination. I was one of the few that passed it. I entered the Consular Service in 1921.

My first post was Valparaiso, Chile. It was a "break-in" post for me and I learned a lot of practical matters there. As an example, I acquired a handgun and it was necessary to register it in the mayoralty. There were seven men and three women waiting in the reception room. I strode up to the receptionist and explained what I wanted. He arose and repeated loudly, "*el señor Vice Consul Americano desea permiso para llevar su pistola.*" The seven men broke out in raucous laughter. The three women bowed their heads and smiled. I asked the Secretary, "Enrique, what in the world did I say?" He replied, "You asked for a permit to carry your penis." He then issued me a "*certificado para cargar revolver.*" After about six months, I was transferred to Iquique to take over from the consul who was going on home leave.

I had a room in the consulate, but ate all meals at the local hotel. Often, I would call the waiter and have him change my soup because it had a fly in it, which he always gracefully did. After many such occasions, I finally decided it was simpler to flick the fly out myself and enjoy the soup. In other ways, I found it simpler and more effective to adjust to local customs and habits and this stood me in good stead throughout my career. I served in Iguique for several months and was then transferred to Guayaquil, Ecuador, where I served for two-and-a-half years (1923-26), most of the time in charge of the consulate general.

There were three of us in the office. I did the economic reporting and general representation. I knew all the authorities and was friendly with them. One of my assistants, an American citizen, took care of citizenship matters for Americans, and the third person, an Ecuadorian, took care of the consular invoices and the routine operations of the office. The three of us ran it. I suppose today in Guayaquil one would probably have fifty or even a hundred people to run it.

As far as living conditions were concerned, it was a hellhole if there ever was one. To give you an idea of what Guayaquil was like in those days, Thomas Nast, the famous cartoonist, was assigned there as consul and died of fever. The wife of the consul general that I succeeded died there of yellow fever. They also had bubonic plague. But, at the time I arrived, the Rockefeller Institute had sent a member to Guayaquil to eradicate yellow fever, and he did it. The principal thing in eradicating yellow fever was to get rid of the anopheles mosquito, which the man from the Rockefeller Institute found was being propagated in the interior water tanks over the toilets, which were open on the top, so he had them all covered.

My period of service there was an active one. I sent a radio report in every week to the Department about the cocoa market, which was the principal cocoa market of the world at that time. On one occasion, I was able to go on vacation to Riobamba and while there I called on the local officials, including the military man. He told me that on the following Saturday he had received orders to keep everybody in barracks. That occurred to me to be very pertinent information, and I took the first available train to Guayaquil and sent a message in code to the Embassy indicating that there was a possibility of a coup on the following Saturday. And actually the coup did occur, and the Embassy had been forewarned by me. I received a highly commendatory letter from the Embassy.

I traveled somewhat through the countryside too on horseback to Cuenca and other places. So I was quite busy. One of the outstanding things was to settle the estate of a Virgin Islander who kept a small grocery there and who had died of bubonic plague. This worried me quite a bit, but after two or three days I got over that. Fortunately, I didn't catch the plague.

We had some problems with seamen and shipping. The governor of the province was in Guayaquil. We had a seaman who came ashore and was arrested. I found out about it later on. So, I went to the governor and spoke to him about it. He said, "Oh, that is quite all right, we will fix that right away." And he did. He released the man that afternoon. And he said to me, "Oh, by the way, I have a pony that I would like to transport by rail." (The railroad was built and controlled by an American company.) I said, "I will see what I can do about it." So, I arranged for the railroad to have his pony shipped up country free of charge.

There were other things that were very amusing, but life on the whole was not very pleasant on account of all the insects, especially the *grillos*, a form of cricket that came in the thousands. Even the streets were covered with them. When the automobiles would go along the street they would crack as you went over them. They could get into your house no matter how tightly you had it screened. We also had scorpions and all kinds of insects. The kitchen at night, when I would come home, would be a menagerie. There would be rats running around, scorpions, and all kinds of insects in the kitchen of the home where I lived, which was attached to the office, so it was a pretty tough life.

FIRST WOMAN U.S. COMMERCIAL OFFICER IN LATIN AMERICA

Aldene Alice Barrington entered the Foreign Service through the Department of Commerce. Her experience points out a now mostly forgotten fact: that the U.S. government, including the Foreign Service, represented one of the very few places where women in the 1920s and 1930s could enter the lower executive ranks and rise to positions of real responsibility and prestige. American business had little to offer ambitious women during this period. Except for teaching and secretarial work, there was almost no opportunity to compete with men. However, if a woman got married while a Foreign Service officer, either to an American or to a foreigner, she was expected to resign. Male officers were not subject to this rule. This meant that there was little future for any woman who wanted to have a family and a career. This gender inequity endured until the 1970s when the U.S. courts ruled it discriminatory.

Aldene Alice Barrington
Commercial Officer, Bogotá, Colombia, 1927–1931

On graduation from Barnard College, I was pointed towards the Foreign Service, because I'd gotten this little glimpse of it and had become acquainted with people connected with foreign endeavors. At that time, the Department of Commerce and the State Department were more or less separated in our Foreign Service. They later combined and correlated their services. But Commerce then appointed its people directly. I knew that they were opening a commercial attaché's office in Bogotá, Colombia. I learned of this through someone I had met in Puerto Rico and who had come from a South American assignment. So I applied. I got a reply suggesting that I please come for an interview. I don't remember the officer's name, but I well remember that, ending the interview, he looked at me and he said, "You know, we have this opening, and your qualifications are all right, but we couldn't think of appointing a young woman to such a primitive country." That was that!

Well, I got a job in New York with a lawyer's office. But I still wanted to get in the Foreign Service. The Department of Commerce took a young man for the Bogotá office instead of me. At that time, one went by ship to Barranquilla, Colombia, and then up the Magdalena River, a long trip. This young man, who got the job, was bored on the trip. There were other passengers, of course, some of them working for the Colombian government. To pass the time they started playing cards. Unfortunately, our young man mostly lost, and lacking cash, he continued to give his opponents IOUs. When he got to Bogotá his office work, which was clerical, included being a disbursing officer, one who could write government checks to pay local employees. With such a source of money, he paid off his gambling debts! That's when I got a telegram from the commercial attaché to me directly, asking, "Are you still interested?" And so that was my first Foreign Service job!

Bogotá was very colonial. In the beginning, I was somewhat unusual. American companies locating there would have loved to have found available English-speaking people to employ for clerical jobs in their offices. I was, more or less, office manager. We had working there a kind of a flunky, an office boy, Rodriguez, who was of an upper-class Colombian family. And we had to do an awful lot of reporting. I started, on my own—I was really pushed into it, because everyone was so very busy—reporting on different commodities and opportunities for trade and investments, because that was primarily what the Department of Commerce wanted. I can remember getting that department pouch off, which was quite a task, every week, and miscellaneous obligations that I was in charge of.

I remember one of the reports that I was pushed into writing was about doing business in Colombia. And you had to answer a lot of questions about their legal requirements and points of view and what the American company had to do in order to establish itself, pointing out the difficulties and the differences, which most Spanish-speaking countries probably inherited from Spain. The government had control of industry, and certainly of natural resources and their many minerals, which included petroleum. Such widespread government ownership was foreign to the American point of view, because we didn't have similar strict controls. We had more freedom, from a business point of view. And one had to explain the differences and difficulties and what the company had to overcome.

There were no big trade difficulties. The Germans and the British were there, as well as us. We were all competing. Our office would put an American exporter in touch with a prospective local representative for their products. The Germans seemed to be very steady and didn't put on a show at all, but had longstanding contacts there that were founded in machinery and various staples. And the British more or less felt that it was their country and that they were long experienced in supplying a wide range of needed imports.

VANCOUVER AS A TRAINING POST FOR A FUTURE AMBASSADOR

For Americans, the 1930s were dominated by the Great Depression, a time of austerity. For most people, there was little interest in foreign affairs. Despite the successful involvement of the United States in the Great War of 1914–1918, the country avoided a strong international role. Rather, a powerful current of nationalism and isolationism prevailed in America. Joining the Foreign Service was first and foremost a job in a time of limited employment.

The United States played a minor role in the world and there was little appreciation among Americans for working abroad. The Foreign Service was small, as was the Department of State, and its members could feel that they were at the end of a long line in regard to the general interest of the power centers in Washington, DC, or elsewhere in the country. Foreign affairs work was not perceived as the road to success for those who wanted to get ahead. The backgrounds and education of those who entered the Foreign Service were not all of wealthy East Coast families or prestigious universities. Once in the service, rising in the ranks depended more on ability and luck as to time and place of assignment than on family connections. But being a graduate of Harvard, Princeton, or Yale was still an asset, as many of those in the upper ranks of the service came from those schools and felt comfortable with those of similar upbringing. Still, the composition of the Foreign Service was changing.

Douglas MacArthur II describes his early years, especially doing commercial work at Vancouver, Canada.

Douglas MacArthur II
American Consulate General, Vancouver, Canada,
1935–1937

In the courses that I took at Yale, my professors and instructors knew that I was headed for the Foreign Service, and I took more than the required number of courses to cover a larger area of study. I had some excellent courses, one given on the Soviet Union two nights a month, each three hours, by a Russian émigré. Russia, at that point, was largely unknown to us students, because we had no diplomatic relations in the 1920s and early '30's. That came only after Roosevelt in 1933.

Every person taking the Foreign Service examination had to take a written examination in one language in which he had to be reasonably proficient. But in addition, he had to pass an oral examination administered by the Department after passing the overall written examination. My last year at Yale, I had a very nice French instructor in an advanced course in French. This was in the days of the Depression. I used to buy him lunch once a week so that we could talk only in French, to get a familiarity with speaking the language. Unfortunately, then as now, foreign languages were taught abysmally badly in the United States. While one could learn to write and read, the fluency to communicate comes only with the practice of speaking. That, except in most advanced courses, you didn't get.

One made a formal application to take the examination for the Foreign Service. The examinations were about three-and-a-half days, and it was all in writing. The subjects included world history, American history, economics, international law, mathematics, and language. The examinations were, I think, extremely well designed. They weren't designed to find out how much you didn't know because, obviously, even if you came out of a university with a master's degree, you could know only so much when you're twenty-two or twenty-three years old. They were designed to see how well you could express yourself in the written language in the subjects which you knew. So you would have, say, a three-hour morning period on American history, and there would be five or six topics, and they would say, "Write on three of the following topics of your choice." Obviously, one had to know something substantively, but the written expression was important, because if you're five-thousand miles away and trying to convey to the people in the State Department what a situation is, if you can't communicate and express yourself appropriately, they aren't going to get a very good picture of what the situation is in that particular part of the world.

The oral examination in the language of your choice, in my case, French, was a very thorough one, administered by a man who was almost bilingual. It was very useful because, even if you didn't go to that country, you had at least one foreign language. And if you speak one language reasonably well, the second one comes easier, and the third comes more easily than the second.

In my family and circle of friends, the Foreign Service was considered a way-out thing—rather exotic in a way—because you'd be living in strange parts of the world. I think some of my friends thought I was a little bit crazy. I had some friends at Yale, I remember, who said, "Come on down to Wall Street. You'll make three times more there the first year than you'll make after you've been five years in the Foreign Service." But generally, one's friends were interested and intrigued. The Foreign Service was considered a rather unusual career, and one that had a certain amount of glamour to it.

I passed my examinations in '32, the year I got out of Yale, but this was the Great Depression, and they took nobody into the Foreign Service until 1935. Congress said to the State Department, "We're not going to appropriate any money for new people for at least two years." So, those who passed the examination were so informed by the Department, and told to go out and find something to do for a couple of years.

I shipped briefly as an ordinary seaman on the Isthmian Line. This line, operated by U.S. Steel, went around the world, or out to the Indian Ocean and back; wages were eighteen dollars a month. It took twenty-two days from Brooklyn to Alexandria, Egypt, nonstop, going about eight or nine knots. I did that and stopped off in Egypt between runs because I thought I'd get further exposure to places that I'd never seen.

When I got back, I received notification that the Army was seeking people for active duty. I had a reserve commission, so I served until October, 1935 in the Army.

When I came into the Service, about a thousand people took the examination. It was the depth of the Depression and some of them, I think, just took it as a flyer. Of the thousand, there were one-hundred and five who passed the written examination. Then following the oral examination, there were thirty-five of us who were selected. You had no training before being assigned abroad. After you passed your examination, you were called down to the Department, given your railroad ticket or your boat ticket and your passport, and told to go out and report to the place where you were sent, usually a consulate general. There you would be exposed to the various types of work that you would get in the Service, except a very important part which I'll touch on, political reporting.

I think of all the thirty-five people who came into the Service when I came in, only two or three had any outside income. The rest of us were dependent totally on what we earned. The salary was twenty-five-hundred dollars a year, less five percent, which ran to about one-hundred and ninety-nine dollars a month. You did get a housing allowance, and that, of course, made it possible to live. It wasn't rich living. There were, of course, in upper positions, a certain number of people who had come into the old diplomatic service, before the Rogers Act in 1924, when the Rogers Act combined the consular service and the diplomatic service. Some of them were rather snobbish and affected, but some of them were extraordinarily capable people. When I came into the service in the 1930s, you felt you were extremely fortunate to have been selected into the Service; you felt that the Service was an elite service, and there was a great deal of pride in it.

So, you arrived at the post, green as grass, with absolutely no experience and no briefing in the Department. You spent about three months in each of the major sections, and then you were assigned to one until you were called back to the Department to the Foreign Service school. You were usually gone about fifteen months on this probationary period. You were not secure in your job until you had passed through the Foreign Service school after this first probationary post.

I was assigned to Vancouver. I started out in the visa section. After about three months in the visa section, I did three months of general work, including shipping; that is, the visaing of crew lists, the discharge of crew members who sought discharge, the signing and stamping of commercial invoices that had to accompany export shipments to the United States, and general protection work. While I was doing this work, the old Seattle-Alaska line went on strike. They were controlled pretty much by Harry Bridges' left-wing union on the West Coast. There were several strikes stranding a ship in Vancouver. I went down to witness the discharge of these striking seamen, and by a sheer coincidence, I found that one of the seamen was one of the people who had been with me on the old Isthmian Line when I had taken that ordinary seaman's job. The shipping job was interesting, particularly the discharge of a striking crew. There was the usual tough-minded labor union labor leader on each ship, if the crew was unionized. The union leader always wanted to be present when a crew member was questioned so he could intimidate any seamen not favoring a strike. I got involved in what the French call a *prise de bec* (nose-to-nose) with union representatives, saying the seaman had the right to speak alone with the consul and the captain when he was asked the question of whether he accepted the discharge voluntarily or not, or why he was striking. But it was an interesting experience where, again, my background on a merchant marine ship taught me a lot in understanding the problems of seamen.

One further observation about training in the first post. In addition to visas, shipping, general protection work, citizenship (that is, passports, registrations of births and deaths, etc.), there was one other very important type of work, commercial work. I spent three months doing commercial work. When you went out to a large consulate general, as Vancouver was, the hard-working corps of the Foreign Service that gave continuity was the non-career vice consuls. They were people who had worked up from clerical jobs. They were not "career", but they were extremely expert and proficient in their particular line: visas, citizenship work, invoicing, shipping and commercial work. I had the great good fortune to work three months with a non-career vice consul, Nelson Meeks. He taught me, for the first time, the tremendous importance of commercial work, which was in those days not looked down on, but not considered terribly important by some "old school tie" boys in some of our embassies. Nelson groomed me, and then sent me out to do several reports. Later, when we were in the Foreign Service school, where one spent two or three days in each of the other departments—Agriculture, Commerce, Justice, etc.—they distributed some of the reports that they thought had resulted in sales. Among them was a report that I had done on the toy industry in Vancouver, under Nelson's excellent supervision. I think that early training in the importance of commercial work and what it means to our companies helped me immeasurably later. I got some very nice letters from the companies that sold some toys to the toy retailers in Vancouver and Victoria.

It was one of the reasons why, in later incarnations, when I became an ambassador, I attached so much importance to the commercial aspect of our work. In the Foreign Service, the commercial attaché is the fellow with the title, but the ambassador is the only one with access to the government at top level, at the prime minister level, at the minister of commerce level, the minister of finance level. So the ambassador is really the chief commercial attaché. The role of the commercial attaché is to prime the boss (that is, the ambassador), keep him fully briefed and informed, and when the proper moment comes, prod him into action, to go and raise hell with the prime minister or the appropriate cabinet minister if we're being discriminated against or our industries and our business are being badly treated.

We must remember that the United States Foreign Service was very small. I have here a booklet published by the State Department in 1936. I'd been in the Foreign Service just about a year. The total number of Foreign Service Officers in

1936 was 683. We had sixteen-hundred and nineteen clerks and twelve-hundred and ninety-one miscellaneous employees of various kinds. That's a total of thirty-six-hundred and forty-seven, from janitors to class one Foreign Service Officers. We had diplomatic missions in fifty-seven countries, because in those days—we're apt to forget now—the number of independent countries was relatively small. There were twenty-some countries in Europe, if you include Eastern Europe, Russia, Latvia, Lithuania, Estonia, etc. There were almost twenty in Latin America. That leaves perhaps twelve or fifteen for the rest of the world.

In Africa, we had consuls in places like Dakar and Lourenço Marques and a few other places, but we had diplomatic missions only in the Union of South Africa, in Egypt, Liberia and, I can't remember, but think we had one in Ethiopia, too. But elsewhere, south of the Sahara, the whole continent consisted of colonies. Their borders had largely been determined at the Berlin Conference of 1885 by various European powers. In South Asia, there was no such thing as India and Pakistan; there was British India. Elsewhere there were other dependencies and possessions such as Malaysia, Singapore, and Hong Kong. In the Middle East, there were a few independent countries at that time, but Lebanon and Syria were French protectorates. Palestine, including Transjordan, was in those days a British protectorate. The world was very small in terms of countries.

We came back to the Foreign Service school for about three-and-a-half months. In that school, for the first time, we were exposed to political reporting, because in a consulate general, the consul general did a political report about once a month, unless there were elections or the Embassy wanted to know something about attitudes and the strength of political parties or groups in that particular province of Canada. But the young probationary officer had nothing to do with all that. In the Department, for the first time, you were trained in political reporting, and it was rather interesting the way they did it. They would give you some political reports that had been declassified, to read, and then they would assign subjects, like strength of the American labor movement, or the political orientation of some element of our society, things of that kind, and tell you to come back the next day, or two or three days later, with a draft telegram on that particular aspect. They confined it, obviously, to something that you could dig into and gather some background on, such as the political strength of certain movements or political parties, the political orientation of agriculture in light of the Depression, and things of that kind. This was one of the training tools they used, and it was really quite effective.

The School was entirely run by the Foreign Service. We were briefed by the senior people on the Middle East, Latin America, Europe, and the Far East.

Those are the major areas. Africa, we were not briefed on, because it was basically all colonies. The Middle Eastern part covered Egypt and Arab North Africa. The rest, south of the Sahara, was colonies or dependencies except for the Union of South Africa at the southern extremity. But we were usually briefed a day—a morning and afternoon—on a subject. Sometimes junior officers, somebody below the top, came in and filled in on American exports or commercial or special interests.

To give you an idea on how small our government was when I went to the Foreign Service school, it and the State Department were in what is now the Executive Office Building, next to the White House. Not just the State Department, but the War Department and the Navy Department were all in that one building, with a Secretary of War (we had no Defense Department then) and a Secretary of the Navy (we had no Secretary of the Air Force). The Air Force was part of the Army. The chief of staff of the Army and the CNO of the Navy ? Chief of Naval Operations ? were both there; all of us were crammed into that one building.

We were still passive observers [in the international arena]. We had an interest, but in the one-hundred-fifty-odd years since our independence (from 1781 to 1936) we had followed a policy of isolationism. True, an isolationism with a tremendous expansionist drive in our continent and hemisphere, but isolationism from the great world beyond the Atlantic and the Pacific Oceans. That isolation was still very, very strong.

Although the president [Franklin D. Roosevelt] was obviously a man with no previous real experience in foreign affairs, he had enough understanding to realize—as did our embassies and our ambassadors abroad who reported back to the Department and to the president—that we were moving steadily toward a crisis, a very severe crisis that could lead to war. But we were not players in the international game then. That was one reason, perhaps, that our Service was so small. We were interested observers, but not players. We were not active in taking positions and going and beating on governments' doors or prime ministers' desks and doing other things of that kind. We kept informed, we tried to use our influence for peace and so forth, but we were really just observers.

THE MAKING OF A CHINA HAND

John Stewart Service describes being a junior officer in China, an area of the world where he lived as a youth. Later, as a "China Hand," he would be fired during the McCarthy years.

John Stewart Service
Clerk and Vice Consul, American Consulate, Yunnanfu, China, 1933–1941

I got to Washington just before the oral examination. The examining panel in those days was very high level. There was the man who was executive head of the State Department, named Wilbur Carr; he was the head of personnel of the Foreign Service. There was an assistant secretary, William Castle. There was a man in charge of the exams who had drawn up a new type of examination which they were giving then. This was why my friend Harrison had failed, because he was there the first year of the new type of examinations.

They asked me all sorts of weird questions. If I were offered ten-thousand dollars if I could shake Mussolini's hand within ten days, did I think I could do it and how would I go about it? So, I explained very briefly how to get to Rome the fastest way possible. Then I said that I would go to one of the American newspaper correspondents. I mentioned the *New York Herald Tribune,* one of several there. I explained the proposition to him and asked him to talk to the information minister of the Italian government whom he would have contact with to explain that I would give the money to charity if Mussolini would do this. I said I thought Mussolini would go for the story and publicity.

They said, "You wouldn't go to the American embassy?" I said, "Oh, no. I wouldn't go near the American embassy." They were obviously pleased!

I had told them that I could speak some Chinese; they sent me around to see a Foreign Service officer up in the Division of Chinese Affairs, who turned out to be someone my parents had known and I had known slightly in Shanghai. He was rather busy and surprised. He said, "Well, I haven't spoken any Chinese for a long time." A lot of people didn't keep up their Chinese very well. He said, "Just tell me something about yourself, where you were born, where you went to school, and what you're doing." So, I rattled on for a while in my terrible Szechwanese. He said, "Well, obviously you know some Chinese."

After the oral, the examiners said, "Wait in the waiting room outside, the anteroom." So I went back there and fifteen or twenty minutes later, a clerk came to me and gave me a piece of paper and instructions about having a physical examination at the navy dispensary.

Well, this was a tip-off. If you were sent to get the physical, then you had passed. They didn't tell you officially until some days later. I went and passed my physical exam that afternoon at the naval dispensary.

Then, there was the question of what to do. I had asked the man who examined me in Chinese for advice. This was January '33. He said, "Look, there's going to be retrenchment in the Department. Appropriations are going to be cut. There are simply going to be no appointments of any Foreign Service officers. You've undoubtedly passed the examination since you took the physical, but I can't give you a clue when you may get appointed."

I mentioned that I was thinking of going back to China anyway. My father was going then and my mother was going to follow later. He said, "Well, that would be an excellent idea. If you go to China, apply for a clerk's job, a clerkship. You'll probably get one if there is a vacancy because you will have saved the Department of State money by being already in China; and the fact that you've passed the examinations and are on the waiting list for appointment will also be in your favor. So that's what we did. I went with my father to China. Almost as soon as I got to Shanghai in 1933 I went to call on the American consul general, a very elderly gentleman who had been in Shanghai a long time, and applied for a clerkship.

It wasn't too long—I think it was only about six weeks—before the consul general asked me to come and see him. He said, "Would you like a job as clerk at Yunnanfu?" In those days, Yunnanfu was considered the end of everything, I mean to hell and gone, a remote and isolated post in southwest China. He said, "You don't have to say today." I went back to him I think the next day and said that I'd take the job. So I went to Yunnanfu, which is now known as Kunming.

When I first got there, there were two officers: two vice consuls, actually. We reported to the legation in Peking. We generally reported by mail, which might take two or three weeks, because the only way to get to Yunnan was a long trip through Hong Kong, then down to Haiphong, then by train, the French railway, from Haiphong—which in those days was a three-day trip because they didn't run at night—up to Yunnan. You could come directly overland but it would have taken you weeks to make the trip. You'd go up the Yangtze to Chungking and then overland to Kunming, but it would take you about four weeks to do it.

I did everything. I established and maintained the files. I did all the typing and I was not a trained typist. This was to create a lot of grief because the other vice consul was terribly worried about promotions and much concerned about almost everything, especially social position. He couldn't stand any erasures or any mistakes on a page. I was always having to retype things so they would go in looking perfect. I myself don't mind little things like that.

He had me do commercial work, such as trade letters. But there really weren't any commercial opportunities in Kunming. There couldn't be because the French were not about to let any Americans, or any other foreigners except themselves, do business in Yunnan. All goods had to come through French Indochina.

We would get trade inquiries: what is the market for beer, for instance, in your consular district? The only real letter to send them back was just, "There isn't any." But not my boss! He insisted that we write them a full-dress discussion of the market and procedures for importing and the desirability of getting a local agent, the desirability and necessity of getting a forwarding agent in Haiphong, and all the rest of this. Every trade letter had to be a certain number of pages.

Some foreigners smoked opium. The Frenchman who was the local representative for the Salt Gabelle, which was the third Chinese organization run by foreigners (others were the Maritime Customs and the Posts) smoked opium. After dinner, he would generally retire and smoke.

The whole life style, the daily schedule of a city like Kunming, was tied to opium smoking. People got up very late in the morning, and late in the evening they would come out in the streets to get a snack. The whole town was geared to the prevalence of opium smoking. You saw it everywhere you went. If you traveled, the inns were full of the smell of it. Your chair bearers and so on would smoke. It was a very commonly seen thing. We took trips on ferry boats on a lake near Kunming. For instance, I remember watching an old man curl up on deck and then smoke.

One thing I may not have stressed was the fact that Yunnan was one of the principal opium-producing regions of China. It was an important cash crop. The opium was shipped out through various other warlord domains down the river to Shanghai, Hangchow, and also particularly down the West River to Canton. Of course, some of it went into Indochina and some of it, we suspected, was processed into morphine and heroin. Exporting soldiers and exporting opium were what Yunnan really lived on.

The United States Government was very much interested, then as now, in stopping opium and narcotics traffic; so, we were supposed to report on that. If you saw the countryside around Kunming in the springtime when it was just a mass, a sea of opium poppies, you could believe an awful lot was produced. You had ideas of the magnitude of the trade through the size of military convoys that would take it out of the province, for instance. It had to be by military to give it safety. Most of it moved in very large shipments, one warlord shipping it through the territory of another warlord, by arrangement, of course. There would be a pay-off. But you would hear, for instance, of convoys of a hundred or two hundred mules. Well, we're talking here about ounces, so you'd convert that to pounds, into mule loads. A hundred mule loads is a lot of opium.

There very definitely was a local warlord named Lung Yun ("Dragon Cloud"), who was part aborigine, probably mixed Chinese and aborigine. But he had gotten Yunnan very firmly in his grip. Of course he worked with the French, but I think the French were quite content to let him govern.

We didn't have a great deal of business. We were there mainly because it was so remote; there was no other way for Americans to get the protection or consular services, passports, and so on, except by having a consulate there. But, also, we were there to watch the French. In earlier, more actively "imperialist" days, there had been concern about what the French were up to.

2

World War II

As Douglas MacArthur II remarked in the previous chapter, the United States was mainly an observer on the world diplomatic scene prior to World War II. The work of the American Foreign Service changed with the advent of that war. Major foreign policy initiatives were in the hands of the president, Franklin Roosevelt, and everything was subordinate to the needs of the American military. Those Foreign Service officers serving in the embattled countries of Europe and Asia felt the full weight of the war, but most were acting in peripheral roles.

France fell to the Germans in June, 1940. But the U.S., still a neutral nation, maintained diplomats in the part of France titularly controlled by the French regime at Vichy. Even after the U.S. went to war with Germany in December, 1941, U.S. diplomats remained in France, accredited to France until the Allied landings in North Africa in the fall of 1942. The presence of these diplomats, under the noses of the Germans, gave rise to some real derring-do.

This World War II chapter ends with John Melby, Parker Hart, and LeRue Lutkin, who worked in Latin America.

SPYING FOR THE ALLIES

In unoccupied France, Constance Harvey used her position as consular officer in Lyon, to provide intelligence that was passed on to British as well as American consumers. After the Allied invasion of North Africa in the fall of 1942, the Germans ended the fiction of Vichy's independence and occupied all of France. Harvey was interned, along with many other American diplomats, including Douglas MacArthur II, who had been serving at the U.S. embassy in Vichy.

Constance R. Harvey
Consul, American Consulate General, Lyon, France, 1941–1942; German Internment, 1942–1943

I left Bern on New Year's Day 1941; I was transferred to Lyon. We were not yet at war, and were neutral. Then, I began my nefarious life.

Our military attaché in Bern, General Barley Legge, and his wife were very close friends of mine. Soon after I got down to Lyon, he asked me if I would help him with some things. So I said, "You bet I will. No problem." And so I did. I got into a whole lot of business for our military attaché in Bern, which did not go through the embassy at Vichy.

It went on until I left to be interned, and after the war I was given the Medal of Freedom by General Legge. Quite a few other people had been up to some monkey business, just to help out. The citation had to be changed in the War Department, because at first it had been written that I'd been of great assistance, etc., etc., since my arrival in January of 1941 in France. They changed it to December 1941, cutting out the time when we were supposed to be neutral.

Well, it wasn't legal! Quite obviously it wasn't, but it was leading towards the legality pretty fast at that time, but I've always been glad that I could do it. I learned in Washington, after I got back and lived there a while, that our government—that is, the War Department—had the very best information from any source from Barley Legge on what was going on on the Russian front. It wasn't exactly an underground. When I got to Lyon, I was immediately put in charge of Belgian interests. We had British interests. One of our employees was a Belgian who had worked with our embassy in Brussels. He and his wife were stationed there and were part of our whole Foreign Service network.

I helped General Legge in various ways. I got lots of information from the northern part of France from various quarters and people. That went to Legge as fast as we could get it to him, with the pouch going immediately—like that! Right from Lyon, not through Vichy. Also, we didn't like things getting into Vichy; sometimes things got mixed up. Everything was quicker right from Lyon.

I took things in. I went back and forth quite a bit to Switzerland. Sometimes I wouldn't get further than Geneva, but an American attaché would come down and meet me in a field near Geneva. Once I took him a plan of all of the German anti-aircraft stations in and around Paris. He turned pale and said, "I'll remember this!" I thought it was pretty good, too.

I didn't have any problems. There was always a Gestapo at the border. The Gestapo came right into our office all the time. Our principal in our little office there said, "Never inquire about anybody who comes in." Just don't know who comes in and who doesn't; it's better not to know. I know quite often you could spot them because they were all over the place. But they were always right with the French official as you left and entered France. This was not occupied France, either! But, nevertheless, he was there. I had a Ford at that time; I didn't always use it. I also used a French car, but I always went up to Switzerland in my Ford. Fortunately, I've never seen another car that had the same—the key to the glove compartment was completely different from any other key to the car. So, when I got out to show my papers to the *douanier* [customs officer], I would leave my keys conspicuously dangling in the ignition. The other key was down here around my neck under my dress. And I would go in—I probably turned off the engine, but I left everything open—and soared right through. I learned all the tricks. Everybody had to. I was so fascinated; I was so interested, so determined to do it. Of course, I've been frightened in my life, but not doing that sort of thing, not a bit.

I myself wasn't involved in any escape routes. However, the Belgian radio in London, which went to Europe and to Belgium said every day, "Come, we need you, we need you in the army here. Try to get to North Africa. Go first to the American Consulate in Lyon." We looked like a recruiting office. Young people came in all the time. All these young, round faces would appear! And we shoved them out because the Belgians had their lines pretty well fixed up.

What we did do, what I did a lot—or at least let it be done for me—was to get out practically the whole Belgian government in exile. We got out the man who had been the Belgian attaché at Vichy. We got him a nice Belgian passport with a picture on it that was his, but with the name of somebody completely different, with a whole different life story, all signed by C. R. Harvey. We got him out on a train through Spain. This is where these people were going then, because they were too old to climb the Pyrenees Mountains. We thought we'd done pretty well!

I remember very, very well the 7th of December, 1941. It was a Sunday, I was preparing to go out and have lunch in the country with some good French friends. I heard on the radio about Pearl Harbor. I knew pretty well what that meant. I telephoned and I said, "I'm sorry, I can't come." They said, "Why not?" I said, "Turn on your radio. Goodbye."

I was ordered back to Bern, because they were desperate to get as many people into Bern as they possibly could. They were sure that the Germans were going to occupy Southern France and that Franco was going to join Hitler. I knew better, because I had a good source for knowing that would never happen. But in any case, I and also the consul, who was a very young man, were ordered to go to Bern along with several other people from different offices in France. Allen Dulles got in just before they thought the frontiers would close. We all rushed. I finally made it, with my Persian cat and just barely enough gasoline to roll into Geneva on Christmas Eve of 1941. I was glad that the head of the Swiss government had said this was the one night of the whole year when there wouldn't be a black-out, because a black-out in Switzerland was blacker than it was anywhere else—London or Paris or anywhere else. It was black!

But this year, there was a great big Christmas tree—full of lights all over the place. I spent the night there and then finally I got up, having left my car behind because I couldn't get any more gasoline. With the cat in a basket, I went up on the train to Bern, where we were supposed to report the day after Christmas. I wasn't very pleased to be there; I didn't want to be there at all. Pretty soon I said to the deputy, "I think I'd better go back. The consul general down there hasn't got anybody with him. It's very bad; he needs people back there. I think I should go back. There's not going to be this business of Switzerland being shut off." They didn't believe that. After a couple of days they said, "Now you people are all keyed up. You've got to relax. This is now a quiet country. You've got to pull yourselves together, and we've got plenty of interesting work to do here. You can review newspapers."

So I reviewed newspapers for a few days. Then I went back and talked to the deputy. I'd known him before and he was a nice man. He said, "No, no." I pounded on his table and broke his inkwell! And then he said, "I'll telegraph." He telegraphed to the Department and they said, "Yes, send her back." So I was sent back. A year later, I got interned, but I never regretted it.

This intelligence work in Lyon was my own independent enterprise, until we got into the war. Then the consul, who had come out fairly recently, called me and Vice Consul George Whittinghill into his office. He said, "I know all about you kids, what you've been up to. You can take me aboard now. We can share it together."

I had control of the pouch just as it left. I got anything I wanted into that pouch. Some of those very necessary things were often industrial diamonds. They traveled up to Switzerland in that pouch quite frequently. They had been purchased by a Swiss who had been in the business, who became a very good friend of mine, who had been asked by the British to help with the cause for Americans to get industrial diamonds. He said, "No problem, I go back and forth all the time, but I just can't carry them into Switzerland." But they got to Switzerland without him! You couldn't get any from South Africa. That was just one of the little things. Once, at least—well, more than once—I got a whole great box of gold sovereigns, which was to pay part of the British secret service. I can't quite remember how that got into their hands, but it did.

The Embassy didn't know anything about that either. It just had to be done; these things had to be done, that was all there was to it. I just knew that any kind of information would get out from Legge's office faster than from any other area, and it would go by telegraph or whatever we did then, right straight to the War Department, which of course would pass it right on to the Department of State. So they did know in the Department, before long, that I was up to shenanigans, but Vichy didn't know.

We had all kinds of people coming. I had someone coming in from the Belgian secret service who was parachuted in. I think his name was Dewind. Usually we didn't know their real names. He used to come to my apartment and have a drink or a meal with me in the hotel, and tell me all about his wife and children.

This Belgian, who worked so hard for Belgian interests with me, was arrested. The Vichy government, probably on orders from the Gestapo, took him to a military hospital where he stayed a week. Then, we heard on a Monday that he had been put on a train to be taken to a concentration camp! I said to my chief, "I've got to go and see the police. I'm going at once." He said, "You can't do anything. How can you?" I said, "I've got to go; I _must_ go." So I went, and I spent an hour and a half or two hours in the police chief's office and refused to leave. He said, "No, no, you can't, absolutely."

I said, "Look here. I went to school in France. France is a second country to me. If you don't get this man back to the hospital so that he can have the operation which he's scheduled to have, I'll spend the rest of my life working against France." Finally he said, "I'll telephone." So ten minutes before the train left they got him off and put him in a car.

I cried. I didn't have to act very much; I felt absolutely inflamed with fury. I said, "I will not go to a comfortable, diplomatic internment and let that man go to a concentration camp. I won't take it." So, we got him off the train and he was taken in a police ambulance back to the hospital. I followed in my car, with his wife. By that time we had gotten together.

We got in, and sat down on his bed, and laughed and laughed, and ate up all the Belgian's dinner. Poor thing, he didn't have any. Then we were interned and went away. We knew that we were going to be interned by the Vichy government on the Wednesday after our landings in North Africa. That day, things happened in the south of France. People who were not going to help started to help. One of the nurses, a nun in the hospital, dressed the Belgian up in her sister's garb and got him out of the hospital. He, who was an atheist, I guess, fled to the Archbishop's palace, where he was tucked away until some of his friends could take him. Somehow they smuggled him into Switzerland, where he spent the rest of the war. His wife finally joined him in Switzerland, I think, also by being smuggled through the barbed wire, or something similar. So that was something. He was a very brave man. He never would have lived; he was in bad health as it was. I had eight people I knew go to concentration camps, and four did not return. Two of our clerks went. One came back and lived a few years, but the woman died in Mauthusen. The Germans occupied all of France at that time [after the Allied invasion of North Africa], you see. Vichy then more or less did what they told them to do. In any case, we were all interned and we were sent to Lourdes. We spent about two and a half months in Lourdes. We were interned on the 11th of November of 1942, and had a dreadful time getting out of Lyon.

The trouble was that the police came to take us away from our hotels. They scooped us up and took us down to the station and got us onto the train. These were the regular police. The luggage had to go by another route; it couldn't go in the police car. I said, "I'm not going without my luggage. After all, it will probably never reappear, and I will not go on this train." My chief and this elderly non-career vice consul were with me, it was just the three of us. I had British interests as well as the others, at the end. In any case, I said, "I won't go. I'm getting off the train."

They said, "Well, we'll get off with you." By that time, the police who had taken us there had disappeared! The Germans were flowing through. There was nobody on the streets, nobody looking at all. I said, "I think we'd better telephone the police and tell them we're still here. Otherwise there will be trouble, sooner or later." I did, and the police said, "Well, you'll just have to go on the afternoon train, which will hook up with a sleeper. You can get on that to Lourdes, but it won't go for several hours." It didn't leave until about five o'clock in the afternoon.

How to get lunch? We were hungry by that time. There wasn't a bit of food within sight. We were miles away from anything. For months, you couldn't eat in any restaurant anywhere unless you had a reservation two or three days in advance, because there was no food. There was no place to get food except in a black-market restaurant.

We started walking, because there were no taxis, and no kind of transportation. Three of us started walking back to where we thought there was a little restaurant that we had been in, a good one, too! As we walked along, we passed a small group of about three Poles, whom we'd known. They looked at us as if they'd seen a ghost!

But we didn't look as if we knew anything about them, or they about us; we just went past each other. But they looked scared, almost, to think we were still there.

We got to the little restaurant, where they said, *"Oh, non, non, complet. Pas de place. Rien à manger. Rien à boire."* (Oh, no, no, we're full. No room. Nothing to eat. Nothing to drink.)

I stuck my head in and I said, "Is Mr. So and So (I don't remember his name now) here? Does he really want to have the consul general, Marshall Vance, and his two officers who are going to be interned not have anything to eat before we leave for internment?" A man stuck his head out and he said, "Come in behind the curtain." He whisked us in behind a curtain, where we had a banquet with champagne, and I can't tell you!

I was lucky. In any case, that was terrific! We enjoyed ourselves very much. To our amazement, a couple of our friends came to find out where we were. They stuck their heads in and had a cup with us. One of the Quakers was interned with us later. In any case, we finally got on our train. The luggage arrived! Before I had gotten into this awful temper and left the train, several of my crazy friends had come to say goodbye. One was an Alsatian gentleman who had been the head of the Chamber of Commerce of Strasbourg before it relocated to Lyon. A great many people from Strasbourg were in Lyon at that time. He had come with a great bouquet of flowers to present to me before I left. I heard of this, and said to one of my women friends there, "Get that man off the platform with his flowers, as fast as you can. Don't let him come anywhere near me. He must be out of his mind!" You know, "Beware, beware!" They finally persuaded him to leave. Twenty-five years later, I met him again in Strasbourg!

You really wouldn't think that any sensible man would go and get himself interned twice in the same war! But this was the case of Phil Whitcomb, the correspondent of the *Baltimore Sun.* He was interned in Berlin in 1941. They had only something like five months' internment. He'd already been very much interested in adult education there. It was his hobby, and he started what he called "The College of the Internees."

He came back after they were disinterned and went back to the States. He came back to France, and married a French woman he'd been in love with for some time. Then, he got interned again with us! He was delighted, because we were going to be interned and he would immediately organize a college for us.

Inside of 24 hours, he had a bulletin written up, and everybody was supposed to sign up for various classes to teach and classes to learn. You were to get yourself signed up for both. This was the only way we could get through our internment, which (we thought) probably wouldn't be long. It turned out to be 13 months.

We laughed and laughed, and we signed up just to please Phil. It was our godsend. Everybody did do things; that was very nice. I had a class in American Literature, for which I had one Bret Harte book and a very small anthology. I had four elementary school kids to teach, who had never been back in the States, but were Americans. I also taught Italian to adults. And, of course, I took many other interesting courses. We had practically no books, and everybody had to remember what they could. Books came later.

After being moved to the Black Forest in Germany for internment, we were told we were going to get prisoner-of-war parcels twice a month from Geneva. We had been there only a few days when we heard this. Most of us felt that was wrong. Here we were in a regular, proper, diplomatic internment. We shouldn't eat up these parcels of food. Kippy Tuck said, "You will take those parcels. They'll be no arguing about it!"

We were very glad that we did, because they certainly helped. We got various interesting things. We began getting, after a while, a special meat substitute called "Spam." We had that for a while in the parcels, but then we started giving it as presents to the German servants. After a while they wouldn't take it anymore!

One thing was very good for some of us who were non-smokers: cigarettes. During the war, money—dollars—got you nowhere. Nobody wanted the dollar bill. What could you do with that? But cigarettes were currency! Any package of cigarettes would buy a week's meat ration, or a whole loaf of bread. We used cigarettes to augment our diet and we managed pretty well. We seemed to have the same pudding, though, in various shapes and manners, week after week and month after month. Sometimes it was like a gelatin and sometimes it was fluffy and sometimes it was liquid, but it was the same pudding!

One day somebody shouted to me, "Get into the river. There are lemons!" There was a little stream that went past the garden. Several of us rushed in with our shoes and stockings on, and I captured three lemons. A crate must have fallen off one of the army trucks going over a bridge upstream, and broken. Several of us were able to get a few lemons. I had three lemons during all the time I was there.

We were allowed to pick blackberries when we were on walks in the Black Forest! They were put into the milk cans which we carried with us. My chief, Marshall Vance, said it was a good idea to make them into jam. I put a cane across my bathtub and hung a sack from it, as I remembered they did at home. Jelly dripped through it into a container. It made quite good jam, because we did get some sugar in the parcels. But I was horrified when I took it up, because there were some black stains on the bathtub! I scrubbed and scrubbed, and they never came off; they got better, but not much. I wondered whether they thought I'd been killing somebody in that bathtub, but nobody said anything about it. That was our food situation. We were nourished; we kept alive. People had been allowed to keep their dogs. Doug MacArthur had his dog with him, but he had to give up quite a lot of his ration for his dog. Anybody with dogs did, and went a bit hungry.

We got along quite well until almost the last weeks before we were disinterned. Then, some real rows broke out. Somebody threw somebody down the stairs. I can't remember who it was. It was curious: the fact that we were about to leave upset us emotionally more than anything else. It was extraordinary. We didn't know much, but we were allowed to read the German newspapers and we could listen to the German radio. Any radios had been taken away from us, but one was not found. One of the military had kept it, and we did get a little bit of news that way. I would read the German newspapers published in the occupied territory. We began to notice that the news from the eastern front was always victory. The victories began to get nearer and nearer to the German border.

Then one Sunday a thrilling thing happened. It must have been in October of '43. We had often seen bombers go over, and we knew they were British. We saw a whole group of bombers very high. We knew immediately they were American. Don't ask anybody how we knew, we just knew.

Finally, the Germans said they would exchange us for the diplomats who were at the Greenbriar [a resort in West Virginia used as an internment center for foreign diplomats]. German diplomats spent their time at the Greenbriar. I guess there were some Vichy French at Hershey, Pennsylvania, but I don't think the French were part of the exchange. By that time, there were very few.

There were masses of German businessmen who had been raked up all over Latin America and brought to the United States. These countries turned them over to us because they thought it was not wise to let them stay around. They had been interned with the regular German diplomatic officers.

We were taken by train by the German Army, which was very tough with us. A number of people on that train had relatives who wanted to give them some food or something else. They were waiting for us at the big railway station just south of Paris. It's what the French call a *plaque tournante* (hub). One French woman with us, who had been interned with the Quakers, saw her grandchildren there with things for her. Yet, they were not allowed anywhere near the train. She was able to wave to them, but that was all; she couldn't even speak to them. We weren't allowed off the train, and none of these people could give us anything at all.

Then the Germans put us up in a very good hotel at Biarritz. It was a city I knew already, because I'd been there years before with my mother. After we got our rooms, we were waiting for the *Gripsholm* to arrive in Lisbon, and then, just before they entered the port of Lisbon, our train would go and enter Spain. And when each conveyance reached neutral territory then that was the exchange. The train entered Spain and the ship entered the port of Lisbon.

In any case, we were in Biarritz for three days. When we had been in our rooms for about twenty minutes, somebody came and said, "We have to shut all the windows looking out over the sea. No one is permitted to look out on the Atlantic Ocean." Just what there was out there we wanted to see? Well, we guessed. That was part of the big wall, the enormous fortifications. I didn't see them; they weren't outside my window. But in any case, we never got any light into our rooms. The dogs had to be walked, and that was the only way we got any air.

The people who owned the dogs could walk them outside, and then they rented them out. For a bottle of champagne you could walk a dog for twenty minutes, on the land side of the hotel, and get a little fresh air. How we got champagne I don't know. I don't know how we paid for it. I remember when we finally got on the train to get out of Biarritz I was sitting next to an American soldier who was being repatriated from a prisoner-of-war camp because of his disabilities. He was trembling. He said, "When we get to the border, you wait. They'll stop us. They'll never let us out." He just didn't believe it.

We got to Portugal and embarked on the *Gripsholm*. We went with blazing lights at night. It wasn't a very rapid trip. After we arrived in New York, I stayed there only a couple of nights before I went to Washington. Believe it or not, there was a cocktail party given for us by the "Spam" company!

LEARNING TO HATE THE SOVIETS

The experiences of James McCargar, a new Foreign Service officer on his first assignment to the Soviet Union at the height of the war, are illustrative of the disillusionment and disgust most professional American diplomats felt when encountering the Soviet communist regime. Americans on the home front generally had a high regard for Soviet military sacrifices and the ability of their armed forces. They saw the Soviet Union only as a brave ally and many thought kindly of "good old Uncle Joe" Stalin. On the other hand, the brutal treatment of Soviet citizens and the restrictions and suspicions directed against Allied diplomats inculcated in the Foreign Service a lasting realization of the cruel, authoritarian nature of the Soviet system.

For the Foreign Service, the Cold War—at least as seen from the vantage point of the Soviet Union—started much earlier than the post-war period when the American nation came face-to-face with the real intentions of their former ally. James McCargar was posted to Moscow in early 1942, when most of our embassy staff had been evacuated to Kuibyshev because of the German threat to Moscow. Later, he was assigned to the American Consulate General in Vladivostok, the major Soviet port on the Pacific.

James McCargar
Political Officer, American Embassy, Moscow, Soviet Union, 1942, and Consular Officer, American Consulate General, Vladivostok, Soviet Union, 1942–1943

I was very excited about getting to Moscow, which even in grim wartime had a certain magnificence to it, a great weight of history. The embassy in Moscow, at that moment, consisted of Tommy Thompson, myself, and two clerks—Newt Waddell and another whose name I've forgotten. All four of us lived at Spasso House, the ambassador's residence, as did Captain—later Admiral—Jack Duncan and two assistant naval attachés. The U.S. Military Mission was located right across from the Kremlin in the Mokhovaya building, a part of Moscow University, which the U.S. Government rented from the Soviets as our combined chancery and staff residence. A very old friend from Stanford, by then a major in the army, was on the staff of the military mission.

Brigadier General Philip Faymonville headed the military mission. Faymonville was a very controversial character. He was a San Franciscan, and reputed to be held in high regard by the White House—more narrowly attributed by rumor to mean either Harry Hopkins or Mrs. Roosevelt. As important, he was a very close friend of Lavrenty Beria, who was not the kind of person you want to be close friends with. He was the People's Commissar of Internal Affairs (in succession to the murderous Yagoda and Yezhov). Faymonville was extremely pro-Russian. He wouldn't listen to a word against the Soviet Union, or anything that went on there. This caused a lot of tension.

There was dissatisfaction on Stalin's part, and constant pressure for the Second Front. The delays, until 1944, in the invasion of Western Europe, the 1942 North African and 1943 Italian campaigns were regarded by many high-ranking Russians, both military and political, as diversions, if not actually evidence of an underlying ill-will towards the Soviet Union.

However, FDR and those who were running affairs were giving the Russians every possible aid they could summon, sometimes even at the cost of other theaters of war. For example, they had built a whole transport and infrastructure system across Iran so that cargoes unloaded at Abadan could go to the southern Soviet border stations. Planes unloaded from ships at the Persian Gulf could be flown off directly by Soviet pilots to the Russian front. From there, Russians could take the stuff and make use of it.

We made one of the bedrooms at Spasso into a code room, and I slept there. Once we got a message from Laurence Steinhardt in Ankara, where he had been transferred as ambassador after leaving the Moscow Embassy. It took us half a day to decode this missive. It contained an entire list of Steinhardt's belongings, which he wanted sent from Moscow to Ankara in wartime. It included—and this is not a joke because I saw it with my own eyes—"a box with string too short to use but too long to throw away." We found that box. To his eternal credit, Newt Waddell was later detached from the Moscow Embassy and sent down the Volga to Astrakhan with all of Steinhardt's belongings. I think he then went by ship to Baku, and from there the Russians got him over to Leninakhan on the Turkish border. From Leninakhan, Newt and the Steinhardts' boxes and boxes of belongings were trucked to Ankara—in wartime!

Thompson was working through Stalin's Kremlin offices. I don't think Tommy ever went to see him. When Stalin would give a dinner for visiting American dignitaries, Tommy went. I was too junior to go. By that time, Tommy was already extremely capable. And he was very astute in avoiding any impression on Ambassador Standley's part that he was usurping his position in any way.

There wasn't a lot of connection with the local citizenry. We were all subject to the wiles of the NKVD's (secret police under Stalin) "swallows," as the Russians themselves called these young girls who would call you on the phone, the minute—it didn't matter where you lived—you moved into one apartment or another. Some girl would be on the phone and she'd want to meet you at the well-known "National Corner"—the corner of Gorki and Mokhovaya Streets, where stood the National Hotel, just down from the main Post Office.

Being very hierarchical, the Russians arranged things in orderly fashion. Top ranks—but top ranks only—had access to a ballerina. I was honored with a circus acrobat. These young ladies were very forthright. They'd say, "Look, tomorrow I have to go to the NKVD. I've got to tell them what you've been doing. What do I tell them?" I don't mean to be flip about this aspect of wartime life; some Americans were fortunate to make the acquaintance of extraordinary Russian women of great talent and character, and even more fortunate to be able to marry them and get them out of the Soviet Union. Ultimately, of course, all this changed.

Moscow was much easier than other places once the Germans had been driven back. I was told then that the greatest place any of the people who had been in the Moscow embassy had ever been was Kazan. At the evacuation of Moscow, they were first sent to Kazan. The NKVD hadn't had time to get down there, and a great many of the citizens of Kazan were absolutely friendly and delightful. It was like living in a normal city. Then the embassy staff was sent on to Kuibyshev. By this time, the NKVD was there and the embassies were squeezed back into their diplomatic ghetto. Moscow was easier until the diplomatic corps came back. I don't recall meeting any male Russians in the time I was in Moscow. And I was there for over two months—coding and decoding, coding and decoding.

We got queries from the Department. "Do you think that when the Russians reach their former borders that they will get out of the war at that time?" People in the Department were thinking ahead and the embassy was getting a lot of queries of this kind. To that extent, they were very useful. Also, through the other diplomatic missions, and this leak and that, the embassy could pick up quite a bit.

This is the period, incidentally, when Kremlinology got its start. When people learned to figure out what was going on in Russia from these abstruse signs that you got: bird droppings, so to speak. Years later on his first assignment to Moscow, Walter Stoessel had to cover the cultural world. He got onto it. At that point I was back in Washington reading some of these materials. I was struck by the extent to which Walter had caught on to this technique. He could tell you about a performance of "Swan Lake" at the Bolshoi and draw from it the correct political conclusions about what was going on inside the Kremlin. To people who don't know the technique, it seems extremely weird, but it's a perfectly valid thing that worked for a while. It went beyond just looking to see who was at Lenin's Tomb on the First of May or November 7th. For example, the Vladivostok paper we had was not much of a paper, but we read it faithfully. We had a

Russian woman working at the consulate general: Ida Borisovna Minovich, our only secretary. A bird-like woman, very bright. She came into my office one day with the paper, and said, "Did you see this?" There was the announcement by the Kremlin of a great honor, a medal, given to a man named Ramzin. If you knew Bolshevik history, this was absolutely astounding. Ramzin, a brilliant engineer, was the head of what they called the *Promyshlennost' Part*, the Industrial Party, which supposedly opposed Stalin and the Bolsheviks in the thirties. There had been a big show trial of those people. The British got involved—not to their benefit. Ramzin then disappeared. It was assumed that he had been executed. He was not; he was put in a laboratory with all the equipment he needed. He worked throughout the whole war producing what the leadership wanted. He did so well that they publicly decorated him. You could pick up strange things like this all along, great insights.

In any event, after my Moscow experience, I got on the Trans-Siberian, which then took twelve days to get from Moscow to Vladivostok. You had to get on with a lot of supplies. I had diplomatic pouches, mail sacks, and boxes and cartons of food. But everyone in the embassy was after me before I left. The agricultural attaché took me aside and said, "You've got to tell me how the corn crop is." I said, "I'm a city boy." I'm afraid I wasn't of much use to him. The military, and just about everyone else whispered to me, "You've got to look for the BAM railroad." The BAM railroad branches off from the Trans-Siberian and goes north of Lake Baikal, ending up on the Pacific Ocean or, more properly, Tatar Strait at, I think, Nikolaevsk-on-Amur, which is just opposite Sakhalin Island. In other words, it's a route much less vulnerable to the Chinese and Japanese. Everyone urged me, "You've got to look at Bodaibo and see if there's a switch leading out to the north from there." Another one that excited everyone was the possibility of a tunnel under the Amur at Khabarovsk. All of us who made this journey leaned out the train window in Bodaibo. Tracks went this way and that way. At Khabarovsk, everybody got out and peered into the darkness. What amuses me is in 1992 the Russian Government announced the opening of the BAM railroad.

We were really prisoners in Vladivostok. We were allowed to go to the restaurant of a single hotel, the Chelyuskin, named after the great Soviet polar explorer. It was formerly the Versailles and now has been given back its original name by its Japanese owners. The clientele was limited to foreigners, high party functionaries, senior military, etc. The food and vodka were accompanied by the saddest Polish orchestra I have ever heard.

Great parts of the city were closed to us. We couldn't go to the port, for example. We could go outside of town—towards the north—on one designated road, but only 19 kilometers. There was a barrier with an armed guard, and we could go no farther. We'd go out sometimes in good weather and have a picnic, just short of the barrier. Always we were followed.

My Stanford friend Major Olson from the military mission (later an FSO and ambassador to Sierra Leone) came out from Moscow in early 1943 to inspect the port. The object was to see if it was capable of handling the amount of Lend-Lease material which it was being planned to send through it (with the Northern Route to Murmansk now abandoned). Olson judged it to be capable. But after listening to our complaints about our isolation in Vladivostok, he said, "Oh, you guys are all exaggerating. We don't get treated that badly in Moscow." So we said, "We'll show you."

We got together seven Americans from the consulate general: two non-career vice consuls, three personnel from the naval observer's office (always in civilian clothes), Olson, and myself (we didn't try to include Angus Ward, the consul general, who was not one for jokes). One of us left the building and turned left. From across the street a man emerged and followed him. A second American left, promptly followed by another NKVD man from across the street. Then another, and so on, until we were a procession of fourteen people, discreetly separated one from the other, trailing through the city in single file. Olson was convinced. We had a car, a station wagon, but if we tried to get too clever and dodged the NKVD car that always followed us, we paid. If, after such a success, we would park outside the Chelyuskin and go in for a mild celebration, while we were upstairs the NKVD would puncture our tires with an ice pick. This was no joke because we couldn't possibly get another tire. We did a lot of repair work. That was a minor example of what we lived with. A more striking one was provided by a man named Bill Wallace, who came out from Moscow to replace our non-career vice consul. On Wallace's train from Moscow to Vladivostok, there was an absolutely stunning strawberry blond Russian girl on her way to the Soviet naval attaché's office in Washington, DC. She had to stay in the Chelyuskin Hotel for about a week until her ship sailed. Wallace was also staying in the hotel, until Nichols' quarters in the consulate general became available. He and the girl were together all the time. Everything seemed happy and pleasant; Wallace was so taken with the girl, and spent so much time with her in that one week, that he had no time to absorb our complaints about life in Vladivostok.

One day we took this girl, along with Olson—and Wallace, of course—in the station wagon for a tour of the city, or one of those parts where we could go. One place I knew how to reach was a road on the crest of the range of hills at what was then the northern edge of the city. From there you could see the entire port, the bays, the islands protecting the approaches from the sea, and the sea itself. Sure enough, as we gazed at this splendid panorama, a man in a naval officer's uniform came up to the car, and said, "*Dokumenti*," meaning, "Show me your papers." I said, "I don't believe we have to," and argued with him. He said, "According to Soviet law, an officer in the armed forces may ask anyone, including diplomatic personnel, for their documents at any time." I don't recall whether he alleged that this was especially so in wartime. But there were others passing by. So, in the end, I showed mine, and the others in the car showed theirs. Then Wallace's beautiful girl, who by now began to realize what was coming, had to show hers. The Navy officer wrote something down and handed her papers back. With a palpable chill in the car, we returned to the Chelyuskin Hotel.

The next morning she was called in by the NKVD, fired from her post in Washington, and sent back to Moscow by the next train. Wallace supported her financially from Vladivostok through friends in the Embassy. Eventually, a year or two later, after he had been transferred to Moscow, they were married. They had a child. But there wasn't any hope of getting Wallace's wife, or the child, out of the Soviet Union. The war was over; life, and relations with America, had become even harsher. Wallace's wife was taken first by the MVD, successor to the NKVD. The child stayed with the grandmother. Then, the grandmother was arrested. With the arrest of the grandmother, Wallace, who had meanwhile been transferred from Moscow, never knew what became of his child.

As a vice consul, besides the visas that I issued, I also issued crew list visas covering the crews of the Soviet Merchant Marine then beginning to go to our West Coast for Lend-Lease supplies. I read the papers, monitored the radio (Vladivostok was a place where radio signals bounced, and one of our duties was frequent monitoring of broadcasts almost entirely incomprehensible to most of us), and tried to see as much of the city as I could.

With Consul General [Angus] Ward away, I was left in charge. The first thing I did was to institute a weekly round-up of what was going on in our area. We had a naval attaché, in civilian clothes, there at that time with a yeoman and a secretary. We would put together whatever seemed noteworthy, such as, "A cruiser is in harbor, this has happened, the paper says this, Comrade Pegov is running for First Secretary of the Krai Party," and so forth. This went on for the whole two months that Ward was gone. When he came back, he didn't say a word. But he did not continue the weekly political cable. I got the point that he wasn't happy about my little innovation.

For the department store or the movie house, we were obliged to write a letter to the Diplomatic Agent of the Commissariat of Foreign Affairs, who would then issue us tickets or passes. The citizens of the town had free access to all these oases, except the ports.

There were two instances of the cost of mixing with Soviet citizens of which I had personal knowledge. We always flirted with the waitresses in the Chelyuskin restaurant, who were responsive and always joked with us. One of the waitresses, a very pretty girl who had a small son, one night asked me to go to the movies with her. Her name was Valya. I said, "Valya, I can't do that. I have to ask permission to go to the *kino*." She was very offended—not at me—but that any such thing should be possible. She said, "I am a Soviet citizen, and if I want to invite you to go the movies with me, I can do so." So I went. The film was "One Hundred Men and A Girl," starring Deanna Durban. You had to see the Russian subtitles on the screen to see what the *agitprop* people could do with a relatively silly movie, designed mainly to give Miss Durban a chance to sing. The bloodstained capitalists were grinding this lovely young girl and an entire symphony orchestra into misery.

It was mid-winter and the theater smelled something awful (no one removed his or her coat in a Russian theater in cold weather, since there was no heat). When at last the show was over, I walked Valya home, which meant going straight up a mountain. We parted at her doorway and I slid back down to Lenin Street and home. At five or six the next morning, she was arrested. She and her child were taken away. They were sent, I later found out, to a concentration camp near Khabarovsk. Then they were relocated to Novosibirsk. It was put in their dossier that they—she and her child—could never go again to the Primorsk Krai, not even to visit.

I think much of all this helps to point out why the State Department personnel, at least those who had served in Moscow, or Kuibyshev, or Vladivostok, had a very definite anti-Soviet bias (but not an anti-Russian bias). The officers that served there came away from this experience of Soviet treatment—in the midst of a major war in which we were supplying them with all sorts of things and they were our allies—with unavoidable resentment. For those in the State Department who knew, the experience on the ground was that we were basically being treated like enemies. As the revisionist historians get into all this, they should get a feel for the atmosphere at the time, and for how the Soviets operated. If you worked for the American embassy, or the American consulate general in the time of Stalin in the Soviet Union (of course it was true even under his successors but particularly so under Stalin), you learned very quickly that the only methods which would help you to get your work done were clandestine. Open diplomacy? Forget it.

THE DIXIE MISSION TO THE CHINESE COMMUNIST LEADERSHIP

In contrast to the repressive treatment experienced by James McCargar in Moscow and Vladivostok, John Stewart Service spent an exciting time in Yenan in 1944, with the top Communist leaders of China. Having observed first hand the incompetence, corruption, and suspicion of the Chiang Kai-shek regime in Chungking, Service and his fellow officers found a seemingly open, egalitarian society in the depths of China. This picture of the leadership-to-be of Communist China was not a harbinger of the future. The adage "power corrupts and absolute power corrupts absolutely" was shown during the tyranny of Mao Tse-Tung and his coterie once they achieved power.

Service and his fellow Foreign Service officers, who specialized in relations with China, were to suffer at the hands of the right-wing followers of Senator Joseph McCarthy for reporting on what they saw, regarding both the Nationalist Chinese and the Communist Chinese. The Foreign Service took note of the lack of support by the administrations of President Truman and President Eisenhower during what became known as the McCarthy period in the 1950s. This had an unfortunate impact on reporting, especially in regard to areas of domestic political sensitivity, such as developments in the Middle East concerning Israel or Greece/Cyprus. There were powerful pro-Israeli and Greek lobbies in the United States and one had to take into account that supposedly classified reports were too often leaked, and became political footballs.

John Stewart Service
Political Officer, American Embassy, Chungking, China, 1941–1944

The work of the embassy started snowballing after Pearl Harbor. The embassy staff in the summer of 1941 was tiny. No women were permitted. Four men out of the nine were clerks. Those four had to take care of all the coding and decoding, filing, and typing of anything confidential; most of it was classified. Then there was the ambassador and four officers.

The smallest country now has an embassy twice or three times this size. But this was in China, in Chungking. We had the ambassador, and the counselor,

John Carter Vincent. We had a second secretary named John McDonald, who was the economics man. He knew no Chinese and had never served in China. All he could do was to take the handouts.

I was third secretary, and a Chinese-speaking officer. Vincent was a Chinese-speaking officer, but his language was weak because he'd been out of China for most of his service. He'd been in Switzerland, at the League of Nations, for a long time. Then there was a very young Foreign Service officer named Boise Hart, who was not a China man.

I was interested in political reporting—the gravy, you know; this was the way to fame and fortune. It's also for most people the interesting part in Foreign Service work. I had been very much impressed by talking to old hands like Edmund O. Clubb, who had advised me to make a specialty of something, to be known as an authority on some particular subject.

After I got to Chungking it was quite obvious—to me, at any rate—that the big political issue in the future was going to be the Kuomintang Communist problem. There were very few China language officers in the embassy at that time. It was taken for granted that the Communist contact would be maintained, and that I would be the one to maintain it.

We had been working on the question of getting permission to go to Yenan. When [Vice President Henry] Wallace was coming we thought that this would be a good time to make one more try. We drafted a message referring to previous messages. The White House had earlier sent a request, which the Chinese had agreed to. They would let us go to north China, at least to any areas under Kuomintang control. Of course, this was not what we wanted.

We drafted a message to the War Department for General George Marshall summing up all this, and suggesting that Wallace's visit would be a good time for a push. We got a message back which, as I recall, simply said that the White House had agreed that our message could be given to Chiang Kai-shek as being from the White House. In other words, all we had to do was to change the head and tail, and say that this was from the White House.

When we got permission, we immediately canvassed the various operating agencies in the theater to see if they wanted to be represented: the Twentieth Bomber Command, the people in Chengtu, the B-29s, the Fourteenth Air Force, and the OSS. There were various OSS groups that were put under Fourteenth Air Force, air ground rescue service, and photo—something like photo—specialists that the Fourteenth Air Force didn't have, that OSS was able to supply.

The Fourteenth Air Force would not officially send anybody to join our group, because [Major General Claire] Chennault [its commander] was playing

the Chiang Kai-shek game. He wasn't going to do anything that would complicate his relations with Chiang Kai-shek.

We finally got up to Yenan on July 22, 1944. What surprised us was the difference in attitude in Yenan. Chungking was simply waiting for the end of the
war to come. Most of the people were from downriver, and they were waiting so
they could go back to their homes and their families in Shanghai or Nanking.

In Yenan, they had nothing. The whole atmosphere was full of confidence and
enthusiasm. They were absolutely sure that they were winning. As the Communists always say, "The situation is excellent." Talk about your YMCA sort of
spirit of optimism; this was it to the nth degree. Everything is positive, everything
is good, we're going to win, and we <u>are</u> on the winning road. They obviously
expected, as we got to talk to them more, to be very important in the post-war
era, and to share power, at least, with the Kuomintang. They were quite confident that, "The Kuomintang can never whip us, can never take away these territories."

Their whole attitude was a very different one. It was very much like my own
new feelings that I had found with my Chinese friends, of acceptance, of hospi-
tality, of <u>not</u> being guarded, of <u>not</u> holding people off. Their liaison officers came
and sat and joined our mess. People would drop in to see you. It was all very
informal, like a Christian summer conference atmosphere. People were living
fairly close together.

Mao Tse-tung might drop by for a chat in the evening. Or we could go over
and see them almost at any time, and on very short notice. They had some telephones, very poor ones. But, you could call over to the headquarters and say,
"Can I come on over?" If you came, it might be a "stay for lunch" sort of thing. It
was all a very congenial, friendly, frank sort of an atmosphere. Of course, there
were things they didn't tell us, but we didn't know what they were.

We tried very hard, I think, to avoid [being won over to the Communist side].
We didn't draw our conclusions immediately. We tried to wait until people had
traveled in the areas and gotten out and seen what the guerrillas were doing and
what things were like.

But the confidence that we ran into, the difference in the morale, the *esprit*
and the ways things got done hit us right away. If you asked for things, yes, they
said they'd do it, and it was done, promptly, in fact, efficiently. In Chungking,
nothing was efficient. Nothing seemed to work and everything took a long time.

If we wanted to talk to Japanese prisoners, "Oh, yes, we've got a lot of them
down the road. You're welcome." In Chungking, it was the hardest thing in the
world to get a hold of Japanese prisoners. But, almost anything: "Newspapers,

yes, we can get them for you." We started getting newspapers from Peking and other occupied cities in a surprisingly short time. For instance, they had been publishing a paper all through the war in Yenan, a party paper. I asked Zhou Enlai whether I could possibly get a set of back copies. "Certainly!" he said. A couple of days later, bales of papers arrived: he sent them up. Almost anything. They were very outgoing, cooperative.

We had an elaborate briefing when we first got there. We told them: "We're not in a position to negotiate. We're not in a position to promise. We're here to observe. We want to find out all we can about you, what you've been doing, what the war has been like, what you think of it." So, they arranged a very extensive series of briefings.

The Chinese didn't seem to mind any length of talk or briefings. Each day we'd have another Communist leader come and spend the whole day, more or less, briefing us. Sometimes, it was two days. Chu The, Yeh Chien-ying, all the top military people, Peng The-huai, Lin Piao, and then people from the various areas. A lot of them were already in Yenan.

They were talking about having their seventh party congress, apparently waiting for the opportune time. A lot of people had come in from outlying places. It might take them a month or two months to get there. They were already in Yenan waiting. A lot of these people gave us briefings. I took heavy notes on all this. I was interviewing people, going and talking to people.

Mao said at one of the very early meetings, "I suppose you want to see me," you know, with a smile on his face. I said, "Why yes, certainly I do." But, he said, "I want to see you also, but I think maybe that it's better if we wait till we get acquainted a bit; know more about us, and then our talk will be more useful."

Just a month later I got word, "Could I see the Chairman the next day at two-thirty" or something. I think it was two o'clock. I said, "Of course, I can." The talk was one that lasted from two till ten at night.

I'd been in Chungking a long time, maybe too long. Maybe I'd lost my perspective a little bit. Chungking was discouraging, gloomy place to be. People were waiting for the end of the war, or they were trying to do as little as possible in prosecuting the war. There was rampant inflation with all the suffering and dissatisfaction and complaining that it caused. With the rampant inflation nothing was really being done to check it. There was no rationing. Wealthy people did not get conscripted. Young people stayed in universities all through the war, because university students were not subject to military service.

The attitude of the Chinese officials that you met was generally rather resentful. They had a feeling that you were critical of them. There was beginning to be criticism of China at this time in the American press, so they were rather on guard—rather prickly. They felt that we weren't giving them very much; we weren't doing what we should for China. So, most of our official relations in Chungking were uncomfortable, uneasy. They were particularly suspicious of me. The fact that one could speak Chinese, read Chinese, was something that made them suspicious.

I was talking about the Kuomintang attitudes. We got to Yenan and, of course, we were welcomed. They had been isolated—blockaded. They had already gotten some press people up there just before we arrived.

Just going there was a form of American recognition, and this was tremendously important and very welcome. We were treated with open arms and red-carpet treatment. Barrett and I could speak Chinese. Six people in our group of sixteen had spent time in China and knew some Chinese. A bunch of us had been in China teaching, or had grown up in China. So, there was immediately a very warm, cordial atmosphere. They were interested in what was happening in the outside world. They'd been completely isolated. They wanted to talk to us. They asked us all sorts of questions.

They were quite well informed, actually, as far as the news reports went, because they listened to radio news. They got newspapers from free and from occupied China. They got Japanese publications, but they had very little in the way of foreign publications. They were very eager to read anything we could get them. We got *Time* and *Life* and things like that; very late, of course, but this sort of stuff they were very happy to get.

They tended to follow the Russian line, although they didn't completely on the war because they'd been attacked themselves. In other words, they didn't buy the "phony war" line completely in the '39 to '41 period. They paid lip service to it; it was an imperialistic war, but they were anxious for the war to reach China.

I would say that under the circumstances they were quite realistic. In some ways they had a fairly good understanding of the United States. They realized the effect of the political campaign coming on in the fall of '44, and that this was not a time for Roosevelt to make commitments. They said, "We realize this. We'll wait till after the campaign is over." After the campaign was over they wrote to Roosevelt and congratulated him. Roosevelt wrote back. It was quite a cordial letter.

They were astounded at Truman's nomination, but then so were we all. I mean we were dumbfounded when it came over the news that the Democratic convention had nominated Truman as vice president.

We were having dinner that night with the leaders over at the army headquarters. There were two tables, as I recall. Generally, I was regarded as the civilian leader and Barrett as the military leader. I was generally put at the table or place of honor with Mao Tse-tung, and Chu The gave Barrett the honors.

I could sense that Mao was very impatient to get through with all the folderol about getting into our places and getting seated. As soon as we sat down he came out with it. "Who is this Too-lu-mun? Who is Too-lu-mun?" Who is this man Truman? Most of the dinner was devoted then to trying to explain how it was possible that someone completely unknown, or almost completely unknown, with no great record of war or political service, could suddenly be chosen as vice president.

Wallace, of course, had been vice president. Wallace had made a trip to China. Everyone assumed Wallace would be re-named. The Chinese were worried that Wallace's visit to China had been what did him in, because it was during his visit that we got permission to go up to Yenan.

They were concerned what this meant about attitudes toward China and the Soviet Union. They could imagine all sorts of things, because they didn't have any comprehension of the domestic political situation in the United States.

We didn't know much about it either, so we were sort of helpless. It was an amusing incident. Obviously, Mao had given a hard time to Zhou Enlai, because they were quite relieved when they found we were about as confused as they were.

This is typical of the intellectual atmosphere. Most of them were intellectuals. Some were military men, but even most of the military men had had an intellectual period in their lives. Ch'en Yi, for instance, whom I got to know very well, always referred to me jokingly as his teacher's son, because he attended the YMCA school in Chengtu.

We had been given some games, including a game of Monopoly, by special services in Chungking. Some of the Chinese who were attached to the liaison offices saw us playing Monopoly. The next thing we knew they had gone away and manufactured a game of Monopoly, all based on Shanghai real estate! These were all downriver people. It was Nanking Road and the Bund and the Park Hotel and Cathay and all the rest of the hotels. They just thought it was absolutely hilarious! Monopoly, by the way, was banned in the Soviet Union.

We played baseball. Barrett was insistent on having baseball—some exercise, some organized recreation. Usually in the afternoon before supper, he liked to have a baseball game. There was enough to make up two teams. I was a very poor baseball player. I never learned in my youth, so I couldn't catch a fly properly. I was always put out in right field, among some apple trees, so that there wasn't much hope of catching any flies anyway. I could only chase them.

We eventually had a baseball game with these Japanese prisoners, which was very amusingly written up by an OWI [Office of War Information] man, Adie Suesdorf, many years later, in the *New Yorker* magazine. I expect it was the only baseball game during the war between Americans and Japanese prisoners.

Mao himself was very apt to say on some subject, "You want to talk about economic policy. Well, the man for you to see is Po Ku. Go talk to Po Ku." Or, if I wanted to talk about the party and party work in the occupied areas. "Well, the man to see on that is Liu Shao-ch'i." So, arrangement was made for me to go to talk to Liu Shao-ch'i. As far as I know, I'm the only American that ever really had any lengthy talk with him. None of the newspaper people saw Liu Shao-ch'i at that time.

I talked to lots of people. I went to Lu Hsun Academy. I talked to some of the young intellectuals from Kuomintang, who had come into the Communist area and had been sent out to work in the villages. It's just exactly the same thing that's being done now. When these people came and wanted to volunteer they'd hear, "Well, you've got to go out in the villages and stay for a year to prove yourself." A lot of these people were pretty starry-eyed about it.

It was an informal atmosphere, and everything was possible at the time we were there. Later on, things changed of course. It became obvious that we were not going to go ahead and give them anything, that [Ambassador Patrick] Hurley was going to be rigid and insist on everything being done through Chiang Kai-shek.

"Stop That War!"

While some members of the Foreign Service were engaged in matters directly pertaining to the war that raged in both Europe and Asia, a significant number of United States diplomats and consuls were engaged in Latin America, where they had been assigned to keep normal relations with the countries of the Western Hemisphere and to make whatever contribution they could to the war effort.

Rather than the exciting duty of the war front in France, the USSR and China experienced by Harvey, McCargar and Service, Latin American duty for the Foreign Service in World War II was but a continuation of the past policy of the United States toward its Latin neighbors. John Melby describes his time in Venezuela and then in

Latin American Affairs in the Department of State where he was called upon to settle a "war." He later was assigned to Moscow where a real war was under way.

John Melby
Political Officer, American Embassy, Caracas, Venezuela, and Peru-Ecuador Desk, Department of State, Washington, 1939–1943

Unfortunately, the embassy in Caracas was a little bit over-staffed; there wasn't a great deal to do. The main problems involved the Venezuelan oil industry, with a great deal of American investment. Obviously, the ambassador handled most of the negotiations involved there.

As it happened, not long after I arrived, war broke out. It was early '39. Some clown in the White House had a bright idea: with the outbreak of war, one Foreign Service officer should be assigned to keep track of and watch every German ship in the world. There was one in Puerto Cabello, on the coast of Venezuela. And I, as low man on the totem pole, drew that assignment to go to Puerto Cabello and sit there and look at that German ship.

It was in the inner harbor in Puerto Cabello, so it had a great deal of difficulty getting out. In addition to that, the engine had been taken out of it, so it couldn't move anyway! But it took six months to get that order countermanded from the White House. So for six months, I sat there. I sat there, overlooking the harbor, where I could look out and see the ship from the Hotel de los Baños, and I wrote my doctoral dissertation. That's the way I got my degree!

When I got to Washington, I wanted an assignment in the Department, and I conned my way into being assigned to the American Republics Division. I was put on the Peru-Ecuador desk. This was July, 1941. I was there on that desk for two years. I'd been out to dinner with some friends, on the evening of July fourth. And when I got back to my apartment, I turned on the radio. There was an announcement that Peruvian forces had invaded the Ecuadoran province of El Oro and had pretty much wiped it off the map. Not that there was much there, but it was all the people had.

I figured the next morning I'd better get to the office early, which I did. And when I walked into my office, the phone was ringing, and [Under Secretary of State] Sumner Welles was on the phone. And he said, "John, you've heard the news?" "Yes, sir." "Well, stop that war!" and he slammed the phone down. And that's what I did for two years: stop that war!

It was a question of getting the Peruvians to stop buying off the Ecuadorans. As well as arranging for concessions to them. It was a very complicated problem, actually. I worked with the Ecuadoran and Peruvian embassies in Washington. We had the first aerial survey done of that boundary. Nobody knew where the boundary was! I had to arrange with the Pentagon to get the American Air Force to go down there. They photographed the whole boundary. The argument on the boundary went on for years after that.

Part of the settlement had to be that Peru wanted half of Ecuador's territory, the Amazonian part of it. This is what Welles had to deal with at the Rio conference in 1942: to con the president of Ecuador into agreeing to give up half of his territory. Peru had the support of Brazil, Argentina, and Chile. The blackmail that Manuel Prado y Ugarteche, the president of Peru, was pulling on us was that if we didn't somehow force the president of Ecuador to agree to those terms, Prado would keep Peru out of joining us in the war effort. And he would keep Brazil and Argentina out as well.

So Welles just had to take the president of Ecuador aside at Rio and say, "Look, these are the terms. You've got to do it. This is your contribution to prosecution of the war against Germany." And the president said, "Mr. Welles, you know you're asking me to commit political suicide." Mr. Welles said, "I know. And I'm still asking."

The president agreed, "All right, I'll do it." And that's the way Peru got the additional part of the Ecuadoran Amazon. And they thought there was oil there, which, actually, there was, as it turned out. Even Ecuador has some oil now, too. Ecuador has lived on that oil.

THE DOLDRUMS: BELÉM, BRAZIL

Parker Hart was indeed at the far edge of United States interests in World War II. As consul in Belém, Brazil, he served far away from the battles, but still was concerned about Nazi interest in Brazil. He even went up the Amazon to check out a rumor that the Germans might have been looking for a back door to the Panama Canal.

Parker T. Hart
Consular Officer, American Consulate, Belém, Brazil, 1940–1943

I went to Belém. There I was asked by the War Department to do some scouting on infrastructure and landing beaches. They were afraid that Hitler's forces—his Luftwaffe, which seemed to be invincible—might come down to Senegal. There was an African program in the Nazi plan of conquest and they might cross over to Brazil and try to see what they could do there. Brazil was totally defenseless. They didn't have any forces of any consequence.

Later on, I was sent to the Upper Amazon to the Rio Branco, far north in open savannah country, to see if there was anything to the rumor that the Germans were interested in building an airfield from which they could bomb the Panama Canal.

THE DOLDRUMS: CUBA

LaRue Lutkins, on a rotational assignment to the sleepy pre-Communist U.S. embassy in Havana, did pick up some activity in the consular section as a result of World War II.

Since the war made entry into America difficult, many European refugees transited Cuba to obtain entry visas or permits. As the country was, for practical purposes, an economic dependent of the U.S., Lutkins made certain the Cuban government, unlike some Latin American nations, did not assist German interests in any way.

Lutkins was sent off for a year to the Isle of Pines, where Axis nationals were being kept. He kept an eye on the situation there and looked out for Nazi submarines. Probably his greatest excitement was getting to know Ernest Hemingway.

LaRue R. Lutkins
Political Officer, American Embassy, Havana, Cuba, 1942

I was initially posted to Havana, the capital, in 1942. It was primarily a training experience. They rotated us around. I did work in the economic and commercial section, writing up the traditional reports on business opportunities.

Then, I spent quite a bit of time in the consular section, which was quite busy at that time. Because of the war, there was a large number of European refugees who couldn't get directly into the United States from Europe and who made Cuba their transitional stopping place. They applied for American visas there, which made that section fairly busy and active. And then, it being wartime, there was a certain amount of economic warfare work. We were trying to deny the flow of certain products to the Axis powers. And that involved, wherever one might be stationed, working with the local government to try and prevent business contacts and commercial contacts involving the shipment of scarce materials, metals and that type of thing to the Axis powers.

Cuba was not a particularly difficult post in that regard; in those days, Cuba was really an economic colony of the United States. It was overwhelmingly dominated by the United States' financial and industrial interests, so that we never had much trouble persuading the Cubans to cooperate with us. I think we may have had more problems elsewhere in Latin America, where the Germans were a little more firmly entrenched, but in Cuba that wasn't a major problem. Spain was another example, being a neutral country, which was extremely important in that regard.

For a year, during the two years I was there, I was put in charge of a one-man listening post at a place called the Isle of Pines. It's one of those things that is done in wartime that, in retrospect, seemed rather unnecessary and unimportant. But I guess in the heat of war, precautionary steps are taken that seem advisable at the time. I think the reason was that there were a number of Axis nationals—Germans, Japanese, some Italians—who lived in Cuba when war broke out in December of '41. The Cubans, at our request, locked them all up, and they put them in a federal penitentiary located on the Isle of Pines.

The penitentiary was a modern, up-to-date facility that had been built by a fairly enterprising Cuban military man a few years before, for other reasons. But in terms of penal institutions, it was modern, clean, and well run. In addition, there were a few Japanese farmers throughout Cuba, and some perhaps on the Isle of Pines itself. They also were locked up and put in this penitentiary. The idea was that they wanted somebody on the spot to make sure that the Cubans were doing what they were supposed to be doing in keeping these people locked up and not engaging in any hanky-panky. I guess some of the Germans and the Italians were fairly well heeled, and perhaps had money that they conceivably could have used to get special privileges. In addition to that, in the early days of the war, this was at the height of the submarine scare. There were numerous reports of German submarines appearing, and they wanted to have somebody around to keep an eye on that particular area.

When I came back to Havana after the year on the Isle of Pines, one of the jobs I did was to serve as the ambassador's private secretary: scheduling appointments, and so forth. In that capacity, I sat in on some staff meetings. One of them was attended by a famous American resident in Cuba, Ernest Hemingway, who had a home there for many years and whom I got to know reasonably well. He was a great fisherman and he had—I guess for those days—a fairly big, expensive fishing craft that he used to go out in. During the war, of course, gasoline fuel was rationed and it was very difficult for the layman to get hold of. One of the items addressed in the staff meeting, which Ernest Hemingway sat in on, was to explain his proposal. In return for getting fuel for his fishing boat, he would go out and be a decoy to spot any possible submarine surfacing. This was taken very seriously, and the Embassy actually went along with it and gave him the fuel, which I thought was a bit of a scam.

In the early years of the war, the State Department requested the local draft boards to defer all its officers, because it was a very small service in those days. I think we were 750 officers. Because we were expanding the service during the war to cope with new wartime demands, the department wanted to keep its officer corps. But the political pressures grew on the White House over those years. The story was that, (I think it was Judge [Samuel] Rosenman who was the counsel to Franklin Roosevelt), eventually prevailed, in 1944, on the president or whoever made the decisions, to get the State Department to alter that policy of requesting deferments. So, a compromise was reached whereby the Department no longer requested the deferment of its younger officers, I think ones who were under 30 years old and particularly if they were unmarried.

There was also, from the Foreign Service point of view, a rather infamous agitation in the local press, in the old *Washington Times Herald* that Cissy Patterson published. At some point in mid-1944, a whole page appeared in the *Times Herald*, with pictures of about two dozen Foreign Service officers. The headline said: "THESE FOREIGN SERVICE OFFICERS DO NOT CHOOSE TO FIGHT." The department was rather weak-kneed in its response to that.

In any case, the upshot was that, although the Department ceased to request the deferment of quite a large number of officers, I think there were only about thirty or forty actually drafted as a result, one of whom was myself. Most of us ended up gravitating into being selected for work either in the Army, the Navy, or the Office of Strategic Services, which amounted to virtually what we were doing in the Foreign Service except that we were doing it for much less pay.

So, what happened was that I came back to Washington. I applied to the Navy at ONI [Office of Naval Intelligence], but I was turned down for eyes. I was inducted into the Army. I went partially through basic training at Fort Belvoir. And then, in the middle of that, I was pulled out by the Office of Strategic Services, which I had also put in an application for. That must have been November or December of 1944. Then, I spent the rest of my very brief and inglorious career in the military with the Office of Strategic Services, initially in Washington, and then I was sent overseas to Cairo.

3

Soviet and Chinese Challenges, Beginning of U.S. Support in the Middle East

The end of World War II in 1945 found a small, lean Foreign Service that had been all but brushed aside by the demands of a global war. There was little understanding by the American public, but much by the political leadership of the need for diplomacy. Much of the wartime diplomacy had been put in the hands of presidential envoys, or subsumed by the U.S. military. This began to change, slowly, when the fighting ceased and the American armed forces went home. The military occupation forces in Japan, Germany, and Austria were the exception.

While only a tiny cadre, the professionals of the Foreign Service were preparing for the new world order. The broad outlines of future American foreign policy were apparent to those who had been concerned with foreign affairs before and during the war. First, the United States could never again afford to be just an observer in the international diplomatic sphere. Two world wars had shown that American vital concerns were at stake. The old empires were falling and America was involved in all aspects of world affairs: security, trade, finance, and evolving political and social ideologies.

In particular, the United States could not leave Europe to operate alone. Twice in most diplomats' lives, Germany and France had gone to war and dragged in the United States. Whatever else was to be done, the German-French relationship had to be peacefully stabilized and made long lasting.

While the challenging problems of the Soviet Union were not yet clear to most Americans, the Foreign Service—through its own first-hand experience—had no illusions about the ambitions and overriding Marxist-Leninist ideological intentions of the Soviet system. Despite the wartime alliance, the Soviets were seen by many of our professionals as an expanding, ruthless power, whose hold on people subject to that power was terrifying. Perhaps an accommo-

48

dation had to be made with this wartime ally and world power, but it should be done with caution and due realization of the newly evolving Soviet strength and intentions.

The career diplomats dealing with China understood that the Chiang Kai-shek Nationalist regime was weak and hopelessly corrupt. After the Communists won the civil war in China in 1949, "Who lost China?" became the political battle cry of Congressmen questioning the loyalty of the State Department's Foreign Service. China's civil war between Chang Kai-shek and the Communists was portrayed to the American public as an area where the loyalty of the Foreign Service was in doubt. A number of its "China Hands" suffered because of this portrayal.

Japan had been thoroughly defeated. While care had to be taken to see that Japan did not rise again as an aggressive Asian power, the MacArthur-led occupation looked promising. A number of Foreign Service officers were detailed to work under MacArthur to rebuild a peaceful Japan. Future developments in Japan seemed controllable. The parallel occupation of a defeated Nazi Germany led to considerable Foreign Service involvement.

The full impact of de-colonization through the fall of the European empires in much of the world was not yet clear. Latin America had been one part of the world where the United States had always perceived tangible interests, mostly commercial, and these would continue. Only later would the specter of expanding Communism become a factor in the Western Hemisphere.

Finally, the newly created United Nations seemed a promising development in the post-war world. The major powers of the time—the United States, the Soviet Union, Nationalist China, Great Britain, and France—had control over the Security Council, although in truth there were only three major powers: the United States, the Soviet Union, and Great Britain.

America came out of World War II much stronger than it went in, but would it have the political will in foreign affairs to exercise the role of a leader? The post-war Foreign Service was equal to the task. The Foreign Service Act of 1946, the most significant legislative follow-up to the 1924 Rogers Act, provided for a much more structured organization, based on the experiences of the U.S. military during the war. Clear lines of authority were established between the State Department and subordinate diplomatic and consular posts overseas. The model used in the Act for embassies and consulates was the U.S. Navy's ship command organization: captain, executive officer, and heads of ship's departments. Diplomatic missions were under the executive command of the ambassador or Chief of Mission. The executive officer, next in command, was the DCM, Deputy Chief of Mission. The ambassador, often a political appointee, received authority directly from the president, but was under the "command" or direction of the Secretary of State. The DCM was a State Department career officer in virtually all cases. Section chiefs, Counselors of Embassy in larger diplomatic missions, were parallel to department heads in a ship's officer structure. With defined command lines of authority, the structure of the service was much clearer.

Under the 1946 Act, travel and family accompaniment as well as home leave were provided. Prior to this, the service seemed to accept the fact that either its officers had their own money, or that the officers and family would accept long separation from the United States.

More than anything, the Foreign Service profited from the military service of young American men. The war was a crucible which molded many Americans into persons attracted to working abroad for the United States, used to discipline and difficult conditions, and dedicated to seeing that the United States was not dragged into another world war. Many of the men who were to enter the Foreign Service first learned of it from a bulletin board at a military discharge center.

The period from 1945 to 1955 showed the Foreign Service moving onto center stage. Some of the issues it faced would shape the core of American foreign policy over the next forty years. Examples in this chapter are: the confrontations with the Soviet Union (Thomas Dunnigan in Berlin, Claiborne Pell in Bratislava, Bill Kontos, serving with the Marshall Plan at its inception in Athens, and Theodore Achilles with the creation of NATO), the Arab-Israeli conflict (Wells Stabler in Jerusalem), and the hostility of Communist China (Eldon Ericson). With the exception of Theodore Achilles, these are the experiences of young Foreign Service officers facing up to new problems they had not anticipated when they entered diplomatic life.

BERLIN BLOCKADE

As a junior officer, Tom Dunnigan was fortunate in his assignment to the office of U.S. Political Advisor, Berlin. He reported on the Soviet Union's activities and intentions in East Germany, then called the Soviet Zone of Occupation. This truly was the beginning of the Cold War, but long before the erection of the Berlin Wall. The German Democratic Republic was established while he was there. During the time Dunnigan was in Berlin, the eyes of the world focused on that city, because of the Soviet blockade and the subsequent airlift. Many believed World War III might start then and there.

Thomas J. Dunnigan
Political Officer, Office of U.S. Political Advisor,
American Embassy, Berlin, West Germany,
1946–1950

I was assigned to the Office of the United States Political Advisor, Robert Murphy. After about nine months of general administrative work, I was given my first job in political reporting. I was assigned to follow developments in eastern Germany, in what we called the Soviet Zone of Occupation at that time. This was fascinating. It was when the East Germans were founding what they called, euphemistically, the People's Police, but which was really an army, officered by former high Nazi officials. We got information on this that allowed us to complain to the Russians, but they pooh-poohed it, of course, saying it was merely a strengthening of the local police. We had tangible evidence of military units parading and drilling. We considered it worrisome.

I reported on developments within East Germany. Occasionally, in those days, German politicians could leave the Soviet zone and come to West Berlin to talk to us. This was, of course, long before the Wall. They often did so at their own risk, but they wanted to talk. We got some very interesting stories about conditions in Saxony and in Rostock. The clergy were good that way, as were some of the university people, and politicians.

They were definitely disturbed, because they felt powerless. They said all control was exercised by the SED, the German Communist Party in East Germany. And while they belonged generally to either the old Christian Democratic Party, which had existed there in '45-'46 and still existed in the shadows, or the Liberal Democratic Party, they were merely tolerated. They had no authority, no power. Everything was done by the Communists. The only way to get ahead in East Germany was to be a member of the SED.

This was a fascinating period because it was at that time that the German Democratic Republic was established, in October of 1949. We saw signs of it coming by reading the papers from the Soviet zone, which would contain reports of slogans adopted by factories, saying: "We must have our own government. If they have one in Bonn, why can't we have one?" One began to wonder why this was being orchestrated all over the zone at the same time. And it was quite clear that they were preparing a move, which they made on the 7th of October.

I was assigned to a different responsibility: to represent the U.S. on what was called the Civil Administration Committee of the Allied Control Council, the group that ran the city. It was ostensibly four-power, but by the time I got on it the Russians had been out for over a year. It was basically French, British, and American. We reported to the commandants. The Civil Administration Committee handled the basic details of running the city. The German authorities would report to us, ask our permission to do things. We would give it, usually, if it were sensible; otherwise, we would explain why it wasn't possible. Many of the things had to do with legal matters, going back to German law, so we had a legal subcommittee. We had a labor subcommittee, because we had to look after labor affairs. This was a fascinating job, and I did that for the last year I was in Berlin.

The blockade started on the 24th of June, 1948, and lasted until the 12th of May, 1949. We maintained, outwardly, that Berlin was a four-power city and that we, as a member of the occupying powers, could go anywhere we wanted within the city. We could not go outside the city into the Soviet zone except on one road that linked us to the West, the autobahn through Helmstedt. There was a train line. We could go by train either to Frankfurt or to Bremerhaven, but we could not go outside the city in any other direction. But we deliberately went into the Soviet sector of Berlin, as it was called, frequently. In fact, they had the best opera there. And we would drive around, just to be seen, in American cars. We didn't want the Russians to say they had shut us out of there, or frightened us out. In those days, you could take the subway or the elevated train. There was no problem right in the city.

It began to get a little dicey in April, 1948. The Russian representative Marshal [Vasily] Sokolovsky had walked out of the Control Council at the end of March, 1948, over a dispute about currency reform. The Russians didn't want any reform. The Western powers had said, "Look, nothing will ever get this country off its back unless they have a solid currency." There was a to-do about that, and Sokolovsky never came back. About four weeks later, a British plane coming into Berlin was, as I recall, shot down by the Russians, who said it had strayed out of the air corridor (which was nonsense) and crashed. This told us they were ready to play hardball. They stopped the trains from Helmstedt around that period, on the pretext that the bridge across the River Elbe needed repair and would be closed for some time. So the noose was tightening. We still had the autobahn to drive back and forth on; but they could have said, at any time, that the autobahn bridge needed repair. I think it was on the 21st of June that we declared currency reform for West Germany and West Berlin. The Russians then declared a blockade on the 24th, and we started the airlift on the 26th.

The situation didn't get questionable until the fall. The airlift worked fairly well in the early months. There had been enough supplies there to last, but it soon became evident that the two great needs over the winter were going to be coal and potatoes, so the planes began to bring those in.

The worst time of all came in November, because for about ten days in a row, there was heavy fog and planes couldn't get in. We didn't have the sophisticated radar or landing-guidance equipment we have now; it was very primitive. And also, most of the time we were using Templehof Airport, right in the city of Berlin. It wasn't built for very large planes. It took some skill. Later, with the French and the British, we built a much larger airport, Tegel Airport. But that wasn't completed until February or March. It was amazing to see the planes come and go—land, unload, and be gone in ninety seconds. Incredible!

It certainly solidified the relations with the Germans in Berlin, because there was a feeling: "We're all in this together." Now, as occupiers, we lived much better than they did. We were still getting PX supplies, although sometimes electricity went off. We were given, as I recall, five gallons of gasoline a month for our cars, so everybody was car-pooling. I had a bicycle along with my car which I used a great deal during the blockade. It got to be a stick-it-out thing, with everybody saying, "By God, we're just not going to let them do this to us." And we did it!

We were always aware that a military threat was there. The Russians, in my recollection, never particularly threatened to come in. There didn't seem to be any large movement of their forces that would indicate they were planning something. All three powers had small garrisons in Berlin. They would have been overrun, but it would have been a pretty stiff fight for a few days. And the Germans would have sabotaged everything the Russians did anyhow; they hated them.

It solidified our relations with the West Germans. In the airlift, the manual labor was being done by Germans at the airport, unloading that coal, unloading the potatoes, telling the plane when it could move out again. Pretty soon the spirit of cooperation replaced that of sort of occupier-occupied.

We still went into the Soviet sector. They never stopped us. They had thrown the city government of all Berlin out of East Berlin, but we wouldn't let them stop us going there. Although, just because of the lack of gasoline, we probably never went there as often. We could go by subway, though, when the subway worked.

With the introduction of the new currency reform in West Berlin, prices meant something. Items began to have value again. West Germans had things that East Germans could only admire. Gradually, there became a cleft between the two that grew wider over the years and ended, as we know now, with tearing the Wall down.

Robert Murphy worked extremely closely with General [Lucius]Clay, the military governor, and he was a most kind and considerate chief to the junior officers. As I recall, he did not hold staff meetings that included everybody, but we would hear from others what he wanted. I'm a great admirer of his, and I think he did a splendid job there. We know, because I could read the telegrams, that he was cautioning firmness in regard to the blockade.

General Clay had wanted us to send an armored unit up the autobahn to shoot our way in when the Russians stopped our land transit. Murphy seemed to go along with that, but I don't think he was completely sold on the idea, because he realized the dangers.

The truth of the matter is that we had little military. We had gutted this wonderful force we'd had in 1945. We had occupation troops there. Most of the combat troops had long since been discharged from the Army. We had a force that was called a constabulary in West Germany. It wasn't until the Korean War, a year after the end of the blockade, that we began to build up our forces again. Clay and Murphy were well aware of our weakness in that regard.

COMMUNIST TAKEOVER IN CZECHOSLOVAKIA

As Dunnigan faced Soviet Union pressure in Berlin, Claiborne Pell witnessed the Kremlin's expansion in Czechoslovakia through the Communist Party in that country. His experiences in Czechoslovakia in 1948 profoundly influenced his thinking about the Soviet Union in later years when he became a United States Senator.

Claiborne Pell
Vice Consul, American Consulate, Prague/ Bratislava, Czechoslovakia, 1946–1948

Prague was just a random assignment. I know I would have loved to have fulfilled my original assignment—that was as third secretary to Tirana, Albania but unfortunately our mission was closed at that time and I was sent to Czechoslovakia. Albania is the only country in Europe that I have never visited.

I was in the consular section and my duties were to determine who was an LPC (Likely Public Charge: could they support themselves in the United States and were they healthy?)

Ambassador Laurence Steinhardt was very much an individualist—tough, competent, a lawyer. He started out as a political appointee but acquired a great deal of service and expert knowledge. He was a pretty darned good ambassador although a fundamental mistake of judgment was made towards the end of my tour of duty there. It was inevitable, to my mind, that the Communists would have to have a *putsch* because they were not going to do as well in the upcoming elections [spring 1948] as they had previously. They and the Soviets could not afford to do worse because they felt that Czechoslovakia was, as the Russians termed it, a "dagger in their side."

I predicted such a *putsch*. I sent a memorandum, which is a matter of record, to the embassy from Bratislava, to the effect that I felt that there would not be a peaceful turnover of government when the Communists were forced to reduce their strength by the vote. This refers to the scheduled spring elections of 1948, which never took place due to the Communist takeover in February. Therefore, there would have to be a military *putsch* to avoid such an election. This is just what occurred, but this prediction of mine from Bratislava was not forwarded by the embassy to Washington. I think that the people in the mission put a little too much faith in the Social Democrats and thought they would prevail. They probably would have prevailed if there had been, as I foresaw, a fair election. But the Communists would not permit a fair election. The Czechs wanted to join the Marshall Plan and the IBRD [International Bank for Reconstruction and Development].

Actually, I had resigned from the Foreign Service at that time. However, when the opportunity to have my own post—Bratislava—came, I requested the Department of State to withdraw their acceptance of my resignation, which they were nice enough to do. I was stimulated by the thought of having my own post; it was a real challenge.

We have many Americans of Slovak extraction. I think more Americans are of Slovak extraction than of Czech extraction. It was a very important political listening post for Eastern Europe and an important historic city. Bratislava was called Pozsony, Pressburg, and Bratislava, respectively in Hungarian, German and Slovak.

We had to live in a hotel when we were getting it going. Eventually our Government had a good building, which we still own. I had sort of my own USIS [United States Information Service] operation on the ground floor with magazines and books, and offices on the next two floors. My wife and I rented a house not too far away.

The major work there was political reporting. The Slovaks were independent, conservative, and religious. For the Communists to get anywhere there they would have to do it by force—by *putsch*—not by popular election. The election of 1948 was coming, which would have had the Communists doing much worse than they had; the Communists and Russians could not permit that to occur. They had to intervene to make sure they had control of Czechoslovakia.

Of course, I was followed wherever I went driving. I used to go walking or running and they would keep tabs on me. They did arrest a couple of my people: one man who was working for me as an interpreter was terribly beaten up and abused and a couple who had worked for me were arrested and badly maltreated. One man who had driven for me was reported to me as having been beaten to death. So, it was a grim business when the Communists took over: about half my staff was either put in jail or fled.

AMERICAN ASSISTANCE IN WAR-TORN GREECE

The postwar world saw a large expansion of the Foreign Service. The greatest challenge facing the United States and its democratic Western Allies was to enter immediately into an assistance program to rebuild Europe's infrastructure. Thus evolved the dramatic and enlightened Marshall Plan, nearly unbelievable coming from a nation historically so introspective. The Marshall Plan's creation under President Truman, with support from the Congress and the American people, resulted from the clear intention of the leadership of the USSR to expand communism in Europe, especially in Greece, where a civil war raged.

New FSOs and supporting staff personnel came to Marshall Plan headquarters, located in an annex to the American Embassy in Paris. They were assigned to Paris and other European posts in economic, political, management, and administrative positions. After the initial success of the Plan in Europe, a new approach emerged stressing technical aid and development projects for non-European areas of the world. Ultimately, the Agency for International Development (AID) inherited the Marshall Plan's ideas and ideals for promoting economic development. An early participant in the late 1940s was Bill Kontos, who recounts several of his experiences in Greece.

C. William Kontos
Marshall Plan, American Embassy, Athens, Greece, 1949–1953

One of my former Chicago professors, Leonard White, a professor of public administration, had once suggested my name to a friend of his who was responsible for staffing the Marshall Plan missions overseas. One of our classmates was the daughter of a Mr. "Skinny" Holmgren, an official of the Marshall Plan. Holmgren had just been transferred from Greece to London, where he was part of the Marshall Plan team. His daughter had asked him to come to give a talk at a tea. I met Holmgren there; we chatted and he kindly invited my wife and me to join him for dinner. He talked to me about the extraordinary initiative that the U.S. was taking in Greece. He gave me a real sense of what was going on and what needed to be done. I mentioned that I spoke Greek. He said that the Marshall Plan Mission in Athens could really use someone like me. He wanted to know if I would be interested. I said, "Of course!" He said he would communicate with some of his friends in the mission in Athens and suggested that during the next break at the School of Economics, I go to Athens to talk to them. I was received very warmly.

The head of the mission was John Nuveen, a Chicago financier and founder of the family of municipal bond funds that now bear his name. He was then on the Board of the University of Chicago. The fact that I was a graduate of that institution undoubtedly endeared me to him. The other members of the staff whom I met were also very encouraging and decided that I should be assigned to the Civil Government Division, engaged in assisting to reorganize the Greek government. The Marshall Plan mission had been opened for only a relatively short time, although the Truman Doctrine had been enunciated while I was still at the University of Chicago. U.S. involvement in Greece and Turkey came about, partially at least, because the British had come to the conclusion after the war that they could not maintain responsibility or even a major presence in Greece. In fact, they turned the eastern Mediterranean over to the United States.

Soon after British withdrawal, there had been established an American Mission for Aid to Greece (AMAG). It was later incorporated into the Marshall Plan, announced in 1948. When I visited Athens in late 1949, the mission was perhaps a year old. One of the sections of the mission, called the Civil Government Division, was staffed with public administration experts. The section then had five professionals and I became the sixth member, the most junior. This staff was involved in helping the newly formed Greek government, which was just rising out of the civil war, to reform and streamline itself. This kind of assistance was brand new to Americans; we had never been called upon before to provide technical assistance, particularly in the field of public administration.

We had Greek employees, some of whom were professionals. I had an assistant who helped me as translator when my Greek did not convey the full sense of my remarks. The Civil Government Division was fairly well established when I reported for duty. It added one more American employee later when we needed an expert on local government. That was Professor Harold Alderfer from Penn State University. Our big effort was to decentralize the government. Historically, it had been highly centralized, based on the French model. The Greeks used the French system of regional prefects or governors ("Nomarchs" in Greek), appointed by Athens. We wanted to give the Nomarchs greater independence from the center. To show you the extent of that centralization, I well remember that before we got involved in Greek administration, a local school could not even replace a window without permission from the Ministry of Education. Greek centralization was ridiculous. So, we put great stress on decentralization, and Alderfer was instrumental in developing a new code for local government.

The Civil Government Division helped the existing Greek government to develop a new organizational scheme. We helped to determine the number of new ministries, their functions, and activities. In looking back, while our efforts were useful in discrete areas such as the reorganization of the civil service, including a new commission and new laws and regulations and the codification of local government, there were no fundamental shifts. It was not the sort of "starting from scratch" that we brought about in Japan, partly because in Greece we did not have a military government as MacArthur did. Many of us felt that the U.S. government, given the Marshall Plan's enormous resources and the U.S. influence it generated, could have done much more to shape and mold reform. We did not take full advantage of our extraordinary influence and when we did apply pressure, the Greeks were very skillful at evading and modifying our suggestions and recommendations.

Change is difficult. We were proposing ideas that would shake up existing practices and hierarchies, the norms with which the civil servants were familiar. What the Marshall Plan group found was a government that had emerged from a difficult war and a severe occupation, first by the Italians and then the Germans. There had been great food shortages causing many deaths. Immediately after the departure of the Germans, a major communist onslaught took place in an effort to take over the government. That was forestalled by the British through Winston Churchill's strong actions. By the time we replaced the British, the attempted takeover of the government had been stymied, but the communists took to the northern mountains from where they conducted a raging civil war for several years.

During the AMAG period and into the first year of the Marshall Plan that replaced it, there was a war going on which called for a significant U.S. input. We gave considerable military assistance and supplied many advisors. General [James A.] Van Fleet, who later became well known in Korea, was head of the U.S. military mission. He was highly influential in shaping the tactics and training of the Greek army for fighting the communists in the mountains.

By the time I arrived, the Greek government was just emerging victorious from the civil war. It had pretty much abated and was rapidly coming to an end in October 1949, when I joined the Mission. We were able to carry on with very modest constraints, although small pockets of resistance still remained in the north. The Greek government that was elected faced deep-seated rivalries between the old Republican and the Monarchist factions. In the late 1940s, Greece was still a monarchy. The conservative pro-monarchy faction of the Greek political spectrum was in control. The principal *modus operandi* of the government was to control everything from the center; all decisions were made in Athens and the civil service was controlled through the ministries. One of our principal objectives was to break this central stranglehold which, as I said, was based on the French model. The resistance to our concepts that developed came essentially from people who didn't want their perks, their control, their power, and their influence upset by these Americans who had ideas that didn't fit into "the Greek reality."

The situation on the ground was extremely difficult. The wars had left the country in a shambles. There were very few first-class roads, the communications system was mediocre at best; and the power supply was erratic. The Greek countryside was in terrible disarray; many villages had been bombed, particularly in the north. There was severe damage. That made a relief and reconstruction effort urgent. It had to be mounted just to provide minimal shelter and get food into the country. Much of that work was done by the Marshall Plan. We imported vast quantities of wheat, flour, and other food stuffs. But in some ways, these rather chaotic conditions gave further impetus to the notion of decentralization. Greece had Nomarchs who knew well their provinces and their problems. Given any kind of sustenance and resources, a Nomarch could apply remedies effectively to the problem areas. To a certain extent, although it went against the grain, we were successful in strengthening the hands of the Nomarchs. And perhaps as important as decentralization was the grudgingly accepted principle that the Nomarch would be chosen on merit. They needed to be people of proven ability to resolve these very difficult problems. They were not to be chosen because of their political connections, as in the past. Before, they had been appointed by the government and had been friends of the prime minister or some minister. That happened, unfortunately, even during the Marshall Plan days, but we insisted and I think successfully managed to increase greatly the number that were appointed for their abilities. The jobs were of some status, position, and importance.

When you are confronted with a situation in which the local people can deal with their own problems with greater efficiency and understanding than a bureaucrat at a desk far away, it is obviously more efficient and effective to give the authority to the local officials who know the problems first hand. The people in Athens rarely left their offices. I was in Greece for a little less than four years. By my third year, however, I had traveled all over the country and knew more about the conditions of Greek villages than the officials in the ministry of Interior in Athens. In part, they were over burdened by paper work; in part, they were inclined to give orders from their desks. Our support of decentralization was a practical approach. We strongly believed in local government and in the ability of people to order their own affairs with greater efficiency and equity; to that extent, we supported decentralization on philosophical grounds. But essentially our support came for practical reasons.

My two years with the Civil Government Division were busy and exciting. Shortly after I arrived, we had a major postal strike in Greece. The Athens central office was filled to the ceiling with packages; it was absolutely chaotic, since the workers were on strike for several weeks. The strike was economically driven; the workers were hurting. The government had been inept in dealing with its finances, partly because of the lack of resources and partly because it kept running the printing presses, causing serious inflation that, at the time, created unrest and hardships for the workers. I should add at this point that later one of our great successes in Greece was to bring about a stabilization program, which brought inflation down to reasonable levels and made the Greek drachma a stable currency.

I was asked to provide assistance to the Post Office in its efforts to reorganize itself. I was barely out of graduate school, and I was supposed to help reorganize a whole country's postal system. I established a very close relationship with the Director General of the Post Office, Mr. John Frangakis, a man from Crete. He and I were able to get some counterpart funds which went for new equipment and for rebuilding some of the post offices destroyed in the war. We worked out new systems for mail distribution that made some sense. We traveled around Greece together. It was a very rewarding experience. In the end, it was the Post Office that reformed itself; I contributed a few ideas, but Frangakis and his staff really did the job. We managed to buy some needed equipment, and that which was already available was used more effectively. Some of Athens' post offices were enlarged; new branch offices were built in addition to those that were repaired. My experience in reorganizing the Greek Post Office was a good illustration of the extent of the influence of the U.S. government.

CREATING NATO

Despite the clear economic successes and increased political stability brought to Western Europe as a result of the Marshall Plan, the growing Soviet military threat to the West produced the need for a specific alliance with many of the former European allies. The North Atlantic Treaty Organization (NATO) resulted. This organization, within the general authorization of the recently formed United Nations world body, was headquartered in Paris.

Participating were a member-nation international staff and separate member delegations, all located in Paris. The United States had two more ambassadors, one to the OECD (Organization of Economic Cooperation and Development, an outgrowth of the Marshall Plan), and the other to USRO (United States Delegation to Regional Organizations), which included our diplomatic mission to NATO and our representation to a specially set up group responsible for tracing and controlling security trade in various materials of military value. Paris had many ambassadors—even one to the United Nations Educational, Scientific and Cultural Organization (UNESCO). All of this brought in officers who contributed enthusiastically to the new post-World War II Foreign Service.

Theodore Achilles describes how he worked with John Hickerson, another veteran Foreign Service officer, on the creation of the NATO treaty. Achilles also points out the disdain in which Secretary of State James Byrnes held the Department of State. Both Hickerson and Achilles are examples of the senior and experienced "old school" Foreign Service officers who participated actively in foreign policy and trained young FSOs to deal with the post-war world. With Achilles and the creation of the NATO pact we see the old Foreign Service at its best: an officer savvy about the ways of Washington and adept in dealing with diplomats of other countries.

Theodore C. Achilles
Political Officer, London/Brussels, Department of State, Bureau of European Affairs, Washington, 1945–1949

In September of 1945, I was assigned to London and also detailed as secretary of our delegation to the first Council of Foreign Ministers, which met in London immediately after V-J Day to try to negotiate peace treaties with Italy, Germany, and the eastern European countries. Secretary of State James F. Byrnes, who had just become Secretary of State, was chairman of our delegation. John Foster Dulles went and represented Senator Arthur H. Vandenberg, who was then Chairman of the Foreign Relations Committee. Jimmy Dunn was the second-ranking member of the State Department. Chip Bohlen was an interpreter and also an adviser on Soviet affairs. Jimmy Byrnes was quite new to the process; he had been in Congress, in the Senate, and had served as a Supreme Court Justice.

At the end of the first day's meeting, as usual I typed up a telegram to the State Department reporting what happened that day. I took it to Jimmy Dunn, who initialed it, and took it to Secretary Byrnes for signature. Secretary Byrnes looked at it and said, "What's this?"

I said, "This is the usual telegram to the State Department reporting what happened."

Byrnes said, "God Almighty, I might tell the president sometime what happened, but I'm never going to tell those little bastards at the State Department anything about it."

After a year in London and a year in Brussels, I returned to Washington as Chief of the Division of Western European Affairs, and it became my duty, with Jack Hickerson, to concentrate for the next year-and-a-half on negotiating the North Atlantic Treaty and getting it ratified.

On that New Year's Eve, December 31, 1947, I was sitting at my desk, slightly drowsy in the middle of the afternoon, when my immediate chief, Jack Hickerson, Director of the Bureau of European Affairs, came into my office and said, "I don't care whether entangling alliances have been considered worse than original sin ever since George Washington's time. We've got to negotiate a military alliance with Western Europe in peacetime and we've got to do it quickly." I said, "Fine, when do we start?" He said, "I've already started it, now it's your baby. Get going."

Hickerson sat down and elaborated. He had been with General George C. Marshall, who succeeded Jimmy Byrnes as Secretary of State, at the last meeting of the Council of Foreign Ministers in London in December, 1947. That meeting had broken up with no progress on negotiating the treaties, which they had been trying to negotiate for the last two years. The night it broke up the British foreign secretary, Ernest Bevin, invited General Marshall to dinner alone in his apartment. After dinner, he made a statement to General Marshall, which was almost word for word the same one he made in the House of Commons two or three weeks later. He said, "There is no chance that the Soviet Union will deal with the West on any reasonable terms in the foreseeable future. The salvation of the West depends upon the formation of some form of union, formal or informal in character, in Western Europe, backed by the United States and the dominions. Such a mobilization of moral and material force will inspire confidence and energy within and respect elsewhere."

At that point, Western Europe was devastated, prostrate, and demoralized and it badly needed confidence and energy within. With the Soviet armies halfway across Europe and still at their full wartime strength, and the Communist parties the largest single political elements in France and Italy, something was equally essential to inspire Soviet respect.

To deter adequately further Soviet expansion, the only moral and material force was a combination of that of the United States and Western Europe together. Some form of union was definitely essential, but there was a great question as to what form and between whom.

The next morning, Secretary Marshall told Dulles and Hickerson of Bevin's words. He was impressed, but he thought that the union should be purely European, with the United States supplying material assistance. He had made his famous Marshall Plan speech at Harvard only six months before and was still trying to get Congressional authorization for it. He did not want to complicate that task any more than was absolutely necessary.

Secretary Marshall flew home. Dulles and Hickerson came by sea. Jack Hickerson was convinced that a European union backed by U.S. material assistance would not be enough, that only a moral commitment by the United States to do whatever was necessary, including to fight if necessary, to restore and maintain a free and solvent Europe could create that "confidence and energy within and respect elsewhere."

By the time they reached Washington, Foster Dulles had substantially accepted that line of reasoning. Dulles undertook to convince Senator [Arthur] Vandenberg—then Chairman of the Foreign Relations Committee—and Hickerson undertook to convince Marshall. Jack Hickerson and I had both read Clarence Streit's *Union Now*, and had been deeply impressed by it. We shared enthusiasm for negotiating a military alliance and getting it ratified as a basis for further progress towards unity.

Early in January, Bevin made his historic speech in the Commons, saying substantially what he had said to Marshall, and he inquired in a private message to Secretary Marshall what the U.S. might be prepared to do about it. Jack Hickerson drafted a reply, but Marshall balked. Jack's draft reply would have given Bevin very substantial encouragement. The reply Marshall finally signed insisted that the nations of Western Europe first show what they were prepared to do for themselves and each other, after which we would consider sympathetically what we might do to help. That was to be our theme song for the next few months: "Show what you're prepared to do for yourselves and each other, and then we'll think about what we might do."

Bevin's message also stated that he hoped to realize a network of bilateral alliances between Britain, France and the Benelux countries (Belgium, the Netherlands, and Luxembourg), each ostensibly aimed at any new threat from Germany but actually and equally valid against any Soviet aggression. We had recently concluded, and the Senate had ratified, the Rio Treaty, by which the nations of the Western Hemisphere constituted themselves a collective defense arrangement under the UN Charter to respond individually and collectively to any armed aggression. Jack's draft reply to Bevin, which Marshall accepted, contained the suggestion that a similar collective defense arrangement between Britain and France and the Benelux countries would be far preferable to a network of bilateral alliances. Bevin bought the idea. Senators Vandenberg and [Thomas] Connally, who had been on the delegation that negotiated the Rio Treaty, and had fought at San Francisco for authorization for collective defense arrangements under the UN Charter to safeguard its provisions, heartily approved.

It would be a long time before anyone would admit publicly that we were even considering a treaty. But Jack and I knew clearly from the beginning what we were working for. As far as we were concerned, right from the beginning Jack laid down two important ground rules. One was that the Senate, through the Foreign Relations Committee, was to be involved from the start. Its "advice" was to be sought all the way through, rather than merely its "consent" to a signed and sealed treaty. The other was that the process be kept thoroughly bipartisan, essential in an election year with a Democratic administration, a Republican Congress, and the chairman of the Foreign Relations Committee a potential candidate for the Presidency.

During January and February of 1948, having accepted our suggestion of a collective defense arrangement, Bevin pushed on with negotiations with the French and Benelux governments, resulting in the Brussels Treaty, signed on March 17th. Our official position was still, and continued to be, "First, show us what you are prepared to do for yourselves and each other, and then, we will see what we can do." Yet, we had been pushing quietly ahead on two fronts. One was ultra-secret political and military talks with the British and Canadians about a treaty. The talks were held in the Joint Chiefs of Staff war room in the bowels of the Pentagon. The very existence of the talks was so secret that when staff cars picked up the various participants to deliver them directly to a secret entrance in the basement, one Pentagon chauffeur got lost trying to find it.

The United States was represented by Bob Lovett, then Acting Secretary of State,; General Alfred Gruenther, then director of the Joint Staffs; Jack; and myself. The Canadians were represented by Hume Wrong, the ambassador; General Charles Foulkes, chairman of their Joint Chiefs; Tommy Stone, minister in the embassy; and Louis Rogers, second secretary. The British team was Lord Inverchapel, the ambassador; Sir Derick Hoyer-Millar, the minister; the chairman of their Joint Chiefs of Staff; and Donald McLean, second secretary of the embassy.

The talks—even their existence—were ultra secret, and to this day I don't believe anything has been written or said publicly about them. Yet it was only two or three years later that Donald McLean defected to Moscow. The Russians must have been getting a daily play-by-play account. The talks lasted about two weeks and by the time they finished, it had been secretly agreed that there would be a treaty. I had a draft of one in the bottom drawer of my safe. It was never shown to anyone, except Jack. The eventual North Atlantic Treaty had the general form, and a good bit of the language, of my first draft but with a number of important differences.

The other front was the senatorial one. With reason, the Europeans were becoming increasingly frightened of Soviet expansion. Their pleas for U.S. action were becoming increasingly insistent. Hungary, Bulgaria, Romania, and Poland had been taken over by the Communists by the fall of 1947. The Czech coup came in February, 1948, and the murder of Masaryk came in March.

After the signature of the Brussels Treaty on March 17th, Bevin and [Georges] Bidault, the French foreign minister, said in effect, "Now we've shown what we expect to do for ourselves and each other, what are you going to do? For God's sake, do something quick."

We were all deeply disturbed by the Soviet westward pressure, but to the Europeans we still kept saying, "You made a start, but it's still a small start. Put some military 'bones' on that Treaty, preferably some collective ones." We were sufficiently disturbed, however, to contemplate a declaration by President Truman that he was prepared to negotiate a military alliance with the parties to the Brussels Treaty and that, should there be Soviet aggression against any parties to the treaty, pending its negotiation and entry into effect, the United States would consider it an unfriendly act.

Lovett tried that out on Vandenberg, and got a resounding "No!" "Why," asked Vandenberg, "should Truman get all the credit?" It was not an unnatural reaction on his part, for it was an election year and Vandenberg was interested in being the Republican candidate. But he was a statesman as well as a politician and his counterproposal was excellent. "Why not," he asked, "get the Senate to request that the president negotiate such an alliance? Wouldn't that give you a long start toward eventual bipartisan Senate approval?" How right he was!

We accepted his approach with enthusiasm. He and Lovett set out to draft a "sense of the Senate" resolution with Jack's and my assistance. Vandenberg had played a substantial role in San Francisco during the negotiation of the UN Charter, and in the Senate for its ratification.

At the end of April, the Benelux military authorities began discussions, but only in September was the Western Union Defense Organization created, with Field Marshal Montgomery as Chairman of the Commanders-in-Chief Committee at Fontainebleau. Montgomery did not mince words. The British showed us one of their early secret telegrams from Fontainebleau. "My present instructions are to hold the line at the Rhine," said Montgomery. "Presently available allied forces might enable me to hold the tip of the Brittany Peninsula for three days. Please instruct further."

I worked all day for two or three weeks drafting the committee's report on the resolution. There were ulcer lunches of stale sandwiches or gummy beans from the scruffy newsstand snack-bar across the hall from the committee room. Francis Wilcox, Chief of Staff of the Senate Foreign Relations Committee, was an exacting taskmaster and a stickler for detail, but able as hell and he knew his committee thoroughly. They adopted the report unanimously and the Senate approved it by the highly satisfactory vote of, I believe, eighty-four to six, on June 11th. Now we could move.

A similar resolution had been introduced in the House and approved unanimously by the Foreign Affairs Committee. We waited a bit, hoping the House would pass it, but the House adjourned for the election campaign without action. We didn't care too much; it was the Senate that counted.

On July 6th, talks began between Acting Secretary Lovett and the ambassadors of Canada, the United Kingdom, France, Belgium, Holland, and the Luxembourg minister, ostensibly on problems connected with the defense of the Atlantic area, including the possibility of a treaty of alliance. It would still be several months before we would admit out loud that we were negotiating a treaty.

The acting Secretary and the ambassadors met once in a while, but the treaty was actually negotiated "despite them," in Jack's words, by a "working group" whose members became lifelong friends in the process. Many of them have since subsequently been prominent in their own foreign services, in their own foreign offices, or as ambassadors, or in the United Nations. We met every working day from the beginning of July to the beginning of September. That was before the days of air-conditioning and we all worked with our coats off. Most of us were already on a first-name basis, and we all were by the third day. No records of any kind were kept.

The NATO spirit was born in that working group. Derick Hoyer-Millar, the British minister, started it. One day he made a proposal which was obviously nonsense. Several of us told him so in no uncertain terms, and a much better formulation emerged from the discussion. Derick said, "Those are my instructions. All right, I'll tell the foreign office I made my pitch, was shot down and [will] try to get them changed." He did.

From then on we all followed the same system. If our instructions were sound and agreement could be reached, fine. If not, we worked out something we all, or most of us, considered sound. Whoever had the instructions undertook to get them changed. It always worked, although sometimes it took time. That spirit has continued to this day, I believe, although the size to which NATO has grown makes it far less easy.

Two years later, we began in London to put the "O" on the NAT by creating the organization. Some of the members of the delegations had been members of the working group, some had not. I was our representative on a committee; the French representative had not been. He made some unacceptable proposal and I told him it was unacceptable. "Those are my instructions," he said flatly. From force of habit I said bluntly, "I know, but they're no good, get them changed to something like this." He was sorely offended. A little later in the meeting I made a proposal under instructions I knew to be wrong. He and several others objected. I said, "I know, those are my instructions. I'll try to get them changed." I have never seen a more puzzled looking Frenchman. "What," I could see him thinking, "is this crazy American up to? Is he stupid, or Machiavellian, or what?" But he got the idea in due course.

The French, of course, were difficult. They always are in a working group; they balked at everything. For weeks they insisted on a treaty having a duration of fifty years. I thought of that often in the years when de Gaulle had the world wondering whether France would pull out as soon as she legally could, after twenty years.

We did not think the Senate would take a duration of more than ten years and told [Armand] Berard, the French minister, so repeatedly. He said France would not sign unless it ran for fifty years. We told him bluntly that we didn't give a damn whether or not France signed, that we couldn't go beyond ten, everybody else would sign, and that he knew damn well the French Government was wetting its collective pants at least once a day for fear the U.S. wouldn't sign or ratify if it did. That was the informal nature of our negotiations.

More than any human being, Jack Hickerson was responsible for the nature, content, and form of the treaty and for its acceptance by the Senate. He had insisted from the beginning that we consistently seek the advice on a bipartisan basis of the Foreign Relations Committee. He was the one who insisted that it be a collective defense arrangement as authorized by the UN Charter. He was determined that it be a binding military alliance with real teeth, but in deference to the Senate, he was very careful about saying so. He was convinced, and succeeded in convincing many others, that World War III could best be avoided by convincing the Russians, in advance, that an armed attack on any country in Western Europe would bring in the might of the United States, "including the industrial might of Pittsburgh and Detroit," as he said, "immediately."

Jack also insisted that we not waste time arguing about a preamble until the rest of the treaty was finished. "No applesauce until we finish with the meat and potatoes." And he insisted that the whole treaty be short, simple, and flexible, permitting maximum freedom for evolution, development, and response to unforeseeable circumstances. Early on, he read a newspaper correspondent's comment that treaties should be drafted in language that the Omaha milkman could understand. Whenever anyone proposed any complicated language, Jack would remind him of that Omaha milkman, who thus became the spiritual stylist of the treaty. It was a one-man Hickerson treaty.

UNDER SIEGE IN JERUSALEM: OPENING TO JORDAN

The period of American foreign policy in the early post-World War II years introduces one more vital, ongoing, and most unsettled segment of American diplomatic history: the Middle East conflict. America's immediate support of a new state, Israel, set the stage. The American Foreign Service played a key role in the independence of many Arab former colonies. The East-West competition and confrontations extended to the Middle East and oil became an important factor. FSO Arabists and specialists in Israeli affairs were at the forefront of the evolving policy issues.

Wells Stabler, a junior officer in the American consulate general in Jerusalem under dangerous conditions from 1946 to 1950, deals with our relationship with Jordan in the early days. He was an example of an FSO thrown in as an "innocent abroad" to work on the evolving American foreign policy in the Middle East

Wells Stabler
Vice Consul, American Consulate General, Jerusalem, 1945–1950

I was told that I was going to be vice consul in Jerusalem. Obviously one knew about Palestine and Jerusalem, but I really had to go look it up on a map because I had it in mind only from Biblical terms.

I left from Philadelphia in a Portuguese freighter in early November, 1944. We crossed the Atlantic flying the Portuguese flag with a big spotlight over it at night hoping that the German U-boats would see the flag of neutral Portugal and leave us alone. We crossed without incident, stopping briefly at the Azores, but we were not allowed ashore. We finally got into Lisbon two weeks after leaving. I had to go by Portuguese airline via Tangier and Casablanca, from which one went to Cairo.

I thought I would not wire ahead, but just arrive in Jerusalem and go up to the consulate and present myself. I got to Lydda and wondered how I would get to Jerusalem. At that point, a very nice British Army officer who saw me stranded said he was going to Jerusalem and offered me a ride. I rode in his car through beautiful country. The orange blossoms were out. It was a beautiful day—cold, but beautiful. We drove on up into the hills and arrived at the consulate, where I presented myself.

I set myself up in the YMCA and there began almost five years between Jerusalem and Amman. The war was still on. The U.S. had camps in Palestine. The British had substantial forces there, although by that time the war was over. The Middle East was no longer a theater of operations. It had shifted basically to Europe.

The Jews and the Arabs were in an uneasy truce during the war. Most of the terrorism and the civil disorder that existed prior to the war had come to an end. There were incidents. The Jews were bringing in illegal immigrants, which were annoying the British and the Arabs. The Arabs had resented British efforts to let even some of the Jews in legally. They felt the British were being unfair to the Arabs. The result of that was that there was a certain number of Palestinian Arabs who openly declared themselves for the Nazis.

There was a truce. I traveled extensively in Palestine and it was perfectly safe for anybody to do that. Curiously enough, it was on the 27th of December, 1945, exactly one year to the day after I arrived in Jerusalem, that I almost got blown up. A Jewish bomb had been placed in a British police compound. That began again the whole cycle of violence that went on right up until the British got out in May, 1948. The truce had broken down. The Arabs and the Jews started against each other again. The Jews started against the British particularly, as a protest against British efforts to stop Jewish immigration from Europe into Palestine. They ran many ships in illegally, and beached them. The immigrants would get off and disappear into the Jewish areas of Palestine along the coast.

The Arabs were aware of this and they objected to it. The level of violence escalated. Later on, maybe 1946, there was the King David explosion. The Stern gang [secret Jewish organization] had brought explosives in milk drums into the basement of the King David Hotel, which also housed the British Secretariat for the Mandate, and blew it up. It was a ghastly scene.

The U.S.'s main effort really was to observe what was happening. The consulate general was one of two consulates general that reported directly to Washington, it and Hong Kong. The exequaturs [official documents to a consular officer] were issued by two foreign powers, Great Britain as it related to Palestine and then, even though Transjordan (the West Bank) was not independent, we were commissioned vice consuls for Palestine and for Transjordan as well.

At that point, Transjordan was still an emirate. There was a British resident there. Abdullah, King Hussein's grandfather, was the Emir at the time. But he also had certain authority and we had an exequatur from Transjordan as distinguished from the exequatur signed by King George for Palestine. In 1946, Transjordan became independent.

In any event, the role of the consulate general at that time was one of tracking what was happening there. The consul general, Mr. [James] Pinkerton, was someone who played his cards quite close to his chest. I really never did know to what extent he was turned to for advice as to what we should be doing about Palestine.

My role at that time was simply as vice consul in charge of visas. In addition, I handled cultural matters. I used to take films out to kibbutzim and Arab groups and give little talks about American history. It was interesting going to some of the kibbutzim and showing films produced by OWI [Office of War Information] on a variety of topics related to the United States. The visa work was tremendous. Not so much the first year, because no one went anywhere due to strict regulations and lack of transport. When the war ended, however, there was an overwhelming number of passports that had to be issued to get people back to the States. There were ships that came in to take people back who had been stranded.

Shortly after I got to Jerusalem, during the early months of 1945, Mr. Pinkerton apparently had learned that the Emir of Transjordan was unhappy with him because although he was accredited to Transjordan he never went there. He decided that he better go see the Emir. Abdullah had winter quarters in the Jordan valley, on the other side of the Jordan, not terribly far from Jericho. He was down there and Pinkerton decided he would go, but he seemed to think he needed an excuse. The excuse was to present me as a new vice consul.

To a twenty-six year old, seeing an Emir was pretty heady stuff. Abdullah was very nice and it was very pleasant visit. The following Sunday, I decided that I would go back and personally sign the book. I got to Shunah and was very much impressed by all the Arab Legion soldiers who would snap to attention and salute when they saw a consular license plate. When I got to the winter quarters I said to a guard that I wanted to sign the book. He disappeared and came back a few minutes later and said, "I am terribly sorry that the book is in Amman, but the Emir is here; would you like to see him?" I said that that would be splendid. So, I went in and had a nice chat with Abdullah and told him how impressed I had been by the Arab Legion that I had seen along the roads. He said, "Well, I am having a maneuver in about three weeks' time and I would like you to come as my guest." I said, "That is very kind of you, Your Highness; of course I would like to come."

After three weeks I had still heard nothing at all. One morning I was in the file room of the consulate hunting for some document and I came across a letter from Glubb Pasha, who was then the British Command of Arab Legion, addressed to Pinkerton saying that the Emir was holding a maneuver on such and such a day and had commanded him to invite Pinkerton to come to the maneuver. I was crestfallen that I had been forgotten by my new friend.

The appointed day for the maneuver came, and I went to my office in what used to be affectionately called "the turnip shed" of the consulate general, a horrible little shed that was attached to it, heated by a big potbelly stove. I had been in my office not more than 15 or 20 minutes when the phone rang. It was Mr. Pinkerton down at the winter quarters saying, "You get on down here as quickly as you can. The Emir said that the invitation was for you and he won't start until you get here." I thought to myself, "That's a lot of fun, but the end of my career."

I pulled myself together and drove down. As luck would have it, I got a flat tire and got stuck in the sand somewhere. By the time I finally got to the maneuver it was over. The Emir was very nice and invited Mr. Pinkerton and me to lunch in his tent. That was the beginning of a long relationship and friendship that I had with Abdullah, his son, and his grandson, King Hussein.

Consul General Pinkerton spoke no Arabic. I don't think he spoke any foreign language at all. He got along well with the British; they liked him. But he had no real interest in the Transjordan situation. He left in 1946.

I traveled extensively and saw lots of both sides. I did a good deal of work on the Arab side, too. But, curiously enough, during the period Pinkerton was there, I never ever prepared any sort of political report. I went around extensively and talked to people but my role was not that of a political reporter.

For those of us who were serving in Palestine, it was clear that the majority of the residents of Palestine were Arabs. There were about a million-and-a-half people in Palestine, of which about a million were Arabs and roughly five-hundred-thousand were Jews. On the other hand, as you drove around Palestine, which I did extensively at all hours of the day and night, you couldn't help but marvel at what the Jews had produced in their part of Palestine, along the coast in particular. It was a miracle what they had done agriculturally, and to some extent industrially. They had done this aggressively because it wasn't easy to do. They worked terribly hard. They were aggressive in terms of what they hoped to ultimately achieve. One probably didn't know at the onset a great deal of what had been happening in terms of the genocide in Germany. I happened to live part of the time in Jerusalem in a small apartment in a Jewish house. The owner was a marvelous woman who was a Dutch Jew, and who, after I left, unhappily was killed in one of these horrible terrorist actions where the Arabs shot up the bus in which she was traveling. You couldn't help but have great admiration at what they had done, but also you recognized that there was this constant encroachment on what was a demographic majority in the area. You couldn't help but be rather disgusted by some of the terrorism they pulled off in Palestine. A lot of one's British friends were killed as a result of incidents like King David.

There was this constant friction involving British, Jews, and Arabs which got fairly tiring. I have to admit it was very hard to be entirely neutral. You invariably felt more one way than you did another way, although our official position was that of being entirely neutral between the two. I always cite what happened to me on the 15th of May, 1948, when the British left, as evidence of my following instructions to the letter. When I was caught in the crossfire between the Jews on one side of the street and the Arabs on the other side, I ended up with 37 bullet holes in my car. Still being alive, at least, I was neutral to the extent of saying, "Who shot at me?" It was very tense. You had the feeling that the British administration was more sympathetic to the Arab cause than the Jewish cause. And the Jews knew that.

We had difficult moments. Pinkerton left and [Robert] MacAtee came—it must have been in 1947—after the partition resolution. The consulate was not very far from the Jewish Agency building. One morning, there was an enormous explosion. It was quite clear that it came from the Jewish Agency [the official agency representing Jewish interests in British Palestine]. One was sorry that this had occurred but we were even sorrier when we realized to our absolute horror that the consulate car had disappeared. What had happened was that one of our Arab drivers had taken the consular car, had it loaded with explosives, drove into the Jewish Agency courtyard (allowed in because of the consulate plates), got out, disappeared and the car blew up. So it was the consulate car that was responsible for a lot of damage; fortunately, nobody was killed. This gentleman disappeared and eventually ended up in Honduras. I went there some years later and discovered there was a large Palestine population there. A constant tension existed, which took its toll on people. It was hard on people; there were curfews, bombings and God knows what.

The UN came up with the Partition Resolution, which was strongly resented by the Arabs. I would make a good many trips across the Jordan to see what was happening there. When I went over there, I was advised by the British to take my car and have two soldiers from the Arab Legion with submachine guns sitting in the back seat. I did this and got over to Amman. My Jordanian friends asked why I was doing this as I was well known and no one would do anything. They thought it was sort of an insult to come with two Arab Legion guards. So, I never had them again and nothing happened.

There was very strong resentment. Temple bombs increased and we recognized—this was 1947—that the day would come before very long when the British would be out and where would we be? So, we decided that in terms of safeguarding the consulate we would have the British give us an expert estimate as to what would be needed to guard the consulate. They came up with a figure of two-hundred-and-eighty-five marines, which would be twenty-four hour guard service, plus road escorts. We sent a telegram to Washington saying that here is what has been recommended. Washington obviously went into a dead faint because they never answered it.

In their wisdom—which wasn't any, literally—I think it was about a week before the British left. They suddenly threw on top of us something like thirty civilian guards, young men who, after the war not knowing what to do, had answered some sort of ad and signed up as embassy guards. They came from all walks of life. One man had ended up as head of the commissary in Rome, but still was a guard and found himself in Jerusalem wondering what the hell he was doing there. None of them knew how to shoot a gun. I had to take them out personally to a range, although I had never shot a Tommy gun, to teach them how to shoot Tommy guns. They were totally undisciplined. In addition to that, all of the sudden, they sent us, a ten or twelve man navy communications team, which was very useful in that it turned out to be the only way we could keep communications going. I think we had in the consulate general fifteen civilian guards. They drank quite a lot. One of them got mad at me one evening and chased me with a machine gun. It was really chaotic.

We asked for an armored vehicle for the consul general. They had set up a United Nations Truce Organization, made up of consuls general from France, Belgium, and the United States. The meetings were usually held at the French consulate general, which was right under the walls of the old city. In order for our consul to get back and forth he had to go in a car without armor, or walk. So, we requested an armored car. They said they couldn't send a car but could send an armored personnel carrier which doesn't have any armor on top, just on the side and with a canvas top. We never got that, either. The consul general was killed by a sniper's bullet. So, the fact of the matter is that the Department of State was totally not prepared for anything of this sort.

We were left out of the loop on things. There were a lot of conversations between London and Washington which we were not privy to. A lot of things were being done without our knowing what was going on.

I talked about the consul general being killed by sniper fire. It was not MacAtee, it was Tom Larson. He didn't come until just before the British left when all the married men were removed. Tel Aviv didn't exist as far as a U.S. post was concerned. I was the only contact with Transjordan. I was no longer accredited to

Transjordan, because Jordan had gained independence. I traveled there as a friend, nothing official at all. The only thing that existed was the consulate general in Jerusalem. I don't have any recollection that we were really consulted a great deal on these things, that we had much input on partition, or that we were asked very much what we thought. I don't recall that we were kept up on the happenings in the UN. Things would happen, and we would not have advance knowledge. We were really cut out of the loop. I suppose the high commissioner was being queried, because the British are better about these things then we are. Most of what we knew was gleaned from the British.

We were reporting to Washington the views of various communities: the Arabs and the Jews, religious leaders who had an interest in all of this, and also the views of the British. We reported on what was actually happening: acts of terrorism and strong feelings of the Jewish and Arab communities. We let Washington know the tensions that existed between the communities and what might happen if certain things were done. And then, after the partition, we brought them up to date on that.

After Pinkerton left, there was a greater openness in expressing points of view; I mean, not worrying about the political side. One tried to call the shots such as they were. The Arabs expressed very strong views about things; those views would be reported without regard to whether they would upset somebody or not. By the same token, the views of the Jewish agency were also reported, plus those of the British, who were more apt to favor the Arab cause than the Zionist cause. But I don't think political considerations entered into this reporting at all. Although one knew what the feelings were in Washington (with the Department of State on one side and the political aspects on the other side), when the time came for Truman to make his decision to recognize Israel de facto on the first day the British had left, I can assure you that we were neither consulted nor informed. I don't think anybody was. The effort was made at that particular time to persuade the president that if he was going to recognize Israel de facto, he could temper it by recognizing Jordan de facto (even though Jordan had been independent since 1946 and we are talking about 1948). The president declined to do so.

When Jordan became independent, no one in Washington really bothered to think about recognizing it, regarding it pretty much as a British affair. In 1948, it was entirely a political thing. The president made the decision that this would have to be aimed at Israel and not be tempered in any way by also recognizing an Arab state. By that time, the general outrage of the Arab world had already been felt with respect to what was happening with the partition. Therefore, many believed it would be regarded by the Jews as probably insulting to try to balance it in some way. So, the president declined to do that and it was only in January, 1949, when we recognized Israel de jure, that the decision was made to recognize Jordan de jure at the same time.

Obviously, everybody recognized there would be utter chaos and almost anarchy once the British left. We all knew that partition wasn't going to be viable because everybody was against it. It was a big unknown that we were embarking on the day that the British pulled out. The political situation had reached the point where there was no alternative. They wouldn't stay and the UN had no ability or capacity to put a force in there. It was just one of these machines that gathered speed and there was no stopping it. The United States had no power to stop it because we were behind the partitioning. We certainly weren't going to take over from the British. Domestically, it was quite clear that this was what the Jews wanted, because this was the creation by partition of the homeland. As it turned out, they got the whole thing.

In the consulate general, we knew that there was the Haganah (the Jewish army). It was illegal, but the British didn't do much about it. They knew it had some utility in the defense of *kibbutzim*. They got their arms helter-skelter by stealing from British ammunition depots. That was sort of the unofficial army. Then, there was the Stern gang and the *Irgun Zvai Leumi*. The *Irgun Zvai Leumi* was the larger group and the Stern gang was the smaller group. One knew that the Jewish Agency ran a fairly efficient operation and the assumption was that the Haganah would acquit itself pretty well in the struggle against the Arabs.

But as you added up the Arab armies, it was hard, frankly, to see how the Jews would be able to withstand this onslaught. American representatives in all the Arab capitals were reporting that this better not happen because the Jews would be pushed into the sea. At times the "war" between our representative, James McDonald, in Tel Aviv and our representatives in the Arab countries, was worse than the actual fighting. Those in Arab countries took one side, and McDonald took the other.

On the 15th of May when Truman recognized Israel de facto, we set up a diplomatic representative's office in Tel Aviv. James Grover McDonald came to Tel Aviv as the first American representative. Although he was not an ambassador in the strict sense of the word, he was the American representative de facto. The office was set up in Tel Aviv as if it were an embassy, with communications. Messages would be sent also to Tel Aviv and Arab capitals.

On paper, it looked as if there was no way the Israelis could withstand the Arab onslaught. The British pulled out of Jerusalem. Then, they pulled out of

Palestine a day or two later. They moved with the High Commissioner up to Haifa and had an enclave. Shortly after, they pulled out completely.

On May 15, 1948, I was at the consulate general in Jerusalem. The staff by that time had been reduced by many. Officers were all bachelors, including Consul General Tom Larson. It was the policy to remove married men from the danger area as far as Jerusalem was concerned. We had a number of married officers there and they had all transferred. Several officers brought from other posts for temporary duty were bachelors. In any event, on the morning of May 15, Major Andronovich, the CIA representative in Jerusalem, and I drove out in my personal car. The consulate general by that time had no car because it had been blown up. We drove out to a little airstrip called Colombia near Jerusalem and found a small plane and British troops drawn up in battle array with a battery of field artillery with guns aiming in the direction of Jerusalem.

In due course, the high commissioner, Sir Alan Cummingham, a friend of mine, arrived. He was received with full honors at the little airstrip. After saying goodbye to me, Andronovich and his staff took off in his little plane headed for Haifa. The guns were hitched up and bit by bit the British forces also departed. In a very short period of time, Andronovich and I were left standing on an extremely empty airfield feeling really quite lonely. With the departure of the British forces, all public security in Jerusalem came to an end. There was no neutral police force, no security provided by a third element—that is to say, Jews, Arabs, and the British.

Andronovich and I drove back into Jerusalem. At the consulate general, on the steps going up to the office, was a group of members of the staff, including civilian guards who had recently come in, and one other officer, Bob Hutton. They were all rather irritated because they had wanted to go up to the hotel not too far from the consulate general on the main street near the YMCA. When they had walked in that direction, they had been shot at. The British had gone and public order had completely collapsed. They went back to the consulate general and asked to borrow a car, which was refused them. They didn't want to risk walking up again and being shot at.

I said, "Look here, I have my car with a couple of flags on it. Hop in the car and I will drive you there." This was around noon on the 15th. They got in along with me and my little dachshund. We drove up the street around the corner from the consulate general and almost in no time we started getting shot at. I drove the car right up on the sidewalk and let the people in the car get out. They almost fell into the hotel.

As soon as they had gotten out, I started driving up the street towards the YMCA. I was then taken under machine gun fire, on one side by the Jews and the other side by the Arabs. I decided it was a no-win situation and backed my car down the sidewalk and came within a hairbreadth of having a bullet right through my head. It was scary. I was able to get out and also fell into the hotel, literally.

There we were stuck for over twenty-four hours. That night there was virtually no food in the hotel and there were no lights. We were concerned that during the night either a Jewish or an Arab patrol might come into the hotel, shoot first and ask questions later. Things were very tense and the Jews and the Arabs were really after each other.

It was while we were all sitting in that hotel—we did have a battery radio or some sort of communication—that we learned that Mr. Truman had announced the de facto recognition of Israel. This made us all even more nervous because there were quite a few Arabs around this area and we didn't think that decision would be very popular.

While we were there one or possibly two men on the consulate staff got rather antsy about being cooped up. Without my knowledge or permission—I was the senior officer there—they went out onto the street and were promptly shot. Fortunately, neither of them was killed. They were picked up by Red Crescent ambulances (very brave ambulance people indeed!) and taken off to hospitals. One of them was a civilian guard who was well into his sixties. He was taken away and we had no idea where. At that point we didn't know whether he was dead or alive.

In due course, the people at the consulate general were able to arrange with the International Committee of the Red Cross—which had people in Jerusalem trying to help in keeping some semblance of humanity in all of this—to come down to the hotel under the protection of a Red Cross flag. I think these were mostly Swiss and extremely brave men because this was a wide open street absolutely visible from any sniper's post. They came down by small groups and began removing the people from this hotel. Being senior officer, I was the last to leave. Just before I left, they started mowing the streets with bullets so we had to hole up awhile. We all got out and went back to the consulate general. Those were the events of May 15th. There then began a period of one month in which we were under siege, the whole of Jerusalem, really. The Arab Legion had occupied the old city and was lobbing mortar shells into the new city. We lived there at the consulate general with our own generator. We had a naval communications unit, just across an alleyway in a convent. This sort of guard force would shoot street lights out and do all sorts of things.

During that period, we had a number of casualties. At one point, a naval communicator was walking behind the consulate general. I don't know why he was there after dark. He ran across a patrol and was shot. We don't know whether it was Jews or Arabs. He eventually died. The consul general, Tom Larson, was a member of the Security Council Truce Commission, composed of the United States, France, and Belgium. As I remember, he was supposed to keep in touch with the Jewish and Arab communities with the idea of somehow getting a truce from the widespread fighting. The Egyptians had come into Gaza; the Iraqis had marched a division into Palestine; the Syrians had fiddled about a little bit up in the north; and the Arab Legion had occupied the West Bank and the old city.

Larson was obliged to walk this distance, which was relatively far and fairly open, between the consulate general and the French consulate. On his way back from one of these meetings he was crossing a street just behind the consulate and the irony of it all was that he was wearing a bulletproof vest, but a sniper—and to this day no one really knows whether it was Jewish or Arab—shot him in the arm, the one area that was not protected by the vest. We got him to the hospital, but he died very shortly thereafter.

So, during that period we were pretty much holed up. I lived in the consulate general and slept with a telephone and a Tommy gun by my bed. We ate "ten-in-one" rations that had been brought in before, enough food for one man for ten days or for ten men for one day. Not the greatest, but it was the only food we had because all the markets were closed. Some people lived outside the consulate general; they could get around.

I was told to return to Washington without delay, by the fastest possible means. I rushed back to the Department to the greeting, "Oh, you are here? Why did you come back so fast?" No one then knew why I had been told to come back so fast.

HOUSE ARREST IN MUKDEN, CHINA

Foreign Service officers don't always enter the service through the "front door" examination route created by the Rogers Act. At the end of World War II, for about ten year—to meet the enormous demand—most didn't. A number entered through the Staff Corps (specialists, especially in consular and administrative work), like Elden

Erickson, or through the Wriston Program and the Mustang Program, similar to the Navy's route for university graduates or otherwise qualified young aspirants.

Erickson recounts his experiences when the United States was dealing with the emerging Communist regime in China. He was assigned to Mukden, China in 1948, while it was still in the hands of the Nationalist Chinese. He was in the middle of the communist takeover. Erickson worked for Consul General Angus Ward, one of the more demanding officers in the service. The story of Ward's Shanghai "cat house" is told here, the authors understand, for the first time.

Elden B. Erickson
Clerk, American Consulate General, Mukden, China, 1947–1949

As soon as I got to Washington, I was put into a training course in the code room for people going to Russian-occupied China. We had to transmit messages from Manchuria through the Soviet Union. I was assigned to Dairen. I thought I would go to China for a year and if I didn't like it I could go back to teaching, which I knew I liked. I had no intention of pursuing a career at all.

We had to have a visa for Dairen from the Russians. Personnel suggested that I take a ship to China because it usually took a long time to get a visa. They arranged everything for me. It took forty-five days from New York via the Canal, Hawaii, and the Philippines. I finally got to Shanghai in October, 1947. I waited there to get the visa. I was made the "meeter and greeter," so I met everybody who came into China via Shanghai. I was also put in charge of the commissary and worked as a General Services officer, in a sense, to help out while waiting for the visa.

The visa never came. I heard it was because of a problem with the communists that I had fired when I was military government officer. There was never an explanation. Finally, in February, the Department gave up trying to get the visa and I was sent to Mukden in February, 1948.

The Communists had still not taken over any major city. By the time I arrived, they had just captured Changchun in northern Manchuria. Edmond Clubb and Al Siebins were the two officers there; they had to be evacuated. Clubb went to Peking and Siebins to Mukden. The Communists were already moving down from the north, with the support of the Russians, of course. After Changchun fell, they kept coming closer to Mukden.

There were five of us young fellows: clerks, plus a vice consul, Bill Stokes; another vice consul, Fred Hubbard, and his secretary; Angus Ward, who was consul general; and a Japanese-American, who was maintenance officer. Angus wanted to maintain as large a staff as possible in case we were taken over. It was obvious that that was what was coming. He wanted to be able to send one person out as courier every couple of months. We were all volunteers. He wouldn't keep anybody unless they volunteered to stay on. The government figured that we would either be able to work out some sort of deal with the Communists, or we would just be expelled and that would be it. They didn't anticipate what actually happened.

I arrived in February, and the Communists didn't come in until the first of November. The Chinese Nationalists had a million troops in the city; it was active and congested. The Communists would move up to the perimeter of the city and then be forced back, an expanding and contracting of the defense perimeter.

We had regular dealings with the Nationalist government: political, military and economic. We had an aid program at the time, too. We were flying in grain to try to support them. We weren't idle at all during this period.

We had very little confidence in the Nationalist regime. One, because of corruption and two, whenever the defense perimeter would get broader and Chiang Kai-Shek thought he could have a major victory, he would come up to take charge. Whenever he appeared, everything collapsed, every single time. We had no confidence at all that the Nationalists would keep the territory.

Angus Ward, the consul general, was very much in charge. He was imposing and autocratic. He had good contacts with the Chinese authorities. He was busy constantly, either with the office or working on his dictionary. He had already done it in Chinese and Mongolian, and was in the process of making it trilingual to include Japanese. He employed a Japanese teacher to help with the Japanese. The whole thing was handwritten in big volume-like ledgers. He had a card file that was amazing, all done by hand.

The Communists came in on the first of November, and we were very apprehensive. We were on the roof of the consulate general and could see them coming down the main street. We watched them start taking over the communications building, which was about two blocks down. Then they came up to our area. I remember there was an old lady that they just shot and went right on. They saw us looking over the top of the building and they started shooting at us. We then ducked down. At that point, they didn't come into the building.

We had lots of food in tins and sacks of flour. Angus was afraid we would get bored, so we would have to take the forty-eight-pound sacks of flour from one room to another. In a month or two, we would move it all up to the second floor. A couple of months later we would move it somewhere else, bag by bag. He said it was to keep the mites out, but it was really to keep us busy. As much as we disliked doing that, it really was a good idea. But it didn't make him all that popular. Mrs. Ward was there the whole time. They lived about four blocks from the consulate general. The rest of us had moved into the Standard Oil compound.

The Communists ignored us totally the first few days. Our compound was about two blocks away. We walked back and forth for the first twenty days. We were totally free to do whatever we wanted. Angus was trying to make contact, but couldn't. On November 20th, they threw a cordon of guards around the consulate building and around the Standard Oil compound and Ward's residence. From then on, we could go only with them. Each morning, they would come to the compound and march us with pistols in our back to the consulate. We would have to show our lunch and they would inspect it. Then, they would bring us back in the evening. Only half of us would go each day, so no one was isolated.

We were doing nothing, but we were showing the flag, pretending to be carrying on normally. We were moving flour part of the time. They always gave us the newspapers. In the beginning, the Chinese staff still came to work. We were translating. What was in the press at that time was interesting. We sent messages the first twenty days, but after that, nothing.

We had transmitters until they came and took all the equipment away. They went into every house, every room, everywhere and got any radios, anything electronic. That we were doing unauthorized transmitting was the pretext for clamping down.

They didn't recognize the American consulate, the American government, or even America. They flatly said so. After the 20th, they would come to the office and demand radio equipment and this and that. Angus stood absolutely solid against their commands.

We were totally incommunicado after the 20th—nothing in or out. We were afraid at times, too, but it was more a wondering of what would happen. The Chinese were told very soon after we were locked up not to have any more communication with us. They still lived in the servants' quarters in the compound. They would bring eggs and various things because we had no way to go to the market, although we did have canned food in the commissary. The servants would leave eggs and fresh vegetables in the basement and we would go down and find them in the morning. But we couldn't have any communication with them. They didn't dare, and we didn't want to jeopardize their status.

We were marched back and forth the whole time, but you weren't sure when they would come or if they would come; sometimes they didn't, and you just didn't go. We got very snotty with them. I would make a sandwich to take and would shove it in front of them to take a look at it and say *hsao paplu* (little Communist). They were furious but couldn't do anything with us without instructions.

There were anti-American demonstrations every day, with singing and parades all along the side of our compound. I can still sing their little chant: "without communism there will be no China."

Another thing that was rather terrifying in the beginning was that every night we were bombed by the Nationalists. That was ironic, too. Here we were being bombed by our own planes. We were hit one evening, quite a few of the windows blown out. Ralph Rehberg was hit and also Franco Cicogna. I remember picking glass with tweezers out of their lips.

We had a regular drill to put water in the bathtub and open all the windows because of concussion. It was already getting cold. It was an eerie sensation. It went on and on. Then they cut off our electricity, which cut off our water supply. We had no fuel. You couldn't take a bath because there was no hot water. You just put on layers of clothing, like the Chinese. They didn't take our clothing away. Each week we were permitted to write a list in Chinese of what we wanted and give it to a couple who would come to the gate. But we couldn't speak to them. We kept ordering needles because our clothes were wearing out. The servants had done all the mending before. So that really became an important thing, to have a needle. Thread was another item.

It was the cold that I remember as the worst. It would get forty degrees below, and that was really cold. Then, the pump would freeze. We didn't have any running water. We would bake bread and the cockroaches would practically line the bread pans as it was rising. We would bake it with the cockroaches in it and then just slice the sides off; they didn't get inside the bread.

What did we do? We played bridge. We didn't have any electricity and nights start very early in the winter time. We did get candles, and that was all we had. We played pinochle five days and couldn't stand it any longer, so we started playing bridge. They always let us buy vodka. The vegetables—carrots and cabbage—we got most of the time. Meat, from time to time, but it would be full of straw and dirt. However, we would just wash it up and boil it well. We were never hungry. That is important in maintaining at least a modicum of morale. If you are cold and hungry that is a lot worse then being just cold.

There is another time frame when Angus Ward and four others were taken away and put in solitary confinement. Tatsumi was treated much worse than any of the others. They would tell him that Angus Ward was killing his wife and his children. They would have women outside who would scream, pretending that all of this was going on. As far as mental torture was concerned, he was probably the worst off. The five of them were taken from the compound, put in solitary confinement and then returned after four weeks. Then, they were tried as criminals for assaulting one of our Chinese employees. There was a lot about that in the Communist paper.

There was nothing to it. Chi Yuheng had been put up to it. He was a very nice man. He wouldn't ever have done this. But he came up to demand his severance pay. Ward said that he had quit and escorted him out. The press said that Ward had mistreated him and was so rough on him that he lost control of his bladder. This was a criminal charge, according to the Chinese. I think that was in April, 1949.

We didn't know if they were coming back. When Angus was taken out to the truck, he insisted I come along. I still did my shorthand. Every time he had a meeting with the Communists, I took it all down in shorthand. So when he was taken out forcefully from the consulate with the other four, he said, "Erickson, you come along with your notebook." I had my notebook and went out the front door and towards the weapons carrier. The Communists kept saying "You can't go. You can't go." And to him, "You go, move on. You go, move on." We got finally to the truck and they took their bayonets and pushed me back into the consulate. Angus said, "You better go back." So, I escaped all the trouble, really. We had no idea what would happen to us, to them, to anybody. They were tried as criminals. So we were very surprised to see them back four weeks later.

In June we were charged with espionage. Up to that time we were not charged with anything. I made some notes at the time:

> "June 1st—the radio announced that we had been closed.
> June 6th—we got a telephone call and letter from Shanghai. I don't know what they said.
> June 7th—a letter from Clubb. We hadn't heard anything from anybody until that time.
> June 20th—we were charged with being spies and read about it in the newspaper."

There was a trial and we were charged with espionage. Only Bill Stokes was permitted to attend the trial. I was charged with espionage. They had the finding ready before the trial, so it went very fast. They read off the charges and the findings and that was it. All of it was bilingual in Chinese and Japanese. When Stokes left for the trial, we didn't know what would happen to him either.

The economic and administrative people got three years in prison. Angus and the political people—Stokes, Hubbard—got five years, as I recall. All the sentences were commuted to immediate deportation and banishment forever from the People's Republic.

I thought I would decide after a year in the Foreign Service as to whether I would stay in; well, I was locked up the whole second year. I wasn't thinking about my career at all, just of staying alive. We sat there and waited. Occasionally, we would get a message or something from Clubb in Peking, but no movement one way or another. When they did finally come, we said that we wouldn't leave without our things. They said, "You can't take your personal belongings."

Finally one day they came in December, 1949, and said to be ready to go in twenty-four hours. We could take twenty kilos each. Everything else was to be left behind. We had to take the cats and dogs. Our captors came early one cold December morning. We got into an open personnel carrier with soldiers at all four corners covering us with rifles. After we climbed in, three more came with pistols to cover us from behind. We got to the railroad station and there was a big semicircle of military or police. We got on board a horse car with six big stalls in it; it was cold as the devil.

We went to Tientsin, forty hours away. There was an aisle and six stalls. All the windows were open despite the cold. Guards walked back and forth the whole time. We didn't know where we were going when we were put on the train. We thought we might actually be going to Siberia. We were told to bring enough food for forty-eight hours. Fortunately, we did go to Tientsin, rather than Siberia.

All the consulates in China were still open at that time. They had sent Phil Manhard over from Peking to Tientsin. The Chinese made one person be responsible so that we would not commit any crimes. He was that person. When we arrived at the train station, one by one we got off and had to go through a little building and sign documents that we had been well treated and had all our belongings. None of us could read it, but Phil Manhard said to go ahead and sign. We all got out and were turned over to the custody of the Tientsin consulate general. We had to stay in their homes and promise not to go out. We could have no communication with anybody.

We were there a couple of days and then had to go to the waterfront to board a little tug. There had been an arrangement for the *Lakeland Victory* to pick us up out at Taku Bar, but we had to go up the Hai River out to open water to board. We got in the tug. We had to go into the hold which was dark and small and sit down. We got on Sunday afternoon and didn't get out to the ship until Monday morning. We couldn't move. My knees swelled. There were no toilet facilities. It was just a totally miserable trip. When we finally got there, they let Angus Ward get off and go on board the ship with the Chinese. The ship was loaded with reporters who had all the good quarters. We had to take what was left over. When some of the photographers started taking pictures, the Chinese said they had to return the film; otherwise they were going to take us back. In the meantime, all except Angus were still stuffed in the hold. Time went on. We thought we weren't even going to get off now. We never knew what the next step was going to be throughout this whole affair. Finally, one of the photographers ripped his film out and handed it over to the Chinese with a big gesture. That satisfied them and saved face for them. At last, they let us get out of the tug and go on board the ship.

The news people were after us the whole time. We resented it because we had to double up in small places so that they could have the nicer rooms. They would come at midnight to ask questions. We were under instructions not to talk about anything because it would endanger the people who were still there. We still had Hugh Redman, CIA, there. He was in the detachment at Mukden, but the rest had pulled out long before. But he stayed on for some reason. I think his mother went over a couple of times to see him. He finally died in prison there.

Tientsin and Peking were still staffed. Anything we said could really endanger people; we were told that right in the beginning. Especially when we got back to Washington, we were told to be careful to just tell the facts and not speculate. I was new to the service and hadn't held a very high position. The publicity was tremendous. We stopped in Korea and got to Yokohama, where MacArthur turned the military inside out to help us. We were met with a band at the pier. We were all given cars and chauffeurs and cards to the PX. Drivers were told to take us anywhere we wanted. We were really treated like top VIPs. They had flown in special cat food for Jeep, Saki, Saihan and Ranger, the Wards' cats. The Wards adored animals, but especially these four pets. My housemate, Wally Norman, and I would go occasionally to the Wards to lunch. They had a long wooden table. The cats would eat at one end and we would eat at the other. We had cat hair in the soup. They had a Chinese scroll with pictures of pheasants on it and the cats would race across the room and claw the pheasants.

Angus wanted to be able to transport the cats when we left Mukden. He sent a cable to Shanghai saying, "Request whereabouts cat house left Shanghai such and such a date." I don't remember the reply. It was the Cat Lovers Society of America which had flown in cat food to Yokohama especially for Ward's cats.

When I was back in Washington and they were still in Michigan, he called me and asked me to find a place to stay when they came to Washington that would take the cats. I went to every hotel in downtown Washington and never found a place that would take the cats. Finally, they left them with his brother in Michigan.

First, I checked into Personnel because I needed to get back to Kansas. It was two or three days before Christmas of 1949. So, I went to Personnel and they said, "Well, we can't give you home leave because you haven't been out of the country for two years." I said, "Where have I been?" They said, "According to your records you have only been…." I then became rather sarcastic and showed them I had been out two years. I don't know if they didn't count Mukden as being overseas or what.

Two of us had flown back to the U.S. All the rest took a ship. Jack Feigal and I wanted to be home for Christmas. When we got here, Assistant Secretary Butterworth called us in and welcomed us home. I don't feel that there was any ignoring of us. I think they were so glad to have the problem settled.

It is foolish now as I look back on it, but I became very idealistic and very anti-communist and wanted to do anything to eliminate communism. When they asked me where I wanted to go I said, "I will go to any border country and do anything I can."

4

Decolonization, Soviet Tensions, and Old Problems

The decade 1955 to 1965 found the American Foreign Service fully engaged around the globe. The Cold War between the Soviet Bloc and the Western Allies was highly ideological and deadly serious. The threat of mutually assured destruction was a reality. Most of Africa and Southeast Asia were going through the early stages of de-colonization and suffering from the instability that newly independent countries seem fated to endure. Had this freedom movement happened several decades earlier, American diplomats would have been passive observers. Given its new role as the leading Western power and the strongest of defenders against the communist incursions and takeovers, however, the United States had to give serious attention and resources to international developments everywhere. This new, preeminent position also made the United States, and particularly its diplomats, prime targets for evolving nationalist leaders and their mobs, despite the generally favorable predisposition America had towards newly independent nations.

In foreign policy, the East-West hostility was an underpinning to most American dealings with the rest of the world. Washington saw all activities by the Communists or the extreme left a potential blow to America's position and a possible gain for the Soviets. The mirror image prevailed in Moscow.

Continuing tensions and conflicts had changed the world. Problems between nations that previously might have been of concern only to their immediate neighbors were now seen as matters to be settled with the help of the major powers, particularly the United States, before they could turn nasty and possibly draw in the Soviet Union or its subordinates or beneficiaries. This chapter gives glimpses of the Foreign Service engaged in various aspects of this turbulent decade.

CIVIL WAR IN THE CONGO

New posts in Africa, as in most newly independent capitals, were seldom staffed with senior, experienced, Foreign Service officers. Such posts were small and called for junior officers. Terry McNamara was but a vice consul in Katanga, a secession-prone part of the huge former Belgian Congo. His political work centered on intelligence and information gathering, often putting him in great personal danger. He was a principal source of information on the local warring groups. The UN performed the peacekeeping work, one of the first such actions in world history. Terry McNamara was present in Africa when a new government in the Congo (later Zaire and now again the Congo) was emerging. McNamara's two years there portray vividly the chaos that was the Congo in this decade.

Francis Terry McNamara
American Consulate General, Elisabethville, Congo, 1961–1963

Katanga was in secession from the rest of the country. Fighting between the UN and the Katangans hadn't actually started in Katanga itself; nonetheless, it was a troubled place and there were plenty of problems.

In those days, you didn't say "no" to an assignment. You went without argument. Even though I had a wife and small children, I went off to Katanga like a good soldier. I arrived in August, 1961. Initially, I went by myself. My wife couldn't come with me. In those days, they didn't provide housing, so I went to Katanga to get established and to find housing for us. She stayed behind while our kids finished the school year in Washington.

Things were far from decided in the Congo. There were two sets of potential secessionists: one was the Katangans, the other was the Lumumbists in the northeast. They were being supported by the Russians and the Egyptians. The embassy was worried that if the Katangan secession succeeded, it would encourage the secession of another Russian-backed group. The Cold War was very much at the center of American preoccupation in the Congo. Understandably, the Congolese did not share our concern. They were focused on their own problems. A politically aware minority, however, was beginning to understand how our preoccupation could be exploited to their personal profit.

American policy was highly unpopular in Katanga. We opposed secession. Our allies disagreed with our efforts to force Katanga to acquiesce. The UN forces were in Katanga. Resolutions had been passed that the mercenaries had to leave and the secession had to end. The forces on the ground were mainly innocuous Irish and Swedish troops, both of whom were ineffective and didn't feel that they were there to perform a combat role, nor were they prepared for it. Their unthreatening presence suddenly changed as the Indians arrived; they were ready to go to war. They were good troops ready for serious military action. Moreover, the [Indian] government wanted to bring down [Moise] Tshombe and end Katangan secession.

Tshombe, at the time, was a creature of the Belgians, the British, the Rhodesians, and the South Africans; in short, a neocolonial creature. He was looked at by the Indians and the more militant Africans as a creature of European capitalist influences which were viewed as also supporting white domination in southern Africa. The bulk of the export wealth of the Congo was produced in Katanga. Like Northern Rhodesia, it was one of the major copper producers in the world. Copper prices were high at that time.

The British, French, and Belgian governments and commercial interests supported a separatist, independent Katanga. They may not have done it openly, but they were generally supportive of secession. They had consuls general in Elisabethville. We were at loggerheads, in a friendly way, especially with the British who were more ambivalent. Our relations with the British consul were very friendly. The Frenchman, on the other hand, was very angry with our consul. I forget the particular issue now, but he felt that our consul had somehow insulted his honor. The Belgians were resentful of our support for the central government against Katanga and for the UN position, which was very much against the mercenaries and Belgian Army people. At the time, they had regular Belgian Army personnel training the Katangan gendarmerie.

The mercenaries were a mixed bag. There were two military groups of foreigners in Katanga. One was made up of regular Belgian Army people who were training and providing cadres for the Katangan gendarmerie. It was called a gendarmerie, but it was the Katangan army. The second group was mercenaries hired from all over the world. There were a number of Belgians, French, British, South Africans, Rhodesians, and a mixed bag from a wide variety of places.

At our consulate there was the consul, there was me, there was one spook [CIA]. In addition, we had a small support staff of about four other Americans. Then there was a couple: the lady was a secretary and the husband was administrative communicator. And then the spook had his communicator and secretary. That was the whole American complement. It was very small. I was writing political reports. I talked to an awful lot of the people in the UN. We were reporting on military and political events. I was also going around town talking to people. I'd been there for only a couple of weeks before the first bout of fighting started, so I didn't have a hell of a lot of time to get prepared to do normal political reporting.

One evening I had dinner and went to bed. At about four o'clock in the morning, I was awakened by noise in the central square just down the street. I looked out the window, and saw UN troops and armored cars drawn up in the main square. The post office had been occupied by Katangan *paracommandos*. Tensions had been growing over the past few days as the UN picked up mercenaries and Belgian officers. They were scooping them up off the streets, and raiding apartments. Groups of Belgians had already been sent home. In response, the paracommandos took over the post office in the center of town. Suddenly, that night, Indian troops came into the *Place de Poste*, in front of the post office. The apartment I was in was just off the *Place*, so I could see into it and hear what was going on. I heard them give the Katangans an ultimatum over a loudspeaker to surrender and leave the post office. When the Katangans refused, the Indians started to shoot. The shooting went on for some time. There was riposte from the Katangans, but they were outgunned and lacked effective leadership. Their mercenary officers were in hiding. The post office was stormed by Indian troops. By eight o'clock in the morning, resistance had ended. The Katangans had suffered some casualties but most were taken prisoner. After seizing strategic points around the town, the UN troops began a search. This is how the fighting started in Elisabethville, based on my own observations.

That day, there were a couple of things that happened. One, the African population began hunting Balubas. Balubas are from Kasai and from Northern Katanga. They were not viewed favorably by tribesmen from southern Katanga who provided the bulk of support for Tshombe's separatist movement. On the contrary, the Baluba strongly supported the central government. The antagonism stemmed, in part, from the large number of Baluba who enjoyed well-paid jobs, especially with the copper company. There was a large colony of them living in Elisabethville. By mid-afternoon, the Baluba hunts began throughout Elisabethville. Groups of young Katangans sought them out, beat them, and often killed them.

I was walking down the main street of Elisabethville that day when suddenly I saw a man peddling like mad on a bicycle, with a gang of youths chasing him on foot. Finally, one guy caught up to him. This gent had a bicycle chain attached to a stick that he used like a whip. It wrapped around the unfortunate's neck. The chaser then yanked the man backwards off the bicycle. He landed with a sickening thud. The chain had cut into his neck and was strangling him. The gang of assailants then proceeded to kick him to death.

There was a quiescent period several hours after the UN made their early morning move. Early in the afternoon, I left the consulate with a colleague named Tom Casselly, who was in Elisabethville on TDY [temporary duty], to pick up the wife of the CIA communicator, Will Poole. We were trying to concentrate the Americans at the consulate and in houses where they would be more accessible, less isolated, and in areas away from points of potential conflict. We picked up Dottie Poole in the consulate Jeep and were bringing her back to the consulate building when suddenly we ran into Katangan troops preparing to attack the UN headquarters. When they saw our Jeep, they began shooting at us. They thought that we were UN, because of the vehicle. Anyway, we pulled into a driveway, jumped out of the car, and got into a drainage ditch.

When the shooting died down, we went to a neighboring house and knocked on the door. A young Belgian couple opened the door and let us in. We all took shelter in their *cave* [cellar] in the back of the house as the rate of firing increased. The Katangans soon surrounded the house. They then banged on the door. When the owner opened up, he was told politely that they wanted us to come out of the house. The man insisted that we were not from the UN. We refused to leave the questionable safety of the house. Surprisingly, they did not force the issue or attempt to enter the house. Instead, they asked the Belgian next door, "Do you think those are UN people?" He assured them that we must be local civilians as our Jeep's license plates were ordinary Congolese private plates.

This seemed to satisfy them, and they went away. But, if they'd grabbed us, God knows what would have happened. Thank God they did not suspect that we were official Americans. We stayed in the Belgians' *cave* for the best part of the afternoon. Just before dusk, we decided to make a run for it. I told Casselly to take Mrs. Poole and head up the street where I could shelter behind some buildings. They shot at us as we were leaving, but the bullets were high above the top of the Jeep. Casselly and Mrs. Poole soon joined me and we returned to her house rather than attempt to cross the town to the consulate.

In her apartment, we had no communications. We simply lay on the floor and hoped the random firing would not penetrate the sides of the building. In the middle of the night, a UN convoy suddenly pulled up in front of the house, complete with armored cars. When we had gone missing, the people in the consulate had organized a search party for us, fearing that we had been taken prisoner by the Katangans. Fortunately, the convoy was able to escort us to the consulate.

The relationship between the American consulate and the UN was very close. We supported the operation with advice and intelligence. I was in the UN headquarters every day during the fighting giving advice and information, crossing lines at some considerable risk, advising on military operations and on the attitude of the population. I gave first-hand accounts of Katangan military dispositions and on their reaction to the fighting. The UN didn't have advisors as we use the term, but here we were; we had our consulate general situated next to Tshombe's palace. I was floating around town, talking to people and moving between the lines. I found a relatively lightly covered back road leading into the UN camp. The Gurkhas would often provide covering fire while I scooted into the camp. It was an incredible situation, and it went on for some two weeks. Finally, a cease-fire was declared. The UN had seriously miscalculated Katangan resolve and mercenary abilities.

The consulate was looked at as the enemy. We were supporting the central government and the UN in their fight against Katanga. The American government supplied the essential element in terms of support for the UN force in the Congo. It couldn't have existed without American support and encouragement. Therefore, we were looked at as an enemy. There had been demonstrations against the consulate, which by this time was guarded by Gurkha soldiers.

In November, 1961, my family came up from Rhodesia. I had three small children. The eldest was about five or six, and they ranged down from that to three or four years.

Essentially, the consulate was trying to keep the peace in a combustible situation. At the same time, we were advising the UN on military and political affairs. They were isolated and without much reliable intelligence. I gave briefings every day to the UN leaders on what was going on in town, the mood of the Katangans, and their military dispositions. Members of the Swedish contingent had cultivated some contacts among the local Belgian population; this seemed to be the extent of their sources of information. Given our greater mobility and wider range of contacts, we were able to brief and advise the UN leadership. At the same time, we reported to Washington and to Leopoldville what was going on on both the UN and on the Katangan sides. We described growing tensions and what we could see of what was happening daily on both sides.

The fighting broke out in mid-December. It went on for about two weeks. The outcome was an assertion of UN control over the whole of the center of Elisabethville. They extended their perimeters to the suburbs of town. The European center of the town was taken over by the UN. The Ethiopians, Swedes, Irish, and Indians were involved. The Ethiopians were accused of some atrocities, killing civilians. They killed some Belgians. I remember a Belgian woman being killed, allegedly, by the Ethiopians. And as far as I could tell, it was true. But it's not unusual in war, and certainly not unusual under those circumstances. What was more troubling was that a lot of Africans were also being hurt, killed, displaced, and not too much notice was being taken.

The second bout of fighting was again inconclusive, aside from the fact that the UN people extended their perimeters and took full control of the center of Elisabethville. They consolidated their positions and took control of the communication between their positions. At this point, they had a large area that took in the entire center of Elisabethville.

During the fighting, things got really nasty as far as Americans were concerned. The Katangans started threatening Americans for the first time. The American missionaries in general were sympathetic towards the Katangans. The Katangans sensed this and were using this sympathy to try to gain a more widespread sympathy in the United States. Then, when the fighting started in the second round, they turned against the missionaries and started threatening them, as Americans, because of the American support for the UN forces.

American Air Force airplanes were coming into Elisabethville, bringing in supplies and non-American troops for the UN. In other words, these were American Air Force planes. No longer were they just hired airplanes contracted for by the UN, and maybe paid for with American money; these were actual USAF airplanes.

Therefore, the American support for the whole operation was much more obvious to the average Katangan. It was also equally obvious that America was certainly not taking any sort of neutral role; we were one of the essential elements in this whole thing. The Katangans controlled most of the African suburbs of Elisabethville, as well as much of the remaining territory of the province. We decided that we had to evacuate the American citizens in Elisabethville, because it was getting too dangerous.

At this time, the Seventh Day Adventists had decided to have their regional convention at their headquarters in Elisabethville. They brought people from the United States and from other parts of eastern Africa to Elisabethville. Their headquarters was across the street from the UN headquarters, a special target of the Katangans. When fighting started, the Adventists found themselves in the crossfire between the two sides. The poor Adventists were really under the gun.

With the help of a journalist who had good contacts with the Katangans, we arranged a cease-fire, from twelve to one o'clock, to get them out of their precarious position. I went from our consulate to get them out. I crawled down a long drainage ditch to the back door of the mission building. The cease-fire took place on time. No more shooting. We had an hour to get out. Both sides had agreed to this. So I told the missionaries, "You've got to leave now."

Over the phone they had earlier accepted that they would leave, as soon as a cease-fire could be arranged. When the shooting stopped, however, they changed their minds. Some decided that no, they wouldn't leave. So, all refused to leave. I said, "Look, you've got to go. The shooting is going to start in another hour. We've got one hour to get you out of here. If you don't leave, you're again going to be in exactly the same situation." "Oh, no, no, no. It's okay now. We can't leave our homes. We can't leave our buildings, all of our work," and so on.

After much fruitless urging, I had to leave without them. I was sure that as soon as one o'clock came, the shooting was going to start again and I would receive another frantic telephone appeal. "Please get us out of here." Predictably, the shooting started at one o'clock, the war began again, and they were on the phone two or three minutes later, saying, "Oh, you've got to get us out of here!"

With some difficulty, we again arranged another cease-fire. This time, they left without serious resistance. That evening, we gathered all of the missionaries, not just the Seventh Day Adventists but the other groups that were in town. The biggest was the Southern Baptist group. I organized a convoy into the UN headquarters, and then, from the UN headquarters, at night, out to the airport, with protection from UN forces. I got protection from the Swedes in armored personnel carriers, and from the Gurkhas.

As a prelude and a test run to the biggest evacuation, I took the families from the consulate out to the airport first. We had three or four families, women and children. I took them out earlier, to see how it would all go. We put them in the back of an open Swedish APC [armored personnel carrier] and drove out to the airport. There were bullets bouncing off the sides and the Swedes fired machine guns in reply. I recall the spent shell casings flipping into the back of the APC; some fell on my sleeping children.

The differing reactions of the several families were very interesting. I was the only male parent present. Otherwise, we had three mothers with their children. Where the mother was calm, her children remained calm. Where the mother was agitated, nervous and frightened, her children reacted in the same way. For instance, my wife, who is very tough, was calm, joked with the soldiers and reassured our kids. My children stayed calm and relaxed with the youngest sleeping soundly. The youngest one fell asleep on the way out, even though the machine guns were blasting away. She hadn't had much sleep the night before. She and my wife had been in our friend Colonel Mitra's house. When the fighting started, and the bullets began bouncing off the outside walls, the colonel put my daughter in the bathtub with a mattress in front of the tub to protect against bullets or shrapnel. She played quietly there for most of the day.

When the fighting started, two of my children had been at school. They were enrolled in a local Catholic school called Marie José School with Belgian and Katangan children. When the fighting started, the wife of the other vice consul, named Whipple, went to get the kids. She got her children and mine and took them to her house. The next day, I organized the evacuation and took the Whipple, Hoffacker, and McNamara kids, their mothers, and one or two other wives to the airport in a Swedish APC under enemy fire. Thank God, the Katangans didn't have heavy weapons.

The next day, I organized a larger evacuation of all of the American community. Most were missionaries. After we'd had the dry run with our own families to see how it worked, we had a better idea of what we were doing. First, we organized the Americans in a convoy using their own vehicles. There were some two-hundred of them. I led the convoy into the UN perimeter. Escort was organized from there for the run to the airport at night. There was some shooting, but no serious opposition. We got to the airport without casualties. The air attaché was there with two or three airplanes.

When we got to the airport, the perimeter of which was now held by the UN, a couple of the missionaries—after the UN soldiers had protected them and gotten them out to the airport, where they were safe and preparing to be evacuated—complained bitterly about the UN "intervention." I got angry with this wanton ingratitude. The UN soldiers had just risked their lives to protect the missionaries and their families. So I told one of the missionaries what I thought of him. I came close to punching him in the nose, but I resisted the temptation. Afterwards, I got a letter from the Baptist bishop apologizing to me for the intemperate things that his colleague had said to me, and for his nasty accusations of the American government.

Ultimately, in June or July, fighting again broke out. This time, the Indians were ready to bring it to a conclusion. The Katangans still held the copper-mining centers of Jadotville and Kolwezi. Only the administrative offices of *Union Minière* were in Elisabethville. The real economic prize was in Katangan lands. To end the secession and restore the country's most valuable economic asset to central government control, the UN had to take control of these towns and their nearby mines and refineries.

The UN got into Kolwezi as well. Tshombe capitulated and the leaders of the Katangan *gendarmerie* (army) fled into Angola. The UN then was in control of South Katanga, and the Katangan secession was over.

The central government brought in symbolic units from the national army, as well as a resident minister from the government, named Joseph Ileo, to administer the reintegration of Katanga with the rest of the Congo. A nasty contingent from the *Sûreté Nationale* arrived to seek out secessionists, mercenaries and other subversives. I remember one poor Biafran being left tied to a tree for four or five days. His body was covered with cigarette burns. Obviously, he was being tortured. The *Sûreté* types grabbed a couple of Americans who happened to be in Katanga. I don't remember quite why they were there. They were being held in the back yard behind Ileo's house. To assure that they were not being mistreated, in the middle of the night I snuck into the yard next to a campfire. The secret police agents were startled by my sudden appearance. I had come armed with several bottles of beer. This seemed to take the edge off their suspicions. We finally wound up an amicable group around the camp fire—the secret police thugs, the American prisoners, and the American vice consul. I suppose this was a dangerous thing to do, but it may have saved our citizens some disagreeable moments. The next day they were released without casualty. We got them out of the country as quickly as possible. I left Elisabethville in October, 1963. I arrived in Washington just before President Kennedy's death.

When I came back, I didn't realize that I was as psychologically rocky as I must have been. I certainly was suffering battle fatigue after two years in that dangerous, unpredictable place. I'd gone through two years of drunks sticking loaded guns in my face. An inadvertent stumble could have blown my head off. Living in a hostile city, crossing opposing lines during combat, evacuating people, and nearly being killed by my own friends had all taken their toll.

READING THE COMMUNIST TEA LEAVES IN INDONESIA

From the height of the Cold War in Moscow, where Robert Martens had honed his Soviet Union/communist political reporting skills, he went to Jakarta, Indonesia, to apply them in a peripheral Asian country. There, the third largest Communist Party in the world was becoming dominant. On his arrival in 1963, like the rest of the American embassy he thought that Sukarno was a nationalist, not a communist. Within six months it was evident through Martin's analysis of Communist Party tac-

tics learned in Moscow that indeed Sukarno was a willing supporter of the Communist Party. In his observation of Sukarno, Robert Martens saw the twilight of one of the major nationalist leaders in Indonesia.

Robert Martens
American Embassy, Jakarta, Indonesia, 1963–1967

My job at the embassy in Jakarta was oriented towards the communist side of things, and to some extent Soviet and even Chinese affairs. It was what in those days we called "peripheral reporting". There were always a large number of junior and middle-grade officers in Moscow, but not very many senior positions. You had a huge body of Soviet and Communist Party expertise building up over the years, but with few places in Moscow for a second tour. The result was that a great many officers with that kind of background were sent out to so-called peripheral assignments. We had three or four in Latin America, for example. I went to Indonesia and I was very happy to go to a different geographic area. I'd never been to the Far East. I really wanted to go there and report on what was then the largest Communist Party in the world after the Soviet and Chinese parties.

I arrived in Jakarta in September, 1963, on a date that is known fondly among the people that were there at the time as Ash Wednesday: the day the British embassy was burned and sacked. My wife—it was her introduction to the Foreign Service—and I arrived in all that confusion. Even the house next door, a British house, had been burned. It was quite an introduction to the city!

Sukarno had given a great deal of trouble to the West already. He had come to a much more complete individual power position only two or three years earlier. In the early days, there had been basically a parliamentary democracy, so his power had been far from complete. Now he was in the process of entrenching that power and carrying Indonesia, in my opinion, further and further in a pro-communist direction. This was not recognized in the embassy when I arrived, nor did I recognize it. I didn't go out with this preconceived notion, but I began running into things that made me convinced in a fairly short time—several months—that Sukarno was totally in league with the communists, and was carrying the country in that direction. I ended up writing a long report in May of 1964, eight or nine months after I arrived, in which I made the then-startling statement that Sukarno was a communist. I could not get that report out without writing a cover sheet, which I also wrote—I was given the opportunity to do that—saying this was only one man's opinion, but eventually the whole embassy came to this view.

Sukarno had the reputation of being an ardent nationalist, which he was. There was a tendency in those days for people to think that these things were mutually exclusive. I think that was a fault of American intellectual thought in the early 1950s where nationalism was called "the great bulwark against communism." This was a misconception, as these two concepts of nationalism and communism can be much more intertwined.

Sukarno had latched onto the British granting of independence to Malaya, and doing so in a form in which the old Malaya was to be combined with several other British colonies in the area along the northern coast of Borneo and with Singapore, and forming this group of British dependencies into a new independent state to be called Malaysia. Sukarno took issue with this, and declared it a neo-colonialist scheme. There were some intimations that Indonesia also had designs on the northern Borneo territories for itself. One could regard the development of this tremendous hyper-nationalism that evolved in the Malaysia campaign, which began in the summer of 1963, as pure nationalism and nothing else. It was nationalism to some degree, but it was much more than that because, in my view at least, this campaign provided the excuse to carry the country internally in a much more extremist and left-wing direction.

There was a strong and visible trend of Sukarno's working in tandem with the Communist Party from then on. The Communist Party was becoming more and more powerful and had already become, by far, the largest element in the country. This was done not from a grassroots approach; it was primarily a revolution taking place from above rather than below. Sukarno and the Communist Party leadership at the top—the Communist Party working with Sukarno's support—tried to project a feeling of inevitability that the Communist revolution was marching to an imminent total victory. Meanwhile, all opposition to the communists was being suppressed by Sukarno, under his guise of being the "Great Leader of the Revolution" and the "President for Life." This continued right up to the famous September 30th affair, the failed communist "coup" that led to the overthrow of communism in Indonesia.

The ambassador's name was Howard Jones. Howard Jones was sent to Indonesia originally as the AID director for quite a few years before this, had gone back to the department, and had been the deputy assistant secretary of state for Far Eastern economic affairs. He was sent back as ambassador and as such had already been there a long time. His total period as ambassador, if I remember correctly, was seven years; he was well established. He had the reputation—which he tended to promote himself—of being very friendly with Sukarno, and one of the few people who had influence on Sukarno. Sukarno catered to this. It was my opinion—and that of most other people—that Sukarno tended to lead Ambassador Jones down the garden path, making him feel that he had more influence than he did. This became particularly obvious in the last year or so of Jones' tour as ambassador. He left around May of 1965, about three or four months before the so-called coup. By that time, we were being thrown out and our buildings were being sacked. Jones had been made to look ridiculous by Sukarno's actions, and by Sukarno even pointing his finger at him and shouting at him to take away his "so-called aid." This was a distinct put-down by Sukarno.

When I arrived, there was a good deal of antipathy towards Jones in the embassy, particularly after the burning of the British embassy; a feeling that he was out of touch. Some of this was rather personal. I felt then, and I've felt since, a good deal of respect for Jones personally. He always treated me well even though I became the sort of opposite pole in the embassy's thinking about what was taking place in Indonesia. Jones always took me with him to meetings with Soviets, or figures that were openly pro-communist in the Sukarno government. I remember interpreting for him in Russian, between him and the head of the main political administration of the Soviet armed forces.

The situation kept getting worse and worse. By the summer of the year after I arrived, 1964, things got bad with the famous "Year of Living Dangerously" speech by Sukarno. That was not the speech of the year in which the coup took place, but rather of the previous year, 1964. But that speech indicated a very strong leftward lurch by Sukarno, followed by a period in which there was a moderate counterattack led by Adam Malik. Malik was originally a Marxist, but he had come back from a tour as ambassador to Moscow disillusioned with communism. Malik was then removed from his position as minister of trade, and everyone associated with him was removed from office or demoted.

The following spring of 1965, in a speech to the quasi-parliamentary body called the MPRS [People's Consultative Assembly], Sukarno announced that Indonesia was "now leaving the National Democratic stage, and entering the socialist stage." This was straight PKI [Indonesian Communist Party] jargon for ending the period in which the communists were still allied with certain groups in the National Front, and would now go for total power for themselves. Sukarno himself announced this. Most people in the embassy didn't understand it, nor were they prepared to understand this kind of esoteric jargon. From that point on, I felt there was going to be an attempt made by Sukarno to make the country openly and irrevocably communist in the very near future. And, in fact, that's what happened.

When I got out there it was very apparent immediately that a good part of the embassy was opposed to Howard Jones' interpretation of events. I think that Jones was wrong in his analysis, but I agreed with him that we had to stay in the game. There were some embassy officers who felt we ought to leave Indonesia, close the embassy, and break relations. I never felt that. I am a believer in trying to stay in the game to the extent possible. This meant a certain accommodation with Sukarno from the standpoint of keeping channels open, just as we did in Eastern Europe with the Soviet Union. I think that Jones had some reason to be hopeful in earlier days that things would pan out better. The West Irian dispute had come to a conclusion favorable to Indonesia to a great degree because of U.S. intervention, as well as the Dutch ending their last colonial possession in the East Indies.

Sukarno identified himself more and more with the pro-communist forces. At that point, it should have become clear that one's analysis of events had to change. This didn't mean that one would get out of the game, but while staying we would have to keep our eyes open (but I don't think from the way Jones talked that was the case). It was in this later period that there began to be differences in the Department over our policy. There were some elements in Washington, particularly on the NSC [National Security Council] staff, which still generally agreed with Jones. Within the East Asian Bureau—and I don't speak on this except second hand—I think it's clear that Country Director David Cuthell began to take a view very similar to mine on what was going on in Indonesia.

Marshall Green was deputy assistant secretary in the East Asian Bureau, and since Bill Bundy, the Assistant Secretary, was so preoccupied with the Vietnam question, Marshall had supervision over Indonesia and many other matters. Marshall Green also began to see things pretty much as Cuthell did; so, views were beginning to change in Washington. Perhaps as a result of this, our policy began to visibly alter after Sukarno publicly shouted at Jones, "to hell with your aid." This was in January, 1965. Sukarno took the country out of the UN at about this time and Jones dismissed its importance in a cable to the department. The political section succeeded in convincing Jones to soften some of the more ridiculous things he was saying in his original draft of that cable, but it was still overly apologetic for Sukarno's behavior.

In the period that followed, early 1965, the Peace Corps had to be withdrawn. Our library in Jogjakarta was sacked by a communist-led mob. Our library in Jakarta, the capital itself, was then sacked as well by a similar mob. AID [Agency for International Development] was withdrawn around April or May of 1965. The embassy was reduced to a much smaller group. USIA [United States Information Agency] was withdrawn except for one or two officers who remained in the embassy proper without appearing to be USIA. They continued there as information officers. This was much like the situation we had in Moscow at the height of the Cold War where we did not have a designated USIA office, although we had a USIA officer. All this was going on and Ellsworth Bunker came out—I forget whether it was March or April—and apparently came to the conclusion that things in Indonesia were rather hopeless. Bunker talked to me for about an hour, presumably to assess the views of a leading dissident voice about where the country was going.

Jones left in May, and Frank Galbraith, the DCM, became chargé for the next two or three months. He came in with a very pessimistic cable right after Jones left. I had gone to Galbraith, incidentally, right after the Sukarno speech that had declared that Indonesia was now entering the socialist stage. I told him my view that this meant that Indonesia was going to go completely and openly communist within the next two or three months. Anyway, Marshall Green arrived in July as the new ambassador, and obviously with a far different view. I'm not saying that Marshall Green accepted all my views; I don't know whether he did or not. I remember when he arrived that as he came down the aisle at the airport or embassy—I forget which—he said something along the lines of, "I have read your stuff, and I agree with you." I don't know if he remembered that afterward or not.

He did have a much more skeptical approach towards Sukarno. It didn't mean that he didn't try to maintain contact; he also tried to maintain contact with Foreign Minister Subandrio, which was necessary, too. But within a month or two after he arrived, we had the communist effort to seize total power, the September 30th affair. And I should add that these final months leading up to the coup were ones in which the relative moderates in the other parties were being purged at Sukarno's urging. The other political parties, other than the communists, had already been or were being taken over from within by communists, or were totally neutralized. Sukarno was also pounding the army leadership to accept what was intended to be a political commissar system with the communists being the commissars. Sukarno was pushing the concept of what he called a Fifth Armed Force, which was basically the arming of the PKI. The army was balking at these measures, which were intended by Sukarno to be the last steps required to carry the country into the communist camp by peaceful means. When the army balked, Sukarno decided to turn to a violent entry into the socialist stage.

This was foreshadowed by a speech he gave on July 25th, which I remember very clearly. I sat near Sukarno while he gave it. His bodyguard was Colonel Untung, who was later the nominal leader of the so-called coup. In that speech, Sukarno praised the earlier communist uprising of 1926–1927 by identifying himself with the PKI of the 1920s, which went underground after the failure of that revolt. In effect, Sukarno was saying that he had been a member of the 1926 PKI. None of this had been known to the outside world. Sukarno then began to browbeat the army to get in line with the revolution, or else. He shook his finger at General Yani, the head of the army in this period, and publicly threatened him along these lines. The so-called coup, starting with the assassination of Yani and his leading generals—which was carried out largely by Sukarno's personal body-guards, the so-called Tjakrabirawa Regiment—was aimed at getting rid of the top army leadership, which was seen as the only remaining impediment to permit "entry into the socialist stage." Unfortunately for them, the coup failed.

The entire embassy staff was a very close-knit group, particularly as the situation got worse and worse. In certain closed societies, you tend to have better rela-tionships with people than you do in some of the more open societies. We knew all those people. They [the CIA] did a certain amount of reporting. It was the kind of reporting that the agency does: non-analytical reports from sources, reporting on what the people they had on their payroll were saying. Some of it was very good, but some of it was off base because a lot of the Indonesians were so terrorized by the flow of events that they came up with rosier views than were warranted, or than what they really believed themselves. They kept hoping that Sukarno was going to save them from the communists. Whether CIA was doing anything operational, I don't know. I don't think they were doing anything sub-stantial, frankly.

From all I was told by them and by others, the CIA was authorized to oppose the communists, narrowly defined, but to do nothing against Sukarno or any ele-ments of the government. If you took the view, as I did, that Sukarno was the real leader of the PKI in essence, this was a totally unworkable kind of thing. They were not doing anything in a major way against Sukarno except reporting. In any event, I don't think one could find any basis whatsoever for any belief that the U.S. was involved in trying to change things in Indonesia. We wanted things to change. Obviously our sympathies were not with the communists, nor were they with Sukarno as he became identified with the communists, but that was all it was. We didn't see any role to be played. In fact, one could argue whether that was right or wrong, but that was basically our policy. We stayed out of it.

Ambassador Green later described how the policy under him was similar to that of a surf boarder riding the waves—keeping out of trouble, basically. The changes that took place were changes that took place because of internal factors. The fact was that the Indonesian people, by this time, were absolutely fed up with the Sukarnoist and PKI system, very much like what happened in more recent times in the Soviet Union and Eastern Europe. There are a lot of parallels. I'd had previous experience in Moscow at the height of the Cold War. I found the terror in Indonesia in 1963 through 1965 greater than that in the Soviet Union in the 1950s.

People were actually scared to death. I remember a young man who had been teaching me Indonesian on Sundays. The last time I saw him he went out the front gate and then came running back to my porch saying that he had seen some people laying for him out there who were trying to kill him. I took him out the back way, and walked him up to a bus stop some distance in the opposite direction so I could protect him as far as I could. But there was obviously no way that I could protect him on a longer-term basis. I never saw this young man again. I'm convinced that he was killed by the communists shortly after he left my house, although I have no direct proof.

And I had some very similar experiences with a professor at the University of Indonesia that I used to see during my first year in Jakarta. Later, he was intimidated by the communists at an academic symposium and his life was threatened if he continued to advocate non-communist views. He became so fearful thereafter that he wouldn't see me anymore. I ran into him by accident on neutral ground later. This was at a third world-country embassy probably, in August, 1965, just before the September 30th coup. Things were really looking bleak for the non-communists. We happened to be standing next to each other on a balcony, and I said—I won't mention the man's name—"So and so, you can see how things are going as well as I can." The man, an ethnic Chinese, started crying and this was a very brave man in the earlier period. He said, "I know how it's going, and if the communists take over, and it looks like it's ninety-five percent certain they will, I will be destroyed even though I have tried to take on a neutral image. But that's not going to work; both my family and I will be exposed to persecution. And if by some miracle that doesn't happen, and the non-communists come out on top, it might very well be in the context of an anti-Chinese pogrom, and I would get it that way, too." But it didn't happen. The man survived. There was some anti-Chinese feeling in places, but it was not on the scale that was anticipated, and most of the Chinese came out all right.

What happened was, as in every closed society, people that have had the kind of experience I've had with Soviet affairs, analysis sometimes called Kremlinology, you try to read the tea leaves and you try to understand the organization of the Communist Party, not through contacts, which you cannot very much have, but through reading the communist press very carefully. One of the things you do is to try to form a structure of the party by carding the names of positions. Not so much the names, as to try to get the positions organized and understand how everything fits together. I'd been doing that for the previous two years when this so-called coup—actually an attempted purge—took place. I had assembled all this unclassified data on the Communist Party structure based on the communist press itself, and to a far lesser extent on other communist publications. Regarding the latter, I went frequently to the three communist bookstores that I knew of in Jakarta from time to time and bought some of their pamphlets, which I reviewed later. Anyhow, I developed this into a sort of structure of the party.

About a month after the coup, a man came to my house who was a chief aide to Adam Malik, a man I have spoken of earlier. Malik, you will recall, had been one of the few leaders who had stood up to the communists, and he now became very close to the army. He was almost a foreign minister in waiting, and he later became foreign minister under Suharto, and still later vice president. This fellow said, "I have been told by friends in the diplomatic corps, not from Americans, that you know more about the Indonesian Communist Party than anybody else. So could you help me?" I said, "Sure." So I talked to him and we hit it off quite well. He became a very good friend, as well as a contact; and we talked about what was going on, as you do with lots of other people. You don't go to foreign countries to sit in the embassy doing nothing but twiddling your thumbs.

I talked with this fellow at some length, and over time I discovered that he didn't have—and perhaps the army didn't have—a very organized collection of data on the Communist Party. Everybody knew the big names. If they could put it all together they probably all knew things individually far more than I did, but I had a kind of structure. For example, the new Central Committee of the Communist Party that had been announced maybe a year or two earlier, had been in the Communist Party newspaper at that time, but whether anybody had that available was problematic because fear and terror had been so great that anybody within the Indonesian system that collected information on the PKI would have been considered an enemy of Sukarno and the state. So, I gave some of this basic newspaper material to him, and he took it to Malik, and Malik apparently gave it to the army. What effect it had, if any, I don't know. It was certainly not a death list. It was a means for the non-communists that were basically fighting for their lives—remember the outcome of a life-or-death struggle between the communists and non-communists was still in doubt—to know the organization of the other side.

To accuse me, or the embassy, of trying to murder masses of people even down to the village level, as was in an article in a U.S. newspaper, is about as sensible as trying to say that anybody that kept data on the Nazi Party in the late 1930s—so that Americans might be able to distinguish between Martin Bormann and Heinrich Himmler and all those people—was guilty of some heinous crime. It doesn't make any sense whatsoever.

Ninety-nine percent of my reporting on the Indonesian Communist Party, its various affiliates, and some of the other leftwing movements was based on reading the tea leaves of the communist press, and analyzing what was happening in the public arena. I did seek contacts and attend events whenever I could. I took advantage of any luck.

We were fairly aggressive at times in pursuing a better understanding, a better knowledge of the country, but not really underhandedly; we had an excuse to do it on this occasion. Otherwise, it was very difficult and the embassy was very isolated by the intense anti-American atmosphere promoted by both the Sukarno Government and the PKI.

Suharto had come to full power, at least in reality if not totally in theory, on March 11, 1966. The government had been formed with Suharto as prime minister, Adam Malik as foreign minister, and the Sultan of Jogjakarta as a third key figure. They were considered a triumvirate, although Suharto was obviously first among equals.

Sukarno was still nominally president, but was not allowed to do anything. It was now clear that this important country was going to go in a non-communist direction. Indonesia had rejected the communists completely. The relationship with the United States was still remote; not unfriendly, just no official contact in the transitional period. The embassy, under Marshall Green's guidance, had rightfully avoided any kind of overt contact in order not to play into the hands of the communists. Suharto and Malik and the others also kept their distance for that reason because they didn't want to support the Sukarno line that his enemies were lackeys of the imperialists.

BERLIN MAN IN MOSCOW

In retrospect, the period 1955 to 1965 was the apogee of the Cold War. The United States and the Soviet Union came closer to war—twice in this period—than at any other time. The immediate cause was the adventurism of the Soviet Premier, Nikita Khrushchev. He repeatedly challenged the United States over Berlin and missiles in Cuba. Kempton Jenkins served in Moscow during the Berlin confrontations. Having just served in Berlin, he clearly was the "Berlin Man" at the American embassy in Moscow during these tense and dangerous years. A high point is the confrontation between Tommy Thompson and Foreign Minister [Andrey] Gromyko, when the latter's threatening bluff is called.

Kempton B. Jenkins
Political Officer, American Embassy, Moscow, Soviet Union, 1960–1962

We arrived, as I recall, in August of 1960. It was a shock. From the air, Moscow looks beautiful. There had already been some light snow, oddly enough; maybe it was September because I remember clearly there was some snow on the fields, although not much. All the pines and the birches, from the air, looked beautiful. When you arrived at the Sheremetyevo international airport, it was three buildings. It was and still is tacky. You hit the ground, and all of a sudden you realize that "this place needs new management!" Everything was run down. The two years that I lived in the Soviet Union and during frequent visits thereafter, it has always been one of the strongest impressions: "God, this place is so badly maintained!"

Khrushchev was in. The relationship was extremely confrontational. The Berlin crisis was in full flower. Shortly after we got there was the ill-fated Bay of Pigs landing. It was a huge embarrassment.

The ambassador was Llewellyn Thompson who is, in my judgment, the finest career officer I ever had associated with. He was not a strong personality like Chip Bohlen had been; he was shy and retiring, but absolutely a splendid and decent man. He had sensitivity to political realities and the Soviet Union, and had a very good dialogue with Khrushchev and his entire Politburo. And he had terrific insights.

As an embassy, our strength was our knowledge. There were a few areas where we were deficient; the Japanese, for example, had a fisheries attaché, but we didn't. But they came to us for our agricultural attachés. The French had a stronger cultural section than we did in terms of the number of people and the diversity of contacts. But in everything else, we were the best informed. Of course, we had an extremely close working relationship with our allied counterparts.

I was the Berlin man in the embassy. Arriving there, it became my responsibility to interpret what I could see in the paper, by attending lectures and traveling. I might interject that we had a "travel program." I was the travel officer in the political section, among my other duties. We deliberately laid out territories, or areas, of the Soviet Union we wanted somebody to cover.

The Defense Department attachés were on the road all the time for their own reasons, but we shared maps. If we wanted to go to Frunze, and Alma Ata, which I did, and the defense attachés had not been able to get certain information about the kinds of factories which were present for their purposes, we would share requirements. And they would come back and give us things like programs from cultural events where we could see who was actually appearing. And we would pay calls on the local editors in the newspapers in these outlying republics, and we'd call on the republic foreign minister, who of course was a sham, but was thrilled when we showed up. That was the event of the year, so we would get something out of that every time. I would say three-fourths of the Soviet Union was off-limits, even though on the official map it was all open. You had to apply for authority, a *propusk*, to go there. Then the Soviets would reply and say, "Sorry, there are no hotel rooms this week," which meant it was a closed area. They didn't want to admit that much of the Soviet Union was closed.

I was in Moscow when the 1960 American election occurred, and I watched the debates between Nixon and Kennedy in the snack bar at the back of the embassy building. We had our western colleagues and journalists in to watch this. We got the tapes; we didn't see the TV live, but it was taped and flown out to us. We shared that, and we were all pretty excited about Kennedy.

We in Moscow initially were all thrilled, but the Russians were scared to death, because Kennedy was a political sex symbol all over the world. They couldn't cope with that. This was popularity. Eisenhower had been disliked by a lot of people, he was regarded as too old and too cautious. He was a military man, so in Third World countries he was looked upon as an American imperialistic symbol. When Kennedy came in, that was dissolved. All of a sudden, the United States became the image and symbol of young, vibrant, creative, peace loving, tough—all the right words. And in Moscow the Russians all felt this way. The people would come up to us in the streets, and say, "*Khorosho* (Good)." It was very satisfying. John Glenn went into space at that time, and that was a plus;

again all the westerners, and the Russians, applauded us. Nobody among the Russian people really wanted us to fail, because we were what they wanted to become.

However, we began to run into the arrogance of the Kennedy White House early on. It was difficult. "Tommy" Thompson was extremely impressive and careful, and he nurtured his ties, and played his hand very carefully. He was very secretive. He didn't broadcast—like George Kennan—his telegrams for everybody to see and to show off. He really wrote telegrams for Kennedy and for Dean Rusk alone.

I think our impression of the Kennedy administration at first was very hopeful. We had felt that Dulles and Eisenhower, and Chris Herter, the former governor of Massachusetts, were weak on Berlin. They didn't seem to grasp that it was our will that was being contested. It was essential, just as in dealing with any playground bully, that when you're tested you have to stand up the first time, or you're just going to spend all your time rolling over. It was that simple. It was never fully taken at face value by the Eisenhower administration. When Kennedy came in, we were very hopeful that this would change. Here was a PT boat hero: young and vigorous. Dean Rusk was solid, and a wonderful man. But Kennedy's White House, like Clinton's, was full of arrogant friends who all were convinced they knew better than anybody. Dickie Goodwin, [Arthur] Schlesinger the historian, and John Kenneth Galbraith were absolutely convinced that they were intellectually far superior to these drones in the Foreign Service and in the embassy.

This attitude prevailed, so we became very nervous. We were competing for Kennedy's mind, we thought. Things like Jack Matlock's airgrams about dissent among the intelligentsia were very important. Kennedy read those, and Jack received a personal commendation from Kennedy for them.

Tommy was very trusted. Kennedy trusted him. Tommy was able to dampen down a lot of the mischief that Bobby Kennedy and all of his cohorts were promoting. Bobby Kennedy was a big part of the foreign policy process in the Kennedy administration including, in my judgment, putting our troops into combat in Vietnam instead of remaining "advisers."

As we went on into this Berlin confrontation, it became more and more serious. We faced the Khrushchev ultimatum. The Soviets began creating incidents in the air corridors which had been sacrosanct up until then. I remember once that Sir Christopher Steele, the British ambassador, flew from Bonn to Berlin in the corridor, and two MiGs came in and actually brushed the wings of his plane. That was a huge confrontation, and it was one of the occasions when our collaboration with our allies was so close.

When Steele's plane was buzzed and brushed, we couldn't wait for our four capitals to coordinate a message and send it back to us. It required an immediate protest in the strongest language. So Tommy and Sir Frank Roberts, the British ambassador, and the French and German ambassadors, all agreed. I took it upon myself to write the first draft with my three colleagues sitting around the table with me. They suggested changes and we ended up with a two-page démarche which we had drafted together. Without waiting for approval, we flashed these back to our capitals, and the ambassadors went in simultaneously with these protests. We informed Washington instead of requesting permission. It was very tough language: "We will take appropriate steps, including the use of force if necessary, and if you want to bring our relations to a crisis point where world peace is threatened, this is a good way to do it." The message was delivered, the Soviets took note of it, and there was never another incident again.

The only reaction out of our capitals came from the British. Lord Hume was then foreign minister. He wrote and commended the drafters of the démarche for an outstanding job demonstrating initiative in the finest tradition of the British service. So Sir Frank and John Tretwell shared Lord Hume's message with Tommy. That was a very satisfying and exciting thing to be part of.

What were they up to? They were testing us, convinced that we didn't have the willpower. They were pushing and slicing constantly—we called it "salami slicing"—to see how far they could get. The goal was to eventually force us out of Berlin. They seemed convinced that we would pick up our marbles and go home, because it was too scary to continue the confrontation. If that had happened, in my judgment, the psychological impact in Europe would have been decisive. I think, instead of the Cold War going our way, it would have, at least temporarily, gone their way.

There was great intellectual unrest at the embassy about the firmness of the Kennedy Administration. Rusk was not that strong at the White House. [McGeorge] Bundy constantly agonized over things; he was more interested in the intellectual process than he was in the substance. The sense of history, which Kissinger (and Acheson in his time), had reflected so well was missing. Rusk had a sense of history, but it was all Asian oriented. I thought Dean Rusk was a magnificent human being, but obviously he was basically mistaken about our role in Asia and the Vietnam War.

We were not comfortable. We did not have the sense that the policy was firm. We were constantly fighting for Kennedy's mind. We had great confidence in Tommy, and we knew that Tommy was very effective in his dialogue with Kennedy, and even with Bundy. We also knew that around them were the Dickie

Goodwins of the world. Goodwin was the Stephanopoulos of the Kennedy White House. He even had the woolly head hair-do, which was not yet fashionable. They were arrogant. Pierre Salinger was part of this, but he wasn't a serious policy player. They were cocky as hell, and convinced that we were a bunch of drones, and that we couldn't be trusted, and if they could only get Khrushchev off in a room with Kennedy for an hour, why, it would all work out; which, of course, they eventually did in Vienna and it didn't work out at all. What we said was true. Khrushchev came in, stepped on his foot, and kneed him in the balls to look at his reaction. The reaction was weak, and therefore Khrushchev ratcheted up his initiative.

We felt the Khrushchev-Kennedy meeting in Vienna in 1961 was the golden opportunity for the president to be charming, to have Jackie charm Khrushchev and then have Kennedy come in and say, "Now look, I want to say this perfectly straight. Get your bloody hands off Berlin or we'll destroy you," but he never did. He was constantly talking about how we've got to find a way out, what we can do to reassure you, how we don't want you to distrust our motives, and how we're not aggressive. He played right into Khrushchev's impression, and Tommy was upset. He didn't articulate that to us because he was just too professional for that. But we knew he wasn't happy with the way it went, and we indeed saw further deterioration in the confrontation as a result of that meeting.

In the key period, the winter of 1961 and '62, with the ultimatum having been raised, the confrontation in Berlin came down to "access." So Khrushchev switched his target and insisted that we accept East German control of the access, which had been part of their focus from the beginning. Dulles originally had this idea that we would accept East Germans as "agents of Moscow," and legally our position would be unimpaired. This was not a legal issue; it was a psychological confrontation, and Kennedy continued to futz around the issue. The Russians got so aggressive finally that we had to have a series of special negotiations on Berlin access with Thompson, Gromyko, and [Vladimir] Semyonov on the Russian side. I went with Tommy. We had these long cables come out from the Department with instructions. I would boil them down and interpret them for Tommy. They were replete with details. I would get the instructions, work out a talking points paper for Tommy, and then the two of us would go in and meet Gromyko. We had five high-profile meetings. They were reported in the *New York Times* on the front page.

The first meeting we held agreed to have consultations on Berlin access (which already made us nervous because we didn't want to consult on something which was a "right"). But that's what Kennedy insisted on. As we arrived at the first meeting Gromyko received us in his outer office and escorted us into his little sitting room. Gromyko was extremely friendly. "Tommy, how's Jane? How are your little girls? Is everything going well? I hope it's not too uncomfortable. It is a difficult time for us, but it has always been a great pleasure for me to work with you professionally because you are so professional." He turned to me—this was all in Russian even though Gromyko spoke beautiful English—and we chatted a little bit, and he complimented me on my Russian, and asked where I lived and where my apartment was. Semyonov was also friendly. They had a translator, Victor, who had been Khrushchev's translator and subsequently became Gorbachev's translator; he attended every meeting.

We sat down and agreed that we would have another meeting the next week, and then we tabled our position, and they tabled theirs; we both agreed we'd study the positions and report back to our government. And we left. It was a very pleasant meeting, about forty-five minutes.

The second meeting took place about a week later. We had long instructions from Washington about what to present. We walked in and Gromyko was absolutely a changed personality. He was cold, hostile, and unfriendly. He abruptly told us to sit down, and then launched into a forty-five minute tirade about American irresponsibility and aggression, and lack of legal basis for being in Berlin at all, and how we're going to do this, and we're going to do that. At one point he said, "You know, you've got to recognize that if you allow Berlin to become the flashpoint for a war, we will incinerate New York City in twenty-four hours." That's pretty heavy stuff! Tommy was sitting there on the couch, and I was sitting on the couch next to him. Tommy was a chain smoker (eventually he died of lung cancer). He was smoking quietly. Gromyko stopped. He gave this oration in a fairly high-pitched voice; it was not casual conversation. He was pounding on the coffee table. Tommy just kept smoking, and there was silence. About thirty seconds went by; Tommy never said a word. Gromyko said, "Well, Mr. Ambassador?" And Tommy very quietly stubbed out his cigarette, and looked up at Gromyko, and said, "Oh, are you through, Mr. Minister?" It was a beautiful deflation. Of all the things I witnessed, that was the coolest diplomatic performance I ever saw. I was sitting there; my blood pressure was going up, of course. I didn't open my mouth but I was taking notes. In these meetings I was the scribe; I wrote down everything that they said, or that we said in response.

Tommy sat there and waited and then said this; Gromyko's face fell. He was clearly embarrassed. Then Tommy very quietly, in about two paragraphs, said, "I deeply regret that you have been required to put on this performance, which I regard as irresponsible, undiplomatic, and certainly below your high level of diplomatic and professional behavior. You know, and I know you do, and I'm sure Mr. Khrushchev appreciates this, that if we ever get into the beginning of a nuclear exchange, that no doubt you can damage an American city or two, but you also know that the entire Soviet Union will become a rubble heap within twenty-four hours. It's your choice of time frame; it will take a lot less than that." And he stood up, and we left. Gromyko's mouth was open. It was a dramatic performance.

In Tommy's interpretive telegram he characterized Gromyko's performance as theatrical, dramatic, "staged," and, as I recall, that it was another deliberate probe of our will—a deliberate attempt to intimidate. The language that Gromyko delivered was reported verbatim, practically. Some people in Washington would dismiss Tommy's interpretation and be paralyzed by the threat. The president had developed confidence in Tommy—like many other people who were on top of it—and realized that Tommy was the best interpreter that the United States had, and that his words were extremely weighty. I think that we helped stiffen the American spine by our interpretative comments. The reaction in policy terms in Washington was reassuring in that regard. But we knew that there were people back there saying: what are we doing in Berlin? We've got to get out of Berlin; this is crazy. We're jeopardizing the United States' security. Why are we there? This is a beachhead; we shouldn't be there. Let's withdraw. There were a lot of people going that way, and they were on both sides of the political aisle. You know, this bully is threatening me; we've got to stand up and whip him. We always felt this was in the balance, and the Russians clearly felt that way. They wouldn't have gone through all this if they'd known for sure it was going to be counterproductive.

Those of us who had been in Berlin, especially me—I guess some people didn't agree with me, perhaps—always felt that World War III could start by miscalculation anywhere, but especially in Berlin. In terms of a calculated military engagement, however, there was no risk at all. Our real danger was to make sure that the Soviets didn't misinterpret our anguished, intellectual approach and massaging as weakness; but they did, frequently, as we saw. Khrushchev in Vienna misinterpreted Kennedy's performance as weakness. It was just his intellectual approach to things: they can't be black and white. But in Berlin, in one of the rare occasions in my career, it was pure black and white. And I reflected that and Tommy reflected that in his own quiet way.

THE SECOND LETTER

William Watt's tour in Moscow overlapped with Jenkins'. Like Jenkins, he details extensively the professionalism and keen insights of Ambassador Llewellyn "Tommy" Thompson. Watt's first-hand accounts of Soviet actions and reactions during the Cuban Missile Crisis are not only clear and exciting, but also his observations of President John F. Kennedy's actions that caused Khrushchev to "blink." The president relied heavily on Ambassador Thompson, then in Washington. Watts found himself a key actor in the affair of the "second letter." He saw history in the making, as the superpower neared the nuclear precipice.

William Watts
Political Officer, American Embassy, Moscow, Soviet Union, 1961–1963

I was in Moscow from the middle of 1961 to the middle of 1963. I arrived in about July-August, 1961, and left just before the Fourth of July, 1963. The ambassador was Tommy Thompson, one of the legendary figures in the Russian field. He was a very distant ambassador to work for. When he was replaced by Foy Kohler, we used to comment that under Thompson the door to the ambassador's office was always closed, while with Kohler it was always open. It was sort of indicative of their styles of operating. Thompson tended to work through a very small number of people.

The missile crisis (October, 1962) was over in Cuba, but this was probably the most dangerous point of the whole Cold War period. Events were developing at the UN: Adlai Stevenson showing pictures of the missiles, there were missile-carrying ships on the way and we were scouting them like crazy. The tension increased day by day. A letter came into the embassy that I was not aware of, the first letter from Khrushchev to Kennedy. That was sent off to Washington. Then, about Tuesday of that week, a second letter was sent over from Foreign Minister Gromyko to Ambassador Kohler with instructions that this letter was to be totally secret and sent top priority—our equivalent of FLASH, which we used very, very rarely. Kohler gave this letter—it was about two pages long—to four of us and said, "Here, translate this." We had to go up to the secure room in the embassy, which was located on the top floor and was an enclosure inside a room that you went into, shut the door and turned on air pumps. I am not quite sure why we did this since the letter came from Khrushchev, but we did.

The interesting part was that each of us, when we got part way through our translations, sort of looked up stunned. This letter was intemperate. I recall—and this may now be memory playing tricks with me—in the segment that I translated at one point it was saying, *"Kennedi, ti sukina-sin"* (Kennedy, you son of a bitch). In any event, this was an intemperate letter by any stretch of the imagination.

We took this back down and gave it to Kohler, who was impatiently waiting for it. He knew it had to be something important. He read it. We used to kid about Kohler being the whistler because when he got a little nervous he would start to whistle; this time he went into a full symphony. I will never forget when he said two things: "Gentlemen, you may not discuss the contents of this letter with anybody, including your wives." And then as he turned to go in and write his cover note, he said, "I think this may mean war." When your ambassador in Moscow says that, that sort of shakes you up.

The message went off. I later was told that in an ExComm meeting [in the White House], the second letter was discussed; there were various accounts of what happened, but the account I got was via Chip Bohlen, who was there. There were lots of different things thrown out as to what to do. Kennedy then turned to Thompson—this was dealing with the second letter and what it meant—and he said, "Well, gentlemen, you are the two top experts on this; I want your advice." This had been agreed before that he was going to turn to them. Bohlen opened this discussion, as I understand the meeting, and said, "Mr. President, we have discussed this at great length and are at complete agreement with what Ambassador Thompson is going to say. He is the senior of the two of us, and speaks for both of us." Thompson, according to this account I got, said, "Mr. President, you never received the second letter. Quite frankly, we have read this over and over and over and we can't tell whether Khrushchev might have been drunk, might have had somebody with a gun at his head, or whether there may have been a coup underway; we just don't know. But whatever it is, if you respond to the second letter, whoever is the cause of that letter is on the hook. They are now committed and we don't know how you deal with that. The first letter you can deal with. It calls for two things: removal of Jupiter missiles from Turkey—which were obsolescent anyway—and essentially a no-invasion pledge, which is no big deal as we weren't planning to invade anyhow." I was told that President Kennedy said, "Gentlemen, that is why we need career diplomats who know their stuff. Well done."

About a week or ten days later we had a reception at Spaso House, the ambassador's residence. I can't remember what the occasion was, but the guest for the occasion was a pretty big deal. We expected absolutely nobody from the Soviet leadership to show up. We figured they would send, at the most, Gromyko for a minute or two. Then the whole shebang marched in: Khrushchev, [Anastas] Mikoyan, [Aleksey] Kosygin, Gromyko, Malinovski. They were all there! Everybody was completely startled. It was obviously some kind of statement. How that was interpreted back in Washington, I don't know. Khrushchev as usual was bubbling around. Finally I went to Kohler and said, "Ambassador Kohler, wouldn't it be interesting to see what Rodian Malinovski, the minister of defense, might say if I mentioned the second letter to him, just to see how he would react?" Kohler said, "Okay, once. You can make a reference to the second letter, once and no more. Don't follow it up. If he starts asking questions about it, just say you don't know anything about it; just that there was one. Get out of it immediately. Just drop it in a sentence and leave it at that."

I went over to Malinovski, who was a caricature of a Soviet general. He was square with medals that went from his shoulders to his waist. You could just see he didn't want to be there; he was obviously there under command orders. They were making a show of amity. We chatted a little bit and then I said, "What do you think about the second letter?" He just froze. He stared at me for what seemed like hours, but what was maybe five seconds. Then, in this deep voice he said, "Now, I can believe in God," and turned around and walked out. Obviously, what he realized was that we did get it and didn't respond to it, and that it may have averted war. It was an amazing thing.

When I left the Soviet Union, my feelings were heavily influenced by the missile crisis and the fact that, as Dean Rusk said, "They blinked," and also, this sense—particularly when I got back to the States—of the incredible strength of the United States compared to the Soviet Union. It just overwhelmed me. In fact, I arrived back just in time for the Martin Luther King march on Washington and went down there when he gave his "I have a dream" speech. If anybody wanted to contrast two societies in their relative strengths and weaknesses, there couldn't have been anything more dramatic: leaving the Soviet Union after the missile crisis where they had backed down and realizing this place was a running outhouse—so badly run, so badly organized, and where the quality of life was so rotten—and to come back to the United States and have this incredible, peaceful march on Washington with a human rights declaration of extraordinary power carefully protected by the police, instead of what would have happened in the Soviet Union. Just looking around and seeing the wealth.... I must say I felt very, very confident as an American at that time.

Nikita Khrushchev's adventurism frightened and angered the Soviet top leader-ship—the inner power circle—so much so that he was expelled from office in 1964.

BORDER DISPUTES, TUNA WARS, AND AN ALCOHOLIC PRESIDENT

In diplomacy, few serious issues between countries are solved permanently. In 1960, Ambassador Maurice Bernbaum was faced with Ecuador and Peru at dagger's point again. Egos of national leaders, especially Latin dictators, are not easily assuaged or manipulated. With Stalin gone, the hostility was not as intense towards the United States, but it was more dangerous due to possible miscalculation and the nuclear threat. Maurice Bernbaum had to deal with the ongoing enmity of Peru and Ecua-dor, and with a difficult president of Ecuador.

Maurice Bernbaum
Ambassador, American Embassy, Quito, Ecuador, 1960–1964

Probably one of the reasons I was appointed was that I had been in Ecuador before. We were having the problem of an inter-American conference at Quito. And we had a boundary dispute between Ecuador and Peru. The political appointee who had been appointed to be ambassador died four days after being sworn in as ambassador. The question arose as to whom we were going to send. People in the Bureau [ARA—the Bureau of Inter-American Affairs] conscious of the need to have somebody with experience and background in Ecua-dor—because of the inter-American conference that was going to take place there, particularly through Ecuador's dispute—decided to recommend me. The first thing I knew about it—I had no indication whatsoever that I was going to be tapped—was a telephone call from Loy Henderson asking me whether I would be interested in being an ambassador. My wife was devastated. She wanted to stay in Argentina; she was enjoying it. She said, "Can't you hold it off?" I said, "Light-ning doesn't strike twice in the same place."

I had not yet been confirmed by the Senate, so after arriving in Ecuador as an interim appointee, I was asked to return to Washington to be confirmed. I was then sized up by the Kennedy group in the White House, who apparently decided I was all right. And so the appointment was renewed and confirmed.

My main concentration when I arrived was specifically the Peru-Ecuador boundary dispute and the inter-American conference, to see what I could do to minimize the friction between the two countries. I felt that we were placed in a very difficult position, because when you get into boundary problems you have a tremendous amount of nationalism and emotionalism. Rational arguments frequently don't prevail. My feeling was that the best way of trying to resolve the problem was to get the two parties to talk. And, if necessary, to go to arbitration, with the idea that if they agreed to an arbitration, perhaps the decision would settle the problem—take, say, the Ecuadorian or the Peruvian government off the hook. This was one of the main things I was trying to do while I was in charge of South American affairs. I became very much involved in the Peru-Ecuador dispute and made a number of trips to both countries. On a few occasions, I almost got them to talk to each other, and then things would fall apart.

This was really the basis of our policy throughout the whole period: not to take sides, but to get them to talk. I remember two conversations. One when I was on my way from Buenos Aires to Quito and stopped off at Lima. I had dinner at our embassy, where I stayed, and the Peruvian foreign minister had been invited so that we could talk. I listened to him, and he said their legal position was absolutely impeccable. I said, "Well, why then wouldn't you be ready to accept some kind of arbitration? You know, wouldn't this settle the problem for you?" He said, "If I were to try that, the government would be overthrown." He continued, "Because Peru has been in the position of having lost wars to Chile, having lost territory, and this is the first time we beat somebody. And we're not going to let the spoils of that victory go, or even take a chance of having that happen. The military wouldn't stand for it."

Later, after I arrived in Ecuador, I made a point of seeing the various past presidents. I mentioned this problem to one of them. He said that he had learned that the only way you could solve a boundary dispute was to have two strong governments in power who could take the flak from a decision which might not be approved by everybody. He said you've never had a strong government in Peru or in Ecuador. They've never coincided and you never could get a decision.

In 1942, Peru invaded Ecuador, and got as far as Guayaquil. They were interested in annexing a large part of Ecuador, and that's when we and the other guarantor countries stepped in. World War II was on. We forced—well, more or less coerced—the Peruvians to withdraw and to accept far less than they had originally wanted, and in a sense we would coerce the Ecuadorians to accept some loss. The result was that the Ecuadorian president and foreign minister, who signed that treaty, were killed politically.

We, the Brazilians, and the Chileans became guarantors of this treaty. The demarcation or boundary, was proceeding when an aerial survey conducted by our Air Force revealed the existence of a watershed that had not been known before. The Ecuadorians seized upon that as a basis for attempting to renegotiate the boundary. This happened before I arrived.

That was one of the problems. The Ecuadorians were interested in revising the boundary so that they would have direct access to the Amazon, whereas under the old agreement they would not have had access. The Peruvians claimed that the old agreement was theirs—signed, sealed, and delivered. The boundary markers were being established and there was no reason not to proceed. They wouldn't talk with the Ecuadorians about it, and our problem was to try to get them both to talk about it.

First, to sign a commercial treaty, because they had no commercial relations across the border. The idea was if we could get them talking on the basis of a commercial agreement, perhaps then there would be more of a basis for continuing the conversation politically. When I was in Peru, at one time, I saw the prime minister and various people. I thought that he had become convinced that this was the thing to do, and I left feeling we were going to have a commercial agreement. But apparently, the opponents prevailed on him and he canceled the idea.

The new president of Ecuador, Velasco Ybarra, made a statement saying that he would not honor the treaty, that the treaty was null and void. That presented us with a problem. The Peruvians were pressuring the guarantors to denounce the Ecuadorian statement as a violation of the treaty. My problem was to try to get our government to abstain and not take a position. We did take a position against the Ecuadorians, however, and as a result the embassy was stoned and attacked. We had quite a messy situation.

I do remember that we made a statement supporting the Peruvian position. I remember speaking with our assistant secretary at the time. I said, "For goodness sakes, you know damn well it's not going to solve the problem. By taking sides we're going to be on the wrong side of a nationalist issue in Ecuador, and we're going to have an awful lot of trouble." And he said, "I know. But the pressure here is too great." The former ambassador to Peru, Ted Achilles, had become Counselor of the State Department, and he was predisposed towards Peru. It was an internal Department of State matter.

One problem the Ecuadorians had was that they were always outmaneuvered diplomatically by the Peruvians. The Peruvians would have an ambassador in Washington who had been there for fifteen or twenty years and knew everybody. They did the same in Brazil. Same thing in Chile. The Ecuadorians were always changing their ambassadors. They never really did have the kind of clout in these capitals that would permit them to get their viewpoints across effectively. The problem between Peru and Ecuador has never been resolved.

After the stoning of the embassy, the Ecuadorians had gotten it out of their system. We had a bill for broken windows and so forth, and as a result we instituted security measures. We built a fence around the Chancery which was very ugly. I always tried to get rid of it, but I think it's still there. Other security precautions were taken. But we never did have another problem of that kind, because this one event demonstrated to me that we should always make every effort possible to stay on the right side of a nationalist issue, and certainly not to be on the wrong side, because the only thing that would get the crowds moving was nationalism. We had other problems. I think of the Bay of Pigs. The left-wing elements in Ecuador used that to try to rally the crowds against the embassy, but they couldn't do it. The people just weren't that interested, whereas they had been greatly interested on the boundary dispute. It was a nationalist issue involving Ecuador.

We were continuously making efforts to try to get the two parties to negotiate a commercial agreement. The Ecuadorians were always very partial to that. We never had any problem with them. The problem was to get the Peruvians to do it. After my effort had failed, the Brazilian foreign office tried it. The foreign minister made a trip to both countries. That failed. Later, apparently, the Peruvians had a change of heart and they sent an ambassador to Quito who had Ecuadorian relatives. I think one of his grandparents had been Ecuadorian, and the idea was that through his contacts, he would be able to work out an acceptable agreement. I worked with him on that, but it never went through.

Very early in my period there, we had the Alliance for Progress. Our prime interest was to further the Alliance for Progress in Ecuador, to get them to accept our assistance and make use of it. We had a problem there. The Ecuadorian government was very much interested in whatever assistance we could give them, but they were always a bit suspicious of our motives. They never could quite believe that we didn't want to get some political advantage out of it. I always tried to assure them that that wasn't so, but one of their big problems was that they had most of their revenues earmarked for autonomous agencies. It was very difficult then for the government to furnish its share of the projects which were being financed under the Alliance for Progress. That was one of the problems that I had all the time. I used to travel around the country pushing for collaboration. I used to spend a lot of time with the president, [Carlos] Arosemena, who was not very pro-American. He had had problems when he was in the embassy in Washington. He was a really complicated individual. His father had been president of Ecuador. He came from one of the first families in Guayaquil. He was more or less a maverick in his community. He was addicted to drinking; he was a dipso-maniac. Somehow or other he always seemed to be interested in stirring things up.

I remember one time as vice president when he insulted the Chinese ambassa-dor; he was a bit drunk at the time. And another time when he insulted the Colombian ambassador. When drunk, he always wanted to stick needles in peo-ple. We used to have some conversations about that. His problem was that he couldn't stay away from the bottle, and that made life with him somewhat diffi-cult.

His politics were to the left. I had a feeling it was more based on his personal-ity than any ideological preferences. He was under pressure from the military to break with Cuba, and he didn't want to break with Cuba. I'll always remember this; I can tell it now.

I was playing golf one Saturday, and his aide came along to say that the presi-dent wanted to speak with me. So I left the course. This was always a topic of conversation between us. He was always kidding me about playing golf. And I said, "Mr. President, you did a terrible thing. I was about to win that tourna-ment, and you pulled me off the golf course."

He said, "In a good cause. I'm being pressured by the military to break rela-tions with Cuba. What do you think about it?" I said, "That's your baby, not mine." He tried every which way to get me, to commit me, to tell him what to do, and I wasn't going to do that. Finally he said, "I'm wondering whether I shouldn't have a plebiscite in the country on that subject. What do you think about it?" I said, "I will then express an opinion. You'd just divide the country. It seems to me that would be silly. In that case, I'd suggest it would be far better not to break than to have a plebiscite." That ended the conversation. Later that evening the minister of the interior visited the embassy to tell me that the presi-dent had broken with Cuba. He was probably trying to be able to say that he was forced by the U.S. to break.

There were two problems. One was that President Kennedy had made an imprudent comment to Arosemena's brother that he might invite the Ecuadorian president to visit the United States. When I heard about it, I wrote to oppose the invitation because of Arosemena's dipsomania and corresponding unpredictabil-ity. So, the invitation was held off for quite a long time. Finally, the Ecuadorian president let it be known that he was waiting for an invitation.

There was another problem: pressure from Washington interests to get me to do something when Velasco Ybarra [the former president of Peru] was overthrown. At that time, there were three candidates for the presidency. The vice president was then in jail, on the grounds that he was plotting against Velasco. The president of the Supreme Court was another candidate for the presidency. I forget whoever else. There were three candidates. The situation looked rather hairy in Washington. I had a few phone calls asking what we should do. I advocated not doing anything. I didn't care who was president. Any one of them was perfectly all right, and there was no reason why we should get involved in any way. They accepted that, and eventually it turned out that way. Arosemena became president, and things worked out well until he was overthrown. We stayed out of it. We just refused to get involved. There was absolutely no reason to get involved.

There were directives regarding the role of the ambassador: one written by Eisenhower, and one written later by Kennedy. The idea was to emphasize the predominant role of the ambassador in embassy operations, in that his views would override those of other agencies that were represented in the embassy. This was a very difficult thing to enforce, but generally speaking, I never had any problems with any of the representatives of the other agencies. We all collaborated very well.

I never had any problems with the CIA. Any time a proposal was made to conduct an operation, I would query them for the reasons. If there was no really serious security involved—say, for example, something involving the Communist Party—I saw absolutely no reason whatever for an intervention, a project by the CIA. Invariably the station chiefs would say, "Fine, we just won't do it." Sometimes they would be asked by their home office to consider the problem, and in a sense I was taking them off the hook. But I never had any problems with the CIA station chief or anybody else.

There was one case shortly after I arrived. There had been rioting in Guayaquil. At that time we had a station chief who seemed to be running for election in Ecuador. He wanted to be a very popular fellow. He was a very attractive personality.

A Jesuit priest was caught in Guayaquil with ammunition and guns, and was accused of fomenting rioting. He was quoted as saying he was doing it under the supervision of the CIA. I asked our station chief about that. He said, "Absolutely not." I never was sure that this was so. I remember the minister of the interior calling me to complain about it. I reminded the minister that some time before, during a previous administration, he had headed a delegation to me asking whether we would support a coup against that government. I then said, "You remember what I said, don't you? Lay off. It's not the thing to do." And I said, "Do you think an embassy that made that recommendation in the past would support any of the activities that this priest said we were engaged in?" He said, "Forget it." But I was never sure about that station chief, whether he told me the truth.

Arosemena had been involved in various incidents due to drunkenness. One of them was when he met the Chilean president at the airport in Guayaquil and was drunk. It was said that if it hadn't been Christmas he would have been overthrown then.

Later, Admiral [Wilfred J.] McNeil, president of the Grace Line, visited Ecuador with his wife. The president gave a banquet for them, because the Grace Line had participated in the inauguration of a new vessel. The president's wife had been invited to visit the United States. His apartment was above the presidential office. I showed up, where I expected the party to take place. He was there with a few of his ministers, including the foreign minister. He was already half gone. As I walked in he said, "Ambassador, have a drink."

I said, "Well, Mr. President, let's go downstairs, we'll have the drinks down there." We got him down there, and he made a speech decorating the admiral. He neglected to mention my presence. Whenever he was annoyed with the U.S. for one reason or other, he neglected to recognize my presence. So, I knew something was up.

During the soup course at dinner, he arose—by that time he was really pretty much under the influence of liquor—and made a long rambling speech in which he attacked the U.S. government for exploiting Ecuador without mercy. Well, of course, you can imagine the reaction at the table. He turned to me and said, "You agree with me, don't you, Mr. Ambassador?" I didn't know whether to laugh or cry, so I said, "No, Mr. President. When you're speaking of the government, you're speaking of the American people." He had spoken highly of the American people as being distinct from the government.

Then, he turned to one of his ministers at the other side of the table, and said, "Paco, you agree with me, don't you?" Well, this minister at that point was studying the molding on the ceiling. Finally, he said, "*No, Señor Presidente.*"

Arosemena got up, and staggered out of the dining room. Dinner continued, and finally we finished. The various ministers came along and said, "You're not going to make anything of this, are you?" I said, "No, not under those conditions. I don't know what brought it on, but I'm sure he wouldn't have done it if he was sober." I remember it was a subsecretary of foreign affairs who came along and said, "It makes no difference what you say. The three chiefs of the armed forces who were at that dinner have just decided that this is it. This man's gone too far." They threw him out of power.

The following day we were giving a farewell luncheon for our armed services attaché. One of the members of the newly appointed *junta*, Colonel Gandara, came over to bring his wife. This is quite a coincidence, but it was interpreted by virtually everybody as indicating that we were in on the overthrow.

I asked Gandara at the time, "What's going on?" He said, "Well, we decided that we just had to oust him. If we hadn't done it, the ranks would have done it." Then he left. Arosemena was flown to Panama. Gandara visited me after the military government had taken over. I asked him what their policy was going to be. He said, "We want to take advantage of the Alliance for Progress. We don't have any great ideas about what to do, and we'd very much appreciate suggestions from the U.S. government, as well as financial help."

I said, "How long will the junta stay in power?" He said, "If we stay in power longer than a year, we will continue in power, because the appetite for the goodies will be too strong. What we've got to do is to get things done and get out before the year's over." I reported that back home. That was encouraging, that this man was interested in implementing the Alliance for Progress. We did what we could, but our bureaucracy was a bit too cumbersome to get many of the things done that we'd hoped would get done.

In any case, we recognized [the government] on the basis of that conversation. At the end of a year I called on the colonel, who had then become a general. I said, "How about it?" He said, "It's too late. The appetite has progressed much faster than I had expected." There was a lot of graft going on. The chief of the Air Force and chief of the Navy were very much involved in graft, and this created some problems with us.

In the 1990s there were further clashes on the Peru-Ecuador border and American diplomats were trying to smooth tensions, again.

5

Turmoil in the Middle East and Indochina, China Reopens to the U.S

The decade 1965 to 1975 was momentous and dangerous for the Foreign Service. The Cold War still dominated international affairs, and manifested itself in varied ways. American diplomats also faced very stressful situations in the Mediterranean and the Middle East. There was a violent coup in Cyprus by Greek Cypriots, instigated by a military junta in Athens, which led to Turkey's response of occupying a third of the island. The U.S. ambassador was assassinated in Nicosia by a Greek Cypriot faction. Nearby, the 1967 and 1973 wars between Israel and several Arab countries continued political tensions over the existence of the state of Israel, tensions unresolved to this day. Many Arab states broke diplomatic relations with the United States over both these wars. Official and private U.S. citizens residing in or near the war zones were evacuated or advised to leave the area, except in Saudi Arabia where the American community remained.

The major professional challenge to the Foreign Service during this decade was in Southeast Asia: Vietnam, Cambodia, and Laos. A significant number of State Department Foreign Service employees, plus those from USIS, AID, and CIA, served in Indochina during the 1965 to 1975 period. Some Foreign Service members were killed while performing their duty under state-of-war conditions. Much of their work was not of the traditional diplomatic or consular nature; they worked in the provinces, dealing with nation building and trying to guide and help the South Vietnamese to form a stable and efficient governmental and economic structure so that it could survive and fight off the North Vietnamese communists. This commitment challenged the ideals and attitudes of the Foreign Service because many of its new recruits were from the generation that was demonstrating in the streets and on the campuses in America and abroad against U.S. involvement in the war. Once engaged, however, Foreign Service personnel in

Indochina proved to have the skills, professional discipline, and fortitude to meet the challenge.

Also in Asia was the secret, and eventually successful, overture by President Nixon and Secretary of State Kissinger to open relations with China. Clearly one of the most important reasons for this venture was the interest on both sides in playing geopolitics with the common enemy, the USSR. What began in tight secrecy for American diplomats soon became highly public. China-U.S. relations dramatically changed.

AN ISLAND DIVIDED BY HOSTILITY

Since the end of World War II in 1945, the Eastern Mediterranean has been a constant source of challenge to the American Foreign Service, both for the officers assigned there, and for those dealing with it in Washington. During the decade of 1965–1975 there were two major foci: the Greek, Turkish, and Cypriot triangle; and the long-standing hostility between the Arabs and Israelis.

The first issue raised in this chapter focuses on the Mediterranean and the Greek-Turkish pressures on the U.S. mission in Cyprus, newly headed by Ambassador William Crawford, sent there to replace his murdered predecessor. In Greece, there was a military coup in 1967. Later, in 1974, the nationalistic government in Athens sponsored an attempt by the Greek Cypriot majority to bring Cyprus under Greek control. The Turkish invasion and occupation of one-third of the island prevented that and, in retaliation, the American ambassador was assassinated by Greek Cypriots William Crawford, hastily appointed to the dangerous post of ambassador to that troubled island, discusses his efforts to calm the situation down, and stay alive doing it.

Fortunately, his previous assignment as DCM to Nicosia had equipped him well. He knew the "players" intimately, including Archbishop Makarios, president and spiritual leader. Crawford characterized him as a master politician and a cat with nine lives. Perhaps as an example of the axiom "it takes one to know one," Secretary Kissinger found the Archbishop most difficult to deal with.

As Crawford quietly but effectively moved in both Greek and Turkish Cypriot communities, he was in many ways more successful in quieting hatreds between the two sides than even the United Nations peacekeeping forces. Less anticipated by Crawford was the increased effectiveness of the Greek lobby in the United States. At the time of the Carter victory over Ford, the lobby saw to it that Ford Administration officials involved in Cyprus policy were replaced. Crawford cites the role of Archbishop Makarios in deciding whether Crawford should remain in Nicosia. He did.

William R. Crawford Jr
Ambassador, American Embassy, Nicosia, Cyprus, 1974–1978

There had been the cataclysmic events in the summer of 1974 in Cyprus, in which the [Greek] junta [in Athens] had made its final desperate effort to unseat Makarios. It had very nearly killed him, but he escaped with his life. I remember I was in the Department, having just talked to Secretary Kissinger. He said, "Particularly at the wish of NEA [Bureau of Near Eastern Affairs], your own bureau, you will be going back to Yemen. You're free to go on your summer vacation."

The day I was leaving the Department happened to be the day that the Greeks moved against Makarios. A couple of senior U.S. officials remembered my Cyprus experience and called to ask my thoughts on the Makarios course of events. The then assistant secretary for IO [Bureau of International Organization Affairs] was one call, and the other was from the NSC [National Security Council]. My first response was to ask if Makarios had escaped alive. They told me the newest reports indicated he might have. I said, "He's a cat with nine lives, and if he has escaped he will be back, because he's beloved by the Greeks and a master politician. Who have the Greeks put in his place?"

"Somebody called Nicos Sampson." I said, "You mean that paranoid killer?" If anything more were needed, that would discredit the Greek effort. I explained that he was a discredited paranoid killer.

The junta had, I believe, gone to a couple of other "respectable" Cypriot political leaders, who had turned them down and said, "We're all loyal Greeks, but we don't approve of your apparently impending action against our president, and we're not going to be a party to this."

Nicos Sampson had been a newspaper photographer and later newspaper editor/owner in the 1960s, just a plain despicable man whose claim to fame in history was that he carried in his newspaper during the period of the fight against the British pictures of a British woman and child blown up or shot in the back, lying bleeding to death on a Nicosia street. The common story was that it was Sampson who had shot them in the back and then stepped up to photograph them and give it more publicity. This was the view that the Cypriots had of him: cheap, unintelligent, ambitious, a killer, a thug. Most sensible Cypriots and foreigners refused, even before this, to have anything to do with him. In Cyprus, as deputy chief of mission from 1968 to 1972, I had refused his invitation to come to his house, he was such a despicable person. The British obviously felt that way and so did many Greek Cypriots. I pointed out to my interlocutors on the telephone that the fact that Sampson was the only man the junta had found to play their game meant their effort was discredited from the start and I doubted Sampson would last.

They said, "Who will take his place?" I said, "In the absence of the Archbishop, probably Glafkos Clerides, the speaker of the house, a fine man who is in the constitutional position to step in as acting president. The next thing that's going to happen is that Turkey is going to invade, and nothing that we do will stop them. We stopped them twice before, and this time they're going to view this as such a serious disruption of the status quo, that under their treaty rights they will almost certainly invade Cyprus. We won't be able to stop them."

The next question was: "How much of Cyprus do they want to take? All of Cyprus?" I said, "No. They'll go for the northern third, which is enough to establish strategic control over the island. Finally, one gratuitous comment, and that is: look for the early fall of the junta, because the Greeks cannot, in their pride, stomach a government which has so seriously misbehaved and jeopardized Greece's reputation around the world. So, look for the early fall of the government in Athens. Is there anything that I could usefully do in this evolving situation?"

"We'll check with the Secretary." The answer came back the following day. "Thank you very much. We've got it under control. The Secretary thanks you, but you're free to go on your vacation."

I did. I went off to hike in Norway sometime in August, and had hardly started when the Norwegian police found me on top of a fiord and flew me back to the capital, Oslo, where I was told by our ambassador that I was to return to Washington instantly at the Secretary's request. He told me of Ambassador Roger Davies' assassination, August 19, 1994, in Nicosia and speculated that this was the reason for the peremptory summons. On my wilderness hike, of course, I had heard nothing of what had happened in Cyprus after leaving Washington. I flew back. I think the fact that Kissinger had seen me just a few weeks before was relevant, as well as my four years previous experience in Cyprus.

President Ford and the Secretary prevailed on Congress to treat Senate confirmation as an emergency. From start to finish, from notification to the Senate to confirmation, took about two hours. I was sworn in, and I was off in just a few days, arriving in Cyprus, as I recall, on August 27. By that time the civilian airports in Cyprus were closed off because of the fighting. The only way to get into Cyprus was to fly into the British sovereign base area located in southern Greek-Cypriot Cyprus. So, I flew to England, and the RAF took me into the British sovereign bases. I came, so to speak, by the back door. I believe I arrived exactly 10 days after Roger was killed. It's curious that there were not any instructions from Washington. I certainly never received any instructions from Dr. Kissinger, except to go out there and get there in a hurry.

On the plane crossing the Atlantic, I decided that the first thing I had to do was get back into effective communication with the leaders on both sides. Makarios was in London, and the acting president of Cyprus was Clerides. In a sense, the first policy thing I did was in my brief remarks on being sworn in by the Deputy Secretary, although I in no way thought of it as making policy and it produced immediate grumbles from Dr. Kissinger. I spoke of an island whose very independence and unity were threatened unless remedial measures were taken soon to prevent a permanent division of the island, to get the communities back into negotiation, to terminate the foreign military presence. Word came down through Arthur Hartman, the assistant secretary for European affairs, that the Secretary had rather blown up about his new ambassador in Cyprus making policy before he even arrived on the island. I said, "It's simply a statement of fact. The island is now divided, and unless somebody does something, it's going to stay divided. I wasn't trying to make policy, Arthur." He said, "Well, the Secretary is angry."

I said, "By the way, Arthur, I'm going to stop and call on Makarios in London." Arthur looked troubled. I guess he realized more than I did at that point the extent to which the Secretary—this does not give credence to those who think the United States was involved in the effort to overthrow Makarios; we absolutely were not—did not like Archbishop Makarios, and vice versa. I actually rather liked Makarios. He was very cagey. There was no pious virtue about him despite his chosen profession. He had tremendous sagacity as a politician: very wily and very tough. You had to admire that. He was shrewd. As Dr. Kissinger once venomously said to him in my presence, "Your Beatitude, we don't have any problem with you, except you're too big for your island." When I repeated that I intended to call on the Archbishop, Hartman said, "The Secretary would not like that."

I said, "I'm sorry, I've already been asked by the Archbishop's entourage to make sure that I stop in on my way out. Although he is not currently the president of Cyprus, he will again be. Clerides is only the acting president. I really have no choice." I did call on Makarios. I'm very glad I did, because it helped pull back on the suspicion, which Makarios really had, that the United States had not only supported the junta, but also its effort to remove him. It helped to get me off on a better foot. At least I didn't have Makarios and his supporters against me.

It was not a direct instruction not to see Makarios. Arthur shrugged and said, "I'll tell the Secretary that the horse is out of the barn door, you've already been asked by the Archbishop's entourage to make sure that you call. It would then be a clear insult not to do so." I emphasized that from my point of view, not to mention my safety, it really had to be done. And I'm glad I did, because that was a calculation. We had just had an ambassador killed by ultra-Greek nationalists and they were still very angry over the failure of the attempted coup. When I got to Cyprus, it was the ultra-nationalist EOKA [National Organization of Cypriot Fighters] types advocating union between Cyprus and mainland Greece, and EOKAB, the second EOKA movement (the first having been back in the 1960s under General Grivas), who were certain to be implacably hostile. It was they who had killed Davies. If, in addition to this group, other Makarios supporters—who constituted the overwhelming majority of the Greek Cypriots and truly adored him as a leader—were against me, I would be zero in effectiveness. Not only a question of physical survival, I wanted to make sure that the word got sent back from Makarios in London to his supporters on the island that I was okay and could perhaps be helpful.

Arriving in Cyprus, fortunately I had a very close, friendly relationship with the acting president, Glafkos Clerides, from previous service. Fortunately also, the same was true of Rauf Denktash, the Turkish Cypriot leader, in his-own-by-then sector of Cyprus.

The first thing I did was to insist on, and gradually gain, freedom of movement. By then northern Cyprus—one third, or a little less—was controlled by the Turkish mainland army. They gave lip service to the idea that Rauf Denktash was the leader of Turkish Cyprus, but in fact he was entirely dependent on the mainland Turks and very much restricted by them in his own movements. The Turkish military wanted none of the messiness that might have gone with an independent local leader.

I went to the Turkish ambassador. There were two or three telephone lines across the line [the "Green Line," which was the UN demarcation]. The first full afternoon I was there, within eighteen hours of my arrival, I got on one of those lines. Ambassador Asaf Inhan had been the Turkish ambassador when I left two years before. After greetings, I told him that within forty-eight hours I proposed to come across the line. He said, "Bill, I'm glad you're back, but I think that would be most inconvenient and probably not possible."

I said, "First of all, in conducting its military operation, Turkey has announced that it is not trying to destroy the unity of Cyprus, nor the independence of Cyprus. As far as I'm concerned, I am the American ambassador to

Cyprus in all of its parts, and I must have freedom of movement. There's an additional reason beyond policy; I have a lot of American citizens in the north whose welfare, under American law, is my responsibility. They have just been through a war and many of them are in trouble. I must be free to visit them." He sighed.

I called him later again to say that we would be arriving at the checkpoint two days hence at four o'clock in the afternoon. I knew he had to check it out with the controlling Turkish mainland military.

The next message from the Turkish ambassador was that I had to have a visa. I said, "A visa to go to all parts of a single country to which I am accredited?" I got them to drop that.

When we got to the checkpoint, as we had said we would, two days later, there was an escort. I said, "I don't have to be escorted. I know my way." The Turkish military said, "Call it an interpreter." So, I had a jeep full of "interpreters" with machine guns at sixteen checkpoints from there out to the northern coast. The Turks were still very much on a wartime footing; they shoved guns in your face. I did establish the principle of freedom of movement, albeit very limited at first. I was able to drive out to the northern coastal city of Kyrenia, call on my American citizens there—which is where most of them happened to be—and bit by bit to extend that every weekend, to expand the area along the coast the military would allow me to visit.

I was able to convince the leadership on both sides that my freedom of movement was in their interest. To the Greek Cypriot Government, which is the only one we recognized—and still is—I was able to say, "Surely, for the sake of the ultimate reunification of the island, it is useful for you to have me insist on this principle of freedom of movement in all parts of the island. Furthermore, I can perhaps see things going on of which you're unaware that may be of interest." Remembering that we were accused by Greeks of having caused the attempt on Makarios and subsequent Turkish invasion, they swallowed and said, "All right, we trust you. We understand why you're doing it, and we'll try to explain to people why you're going to cross that line. We'll try to explain so you don't get shot when you come back."

To the Turkish Cypriots, I offered the chance, and ultimately gave them, some voice to the outside world other than the Turkish mainland military with which Rauf Denktash was very restive. Very early in his career, he had been in exile from Cyprus in Turkey, where he was kept pretty well under lock and key. There, he wrote a book against mainland Turkish policies over the years in northern Cyprus. So, while there was a semblance of Turkish unity, the reality was that Denktash welcomed contact with the outside world and the American ambassador. It gave him a little more elbow room. After the invasion, he initially had no freedom of movement outside his own "capital" of Nicosia. When I insisted on it, as happened on a couple of occasions, he was able to say, "Your insistence has enabled me to say that, of course, I must escort you." It got him and the community moving in areas in which the Turkish mainland military had not allowed him.

The rest of the diplomatic corps—the British, French, and Germans in Nicosia—followed suit. Not knowing how to deal with the situation, they had been cowering on the Greek side for fear of incurring the government's anger. It became the established way for all missions to deal with the confused situation in which there were two declared administrations, only one of which was recognized.

It was not very pleasant living. There were no dependents. Early on, we had to make changes in the embassy staff, because people were pretty demoralized. They'd seen their ambassador killed, gone through a war, and had a very rough time. We removed some, and brought back others who had previous Cyprus experience.

The DCM was Frederick Z. Brown, who had been in Danang. He was wonderful, not familiar with Cyprus, but it didn't matter. I had that familiarity and we had a Turkish language officer who knew Cyprus, and a couple of others whose experience went way back. I flew in with two American bodyguards who stayed with me the whole first year. They lived in the Residence. Because Roger Davies had been killed by shooting through a window, I was never allowed near an open window. The windows were blocked off with sheets of steel, so it was very hard to tell when it was daytime or nighttime. I got out very little. When I did, it was always accompanied by two extra cars of Cypriot police, all armed fore and aft. In the car there was so much bulletproofing, I couldn't see out of my own window. Few Greek Cypriots whom I had known socially in the earlier period came forward to offer anything. Those who did knew they were risking their lives or, at minimum, violent criticism. I was enormously grateful to the brave few who did.

The Greek Cypriots felt that we had caused the whole thing that had happened to them: the loss of their island, the Turkish invasion, and the near killing of their beloved president. They felt, to a large extent, that Dr. Kissinger personally was the cause of it, because to them he was the personification of the maligned U.S. influence. They felt that in his previous position in the NSC, he had unique authority to control the actions of the CIA as well as the overt side of the U.S. foreign policy. They were convinced that we regarded Makarios as a dangerous communist, and therefore supported the junta against democracy in Greece and against Makarios.

They had killed Roger Davies because they felt they had been betrayed. They had been assured by the junta representatives from mainland Greece that this whole thing had been approved by the United States. They felt that it couldn't be motherland Greece that had made this ghastly mistake; it must have been the manipulations of the United States which had caused the whole thing to go awry, and had intentionally created a situation which would permit Turkey to invade.

Sampson had indeed gotten discredited in just a few days and had been run out of town. He wasn't even in Cyprus at that point. I had no dealings with him whatsoever. Clerides, an old and good friend, was acting president by the time I got there.

The Greek Cypriots wanted massive amounts of American aid, which would pressure Turkey to pull out. We insisted that about one-hundred-thousand (one in every five) Greek Cypriot refugees return to their homes in the Turkish occupied area. I sound throughout this as if I blame the junta. In a specific sense, yes. But, in fact, there was a very long history of Greek Cypriot maltreatment of the Turks. This has antecedents going way back.

After arrival, I set about trying to help the whole process of UN-sponsored negotiations between the two and the special representative of the United Nations, Pérez de Cuéllar, who became the secretary general of the United Nations. In reality, the United States had more authority than the secretary general's special representative, because we had more influence with Greece and Turkey and with the two communities in Cyprus. Over the four years that I was there, we tried in countless different ways to nibble away at the intractable situation; it was intractable because Turkey had achieved, in 1974, what it had long wanted: to move Cyprus out of a "waffley" area of Greek-Turkish influence and irrevocably into a zone of Turkish military hegemony. They just never liked the idea that this island thirty miles off their shores might suddenly become hostile and cut them off to the south. The Turkish ambassador expressed it to me in just those terms. He said, "Turkey is an imperial power and a continental power. That we are unnaturally prevented from breathing to the north and the east by the presence of the Soviet Union makes it all the more important that we be able to breathe to the south and to the west. 1974 solved the southern dimension. It remains to solve the western dimension."

I was getting good support from the Department of State all the way up to Secretary Kissinger. I'd like to think that I got along with him quite well. I could deal with him with humor. He seriously wanted a Cyprus solution, no question about that. He felt the whole Cyprus thing threatened to be a real blot on his reputation in history. He really did want it resolved, if it possibly could be, in his time as Secretary. So, he gave me every possible support.

The enmity between Makarios and Kissinger was real. Though Makarios dealt fairly with me, he kept letting his newspapers blame and continue to blame Kissinger for everything that happened. I reported all this. Kissinger finally, quite rightly, could accept this no longer. He said to the archbishop/president of Cyprus, who had by that time returned, "On the one hand, you ask for our help in solving this. You ask for aid. On the other hand, you are against us in every one of your controlled newspapers. You can't have it both ways." So, after the worst of these, I was recalled, at my own suggestion. This was maybe in the middle of 1975 or 1976. It was the only way we could show Makarios we were serious about not accepting continued insults. I was recalled very quickly and sat in Washington for two or three weeks.

Then I said, "We've made the point. I think we should find some way of getting me back to Cyprus." Then Under Secretary Philip Habib asked if I had any ideas. I suggested that I draft a strong letter from the Secretary to the Archbishop, and that to the letter be added an oral message from the Secretary that I would be charged with carrying back, to say, "You can't have it both ways. If there's any more of this violence and insults to the United States and criticism of the American role, we will terminate that role and let the Cyprus situation stew in its own juices." I went back, the dual messages worked, the inspired insults stopped, and I picked up my job again.

By that time, we had established full freedom of movement. For another, we had a massive aid program. This, of course, gets into the whole business of the friends of Greece in Congress and out of Congress. Here I digress a bit. The day I was approved by the Senate Foreign Relations Committee, I went down with Secretary Kissinger, who was giving classified testimony to the Senate Foreign Relations Committee. This would have been sometime before I left, the 26th of August, 1974, or something like that. I went with Secretary Kissinger, who told the Senate Foreign Relations Committee how we saw the situation, what he intended to do, and he introduced me and asked for the committee's earliest possible approval.

After the secretary had spoken, Senator Jacob Javits of New York spoke. A truly remarkable man, I might say. He said something like this: "Mr. Secretary, everything that you've said to us this morning sounds appropriate to the circumstances and we think you're on the right course. We support you. But just a word of advice: rightly or wrongly, I am regarded by some as the leader of what is known as the Jewish lobby in Congress with which you have occasionally taken issue over policy. Whether that is or is not correct, let me just talk to you for a minute about some realities of American politics. Jewish influence in the United States is concentrated in a few key cities: New York, Los Angeles, Chicago. Greek influence in this country is everywhere. There isn't a sheriff, a small town mayor, a state governor, highway commissioner, who hasn't to some extent become indebted to Greek-American financial support and votes, whether Republican or Democratic. Greeks in the United States have an organization which links them, called AHEPA, the Society for the Preservation of Hellenic Culture. It has never been a political organization; it's essentially cultural to preserve the sense of Hellenism and so on. Greek-Americans have never exercised national political influence. Their interest is in the liquor licenses, the highway contracts, restaurant licenses, and so on, to protect their own local position. They've never before exercised this essentially tremendous weight on a national level. But the Cyprus issue has galvanized them as they have never been galvanized before, and they have a structure through which to bring political influence to bear on the national level. If from time to time, Dr. Kissinger, you have had reason in your mind to take issue with the Jewish lobby, just wait until the Greek lobby hits you."

Indeed, it hit him. When the Greeks got behind Carter's campaign, as an alternative to Ford/Kissinger, leaders of the Greek community in this country passed the word to the leaders of Greek Cyprus that, "When our man Carter gets in, we will make sure that anybody who has had anything to do with Cyprus during this disastrous period is eliminated." They specifically said there would be a clean sweep of our ambassadors in Athens, Ankara, and Cyprus. The Secretary of State, of course, would be changed. They said that first. And the assistant secretary for European affairs, Arthur Hartman, said, "We will promise you there will be a complete change of characters." Indeed, within weeks of Carter coming in, they got the change in Athens, got the change in Ankara. Arthur Hartman went off with dignity to be ambassador to France, but they got him out. They did fulfill their promise on that. A couple of other semi-subordinate officials, the Director for Southern European Affairs and so on, were moved. I was, in effect, told by my Greek Cypriot friends that the Greek lobby had assured the Cypriot leadership: "Crawford's next."

Then an interesting, wonderful thing happened, which was reported back to me by the Greek Cypriots—particularly the Greek Cypriot foreign minister, an old friend. He reported these conversations with the constant flow of American Greek principals to the island. So the foreign minister said, "Bill, they've told us that they're going to get rid of you. What would you like to do?" I replied that,

"If there's something useful I can do here, I'd like to do it, to help put this island back together again." The Greek Cypriots went back to their Greek-American friends and said, "If you insist on this, as condition for aid to Cyprus, if you think it's got to be done, fine. But we think that Crawford knows the island, is fair, and we'd just as soon have him stay," including, by the way, Archbishop Makarios.

When I got back, for instance, with that angry message from Kissinger, that was just before Carter came in, Makarios spoke to me. He had this benign, lovely look, with his big tall hat. He said, "Mr. Ambassador, isn't it true that under your system, ambassadors submit their resignations when a new president comes in?" I said, "Yes, your Beatitude, it is." He said, "Wouldn't that be in your case, also, as a career officer, that you would submit your resignation?" I said, "Yes, your Beatitude."

He said, "What are your wishes?" Meaning he was angry at Kissinger; furious, too, at my bearing this angry message, seething. I said, "Your Beatitude, if the time has come when I can no longer serve the cause of peace in Cyprus, I'll be happy to go. If there's still something to be of use based on my knowledge of the island and experience here, I would prefer to stay." He just smiled very faintly, having made the point that he could remove Kissinger's envoy at will. I stayed for another three years.

On one of Makarios' visits to Washington after all of these events—I think he was coming in from London—I was called to be back for the visit. I went up to talk to the Secretary before Makarios' arrival, and Dr. Kissinger said, "Bill, what do I call him?" I said, "Your Beatitude."

We went downstairs to the front entrance. Dripping with cynicism and dislike, Dr. Kissinger greeted the archbishop when the limousine pulled up at the door. "Your Beatitude, I'm so glad to welcome you to Washington, Your Beatitude." We went upstairs, and Makarios was sitting there resting his hands on his scepter, symbol of office, and his lovely hat and all the rest, and that's when Kissinger just started right off saying, "Your Beatitude, I want you to know that we have great respect for you, Your Beatitude. It is only, Your Beatitude, that we feel you're too big for your island. Of course, if you chose, you could, I suppose, be president or prime minister of Greece whenever it suited you. I suppose the one thing that would unify all those Greek politicians, Your Beatitude, would be the prospect that you would come in to be president of Greece or prime minister. Now, on the other hand, if, Your Beatitude, you were General Secretary of the Soviet Union, that would give us real problems to have such an adversary, Your Beatitude." The meeting got nowhere, obviously.

After the meeting as we were going down the elevator—all crushed in there with the archbishop and his bodyguard, Secretary Kissinger and his bodyguard and I, in an elevator that ordinarily holds five—the Secretary said to the archbishop, "Your Beatitude, when I'm with you, I really quite feel that I like you." The archbishop looked at him benignly and said, "Dr. Kissinger, it lasts for just about five minutes after we've parted, doesn't it?"

THE TEL AVIV PRESSURE COOKER: NATIONAL INTERESTS AND DOMESTIC POLITICS, PLUS A WAR

During the decade 1965–1975, Israel and neighboring Arab countries fought each other twice, in 1967 and 1973. American involvement in the preservation of the newly established state of Israel has always had a strong domestic political component. Foreign service officers have had to keep this in mind when dealing with the region. Nicholas Veliotes recounts how these realities bore heavily on his responsibilities in Tel Aviv as DCM in October 1973, especially during the time of the surprise attack on Israel by Egypt and Syria, which became known as the Yom Kippur War.

Veliotes also illustrates the special U.S.-Israel relationship. Both sides are well aware of why it is special and how extra sensitive Israel is to any signs of anti-Semitism or criticism, even when the sources are from Israeli newspaper columnists. It is a given that Israeli officials are always trying to influence the American body politic. Veliotes's principal point is that you must live in Israel to appreciate fully this sensitivity.

The Yom Kippur War was a critical event for Israel. In many ways, Israel was not listening to its own intelligence. The United States had limited information. In general, Israel was seen as near invincible, but was complacent in its self-confidence. Once at war, the shopping list to the United States for weapons was lengthy and not appreciated by the U.S. military, given the heavy demands on it from NATO and its involvement in Vietnam at the time. The USSR was quick to resupply the parallel needs of Syria.

Veliotes felt uncoordinated with Washington, especially because of "Kissingerian" secrecy, including Embassy Tel Aviv's unawareness of an American nuclear alert. Out of the setbacks of the war, bilateral relations improved, especially with $2.2 billion dollar aid packages to Israel which made the United States its basic sole support in economic and military aid. The war also produced an enormous flood of Israelis seek-

ing visas to the United States, and a counter-movement to Israel by American right-wing zealots, such as Rabbi Kahane, who opposed giving up one inch of any Israeli-controlled land to the Arabs.

The DCM in Tel Aviv, Nicholas Veliotes, outlines the issues during the Arab-Israeli Yom Kippur war of 1973. FSOs struggled to keep antagonists separated so that U.S. policy could remain as neutral as possible. As seen in other tales of FSOs affected by Kissinger's style and authority, Veliotes gives many examples of how Kissinger's "enormous arrogance, conceit, and paranoia clouded his judgement." The results were an often ill-informed embassy and strains with Israeli officials.

Nicholas A. Veliotes
Deputy Chief of Mission, American Embassy,
Tel Aviv, Israel, 1973–1975

We were in the sixth year of the post-1967 euphoria in Israel, where there was a widespread belief the millennium had arrived when I arrived in Tel Aviv in the summer of 1973. There was a tremendous amount of belief that Israel was a great vacation spot. As far as I was concerned, it was attractive because I had two teen-aged sons; they had a good school in Tel Aviv. It was essentially an English-language post; you could get by without knowing Arabic or Hebrew. There was a challenge there: I was going to be the senior career officer, with an admirable elderly ambassador, former senator from New York, Kenneth Keating, who had asked me to come.

I realized that, even though Israel was at peace, Israel was never at peace. The energy level in the society was extremely high. There was a feeling of security, of having fought all the wars that had to be fought. There was a not-unattractive sense of optimism, and some arrogance. There was a "sun, sand, and surf" philosophy which, of course, my sons enjoyed immensely in those few months that it lasted.

But even at that time, I realized it was going to be a seven-day-a-week job, exacerbated by the difference in time change, which meant Washington awakened when we closed. There was a high interest in what was going on in the Middle East at this time, as the war of attrition had ended, and the Soviets had rebuilt the Syrian and Egyptian armed services, and Nasser [president of Egypt] had died; Sadat had come in. He'd just thrown out the Russians. What were the Israelis doing? Where were the settlements going? Did it make sense to rely on the Bar-Lev line along the Suez Canal, which was stationary? All these things.

There are times when you go into a situation fresh, where, because your mind is open, you can actually see some things.

In the month before the ambassador arrived, I went around on my introductory meetings; it was fascinating. I went down to see the Bar-Lev line, along the Sinai. It seemed rather strange to stand there and wave to the Egyptian soldiers on the other side, and to see these enormous—what looked like sand ramparts—things up in the sky, and to get a briefing from the Israeli generals. They were impatient with any questions you would ask, like "What are those gigantic sand things?" "Oh, forget about those. If the Egyptians attack, they may cross over at night, but in the morning they will die. In the morning they will die."

There was no conception that perhaps the Egyptians might have the capability to cross and stay, and that there might be a combination of factors that would make it impossible for the Israelis to do in the future what they did in the past with their tanks and their airplanes. When I called on Moshe Dayan and asked his views—at that time he was minister of defense—he described the Arab armies as akin to rusting freighters at anchor, slowly sinking into the water. That was his description of the Arab army: rusting and slowly sinking into the sand. It was only a few months before the war. We had continuing mini-crises. A Libyan plane was hijacked and brought in.

To round this out, Israel closed down from Friday night to Saturday night for Shabbat, the religious holy day. In Washington, of course, any busy State Department office works at least Saturday morning, which means they're in the office from five to ten p.m., Israel time. In any busy embassy, the senior officers go in in the morning on Saturdays. And the Israeli cabinet always met on Sunday, which meant you were getting ready for the cabinet meeting. And it wasn't unusual to meet people on Sunday mornings and try to influence the cabinet meeting, or to go up to Jerusalem on Sunday and get a read-out on the cabinet.

As we saw it, there were always issues that had an impact on us. There were always UN votes. Will there be new settlements? There was always something. How about most-favored-nation treatment for Romania? Would they let the Jews out? Later on, that became the problem with the Russians. The American-Israeli relationship is unique, so that unless you participated in it on the ground in Israel, it's very difficult to comprehend. There is a very symbiotic relationship. The Israeli society is so open that it's a miracle they were or are ever able to keep any military secrets; they can, or at least they used to. There are so many pressure points in the political system. Two or three correspondents, writing in different newspapers, can actually focus public and political interest in such a way that you'll have a discussion in a cabinet meeting, or possibly a decision.

You have to understand that there are three things that interest the Israelis. One: Israel and their own security. Two: beyond that, the state of world Jewry—in Russia and wherever. But anything outside of that—let's call it the Israeli-centric or Jewish-centric issue—the only other issue is three: the United States. What are they thinking in the United States? What are they saying in the United States? The *Kol Israel*, an English-language morning program, is full of the United States. So are their newspapers, front-page stories from the columnists. The best and most important assignment is as a journalist on one of their own newspapers here. The Israelis are always trying to influence our body politic. It's rather silly to talk about the fact that you don't intervene; you always intervene. We try to do it there; they try to do it here. Against that backdrop, it's not unusual. Also, as DCM, one of my jobs was briefing Americans who were in Israel, organized groups of thirty or forty that wanted to come in. We had a big conference room; they'd come in and we'd talk. I was always meeting with American Jewish leaders, not to mention the congressional delegations that would go to Israel before elections, to get support. I've seen it from both the Washington side and the Israeli side, and you can't really appreciate it until you live it on the Israeli side.

Walter Smith was political counselor when I arrived, and Walter was convinced there was a big black book up in Jerusalem, an enormous ledger, and the Israelis made up their minds whether you were a good guy or a bad guy, and you were entered into that ledger. If you were a bad guy, you'd never get off. If you were a good guy, they gave you a lot of leeway. You could move, but even then, it was difficult. Yes, they look at you, they talk to you. The Jews have developed, over the centuries, ways of dealing with their security and the non-Jewish community. I don't want to generalize this, but clearly my conclusion in Israel was they looked at you and they were trying to judge: could you be seduced? Not in a sexual sense, but could you be intimidated? Could you be bought? I understood that, when I got there, when I felt it, when I saw it. I thought some of the things were a little crude, the kinds of pressure that were put on. But there's no doubt that the Israelis seek to take an American official and turn him or her into an advocate for Israel.

I'll give you an anecdote. I was chargé, and it was after the failure of the second Sinai agreement, which failed in March of 1975. My ambassador had died, so I was chargé for six months or so. There was very bad blood between the American Government and the Israelis at that time, because after this failure President Ford announced his reassessment of American policy. The Israeli press was vying with itself on who could describe Kissinger as the greater villain. You heard and read things, openly stated, that he was the greatest traitor to the Jewish race since Josephus, which takes you back to the Zealots' revolt (Josephus was a great guerilla commander who finally gave in to the Romans, became a Roman citizen, went to Rome, and wrote the history of the Jewish wars. He's known as a great traitor). One day, I was called by the Foreign Ministry to come to Jerusalem. There was a very serious problem. So I went up there, and met with my friend, Eppie Evron, who was then, I think, running the foreign ministry. He had the title of director, or deputy director. In any event, he was the number-one guy for the Americans, working with Foreign Minister [Yigal] Allon. He said the foreign minister had asked that he call me in to discuss this very important problem. It was all about criticism of Israel in high places in the United States, that somehow was stimulated by the reporting from the embassy, and how the secretary of state always calls the Israeli ambassador and complains. We were going around and around, and finally I said, "Wait a minute. You say this happens often."

He said, "Yes, sometimes daily." And I said, "Well, we submit a daily press summary, and it's one of the basic reporting tools for the embassy and for Washington. We have a brilliant young girl who comes in, about five in the morning, she assembles it all, and we tell her the five or six subjects that we're interested in. Of course, American-Israeli relations are very high on the list. We send in that summary right to the secretary of state."

He said, "Well, I guess that's it." Then, he hemmed and hawed. I said, "Hey, you're not telling me I'm to censor the *Israeli Times*? *I'm* to censor *your* press so my secretary of state…?" He said, "Well, Nick, it's not that."

Then this man made very clear to me, he said, "Your job here is to explain us to Washington. You've got to explain why we do the things we do." And what he was saying was: "You've got to explain why we should not be held to the same standards as others."

I said to him, "Look, I think I'm as sympathetic as anyone can be, but my job here is to explain you to Washington. That's part of my job. The other part of my job is to try to convince you to support American policies. I'm sorry…." That's the kind of feeling that you get there.

Kenneth Keating should not be remembered as a practiced diplomatist, but as an American who spent over forty years in public life, at every level, including the judiciary, and never had a blemish on his name. This man was a man that I really respected. He had his quirks: he was in his mid-70s; he had a weak heart; he got married again. He suffered from what I call the congressional disease of sometimes confusing policy with the press release. But as a career officer in a position like that, I couldn't have asked for a better political ambassador.

The Israelis remembered him as an extremely sympathetic senator from New York who had been to Israel a half a dozen times, at least, before he got there. He was a pretty shrewd guy. You don't live as long as Ken Keating did and spend all that time in public life without understanding that there are people who are going to try to use you. He understood that. I thought he had remarkable balance on this. I used to draft most of his telegrams, including his first-person telegrams. I tried to understand his style, and I did it.

Every telegram that comes from an embassy is signed with the ambassador's name. A first-person telegram is one in which the ambassador speaks in the first-person singular: "I believe this...," "When I said to the prime minister...."

He would always sign the cables, but he was a very cautious man, and even though he and I had a terrific relationship, the name on the bottom of that cable was "Keating," not "Veliotes." I would go over them. I must admit, this was rather onerous after a while. After working all goddamn day, I'd go over at night and sit there as he went over the cables till midnight or whenever. But, no, he knew what he was doing.

You always had disquiet out there. Something was always happening. And with the Israelis, even though they were in euphoria, there was a certain nervousness, terrorism going on. The Israelis were zapping suspected terrorists overseas. They made a horrible mistake and murdered an innocent man in Norway. These things were always happening.

I should say this about the Israelis, too. They'd love to have you agree with them, but if you don't agree with them, they want you to speak up. The Israelis' national pastime is debating and arguing. It's not a sign of disrespect to have a good, solid argument with them. As a matter of fact, they respect you for it if they know where you stand. They want to make sure you're not anti-Semitic, that you're not uncomfortable around Jews. They pick this up. Blacks pick it up. People pick it up.

We're moving towards October. What's going on? We're picking up signs that the Egyptians, in particular, are engaging in warlike actions, mobilizations and things. The Israeli answer is: "It's all routine. You Americans, don't tell us what's happening. We know. We live next to them. Don't worry about it. We've got it taped. Everything is under control."

A few days before October 6th, the day the Egyptians and Syrians launched their attack, one of our guys went in to see military intelligence. And instead of getting the usual, the Israelis said, "What do you think of this?" All the alarm bells went off. Contrary to popular belief, our guys saw something coming, but we were so mesmerized by the myth of Israeli intelligence invincibility that we never seriously questioned it. After all, in '67, the Israeli intelligence was so terrific that it allowed the Israeli army to win a great victory over the Arabs.

But the Israelis got complacent. It's your mind set; it's how you interpret the intelligence that you have that is important. Look at *Pearl Harbor '41*, the famous book on that subject. I think that was a large part of it, the Israeli overconfidence. So much so, that even a few days before the outbreak of war, Moshe Dayan refused to mobilize the Israeli army. By the time they realized what was going to happen, you really couldn't launch preemptive strikes. It was too late.

On the day of October 6th, which was Yom Kippur, I received an early morning phone call that the ambassador and I were requested to come see the prime minister, in Tel Aviv. Now even though it was Yom Kippur, we had our special car window plaques which would allow us to move. On that holiday you're not supposed to be in a car. Tel Aviv was the tip-off, because that was the center of the Israeli armed services. And that's when we learned that the Israelis knew that the attack was coming. They asked us to get to the Russians, get to the Arabs and tell them the Israelis know, don't do it, it'll be a war that'll go badly.

There was a funny element as we were doing our telegram on this subject. I called the Department's Israeli desk officer, Hayward Stackhouse, who was at home, and I said, "Hey, wake up, there's going to be war." He said, "Don't talk any more, this is an open line!" I said, "Hey, it doesn't make any difference. Wake up [Joseph] Sisco [under secretary of state for political affairs], wake up [Roy] Atherton [assistant secretary for near eastern affairs]," someone better wake up the secretary. You'll have a telegram by the time you get back. Mrs. Meir says the Egyptians and Syrians are going to attack this afternoon. She wants us to stop them, work with the Russians."

As I'm telling him this, he's worrying about security, and I'm shouting over, "It doesn't make any goddamn difference. They know. Get in. Hey, get in!"

I'm not quite sure what happened on the Washington side after that, but then the war started. For several days we were in the dark. It's all well documented. There was an aborted air raid. People didn't really know how close it had come up in the north. Apparently some Egyptian plane got within a hundred miles or something. But there was a very serious concern as to what was happening, and we didn't really know. The Israeli news coverage was distorted, to some extent deliberately so, by the military. There were three very hairy days.

On the morning of the 9th of October, the ambassador and I went to see the foreign minister, who was also deputy prime minister, again in Tel Aviv, early in the morning. And he said, "We stopped them in the north."

And that's when the Israelis gave us their shopping list for re-supply. Then, of course, the Russians re-supplied, and then we started our airlift. As often happens with the best laid plans; none of the equipment that the Air Force flew in worked. So, Bill Foresman, our air attaché, was running that damned airlift with phones and walkie-talkies for days. Things go wrong. And our attachés did a fantastic job. Then clearly the focus was on the south. We did not go down. It was killing the ambassador not to go down. The attachés went down, took a look and then saw what the Israelis were up to. Then we were able to go down freely. I didn't go—my job wasn't there—but our air attachés went, once the Israelis cracked across the Canal the other way. Then you worked continuously. You had people calling you from everywhere. In a fast-moving situation, the telegrams tell only part of the story. You can't record telephones; you can't keep it. That's why if people say, "Well, what are you hiding?" Well, you're not hiding anything; it's just that you frankly are more concerned about doing your job and doing it right than the historical record. If you know anything about Henry Kissinger's operating style, it was utterly maddening to be at an overseas post in the middle of important issues at that time—and particularly in Israel—where you began to believe that he trusted the Israelis, but he didn't trust the Americans.

We knew we weren't getting information. This was very difficult and it became more so as time went on. We were trying to get a little bit of sleep and to reassure a hell of a lot of Americans who were stuck. You know, the kinds of things you do which don't get headlines. The system bogged down, and all we could say to them was, "Look, we don't have the time. We'll let you know if anyone's hurt. But, apart from that, we can't reassure you that those three-hundred-thousand Americans are safe."

The Israeli demands on American military stock were onerous. That showed you the parlous state of the reserves in NATO because of the drain of Vietnam. That really was the issue. Our military got mad at the Israelis; the real problem for the Central European front was Vietnam, where everything was. I'm not sure that our attachés—you're talking about colonels here—were focusing in on the great big picture. They may have been. Anyway, their job was to accurately present the case.

You had a lot of panic in the short run, a lot of El Al airplanes converting and bringing from their own reserves equipment, but less than we initially thought. They lost a hell of a lot. More than the equipment itself, what they needed and what we wanted to convey was the commitment.

You have to understand this against the backdrop of what the Soviets were doing in Syria, in particular. The Soviets were re-supplying the Syrians at an incredible rate. That was when I learned how many new tanks the Soviets had sitting around the Soviet Union. It was remarkafble! We scraped to get fifty or so; I think the Russians re-supplied the two-thousand Syrian tanks in several months. We had another reason for wanting to do it, because the Israelis were so concerned, that they were threatening to shoot up the Russian planes as they came in.

The only one thing that I begrudged then in the lack of communication from Washington was when my attachés came in to see me with one of these interminable military messages, sixty paragraphs. Down in paragraph forty-five we learned the 82nd Airborne had been put on war alert for the Middle East, and that there was a nuclear alert. Why the hell couldn't Kissinger have passed the word to us to go tell the Israelis? To reassure our people, I picked up the phone and I called Roy Atherton and said, "What the hell's wrong with you guys in Washington?" He said, "What do you mean?" I said, "Well, goddamn it, I gather we're on a nuclear alert and you've got the 82nd Airborne on alert to come here. I assume you've told the Israelis. What about the Americans? We are responsible for the welfare of Americans in this place. What are we supposed to do?" You can't just duck it, because this is an important part of our responsibility. If the Israeli foreign minister had called me and said, "What's this about the 82nd Airborne?" I would have felt like an absolute fool. I'm not sure he ever would have talked to me again.

I think we felt that the Israelis had a nuclear device at that time, but it was a rather crude one; it would probably have to be dropped out of a C-130. That was possible to do. But, the distances in the Middle East are such, how do you control fallout from a dirty bomb? Would they kill themselves? They were far from that.

People say, though, that the military did get from Golda Meir the beginning of a nuclear alert. I've never really seen that confirmed. This is still in controversy. When I was in Israel, I never heard it, but only later. While I was there, the only nuclear alert was the one we went through. We claim we responded to the Soviets putting their airborne on alert.

The embassy was coping with the enormously increased desire of Israelis to emigrate to the United States. It was overwhelming. We had to redesign our consular section to accommodate it. We had to enhance the staff; they were under great pressure.

It also was the first time I'm aware of a major demonstration against the Americans by Israelis, led by Rabbi Kahane, of the Jewish Defense League (American JDL). You began to get the emergence of the right-wing transported to Israel from the United States. We almost had a major disaster when these people came screaming and yelling up against our plate glass windows. The disaster would have been if the windows had broken, they would have lacerated dozens of young people. You go to the embassy today and it looks like the same fortress that all other embassies in the Middle East look like, which is too bad.

They were demonstrating against what they saw as American pressure to force them to give back some land to the Arabs and to make peace. These were the zealots, the people who wanted to keep every inch. These were the people who waited at the entry to Jerusalem and, when Kissinger came by, all stood and in unison gave him the finger. Many were Americans. Those forces that were unleashed at that time led to the victory of Menachem Begin in 1977, which has given you thirteen years in Israel of right-wing or center-right-wing government.

There wasn't panic on the part of the general Israeli public, because, fortunately, the general Israeli public didn't know how bad things were in the north, from Syria. There was real heroism of an incredible kind up there that stopped them. By the time the Israelis began to understand (we're talking about only seventy-two hours), that deadly threat had passed. The focus went back to the Sinai.

I remember, one day, Israel's leading gossip columnist (she'd die if I used that phrase) was in the embassy, and I was going down the elevator with her. And as she got off the elevator, she looked at me and said, "Look south." Then, she left. Three or four days later, the Israelis broke across the Canal. This means a lot of people knew that was happening. I think what happened in Israel was not in the first few days; what happened in Israel was in the weeks and months that followed.

One American Jewish friend of mine, a social psychologist, was on a sabbatical. He came to see me, and as he was talking, he started to cry, because he had come to Israel with such high hopes. It was that period of euphoria that I described. He said he couldn't take it, because the society had suffered a collective nervous breakdown; he had to leave.

The casualty figures, for a little country, were just tremendous. I forget, three-thousand killed? At that time, Israel was three million people. Seventy times three, that would have been the equivalent of two-hundred-and-ten-thousand Americans killed in two and a half weeks. The country went into mourning. There were no parties. There was no nothing. Every Israeli family was touched with tragedy. It was a great victory. It was a great victory over incredible odds.

But it destroyed Golda Meir, number one. It put Moshe Dayan's career into an eclipse. You had a reshuffle. You had a new government. The major military figures of the time went off to pasture. I think the head of military intelligence died of a heart attack shortly thereafter. This was a new Israel that was bewildered, felt betrayed by its own people, and had lost its sense of invulnerability. It was a vulnerable Israel again. You had the rise of the right-wing. The only good thing that's happened since that time was Camp David and Jimmy Carter.

Henry Kissinger in those days was larger than life. We were all supportive of what he was trying to do, which was to make a virtue out of necessity and make something good happen out of tragedy. Indeed, he did set the groundwork for Jimmy Carter's later successes. On the Syrian-Israeli border, up on the Golan, I don't believe there have been violations, or, if there have been, very damn few, since 1974. That's sixteen years now, so I'd say he did a pretty good job. He started the process whereby Israel and Egypt made peace.

He was a very complicated person, obsessed with secrecy. Working in the Middle East, you learn to be obsessed with secrecy, because so much can leak. Looking at it, though, from the point of view of the embassy as a contributor, Henry did not use us. His obsession with secrecy with respect to Israel was to exclude the embassy. While he was conducting active oral and other types of negotiations with the Israelis, through the ambassador here, Simca Dinitz in Washington, he did not understand that he was losing a resource.

Let me give you an example. I was the senior career officer there, and the Israelis looked to me as the guy who was running things in the embassy, although I had this marvelous ambassador, Ken Keating. During his frequent visits, Kissinger had this very unattractive habit of cutting you down in public in front of foreigners. Frankly, in order to retain credibility with the Israelis, I had to react in some way to indicate I wasn't irrelevant and I wasn't being pushed around, or the Israelis would figure, why deal with this guy? He should have thought of things like this. I sometimes felt I was being smuggled into the meetings with the Israelis. Henry would have ten people in his entourage.

When everything's going fine, there are no problems. But when it breaks down is when things get tough. I'll give you an example. In March 1974, Henry Kissinger never once talked to us, never once asked for any suggestions. Had he asked for suggestions, we would have argued the next step would have been with Jordan, because we thought the Israeli Government would have been prepared to make a gesture. Even though the Jordanians were saying no, no, no, no, we had reason to believe the Jordanians would in the final analysis accept this gesture. But he'd already made his own agreements with the Egyptians, I learned later, to move ahead on a second Sinai Agreement. In March of '75, you'd had Kilometer 101, Sinai One, the Golan. He ignored the Jordanian front, and went back to Egypt. He never once asked our view as to whether it was doable with the Israelis, what were the factors that were working on the Israelis. He cut us off every substantive telegram. All the exchanges took place in Washington, so the Israeli Government and a small group of people in U.S. Government knew things that the embassy did not. You've got to understand the enormous arrogance and conceit of this man, and his paranoia, which I think clouded his judgment.

We learned, almost by mistake, that Henry Kissinger was going to come back to the Middle East to make a try for a second Sinai Agreement. It's March of '75, and Vietnam is collapsing; obviously, he wanted a success.

One day, I asked the remarkable chief of the political section, John Hirsch, to bring the translations of all the Friday Hebrew papers, which are like Sunday papers. He and I sat down and analyzed them. We could see clear signs of the Israeli position hardening. So we said, "Okay, let's have a few discussions with people, then let's get together later today and write a telegram." We wrote a telegram (as I recall, I was chargé at the time), and I remember starting it out: "We have been told nothing. We don't know really whether the secretary is coming or, if he's coming, what he really hopes to accomplish. But if the aim is to come soon and accomplish a second agreement that would require the Israelis to make certain concessions, our analysis is the Israeli position has hardened in the past week or so, and unless you know something we don't know (I think I used those words), it's highly unlikely that there will be success in this mission." We sent this in. Henry came out. He failed.

Larry Eagleburger, or someone, gave a backgrounder in which he blamed the embassy for failing to keep the Department informed of significant developments in Israel. By the time the press got back to the United States and filed, to follow up that initial story, Kissinger was spreading blame all over the embassy. So much so that the head of the CIA sent the station chief a special message sort of saying, "Don't tell the chargé or the ambassador, but you start reporting politically on this."

My station chief, a remarkable guy, came to me and showed me his reply, in which he said, "There is no disconnect here. My views were fully reflected in the embassy. Here we work in a coordinated manner. Let me refer you to such and such, and such and such. Review these before you come to the conclusion the embassy wasn't doing its job."

I never played games with the Israelis. I said, "I don't know what the hell's going on, but we better talk. I can't get it from Henry." About the only things I used to get from Henry at this time were the continuing complaints from the Department that the Israeli press was mad at him. And the poor Israelis would call me in and say, "What are you reporting?" And I'd say, "Why do you care?

What business is it of yours?" These were people that I knew quite well. (This is the way you talk to the Israelis, by the way, and they talk that way to you.)

They said, "Because Henry Kissinger is complaining every day to our ambassador." So I said, "Well, I thought that was it. Here, I brought you several copies. Here's our week's unclassified review of the Israeli press that we send in every day." The upshot was, the guy said, "Could you send us one of these every day, too?"

It was a very trying time. A delegation of forty members of Congress, led by Tip O'Neill, came out to Israel. While I was riding in the car with Tip and Silvio Conte, a leading Republican, the first thing Tip said was, "Is it true what Henry says, that you guys really screwed up and let him down?" I said, "Of course not." Tip said, "That's what I thought." And he turned to Silvio Conte, "See, I told you." Then he said to me, "Would you mind telling our whole delegation what the real story is?" I did, I was so goddamned mad.

This is the kind of problem you don't need. When you're in that kind of war-peace situation—high stakes and very fast-moving—what you don't need is suspicion lack of meaningful contact with the U.S. Government. No, I didn't like it, but I did my job. Our morale was terrific. Our staffing was great. We did a great job, particularly under the limitations that we had to suffer.

DEALING WITH THE SOUTH VIETNAMESE GOVERNMENT

Richard Thompson served two full tours in the political section of the embassy in Saigon. He saw the ambivalence of many South Vietnamese with families divided over whom to back. He saw also the stress between military control and the civilians to have their say. He also felt a tension between younger officers in the embassy and the senior "old guard."

Richard Thompson recounts his work in the political section during two separate tours, one reporting on the central Vietnamese Government and the other on the provinces. Alan Wendt, trained as an economist, was assigned to Vietnam to work on that troubled country's economy. He was duty officer in the Saigon embassy during the Viet Cong's Tet offensive. John Burns was the Director General of the Foreign Service, in charge of getting officers assigned to Vietnam. He discusses the clashes he had with those who opposed such tours.

Reporting was easy since the South Vietnamese readily befriended Americans. They knew that was where the power lay. Thompson felt he was usually getting solid infor-

mation. He could make his demands without much pressure, including when he had to try to convince the South Vietnamese Supreme Court of a certain action, something he knew no diplomat in Washington would dare to do.

Finally, he describes in some detail the realities of the war on the ground in Vietnam in the late 1960s. He illustrates how this was viewed in Washington, where victory against the communist forces was trumpeted as being "just around the corner."

Richard S. Thompson
Political Officer, American Embassy, Saigon, South Vietnam, 1968–1972

The political section in our embassy in Saigon was very good. The ablest officers—without calling myself an able officer—generally very capable people, were being assigned to Vietnam. It had a priority in the world to get the best people. So, by and large, they were very excellent officers to work with. I think the total number of officers in the political section was something like twenty-five. You had eight on the provincial reports; a similar number working on internal politics at the Saigon level, the various parties and organs of government; you had a labor attaché; a political/military section. It was a very large political section.

When you got up to the top leadership of the embassy, you got into some interesting and sometimes controversial people. Without naming any names at the moment, I think one problem in understanding what was going on in Vietnam was that a lot of the top people had been in Korea. I think there is a very clear difference which these people didn't grasp. In Korea, the communists had virtually taken over the whole peninsula before we drove them north; all Koreans hated the communists.

In Vietnam, on the contrary, the communists had the prestige of having defeated the French. They presented a humane face in the areas which they did control. There was much more ambivalence about the Vietcong even among the people who presumably were on our side, our supporters. We were supporting a government with generals who had sided with the French puppets fighting the Viet Minh communists who embodied the cause of nationalism. There was this concept of *chink nghid*, leading or main principle, which might be translated as "righteous cause." I find it hard to define but you have it or you don't. The communists tended to have it because the driving force of the society was more in their hands because of these factors I mentioned.

Even the people I would deal with that were staunchly anti-communist nevertheless had real admiration for the people on the other side who suffered privation, did not have luxurious living, lived out in the jungle for years, and worked hard. Ho Chi Minh himself was known for his ascetic style of living. They would contrast this with the corrupt life-style of the military government in Saigon. Vietnamese loyalties were often ambiguous; a person would have a brother fighting on the other side, and things like that. The Americans who came in with Korean experience, where things were black and white, did not realize the ambiguity of the situation in Vietnam and how people were not really staunchly anti-communist in a sense, even though all this fighting and dying was going on. The people had a respect if not sympathy for the other side. I think this was an important difference.

Shortly after I arrived, there was a Vietnamese member of the parliament who was calling for a peace settlement involving a coalition government. That was the position of the communists in the north. In the negotiations, he was eventually imprisoned. The senior Americans couldn't understand how the Vietnamese could have any sympathy for a man who was advocating the enemy point of view. But, if you have this more ambiguous view of the war and the conflict, it certainly made sense to the Vietnamese to call for a coalition government which would end the fighting and bring peace and reconciliation to the country.

Of course, you have to feel positively. The president says we are going to hold out here and you do your best to carry out the mission. I think the lower down you got in the hierarchy the more pessimistic you were about the long-term chances because you could see the continuing strength and respect for the VC out in the countryside and the weaknesses on our side. But the view became progressively rosier as you went from the village level to the district level to the province level to the Saigon level and then back to DC.

I was quite startled in the spring of 1969. A high-ranking senior embassy officer had visited Washington and had come back and assembled the entire political section to discuss the situation. He told us that the war was about over, they couldn't hold out more than a few more months, and that you could expect peace that year. That was in 1969. That is an extreme example of how the situation looked different. The realities are hard to define or express in the best of circumstances and you got farther from reality with the chain I described.

During my first tour, I was what they called a provincial reporter covering eight of the sixteen provinces in the Delta. My second tour, I was following Vietnamese internal affairs and had special responsibility for the lower house of the national assembly; certain political parties; a special organ of their government to fight corruption, since that was recognized to be a serious problem; and the supreme court. It was more typical political section work than my first tour.

Americans, especially young political officers assigned to Saigon, were really spoiled because the United States represented power to the Vietnamese. Whatever faction there might be—and there were a lot of political parties and factions there—they all wanted to have an American connection because that was their way of getting their views to the American embassy. It was really easy to do political work, to make contact. In fact, you were being besieged by people too minor to waste your time on. The deputies [national assembly members] were generally friendly. There were very few who tried to be standoffish towards Americans. They were friendly as were all the Vietnamese in the government, because they recognized that they wouldn't exist if it wasn't for American support.

They had a national assembly with a lower house and an upper house. I am trying to remember back now; they did pass legislation, and often important legislation, since they and the government were united in the anti-communist effort. Key pieces of legislation necessary to the war effort that were passed sometimes were changed by the national assembly. What were considered opposition deputies used the assembly as a platform to be consistently critical of the government.

There was a very active press in Saigon and about fifty daily newspapers—maybe thirty-five Vietnamese language and a dozen Chinese language and a couple of English language—representing a fairly wide spectrum of political opinion. There was a pretty free press there. A lot of them were very critical of the government and of the United States presence there, too. They would publish pictures of what were allegedly fetuses deformed by Agent Orange, and things like that. There was more political life and activity going on than a lot of people might suspect from a distance.

You might just think that it was a military government and that was it; but they did have some of the substance of democracy. They had a constitution and an election in which Thieu was elected president. Even though, behind the scenes, the military did retain control through its control of the military apparatus, they permitted quite a significant degree of political activity and freedom.

I remember a time or two I was in a rather embarrassing position of lobbying the Supreme Court to make a decision one way or another. In retrospect, this would be unthinkable in the United States for a foreign diplomat to be lobbying the U.S. Supreme Court. But these were issues relating to what we thought were important political aspects of what was going on there.

I might say two things: in the first place, there were a lot of functioning democratic institutions and the people were used to it and politicians got used to it;

and secondly, there was a lot of progress in making democracy a reality among the political elite of the country. Overall, I think if there hadn't been a communist threat they might actually have become a democratic society.

THE TET OFFENSIVE:
INSIDE THE AMERICAN EMBASSY

Allan Wendt was a newly trained economic officer assigned to South Vietnam to report on that country's economy. He found himself at ground zero in one of the most famous episodes of the War—the Viet Cong attack on the U.S. embassy in Saigon at the opening of the Tet offensive in January 1968. He was the duty officer inside the embassy at the time.

E. Allan Wendt
Economic Officer, American Embassy, Saigon,
South Vietnam, 1968

I had been in the country only about four or five months. Like most large embassies, there was a duty roster. Periodically, your name came up and you were given the duty. It was for a week at a time. Shortly before my turn in January of 1968, the embassy instituted a new measure, which required that duty officers had to sleep in the building at night, instead of just being there until a certain hour and then going home. I suppose they thought that would provide more security in the event of a problem, that it would give you access to all the facilities of the embassy. It makes a certain amount of sense in a situation like that where there was a war going on. That week was my first stint as duty officer. It wasn't the first night. I honestly don't remember which night it was. I was sleeping in a small office where there was a cot, near the communications area. These were the quarters of the duty officer, very Spartan, nothing much there but a cot and a chair. I had a manual of instructions. I had looked at that, of course. One thing I noted right away was that most of the information in the duty officer's manual was out of date. So, I didn't pay a great deal of attention to it. At about two-thirty in the morning, I was half asleep. The sleeping conditions weren't ideal; maybe I was dozing rather than sleeping. There was a loud explosion that really shook the building. We had been instructed in the event of an explosion to take cover immediately. Recalling that instruction, even though I didn't know what was happening or whether rockets were being fired at the building, I dove under the bed.

A lot of people years later thought that was very amusing as a first reaction. I had difficulty explaining that I was simply following the precaution that had been given to us. When you're under a bed, this is a good shelter from falling masonry and debris and whatever. People didn't quite see it that way. But it took me a while to realize what was really going on and that is that we were being attacked. I called a Marine guard down on the ground floor. He told me there was a commando squad trying to get into the building. They had blown open a hole in the wall surrounding the compound—the outer perimeter—and rushed immediately into the compound, and surrounded the embassy. They were firing everything they had at us.

In the beginning, being inside the building and not being foolish enough to go up to a window and look out, I couldn't really know what was going on. Actually, you couldn't look out that easily anyway because the building was surrounded by a concrete lattice work, sort of an outer wall. It was designed to deflect whatever they could fire at us, RPGs, B40 rockets, whatever. I don't think this commando squad had any B40 rockets. But the architect of that structure was a foresighted fellow because he anticipated what could conceivably happen, and it came to pass.

I thought I was living my last moments because I knew there was almost nothing in the embassy that could protect us. The Marine guard had told me that one Marine had already been killed. I think he told me also that some MPs [Military Police] had been killed. He had another wounded Marine on his hands. There he was, all by himself. It looked bleak. I really thought it was only a matter of moments before the Viet Cong would come crashing into the building. We were, for all practical purposes, defenseless. We had no weapons.

As it turned out, there was another military man in the building, an Army communications man, who had a rifle. He was in uniform. Then—I found out much later—there was another Marine guard in the building, but he never appeared. He never materialized. I happened to see him only much later when I went up on the roof. This was a couple of hours later. I didn't even see him on my first trip to the roof. It was a subsequent trip. He was crawling around on his belly. I couldn't figure out what he was doing, or how long he had been there. I guess he had been there from the beginning.

That Marine and the Army communications man climbed on board the first helicopter that was able to land on the roof of the embassy and took off, leaving me and a couple of civilians alone in the building. Ostensibly, they took off to provide additional fire power for the helicopter as it lifted off the roof of the building with the wounded Marine.

Our communications held up very well, so I was able to alert our military in Saigon. That was something I spent a lot of time doing. They had tried earlier to land helicopters on the roof of the embassy, but the choppers were drawing too much ground fire from the guerrillas in the compound. Eventually, they did get one in. They off-loaded a couple of cases of M16 tracer ammunition, which might have been useful if we had had any M16s, but there were no M16s in the building. At that time, in 1968, the M16 rifle had not been issued to the Marine security guards. So, there were no M16s and, therefore, this ammunition was useless.

No one knows for sure why the Viet Cong sapper unit didn't get in. The presumption is that they lost their leader early on and therefore were a little uncertain what they were supposed to do. Or, that whenever they tried to get close enough to the doors to plant satchel charges to blow them open, they got caught in a crossfire. After a while, we had people on the rooftops of adjoining buildings firing down into the compound at these sappers. When I say "we," I mean mostly MPs, some American civilians and presumably also some Vietnamese, although I don't know for sure.

The sappers did duck under the planters in the courtyard for protection. They should have been able to blow open the doors. I often thought that a really professional group of commandos like the kind the British used so often in the Second World War would have been in the building in a matter of minutes, but these fellows never quite made it. Anyway, those were the various presumptions about why they didn't get into the building. I should note that at the beginning, the doors to the embassy were open. They were not routinely closed. But when the incident began, a quick-thinking Marine on duty in another building across the compound saw what was going on, raced across the courtyard, and closed the doors in the nick of time. Interestingly, the one functioning Marine guard on the ground floor of the embassy was not even assigned to the embassy. He had been assigned to a different building. There were two other Marines. One was killed and one was wounded. We were very lucky that this Marine saw what was going on, raced over, and got inside and closed the doors. They were very thick doors made of teak, splinter-proof wood. They stood up well to the pounding they received. A number of rockets were fired into the building and did a certain amount of damage, but it was relatively easily repaired.

I was able to stay in touch with just about everybody I needed to talk to, including people who were responsible for the ambassador. I think they moved the ambassador to a safe house very quickly and set up a command post there. I spoke to those people by phone. I also spoke frequently to the State Department Operations Center and to the White House Situation Room. All of these communications held up very well, under siege. But, it wasn't always easy to call people locally in Saigon.

I often spoke to U.S. military headquarters out near the airport. I pleaded frequently for relief. I had to point out occasionally that the embassy was the symbol of the American presence in Vietnam. The fact that we'd lost control of it was quite serious. I think the same word was coming out from Washington. The military promised an armored column was on its way through the city. I don't know whether such a column existed in reality. It never arrived. The military kept promising relief, but the relief never came. Well, it did eventually, but it didn't accomplish much. Six hours after the attack began, they actually got a platoon of airborne troops onto the roof of the embassy.

What the military said later was that they were under attack all over the place and that the embassy was only one of their problems, albeit a major one. The embassy, I think, was the focal point of the attack. But it is true that at Tan Son Nhut and Bien Hoa Air Base, there was heavy fighting going on. The whole thing was a very harrowing experience. I'm amazed even in retrospect that I lived through it. After about the first hour when I realized that I was still alive and that the worst fate had not befallen us, then I began to think, "Well, maybe we're going to get out of here somehow." Of course, that does help concentrate the mind a bit as well, the notion that you've got a chance at survival. But I was prepared for the worst. As I said, we had no weapons. I did end up with a .38 revolver that I took from the wounded Marine, whom we evacuated. Later, I had a whole arsenal in my bedroom, in the house I lived in. I officially drew two weapons from the embassy: a .45 automatic and an M1 carbine.

I wrote a citation for an award for the surviving Marine. He did get an award. I think he got the bronze star. I really thought he had handled himself superbly in a really difficult situation, where for all he knew, the Viet Cong could have come bursting in at any moment, which is, as I said, what we all thought was going to happen. Miraculously, thankfully, it didn't happen.

I think that what happened eventually was that we stormed the compound and got over the wall and finished off all but two of the sappers, who were taken prisoner. Gradually, they got picked off one by one from all the shooting down into the compound from the rooftops of adjoining buildings. I was still communicating with the Marine guard, and I knew that by the time the platoon of airborne troops landed on the roof of the building in a helicopter, that all of the guerrillas had been killed or captured. When I greeted these troops who were armed to the teeth (grenades, knives, you name it, they had it), I was waiting for them when they got out of the helicopter. The platoon leader was a major. I said, "The action is over. You might as well just go right down to the ground floor and take stock of the situation, but the fighting is over." He said, "Well, you may think it's over, but I can't take any chances and I have my orders." So, they insisted on deploying through the building floor by floor, beginning at the top.

The only problem with that, of course, was how they were going to get out onto each floor. They could go down the stairwell. But each stairwell had a fire door which you could open from inside the corridor to go out into the stairwell, but not from the stairwell to go out into the corridor. It was a security measure. They didn't want to go down the elevator floor by floor. I said, "Okay, just to show you how confident I am that there's nothing going on and that there are no VC in the building, I will take the elevator down to each floor, go down the corridor, and open the fire door for you so you can come out and deploy." That's what they did. I wouldn't have risked my life if I had any reason whatsoever to believe there were Viet Cong in the building.

I knew the entrance had not been breached. I knew from communicating with the people on the ground floor, namely the Marine guard, that the VC had not gotten in the building and therefore deploying through the embassy and securing it floor by floor really was a waste of time, but that's what the troops did. Of course, indeed, by the time they got down to the ground floor, it was all over.

Around eight-thirty, General Westmoreland came to the compound. I greeted him. I explained to him who I was, that I was the duty officer. The compound was a mess. There were bodies all over the place and shattered glass and masonry. He said, "Well, I would suggest you get this place cleaned up and get people back to work by noon or so." That was an unrealistic suggestion under the circumstances. Given all the fighting that was still going on in the city, it was hardly something that we could have recommended to the staff. We did get things going pretty quickly. But still, there was fighting going on in the city and people were at risk. I was kind of a mess; not because I had been wounded myself, but I had blood all over my shirt from the wounded Marine. I eventually went home towards the end of the morning. My housekeeper insisted that I get rid of this shirt right away because the blood on it would bring bad luck. I took the shirt off and she burned it. What amused me at the time was the question of whether or not I was going to be expected to continue my duty. Now that I recall, that was the second night and I had another five to go. I took a nap. I was so wound up I couldn't really sleep, but I did try to get some rest. About five in the afternoon, I got a call from somebody saying, under the circumstances, I would be relieved from my obligation to take the duty that night and, indeed, for the remainder of the week.

It was all an unbelievable incident. It's very hard to imagine that we all got through it. I consider myself extraordinarily lucky. My car, which was in the back of the embassy, was all shot up in the course of this fighting. Of course, that was mere material damage, not important. But I was driving around in a car with no windshield for a while. Fortunately, it wasn't the rainy season. This was the end of January, and it didn't rain at that time of year.

VIETNAM DUTY AND THE FOREIGN SERVICE

Foreign Service participation in the CORDS (Civil Operations and Revolutionary Development Support) program in Vietnam weighed heavily in senior officer John H. Burns' resignation in 1971 as Director General of the Foreign Service. He believed in the discipline required of FSOs, and never doubted it from the many officers sent there—up to four-hundred at any one time—including those on their first tour, who did not want to go because they opposed the policy.

Upon return from a visit to the CORDS outposts, Burns wrote a brief article on his views for the State Department News magazine. The "Young Turks"—FSOs opposed to arbitrary assignments to Vietnam—threatened that if Burns published it they would retaliate with their connections in Washington, including in Congress. He published and the Young Turks carried out their threat.

John H. Burns
Director General of the Foreign Service,
Department of State, 1970–1971

When I was Director General, a great question was the Foreign Service participation in the so-called CORDS program in Vietnam. We were instructed by the White House to second varying numbers of officers to this work, a number which reached about four-hundred at one point, I believe. William Colby, later Director of the CIA, was in charge of the program. He left no doubt in my mind of the value he placed on the Foreign Service officers assigned to him; nor did John Paul Vann, a man of some renown in the Vietnam conflict, when I went there to visit with almost all of our officers at their posts of duty.

Many of these were arbitrarily sent there immediately upon entering the Foreign Service. I do not need to remind you of the views of a large segment of American youth—especially university youth—about the Vietnam War. That many did not want to go was not surprising. It was not because of danger or hardship that they objected; it was because of something much deeper than that and a number of them resigned rather than compromise profoundly held principles. I know this because I had hours of talks with many of them. All of this touched directly my belief in a disciplined Foreign Service, an arm of the executive branch of the government, bound to obey instructions or resign. I cannot deny that our involvement in Vietnam, and my continuing instructions to force young officers into the CORDS program, weighed heavily in the thinking that led to my retirement in 1971.

When I returned from that trip to Vietnam, I wrote a brief statement which appeared, as I recall, on the back cover of the State Department Bulletin. There was an accompanying picture of me with John Paul Vann in front of his helicopter. I gave a lot of thought and time to what was, as I said, only a brief statement. I don't even have a copy of it but I recall the closing lines: "This is perhaps the most difficult demand ever placed on the Foreign Service. Our response will be the one the president has the right to expect."

My heart was not in it. Well, my heart was in it to the extent that I always believed that to be the role of the Foreign Service. But my own heart was not in it. Meanwhile the Young Turks had acquired an advance copy of the statement (they had an active underground) and I had a telephone call from one of their leaders who said, "I'm warning you, Mr. Burns, do not release that statement," to which my response was simply, "It will appear in the next State Department Bulletin." The "Young Turks'" revenge took the form of heavy, and frequently successful, lobbying against any nomination of any officer who had been assigned to the office of the Director General to be chief of mission. They did this through associations they cultivated with the staff of the Senate Foreign Relations Committee. John Stutesman, director of the Vietnam Training Center and as gifted a superior officer as any with whom I worked during my thirty years, was also a victim of this.

To Beijing With Nixon And Kissinger

One of the most dramatic moments in American diplomatic history was the 1973 opening of relations with the People's Republic of China. Marshall Green, at the time one of the most senior FSOs and an expert in Asian affairs, was directly involved in the extraordinarily secret preparations for this venture, and discusses the pressures on him and the subsequent events that led to success at the highest levels.

His excerpts in this chapter demonstrate how essential it is for an officer of such competence and experience to engage all levels of an Administration, in this instance President Nixon and Director of National Security Henry Kissinger. Here, in the throes of the most secretive and stressful situation and one involving sensitive egos, he speaks up firmly and convincingly when he knows a serious error has been committed. Green specialized in Asian affairs, served in Japan as a Japanese language office, and was ambassador to Indonesia, prior to which he served at various lower ranks and several tours in the State Department.

These pages deal with the establishment of relations between the United States and the communist administration of China, with a major focus on ultra-secret negotiations and finally the public and historic Shanghai Communiqué. Green was caught between the very exclusive and small group around President Nixon, who knew of the venture, and most of the rest of his own colleagues. Once the news was in the public domain, Green realized to what extent Secretary of State William Rogers had been excluded from most of the substance of these discussions. A confrontation with Kissinger on a very significant issue (Taiwan) brought out Green's strength of conviction. Green had found a major flaw in the draft communiqué, which was altered accordingly and became the Shanghai Communiqué.

Marshall Green
Assistant Secretary for Middle East Affairs,
Department of State, Washington, DC, 1971

Unbeknownst to all of us in the State Department (except Secretary William Rogers), Dr. Henry Kissinger, Director of National Security, and a few key White House colleagues were involved in highly secret preparations for Henry Kissinger's trip to Beijing in June 1971. The president [Richard Nixon] had a passion for secrecy based, in part, on his distrust of the bureaucracy.

Never was secrecy more strictly pursued than it was over preparations for the Kissinger trip, and with considerable justification. Had word leaked out, it might have raised all kinds of criticisms from the right wing of the Republican Party, not to mention deep concern in Taiwan, Japan, and other countries affected.

I am not faulting Nixon and Kissinger for their secret diplomacy, although not informing people who are expected to be informed can give rise to some real dangers. Let me cite a specific example. I recall meeting one morning in June 1971 with several key members of my staff, one of whom mentioned that it had just been announced over the radio that Dr. Kissinger, who was in Pakistan on a round-the-world trip, had contracted a case of intestinal flu, and was therefore planning to take several days rest by motoring up from Islamabad to the Pakistan mountain resort area of Murree.

I commented to my staff that this was ridiculous that no one with what we used to call "Delhi belly" would take off on a long bumpy motor trip. I then observed blandly that Henry was probably off on a secret trip to China. As soon as I said those words, it occurred to me that my impromptu speculation, if true, would immediately spread to the newspapers, and I would be responsible for the worst leak of the Nixon administration. I quickly excused myself from my meeting, dashed up to Secretary Rogers' office, and told him what had happened. The Secretary paled visibly, for I had uncovered the truth. On his instructions, I rushed back to my office and swore all present to utter secrecy about my speculation. They kept the secret. Such are the dangers of not telling officials of events occurring in their area of responsibility.

The crowning achievement of the Nixon China trip in February 1972 was the final communiqué known as the Shanghai Communiqué, which was to become the charter of our new relationship with China. The format of the communiqué was in itself unusual. Each side—first China, then the United States—presented its contrasting view of the world scene and the main tenets of its foreign policies. This was followed by identifying areas of understanding and agreement. In this section, the U.S. acknowledged that, "all Chinese on either side of the Taiwan Strait maintain there is but one China and that Taiwan is part of China. The United States does not challenge that position." On the thorny issue of withdrawing U.S. forces and military installations on Taiwan, the United States stated this to be its ultimate objective, but related it to a peaceful settlement of the Taiwan question by the Chinese themselves. Meanwhile, the U.S. would progressively reduce its military presence on Taiwan as tension in the area diminished.

Credit for the negotiation of this document must go largely to Henry Kissinger and his Chinese counterpart Vice Minister Chiao Kuanhua. Dr. Kissinger went through the motions of consulting Secretary William Rogers and the rest of the State Department contingent. From time to time, Rogers and I would meet with Kissinger or we would receive sections of the draft communiqué for our comments, but at no stage did I ever see the entire draft until it was already approved by the president, Kissinger, Rogers, and the Chinese leaders.

The first opportunity I was given to read the approved draft was on February 26, the day we left Peking for a one-day rest stop at the scenic city of Hangzhou before our final day at Shanghai. When we reached our hotel in Hangzhou, Secretary Rogers showed me the approved text. I read it rapidly, detecting a major flaw which I immediately drew to Rogers' attention. He agreed with me, and so did Al Jenkins. The flaw was simply this: although the U.S. reaffirmed in the text of the communiqué its support for U.S. security treaty obligations to Japan, the Republic of Korea, the Philippines, SEATO [Southeast Asia Treaty Organization], and ANZUS [the treaty between Australia, New Zealand and the United States], no mention was made of our treaty obligations to the Republic of China on Taiwan. This would almost certainly be seized upon by the world press, and especially by those in the Republican Party who were opposed to the president's trip. Even top cabinet officials like Vice President [Spiro] Agnew and Treasury Secretary John Connally had privately expressed strong concerns over the president's trip to China.

Opponents could charge that the president had sold the Republic of China down the river, that the U.S. had unilaterally terminated without advance notice its treaty obligations to the ROC, and that this could even be interpreted as suggesting to Peking that it could attack Taiwan without involving the United States. Rogers could see my point right away. He too remembered how Secretary of State Dean Acheson had come under heavy fire for excluding South Korea from a map showing those areas in East Asia of primary defense concern to the United States just prior to the Korean War in 1950.

Secretary Rogers immediately put in a telephone call to the president, who was staying at the nearby government guesthouse, but he got Haldeman on the phone instead. Haldeman refused to disturb the president, who was resting; besides, he said, the president had already approved the draft.

I was in a black mood that night at the dinner party given in the president's honor by the Hangzhou Revolutionary Committee. Ziegler noted my mood and asked what had happened. When I told him, he evidently then got in touch with Haldeman.

Around one or two a.m., John Scali beat on my door and said that "...all hell has broken loose in the presidential suite." Evidently Haldeman or Rogers had got to the president about the issue, and the president was enraged.

According to Henry Kissinger's memoirs, the president was furious at the State Department for belatedly coming up with a long series of nit-picks about the Communiqué, and yet failure to correct these nit-picks, the president allegedly feared, might result in the State Department badmouthing the Communiqué. Henry depicted the president as "storming about the beautiful guest house in Hangzhou in his underwear," swearing that "he would do something about that State Department at the first opportunity, a threat he made at regular intervals since my first interview with him...."

Of course, there was no series of nit-picks, just one major objection; a point which, amazingly, no one had spotted until I drew it to Rogers' attention. It is quite possible that the president's fury was directed at Kissinger for having put him on the spot.

The following morning, at breakfast, Secretary Rogers told me that he had managed to reach President Nixon late the previous evening to express our concerns. He said he didn't know what the president would do. After breakfast, we left for the airport to go to Shanghai. While proceeding to my plane, Henry Kissinger intercepted me. He was angry about what he termed my "poor-mouthing of the Communiqué."

For the first time in my three years of association with Henry, I did not hold back. "Since when was the Secretary of State offering constructive criticisms defined as poor-mouthing?" I further reminded him of the constitutional responsibilities of the Secretary of State to advise the president especially on an issue as critical as this, one that could affect the whole outcome of the president's trip.

"But you've been talking to Scali, who has no right to be involved," was Henry's weak retort, to which I replied that Scali had a right to know as press adviser to the president. Henry then did an about-face. He asked with seemingly genuine warmth if I would join him that evening in briefing the world press at the time of the issuance of the Shanghai Communiqué.

I replied that I would do so if the president so ordered. I was not happy about the prospect of being conspicuously identified with a communiqué I found badly flawed, and it was left unclear whether that flaw would remain in the Communiqué.

I arrived in Shanghai in an angry mood until it was revealed to me later in the day that Kissinger had worked out with the Chinese vice minister late the previous evening a way of handling the problem I'd raised. I was also told that the president specifically asked that I accompany Kissinger to the press briefing and that I participate to the extent of summarizing what had gone on in the counterpart talks between Secretary Rogers and the Chinese foreign minister.

Kissinger never told me specifically what arrangements he had concluded with the Chinese side regarding the critical objection I had raised, but during our briefing of a large press gathering in Shanghai at six p.m., February 27, it simply took the form of an agreed removal of the offending sentence from the Communiqué and of Henry stating in answer to an anticipated question from the press, actually Mr. Kraslow of *The Los Angeles Times*, who asked, "Why did not the U.S. Government affirm its Treaty commitment to Taiwan, as the president and you have done on numerous occasions?" Kissinger answered that this issue was an extraordinarily difficult one to discuss at that time and place, but, he then added the key passage: "We stated our basic position with respect to this issue in the president's World Report, in which we said that this Treaty will be maintained. Nothing has changed on that position." Kissinger said he hoped that would be all he would have to say on the subject, and his request was respected.

Thus was adroitly averted what could have been a serious setback. Neither Henry, nor the president, ever thanked me for my initiative. President Nixon understandably acted as though the event never occurred, while Kissinger took it upon himself to leave history with a self-serving account of the incident, one that is misleading and damaging to the State Department, and one that I am now, many years later, moved to refute.

In any event, this red-letter day concluded on a most pleasant note. I was asked to meet with President Nixon in his hotel room at ten-thirty p.m. to discuss the trip which I was about to undertake with John Holdridge, in which we would call on the top leaders of all East Asian and Australasian countries in the course of two weeks to explain American policy in the wake of the Shanghai Communiqué and to answer questions.

The president was warm and gracious. He gave me instructions as to what I should say about his talks in China: their frankness, their lack of double-talk, the fact that there were no secret agreements or understandings it was all out in the open as presented in the revealed record. He also urged that I stress America's constancy of purpose and its continuing search, in consultation with our allies, for "finding the right way to stay in Asia," and that under all circumstances we would stand by our commitments. He also gave me special instructions regarding Korea and Thailand.

In assigning John Holdridge to be my assistant, he ensured that we would be in a more authoritative position to answer certain questions relating to the top level talks with Zhou Enlai, which John had attended as an NSC adviser to Kissinger and as an interpreter. That was the last full day of the president's trip to

China. He took off the following morning from Shanghai with all his party (save for John Holdridge and me) direct for Washington by way of Anchorage, Alaska.

For me, the most exhilarating and important moments of the trip all occurred that last day: my final meeting with Henry Kissinger, which turned out so satisfactorily, our joint briefing of the press (in which he did almost all of the talking and answering of questions), and my final meeting with the president late that evening (February 27). But there was one other event that day which deserves special mention.

In the course of the afternoon, Premier Zhou Enlai made a personal call on Secretary of State Rogers in his hotel room which I was asked to join (Secretary Rogers' suite and mine were on the thirteenth floor, Kissinger's on the fourteenth floor and the Nixons were on the top floor, the fifteenth. The symbolism escaped no one.) In the course of this call, the subject of my flying direct to Tokyo from Shanghai was raised by Secretary Rogers. Our earlier application to the Chinese Government for permission for this flight had gone unanswered. We realized the uniqueness of our application, for no plane of any nation had flown either way between China and Japan in the preceding twenty-three years. So when Bill Rogers raised the question with Premier Zhou in our hotel meeting, Zhou just smiled and said through his interpreter: "Mr. Secretary, you just go ahead and do what you think is right."

Zhou never gave his permission, but he never denied permission. He thereby established no precedent which someone else could invoke. The thought later occurred to me that Zhou's unusual courtesy call on the secretary of state might have been prompted by concerns expressed to him by Nixon or Kissinger over the State Department's "poor-mouthing" of the Communiqué. In other words, Kissinger, in justifying to Chiao Kuanhua the last minute change in the Communiqué that I had urged, had probably talked about how the State Department might otherwise "poor-mouth" (a favorite term of Kissinger's) the Communiqué and thereby undermine much of what the Shanghai Communiqué purported to accomplish. Zhou was also mindful of how shabbily the State Department had been treated by the White House and wished to offset this by his courtesy call on the secretary. Zhou, in typical Chinese fashion, was keenly aware of the need for officials to save face.

It all worked out fine, and when, the next day, following President Nixon's departure, I took off in the president's backup plane for Tokyo, Premier Zhou actually drove down to our plane to say farewell to John Holdridge and me. For the first time, in my hearing, Premier Zhou spoke English: "Goodbye, Mr. Green, have a good trip. Good luck." He knew I faced some difficult moments, especially when I reached Taiwan where I was scheduled to meet with President Chiang Kai-shek. I left China feeling that Zhou Enlai was perhaps the most remarkable of all leaders in terms of his broad command of world events and yet extraordinary attention to detail.

6

Dictators, Portuguese Crisis, Hostages, Murder of an Ambassador, Embassy Bombing, and Trade Negotiations

In Foreign Service parlance, a "challenging assignment" usually means one that is difficult, dangerous, or both. The decade of 1975 to 1985 was arguably the most difficult and dangerous of the seventy-five years of the Foreign Service. It was a challenging decade.

Latin America was still the province of military dictators, but the United States was becoming increasingly less obliging in doing business with them and our ambassadors were tasked with carrying this message. Human and Civil Rights were steadily rising on the United States' list of foreign affairs objectives.

Our alliance with West Europe was considered to be in jeopardy with communist parties in France, Italy, and Portugal seemingly poised to take power, or at least to exert major influence on governments. Particularly threatening from the American perspective was the coup in the 1970s in Portugal which instituted a communist-led government.

The Brezhnev doctrine, whereby no backsliding on the part of states that were under Soviet dominance or influence would be tolerated, was in full force. Nowhere did this seem more evident than in Afghanistan in December of 1979 when Soviet troops overthrew the country's communist leadership because it was not meeting Soviet criteria. The assassination of the American ambassador in Kabul raised deep suspicions of Soviet involvement.

The Cold War was directed from Moscow's position of strength, both in far-flung parts of the world, including South East Asia, and at Moscow's back doors: controlled East Europe and even West Europe, vulnerable in free elections.

At the same time, the Shah of Iran, a long-time American ally, was over-thrown. Some months later, the American embassy was taken over by Iranian students and our embassy staff was held hostage for more than a year.

The Middle East was again in turmoil. The Israelis invaded Lebanon. One result was the suicide bombing of the American embassy in Beirut.

Despite these ominous developments in the decade, the regular work of the Foreign Service went on. Visas were issued, Americans in trouble abroad were helped, a multitude of problems arising between friendly countries were solved, and trade negotiations continued.

HUMAN RIGHTS AND LATIN AMERICAN DICTATORS

George Landau earned two ambassadorships in South America, based, in part, on his reputation of successfully dealing with military regimes in Paraguay and Chile, both known for their highly authoritarian rulers. Once the Ford Administration replaced that of Nixon, such dictators came under the spotlight with Landau instructed to focus on this political extremism. George Landau gained a reputation as a man who could work with dictators in Latin America without coddling them.

George W. Landau
Ambassador, American Embassies, Asuncion, Paraguay and Santiago, Chile, 1972–1980

The only instruction I received in 1972, when I went to the White House, had to do with cleaning up the drug traffic. In 1972, the words "human rights" were never mentioned. When I arrived in Paraguay, I found out that a lot of people were in jail without charges; some had been there for fifteen or twenty years. Nevertheless, I did not get a single inquiry from the Department or Congress for the first year and a half. Then, all of a sudden, it became very much the new thing. What had changed, of course, was that Nixon had left. Human rights started under Ford, not under Carter.

I got a slew of letters from Congress about the human rights violations and the prisoners. I was able to do a number of good things as most of the people were really arrested mindlessly because a middle-level government functionary had problems with the person. When you brought it to the top, to the foreign minister or to some other ministers, they all told me that this was not an important case, but they never did anything about it. They told me that it was a manageable thing for me to talk to Stroessner, that everything had to be decided by President Stroessner.

I saw Stroessner every day, as did everyone else, because at the time Stroessner either inaugurated a school, or there was a parade, or a new highway. There was a public function every day, usually at eight o'clock in the morning. All the cabinet and all the ambassadors were invited. Usually my colleagues went sporadically. I went whenever I needed to see someone because it was the easiest way to do business in Paraguay. The phones did not work too well; moreover, the office hours are from seven to eleven and after that everyone disappears. So, I could talk to the minister of education, the foreign minister, or the president himself, and get matters settled. Then you had to rush back and immediately write a letter because they would forget what they told you on the dusty road.

I used all those outings to tell Stroessner about X, Y, and Z. I told him how there was great interest and how it would affect relations with the United States. There usually was no great problem; he said, "Sure, sure." Then, I had to negotiate his approval to me with the minister of interior, who did not believe me and had to check back, but eventually we got a lot of people out.

My reputation of being able to handle the Paraguayans and get something we wanted, namely the individuals who were in jail, eventually gave the White House the idea that I would be a good man to go to Chile, where the human rights violations were really severe.

I had a totally different relationship with [Augusto] Pinochet than with Stroessner. With Stroessner, I had a superficially cordial relationship. I did not play up to him or tell him he was a great guy. He was a very unhappy man because he looked like a German, like a *braumeister* [brewmaster], and he acted like a German. He was on time, methodical, punctual, and punctilious, all virtues that the rest of Paraguayans do not have. So, he was always annoyed. While you had a meeting with him, he was always calling this fellow or that minister, "Why didn't you come to the meeting? How come you were late again? What is the matter?" He picked up the phone whenever it rang. Once it rang in his office while I was talking to him on a rather sensitive problem. He picked up the receiver and listened for awhile and said, "Sorry, this is the wrong number, you are talking to the president." He was obviously unhappy. The rest of the Paraguayans were very happy-go-lucky and he was not. He demanded action; he wanted to get things done while the others believed, *mañana*. But I saw him all the time.

Pinochet I saw four or five times alone. I saw him occasionally with a lot of people in larger groups. But really a heart-to-heart talk with him, which usually was disagreeable, took place at the most five times.

With Chile, I had very clear instructions. They were to keep a distance from Pinochet—which was self-understood—and to do what I did in Paraguay: get things done. That was the stock in trade; I could "get things done." It started to work out okay, but it did not last very long. By the time I got to Santiago in November, 1977, Pinochet was very worried about the Carter administration. He thought they were out to get him, which, in fact, they were. He had a totally correct appreciation. It was not the president who was out to get him. President Carter was a very decent man and he believed in human rights. That was his platform and he believed in it honestly. However, he did not realize that he had a number of appointees who really used the human rights question only to get down regimes they did not like. They could not care less what Pinochet did; they were out to get him. This, of course, worked against human rights.

There were no high-level visits until Assistant Secretary Terry Todman came in August, 1977. The Chileans were so worried that the day before Todman came they abolished DINA, the secret police, and retired General Contreras, who was the chief of DINA, the main trouble maker. He was involved even before in the [Orlando] Letelier case [A former Chilean ambassador who was assassinated in Washington, DC, on September 26, 1976]. He was probably the most evil spirit who existed in Chile (and for that matter still exists). He is alive and running security companies, which I am sure he can do very well. He bumped off enough people.

Shortly after I arrived, I met Hernan Cubillos, who had run *Mercurio,* the main newspaper during the tough days of the Allende regime. Hernan Cubillos had made a lot of money in legitimate export dealings. He convinced Pinochet that he was a friend of the United States, which he was. Not only through his ties to the Agency, but as he spoke English well, he traveled extensively in the United States and was very well disposed to the U.S. So, Pinochet sacked the Navy admiral who was foreign minister and made Cubillos the foreign minister. Cubillos sold the line to Pinochet that he had to improve his relations with the United States. Everything I asked for was done. We had the Letelier case which was just budding, with an American involved by the name of Townley. We wanted Townley and we wanted him in the worst way. We got Townley; it was not a matter of extradition, he was just turned over to us. It was done through Cubillos and it was sold to Pinochet "to improve relations." At the same time, the U.S. and the UN had already tried for two or three years to allow special rapporteurs to go to Chile, but it had been denied. I talked to Cubillos about it, Cubillos talked to Pinochet, and the group came. It was headed by an Austrian; they had freedom to go around and talk to people. It was very successful from their point of view. It was not very good from the point of view of the Chileans, but they allowed it anyway. We had some labor leaders coming and they wanted to see Pinochet. He had never seen any U.S. labor leaders before and they were pretty rough with him, but he saw them. I reported all this and said these are positive things; if we continued on this line we would be able to make real strides in the human rights field to get people released. The answer from Washington was to be harsher than ever. There was no recognition; and, in fact, it was even about then that at an OAS meeting somebody stuck in Carter's speech the line about "Bolivia's just demands for an outlet to the sea." If there is one thing we should not get involved in is Bolivia's outlet to the sea. It is none of our business. It would be just as unwelcome now to the present government as it was to Pinochet. As it happened, Bolivia and Peru lost the War of the Pacific in 1889 and Bolivia lost the outlet to the sea.

Pinochet had thought that with all these gestures he would get a sign from Washington that there was hope. But he realized that regardless of what he did he would get only the fist in the face. Somehow, the president's speech to the OAS on the outlet to the sea was the last straw for him. In short order, he got rid of Cubillos, whom he blamed for the wrong policy. He fired him, and from then on, if I wanted to get somebody released or found out there was a human rights violation and wanted them to look into it, I got to see the minister of interior or his deputy; Pinochet did not give me the time of day.

That was the type of relations that we had—not very good. But, of course, the Carter administration had thought I had done a good job in carrying out their policy. It would have been better had they responded to the overtures from Chile, but they did not want to do that.

I simply made it very clear that you can't have it both ways. You can't give me instructions to go in and get this and that done if at the same time you don't show any recognition for the things they have done unilaterally to please us. That was really the problem; it was up to Washington to decide. But you cannot have it both ways. They decided not to accept any of the unilateral offerings, so to speak, and hit him over the head whenever they could. At the same time, they were sending me instructions to do a great number of things. Of course, I was rebuffed. You have foreign policy objectives; you have domestic objectives; and you have political objectives. The Carter people were very much interested in political objectives. I don't say they were right or wrong, but I am just stating how it was done. You can't have it both ways; that was the main thing that Washington does not seem to understand.

After Chile, I wound up in Venezuela with no regrets. The string of assignments to military regimes was broken. When I got to Venezuela I did not realize how easy it was to deal with a country that may have tremendous economic problems and all kinds of challenges but did not have this ideological challenge that I had in Paraguay and Chile. There, anything you say will make either the government or the opposition mad, either the Republicans or the Democrats. In Venezuela, it was straight-forward. They renegotiated the debt, there were all kinds of questions (such as petroleum), but it was easy. You did not have to be careful about what you said because it was not that highly charged ideologically. It was wonderful!

THE PORTUGUESE CHALLENGE

Often the question is raised, what good is an ambassador? Why can't the business between countries be done by telephone or by monitoring television news reports from one's own capital? A wonderful example of the importance of an ambassador is the role of Frank Carlucci, coming to Portugal in the midst of a communist-dominated situation. Initially without strong support from his own Secretary of State, Carlucci was able to turn the situation to the best interests of the United States. Frank Carlucci, with knowledge of Portuguese learned in Brazil, was made ambassador to Portugal because of the crisis there after a right-wing dictatorship was thrown out after ruling for decades. The successors were viewed in Washington as communist and, therefore, to be carefully watched and perhaps directly opposed. Carlucci had to walk a tightrope between how he saw the situation in the field and how it was perceived in Washington.

Frank C. Carlucci III
Ambassador, American Embassy, Lisbon, Portugal, 1975–1980

I am not sure why I was chosen to be ambassador to Portugal other than the fact that I spoke Portuguese because I had served in Brazil. I don't know whose suggestion it was. I was in the job of Under Secretary of HEW [Department of Health, Education, and Welfare] at the time, very far removed from foreign policy, even though I continued to serve as a Foreign Service officer. I did know Henry Kissinger and Don Rumsfeld. I also knew the president. Portugal was in a crisis state. The suggestion, I was told, came from somewhere in the State Department. I was asked, and given the circumstances, I decided to accept.

In Portugal, in retrospect, it is quite clear that the president was a communist sympathizer, the prime minister was a communist, the top military structure was controlled by communists, the labor unions were controlled by communists, and most of the government was communist. There was a lot of unrest in Portugal. The feeling was that Portugal might be the first NATO country to go communist. It was quite a tense situation with a lot of demonstrations in the streets. So, it was something that needed urgent attention. Henry Kissinger had been dissatisfied with the previous ambassador, and had summarily removed him. I was given very little time to get out there.

The Portuguese desk pretty much confined itself to the facts of the situation. It was clear that Henry Kissinger felt that the situation was that Portugal was at least a pre-communist state. It is no secret that he called Mario Soares a "Kerensky" at the time. That accurately reflected his views. Henry didn't have a lot of faith in the socialists. He did agree in the outset, however, that we could have some modest aid programs to Portugal. He felt I should have some tools to work with. I gradually became convinced that there were strong forces pushing against the current trend in Portugal. There were a number of considerations. Portugal was not adjacent to the communist bloc. The ties to the West and NATO were fairly strong. The Church was influential, not in the hierarchical sense but at the village level. The people were, by and large, conservative; they were interested in protecting their economic interests. I thought the electoral process could serve to undermine the communist control of the country. There were a lot of skeptics about that. That was, in essence, the nature of the dialogue between Embassy Lisbon and the State Department, with a number of people in the State Department feeling it was probably best to write Lisbon off and teach them a lesson in order to protect the rest of the countries in Europe.

The Azores were essential in those days to any kind of airlift to the Middle East. The Portuguese were very protective of their equity in the Azores. There were elements in the Congress who were intrigued with the idea of Azorean separatism. Some, including one person within my own embassy, were intrigued with the idea of cooperating with the extreme right. I took a very firm stand against that.

Frankly, it took a number of meetings with me and Henry Kissinger in June 1976 for us to reach a meeting of the minds. Henry was coolly critical of what he regarded as my willingness to bet on the democratic parties—which he didn't regard as very strong at that point—and he had made a public derogatory comment about me which emerged as headlines in the press. I think it was something along the lines of "whoever told me Carlucci was a tough guy?" I had a few tense meetings where I told him quite frankly that his statements were pushing Portugal into the arms of the communists and his response was, "Well, if you are so goddamn smart, you make the statements," to which I said, "Fine, I will."

I had some discussions with the White House as well because I believed I worked for the president, not just the secretary of state. I was well acquainted at the White House, having been an Under Secretary of a major department, so I had some discussions there. The next time I met with Henry he said something to the effect that the president had asked to see me. This was in 1976. Quite frankly, at that meeting, Henry did say that he would give my policy option a chance; he would back me. So, I told him there was no reason to go to the White House. Henry couldn't have been more supportive from that day on. He had been highly critical up until that day, but once we reached a meeting of the minds—a joint decision—he gave me practically all the support I needed. It turned out that the electoral process worked, and as history has demonstrated the socialists came in. The socialists ran a campaign of privatization. It was an undoing of much of what the communists had done.

Regarding the embassy itself, when I went out to Lisbon, Larry Eagleburger, who was Under Secretary for Administration at the time, told me it was the worst embassy in the world. My approach was that first of all you try to shape up the embassy. We had to be very precise as to what we wanted out of the staff.

Secondly, I began to work on an AID program. I had a lot of trouble with AID. They wanted to send me flocks of people instead of programs. But we worked that out. I got a good AID director and I started to design AID programs myself. I had had considerable background in the domestic area and began to design some programs in the health area, myself. I started the first emergency medical services program, which is alive and well in Portugal today.

I started a management school at the Catholic University. I moved forward on a housing program. I designed a package for the American military to try to reprofessionalize the Portuguese military. I worked very closely on that with David Bruce, ambassador to NATO, Ed Streator, his deputy, and Al Haig, commanding general of NATO. In fact, it was rather amusing: I went up to USNATO and participated in the drafting of a cable in the evening at Ed Streator's house recommending a military aid package for Portugal, and then went back to Portugal and wrote an endorsement of the USNATO cable!

Thirdly, I began a rather intensive campaign of getting to know the political figures. I would make it a goal of meeting at least two or three political figures a day. I would call them up and set up appointments, invite them to lunch, invite them to dinner. So, I became quite well-acquainted.

Fourthly, I made myself accessible to the press, too accessible according to Washington. But it had a major impact on public opinion, the fact that I was open. The fact that I spoke Portuguese helped. To my recollection, no previous ambassador had spoken Portuguese. That began to create a positive image. There were all kinds of charges about the CIA. The communists put out a book, two inches thick, called "Dossier Carlucci: CIA." There was one press conference where I answered all these charges. The questions were so slanted that even the communist minister of information jumped in at one point and said, "Now look, you can't expect the ambassador to constantly answer negatives to prove that he is not part of the CIA." The fact that I was open, I think, had a major impact.

Finally, I quietly established lines with the Church. Not that I ever asked them to do anything; but I would go over and talk with the archbishop quietly, have lunch with him, and came to understand what the Church's view was. I regarded the Church as being very important and indeed the so-called counter-revolution did start with the village priests in northern Portugal. The Church played an important role.

The first meeting I had with Mario Soares, he came around to my house. I will never forget it. It was an evening and I had been there only a day or two. I think he was foreign minister at the time. He was very down. When he left, Herb Okun, my DCM, and I turned to each other and said, "What have we gotten ourselves into?"

The Portuguese are wonderful people but a little pessimistic and fatalistic by nature. It is always hard to cheer them up and get them to look at the positive side of things. I set about deliberately to do that, to convince them that things were not lost by expressing faith in the Portuguese people and expressing faith in the Portuguese leadership that you can do this. That you can be a free country. That you haven't lost your revolution. It has taken a little detour, but you can work your way out of it. So, the positive outlook, I think, was extremely important.

The Communists had a very erratic leadership. I spent many, many hours in long debates and discussions with the prime minister, Vasco Gonçalves, who liked to argue and had a very Marxist point of view, but was erratic and disorganized as could be. When I had a briefing in the State Department, the desk said that the one hope was the president, Costa Gomes. When I had had about two meetings with Costa Gomes, I went back to my desk and wrote a cable saying, "He isn't any hope at all. At best, he is a dead loss and at worst he may be a sympathizer." Indeed, subsequent events have borne out the fact that he was a sympathizer. So, I didn't have a lot of tools in the government to work with other than Mario Soares, who was then foreign minister but later took to the streets.

There were other democratic parties that I worked with very closely. My theory was that I was not favoring one party over another. What we needed to do was to support all of the democratic parties. The communist leader, Alvaro Cunhal, although capable, was a bit of a Western asset because he was a very vain man who had spent so many years in Czechoslovakia that when he returned he behaved in a very non-Portuguese way. The Portuguese are not vain people. But Cunhal was a little imperious. He felt that the job had already been done. So, the communists overplayed their hand.

Secondly, there were splinter groups basically to the left of the Communist Party: The MRPP, indigenous Marxist groups that did such foolish things as seize the Catholic radio station, for which the Communist Party got blamed. So, you had the head of the Communist Party, Alvaro Cunhal, appearing on television saying that he wasn't anti-Catholic. Well, nobody believed that. They committed a number of mistakes and indeed part of my lecture to my Portuguese friends was to allow the communists to commit their mistakes.

The head of security, Otelo Saraiva de Carvalho, who was a general and one of the original revolutionaries, went on television one night and, in effect, made me a target. There was a coup attempt—I guess it was a right-wing coup attempt; nobody knows much about it—on the 15th of March, 1975. That evening we were all in the embassy and there were demonstrators out in the street. Otelo Saraiva de Carvalho went on television and said that the American ambassador had been behind the coup attempt and had no intention of protecting me. I got him on the telephone and said, "First of all, I want to make sure that is what you said," and he said, "Yes." I said, "Well, you understand that that is the equivalent of declaring the American ambassador persona non grata." He said, "No, I didn't understand that." I said, "Well, that is not your job." He said, "What is my job?" I said, "Your job is to protect the American ambassador and you made me a virtual target." We went on in that vein for a while and he finally said, "What should I do?" I said, "Well, you had better protect me." To my surprise he sent some troops over to my house. I was always nervous as to whether they were there to protect me or for some other purpose.

Sure, there were a number of threats and there were demonstrations virtually two or three times a week. At one point, they were on the verge of breaking into the embassy and I issued orders to use tear gas. At another point, they caught me in my automobile and started rocking it. The State Department sent me a lot of security. We went through all that.

There was an extremely important meeting with NATO. Probably if I had to point to one thing that the United States did that helped to turn the situation around, it was the reintegration of the Portuguese military into NATO—the creation of a NATO brigade, which I worked out together with Al Haig, Ed Streator, and David Bruce. I must say Bruce, Streatorm, and Haig couldn't have been more supportive. Bruce was the ambassador to NATO, Streator was his deputy, and Haig was the Supreme Commander of NATO.

We functioned as a very effective team; we were in constant communication. We came up with the idea of creating a special Portuguese brigade for NATO that we would equip. We provided tanks and APCs (armored personnel carriers). I remember coming back to Washington and trying to sell the idea. The State Department kind of shook their heads and said that was an interesting idea but there was no money for that. I said, "Fine, I will get the money." I went to the Office of Budget Management where I had been a deputy director and managed to get their okay to the money if I could get somebody in Congress to sponsor it. So, I went to Ed Brooke, senator from Massachusetts, who was on the Armed Services Appropriations Committee. He sponsored it and pushed it through. I managed to pick up support from other people who had Portuguese constituents. Senator Claiborne Pell of Rhode Island was helpful.

I obviously focused on them because of the concentration of Portuguese immigrants in Rhode Island and Massachusetts. I had some political experience. If I may say so, it was somewhat unique—an ambassador pushing through his own aid program—but I did. After I designed the program for the army, the air force came in and said they needed a program. So, we designed an aircraft program for them. Finally the navy came in and we ended up designing a frigate program for them, which took something like ten to fifteen years to materialize but it came about. We now have a Portuguese frigate that was built as a result of the aid program that started when I was there.

It was the rabble in the streets that had become important. In fact, I became fairly close to some of the original coup plotters: Melo Antunes and Vitor Alves, even Vasco Lorenzo. I spent a lot of time with them and was convinced that even they were not happy with the turn the events had taken, even though they were all on the left side of the spectrum. I think those contacts at least helped to neutralize them, if nothing else. But, the military was turning rapidly into an uncontrollable rabble and the idea was to restore a sense of professionalism, get them back into the barracks, get them out of politics and enable the elections to take place, and the civilian leadership to take over. And that, in fact, is what happened.

There were all kinds of monitors who came for the elections. In fact, it was rather an inspiring sight. I went around a lot of the polls myself and you would see Portuguese standing in line for hours on end to wait to vote. The Portuguese people expressed themselves decidedly. The results were indisputable. With the monitoring that was taking place, including monitoring by the press, it was very difficult to tamper too much with the elections—not that there weren't irregularities, I am sure.

The socialists in effect won, the communists came in second, and the other democratic parties a distant third and fourth. Eventually Mario Soares was elected prime minister. That was our assessment. It wasn't always believed in Washington and even if it was believed there was considerable skepticism that the socialists were the kind of people who you could work with. But the embassy took the position that the socialists were likely to win and that we could work with them.

I think Henry Kissinger had around him some advisors who were truly skeptical of the position that I was taking. He himself expressed skepticism on several occasions. So it was at the top. Once I got the signal from Henry, everyone fell into line.

I know that I received at critical points some very, very difficult cables. I remember receiving one cable that in essence said to cease and desist and that these guys were bad guys and we are going to drum them out of NATO, or something like that. I wrote a response and Charlie Thomas, my political counselor, came up to me—I had the habit of showing my cables to my senior staff before sending them—and said, "Frank, please do me a favor, put this one in a drawer and don't send it until tomorrow." By the next day I had cooled down and sent a much more measured response.

The media was communist controlled. I don't think I went on TV that much, as it was government controlled. The newspapers were not directly controlled, as such, although the vast majority of the journalists came from the left. I guess that probably is the best way to put it. But, if I gave an interview there were newspapers that would print it word for word. Now, a lot of things I said were distorted, but if you keep saying them over and over again the word gets out. The fact that I became a very visible figure in Portugal meant that the press couldn't ignore me. I didn't set out to make myself a visible figure, I set out to make myself an open figure, but it turned out that I became very visible.

By the time I had been there three years I thought it was time for me to leave, because I had become too much of an actor in the drama and the drama was nearing an end anyway. There was no question I became a player and that is not normally a healthy thing for an ambassador to become.

THE MURDER OF THE AMERICAN AMBASSADOR

Ambassadors rely on the protection of the country to which they are accredited. This principle of the inviolability of ambassadors goes back to the beginning of diplomatic history. It was a tremendous shock to the United States, and particularly to the professionals in the Foreign Service, when Ambassador Adolph Dubs was murdered in Kabul, apparently with the complicity of both the Afghan government and the Soviet representatives in that city.

Bruce A. Flatin
Political Counselor, Kabul, Afghanistan, 1979

Our ambassador, Adolph (Spike) Dubs, was murdered on Valentine's Day, 1979. I was at the embassy as political counselor meeting with Bruce Amstutz, the DCM, shortly before nine a.m. to discuss the staff meeting we'd be holding at nine. The ambassador was not yet in. The security officer and the ambassador's chauffeur burst into the DCM's office to announce that the ambassador had been "arrested by the Afghan government" and was being held at the Kabul Hotel.

By this time in Kabul, one could be paranoid enough not to be surprised that an ambassador would be arrested by the host government. In other places that may strike you as being unusual, but in Afghanistan that was not a concept that was impossible to grasp. I told Bruce I'd go to the Kabul Hotel and call him from there. When I passed my office I told Jim Taylor, my deputy, what had happened and where I was going. His first reaction was, it must have been the human rights report. We'd just delivered it shortly before. It was not a very pleasant report. Once again, it may seem strange, but there it was not out of the question that such an unpredictable government would react in that kind of a fashion.

I traveled to the Kabul Hotel with a couple of other people from the embassy. We used the ambassador's car. I saw letters he had been prepared to post and noted that he had been reading the *New York Times*. When we got there, the hotel lobby was swarming with police and troops. We were told that terrorists had seized the ambassador. They had one down in the lobby as a prisoner, and the other ones—they didn't tell me how many there were—were up in a room with the ambassador on the second floor. (The original report stated that four men had seized the ambassador.) It struck us as odd that the terrorists would come to a hotel in the center of town to hole up with the ambassador. Soviet embassy people were there as well. I was talking to the Soviet official and the Afghan police and military leadership on the scene. They told me that these people were demanding the release of some anti-regime people in return for ambassador Dubs, specifically a man named Yunus Khalis.

The important point to note is that we Americans never ever had any direct contact with the people holding the ambassador. Everything we knew about who was holding him and what they wanted was through the Afghan communist leadership and the Soviets. This is an important point. We brought up our embassy doctor, ambulance, nurse, and the ambassador's blood type just to be ready in case there were problems with his being injured. We wanted to make certain we could take care of him right away.

In the meantime, Bruce Amstutz, the DCM, got in contact with the Department and was told that Secretary of State Vance wanted to ensure that the Afghans did not do anything precipitous. They should negotiate with the people holding the ambassador and not do anything that would in any way bring about any danger to the ambassador. We conveyed this message frequently at the hotel. The DCM was trying to reach Foreign Minister Hafizullah Amin. We sent officers out trying to find him like process servers. He was not available anywhere, and couldn't be reached on the telephone.

At the hotel, I kept telling the police that our embassy was trying to reach Hafizullah Amin with a special message from Secretary of State Vance urging that there be no precipitous action. This was the theme we repeated all morning. I was assured by the Afghans and the Soviets that they would not endanger the ambassador. I was assured they were going to do their best to negotiate. I said that we would like to get someone up to the second floor to talk to the ambassador, so we could reassure him that things were going all right. They did not respond to this initially, but later at a certain point a Soviet officer came up to me (the Soviet I'm referring to was a person whom I knew to be a Soviet security type). He asked me, "What languages does your ambassador know besides English?" I replied, "His best language, of course, is Russian." He responded, "Besides Russian?" I said, "He knows German rather well." He asked, "Do you know German?" When I replied that I did, he went away.

Then a little later, the chief Afghan police official came up to me and he said, "Would you please come upstairs with me?" This was finally the moment to see what the situation was upstairs. He said, "We'd like to have you talk to your ambassador in German so that the people inside the room will not be able to understand what's being said." I replied, "Fine." As we walked down the hallway, I could see a group of troops and police outside this one room. I noted that the suite next to it was open, too. I asked, "Do you want me to talk through the wall from this suite on the other side?" The police official replied, "No, its best if you talk right through the door into the suite where the ambassador is being held." When I looked at this keyhole through which he wanted me to talk, I could imagine myself swallowing a bunch of bullets. I said, "Are you sure the people inside the room have agreed to this procedure?" And he replied, "Yes." I said, "I want to hear you once again talk to them to hear their agreement." So, he talked to them and they appeared to have agreed that this embassy political officer could talk to the ambassador. (I suppose his captors were assuming this was going to be in English, because it was an American officer who would be talking to the ambassador.)

And when that was made clear, I knelt by the keyhole, and I said in German, "Good morning, Mr. Ambassador. How is it with you?" And the ambassador replied in a strong voice, "I am all right." Then the police instructed, "Now ask him what kind of weapons they have." So I asked, "What kind of weapons do they have?" The ambassador started to answer but unfortunately in his German he used words close to "pistol" and "revolver." By that time, his captors caught on to the fact that English was not being used, and they ordered, "Stop this conversation! We won't stand for any tricks. There'll be no further conversation." The ambassador then remained silent. The police tried to get the captors to loosen their controls, but they refused to let any more conversation continue.

Then the police official said to me, "Tell your ambassador that exactly ten minutes from now he's either to try to go to the bathroom, or he is to fall to the floor." I replied, "Just a minute, I want to talk to you elsewhere." So we went down to a cross hallway where I said, "We've spent the whole morning telling you that we don't want any precipitous action here, and you're now telling me to help you light a fuse that's going to go off in exactly ten minutes." I said, "I want to repeat once again that we're trying to find Foreign Minister Amin to deliver an urgent request from Secretary Vance that there be no attack on this room." He shrugged his shoulders, and muttered, "I have my orders."

So then I went to the Soviet security officer, and I said, "Once again, I want to tell you that we have said this many times that we don't want any precipitous action here." The Soviet then talked to the Afghans and that particular raid appeared to have been called off.

But later in the morning—I'd say about an hour and a half later—it was clear they had received an order to hit the room. They got prepared. The Soviets came forward and provided some with special weaponry. They had police and troops on a building across the street who were responding to hand signals from the Soviets in our building. At a certain point there was a loud shot and then a gun fight lasted exactly forty seconds; I checked this with my watch. That's a long time. The floor just shook with the gun fire coming from the hallway where I was standing and from the bank building across the street into the room. When the whole thing was over there could not have been one cubic centimeter in that room that didn't have a bullet pass through it. A gnat flying in that room would have been hit.

In the meantime, other Americans had come up the stairs and were on the opposite side from this cross corridor with me, and they had the stretcher. When the initial burst of firing stopped we were ready to go to the room with the stretcher, and the Afghans told us to wait a minute. Then there were four more loud shots. Then we were told to come.

When we looked in the room, the room had water all over the floor because the gunfire had shot up the radiator. There were some two or three inches of water on the floor. The ambassador was slumped in a chair against the wall, but one half of his body was wet as though he had been lying on the floor. He was taken out on the stretcher, clearly dead. He had many bullet holes in him. There were two men in the room; they were brought out and dumped at my feet. One was probably dead, and the other one looked definitely dead; they were taken away. The third man they had held as a prisoner, who appeared to be a confederate of theirs and had been used from time to time to talk to them through the door, was held nearby in the hallway as alive as you are. They put a brown bag over his head and took him away screaming and kicking.

Then, I went downstairs and saw the police official in charge and said, "I just want you to know our ambassador is dead." He's the one who had kept assuring me that if anything happened there would be a very small chance of any problem. He said, "I'm very sorry." He did not sound very convincing.

I went back to the embassy then and after about an hour I got a call from the Afghan authorities asking me if I wanted to come to the military hospital to see the dead bodies. So, I went there with the security officer and our consular officer. We were brought into a hallway where there were four nude, dead bodies on the concrete floor.

I should point out, incidentally, that one of the earlier reports, including that of the ambassador's driver, was that four people had seized the ambassador. One of our USAID wives thought that she saw four people going into the hotel with him. One of these people, incidentally, was reportedly in a police uniform. He was said to have stopped the ambassador's chauffeured car in front of the USIS building. So, since we were told there were four men, they apparently thought they had to account for this number. As I told you, there were only two "captors" in the room, and both were now definitely dead. The man who was just as alive as you are with a brown bag over his head was now dead, too. He had contusions all over his body, and was turning greyish blue. Then there was a fourth person whom I had never seen before in my life lying there. The police colonel, who was showing us this display, said, "These are the four men shot in the room during the shootout." He and I had been standing together in the hallway, outside the room. He knew perfectly well what we'd seen, but this was going to be their official story.

The ambassador's body was then brought by our medical crew and ambulance to the American AID compound, where they brought him into the dispensary. Afghan troops then entered the AID compound in violation of our diplomatic status. When we complained about it, they said they were in there to "protect" the ambassador. We were very concerned that they would try to seize the body. The White House, responding to the situation, sent a special plane from Washington. We let the Afghans know that it was on the way to pick up the body. So they didn't press us any further inside the compound.

The body was brought back here to Washington for autopsy at Walter Reed. There were many bullets in the body, but the ones that caused death were .22 caliber bullets in the brain, about four of them. The official Afghan incident report to us, in the form of a diplomatic note, had listed weapons found in the room and none of them were .22 caliber. And as you know, police and troops don't use .22 caliber, but certain types of official security agency assassins do use .22 caliber as a favorite weapon. This became a focus of ours. We insisted on seeing these weapons taken from the room, and they promised us we could. We went after this issue time and time again. It must have been ten or eleven different times we insisted upon this in notes and personal conversations. Bruce Amstutz became our chargé, and I became acting DCM. Whenever we saw Foreign Minister Amin or any other appropriate official, this subject would be raised and we would receive slippery answers. On one occasion Amin told us, "We have all kinds of weapons we pick up here throughout the city for various crimes all the time." We were apparently to get the impression that weapons were being thrown in some coal bins somewhere, and that no one could tell which weapons were which anymore.

In June of 1979, we sent a note to the Afghan Foreign Ministry telling them the results of the autopsy at Walter Reed and, in essence, telling them they were liars, and challenging them to give us a straight account as to what really happened in view of the fact that their original note was incorrect. It had conveyed false information. We never got an answer to that note. That was the end of that subject from their viewpoint. We also discussed this with the Soviets, who drew the obvious conclusion that we were saying the Afghans had murdered the ambassador.

Therefore, you couldn't help but reach the conclusion that his death certainly seemed to involve the responsibility of the Afghan government, and probably the Soviets, but it always puzzled us as to why they would do it. Some people said it was because Spike Dubs was a Soviet expert, and the Soviets wanted him out of the way before they went into the next phase of their Afghan adventure. But that made no sense, because we have many Foreign Service experts on the USSR who could have been assigned there. He was not the only Soviet expert we had.

Others said it was because they wanted to terminate our relationship with Afghanistan. And, indeed, that did happen. It did terminate the AID relationship, but that wouldn't have made any sense either, because if I were the Soviets I wouldn't give a damn if Americans were shoving money down that rat hole. I didn't see any communist purpose served by getting us out of our AID programs there. Whatever the reason, he was dead. It was a hardball game there. This occurred, as I said, on Valentine's Day, 1979. Our bilateral relationship went steeply downhill from that time on.

IRANIAN TAKEOVER OF THE AMERICAN EMBASSY

A low point in diplomatic incivility is reported by Bruce Laingen when he and the rest of the U.S. embassy in Teheran were taken hostage by Iranian students, who were sanctioned by the government of Ayatollah Khomeini. There followed four-hundred and forty-four bitter days showing how not to treat diplomats. American FSOs learned, under extreme stress and duress, what playing a world role in diplomatic affairs can mean. No diplomatic crisis caught the attention of the United States and the world more than this period between 1979 and 1981. Bruce Laingen was at the embassy as chargé during this period and explains the events that led to this unhappy action.

Bruce Laingen
Chargé d'affaires, American Embassy, Tehran, Iran, 1979–1981

I had a telephone call from the Director General of the Foreign Service telling me that the secretary wanted me to go to Tehran to serve as chargé d'affaires of the embassy for a period of four to six weeks while the Department and the White House made a determination as to what kind of diplomatic presence we were going to have in Iran in the aftermath of the revolution that had taken place in February and in the aftermath of the departure of Ambassador [William] Sullivan in March and the fact that the chargé d'affaires who had remained in place, Charlie Naas, needed to be relieved as well.

I don't recall if I said immediately on the telephone, "Yes, of course I will go," or whether I said, "I will call you back." I hope with respect to my wife I said at least, "Let me call you back." Having served there earlier, as an old Iranian hand, I and many others were watching what was happening in Iran in the aftermath of the revolution. I can remember talking with Henry Precht, who was then the Country Director for Iran, about what was happening and he, I thought facetiously, saying, "Wouldn't you like to go to Tehran?" I pooh-poohed that and said that I had been away from there too long and was not the one to go. But when I got that call in Minnesota on the farm telling me that the secretary of state wanted me to go to Tehran, as a loyal Foreign Service officer my first instinct was to say, "Yes, of course I will go."

I can also recall feeling excitement. That was where the action was. I am not sure I said that I would call back or immediately said, "Yes." That is important because my wife at the time had reservations. She said, "All right, if you want to go, go." But she was strong in her reservations, and I can recall that she told me that that was not the place to go, that we shouldn't be there at all. What we should do, in her view, was to put a fence around the country and let them sort themselves out rather than take any risks with the place. But she was the loyal spouse, in the days when spouses had less to say, and she said, "Go ahead and go, if you want to go." So I went.

The revolution had occurred in February, 1979. Ambassador Sullivan was presiding in the embassy. The embassy had been overrun in the midst of the revolution. In the zeal and passion and excitement of the revolution, the revolutionary types descended on the embassy and occupied it for six hours. It was restored to Ambassador Sullivan's control by leaders then coming into power but not yet in office, including the future Foreign Minister [Ebrahim] Yazdi. Thereafter, the embassy had revolutionary guards, whom we referred to gently as thugs, on the compound. A squad of them—indeed at the beginning, three squads of them from three separate revolutionary groups—were placed in the embassy for our "protection." Ambassador Sullivan remained on the job for a time, until March.

As far as my own instructions were concerned, in addition to being told that my assignment was temporary, I was to do what I could do in the first place to enhance the security arrangements in the compound at the embassy: do what could be done to get those revolutionary guards, by that time reduced to one squad of about thirty, removed from the compound. They, by that time, were an awful red flag for our proud Marines who didn't think much of the idea at all of having others on the compound and particularly not revolutionaries, sharing the responsibility of protecting their compound. The first item on my list of instructions was to do what I could, even in that short time, to see if we could accomplish their removal.

The second instruction was to do what I could to enhance the morale of the embassy community, largely then confined in their social and official activities to the compound itself. A third responsibility was to again look to how the consular function of the embassy could be rehabilitated. A fourth was to continue to work as Charlie Naas had done to put some order into sorting out our military supply relationships with this new regime.

I guess it was largely that list of instructions, as well, to communicate on behalf of Washington that we fully accepted the change in Tehran, that we had no intention to work with the Shah to restore him to the throne, that we were well aware that circumstances had changed totally in Tehran, and that we accepted it. Those were my instructions.

There was divided opinion in Washington as there had been throughout the time that future relations were being discussed in the aftermath of the revolution in February, but always those who felt that the risk was worth taking prevailed. I think they were a rather substantial majority. That was my opinion of people here. We couldn't just walk out. We still had a great deal of things to sort out on the ground in Tehran, not least the military supply relationship, and it was best that we make that effort.

There was something like twelve billion dollars in incomplete orders placed by the Shah, where the equipment had not been delivered. There was also a substantial amount of spare parts for an existing U.S. supplied military inventory. We had had before the revolution during the Shah's period, a very large military-supply relationship, cash payment, involving hundreds of military personnel on the ground in Tehran handling this complex supply relationship. Most of those had left in the aftermath of the revolution. All of those orders and all of that relationship were lying there untended and we needed to get at it. The Soviet "threat" loomed rather large in the minds of everyone. Of course in the final analysis, that threat and oil interests in the Persian Gulf were the considerations that kept us concluding that to try to have a relationship even with this questionable regime was worth the effort, that we had to be there.

I arrived in Tehran June 16, 1979, and was met at the airport by Charlie Naas and a large entourage of security escorts. This was my first return in a substantive official capacity since I left there in an official capacity in 1955. I obviously returned to a very different Tehran, both in terms of the growth of that city, and in a revolutionary context a very different scene of revolutionaries everywhere, not least at the terminal building in Tehran. I will never forget the impression of traveling into the city from the airport that evening with Charlie Naas in an armored-plated limousine with escort cars both fore and aft. Each of them was loaded with security types who had no hesitation when it was necessary to clear traffic to jump out of their cars and wave their pistols and Uzis [machine pistols]. They were Iranians, waving their guns and Uzis around to clear the way. It was a rather dramatic entry back into Tehran.

I found the morale of the embassy high (in a beleaguered mission it is usually high because it is beleaguered), but this situation, nonetheless, was a little down because the outlook was still very uncertain. They were thrown in upon themselves. They couldn't get out very much at all around the country. They could travel to some extent within the city of Tehran.

My reception by the officials of the provisional government of the revolution headed by secular leaders of the revolution, particularly representing the National Front, was very good. They weren't jumping over themselves to embrace me, but they were courteous, polite, and on the whole very friendly. I never had any difficulty during the months that followed to gain access to see members of the government. I communicated to them a desire to continue to build a new relationship, to remind them that we had no policy objections to the fact of the revolution, and to appeal to them in particular for cooperation in improving security affecting the personnel of the embassy and the compound. That kind of welcome was evident on the Fourth of July, which was less than three weeks after I arrived on this temporary mission. We made a judgment that we would go ahead with an official ceremony celebrating the Fourth of July, which one would normally do in an embassy, of course, but this time it had to be carefully considered because we didn't know what kind of reaction we would get.

So we had a noon-time reception at the Residence, inviting a fairly large number of officials of the Provisional Government, including some military representatives. We had a surprisingly large turn out, including the foreign minister, the defense minister, and I think a couple of other ministers. The reception got some good publicity in the press.

That event on July 4th began the building of optimism among us that eventually became wishful thinking and eventually saw us make some judgments about our durability in Tehran that proved totally unfounded. Behind the scenes, however, we knew there were other elements of the revolution that had brought it about, particularly the clerical elements from the Ayatollah Khomeini on down. Their power, their role, their activity were concentrated in a Revolutionary Council with which I never had direct contact, and which was not a visible organization to the rest of us, any embassy, or for that matter the Iranians themselves. It was very much behind the scenes. It was another element of power which we all knew was there, but with which we did not deal directly. I never did have that kind of contact with them that amounted to much except on some social occasions I would have contact with this or that cleric, this or that mullah.

We were beginning to get cooperation as well in improving the security on the compound. I think it was in August that that effort reached the point where the security group on our compound, headed by a particularly unattractive thug named Mashalla, was removed forcibly by other revolutionary elements. That was a very important development event, because it did a great deal to restore morale on the compound for the Americans who lived and worked there. It was seen as very tangible evidence that the Provisional Government, at least, did want to continue to try to build a relationship with us and let us remain. As this process went on, and we were having some progress as well in discussion in sorting out the military-supply relationship, Washington apparently concluded that it might be a good idea to keep me on not only longer as chargé d'affaires, which of course they did, but eventually to conclude that my being named as ambassador to the new regime would be a positive development. We had a number of visits from American business representatives. We had encouraged them to come to check it out on the ground, but not to stay. We told them that the only way they could hope to begin to resolve some of their problems was to come out and take a look.

I said that we were beginning to have some very serious discussions about the military-supply relationship. We were approaching a point where an Iranian mission of military officers would actually come to the United States and go out to

Omaha and sit down and look at the vast amount of paper and records that had accumulated affecting that supply relationship.

Looking back on it, the one ambassador who was more cautious than others—and in light of what happened, perhaps the best informed—was the ambassador of Turkey. The Turkish ambassador consistently warned me and others in conversations that we were a long way from Nirvana; things could turn badly. He was proven right.

The Soviet "threat" was there and we recognized it. We didn't expect the Soviets to intrude or invade. They obviously needed to be cautious and careful themselves in how they dealt with this new regime, because there was no love lost for communism as an ideology on the part of a regime that was so dominated and motivated by an ideology like Islam. They, and particularly elements of the Communist Party, then underground, remained carefully discreet.

We kept saying that we had no intentions of re-establishing a vast military presence. We knew that was behind us, but we knew that we had to have some kind of very close contact to sort the contracts out.

When I came back from consultations in September, I had instructions to work to find the best possible time to request an audience with the Ayatollah. We never got to that point. But, I was functioning under that instruction when I got back and, conceivably, with a little more time I could have had it. In retrospect, I am convinced that even having done that, possibly even if I had seen him as the accredited ambassador, it wouldn't have made a hell of a bit of difference. The Ayatollah Khomeini was so rigidly opposed to any kind of presence of the United States, of "West toxification," as to make it impossible for us ever to have had a relationship with him.

The Shah had moved from Tehran in January, fleeing with the Empress and a small entourage, and had stopped in various places...Cairo, Morocco...and by June when I came there, he was in Mexico. It was an issue lying there on the table, if you will, in the background for some, what to do about the Shah—the person, the leader, the head of state—for whom the United States obviously had some responsibility, given the previous relationship we had with him. It posed for President Carter a special obligation in the sense that he had reached out to him in such an open, sympathetic way, as the crisis developed in Iran, particularly at the time of the visit of President and Mrs. Carter to Tehran on New Year's Eve in 1977. I was chargé of the embassy in Tehran beginning June, 1979. I was asked on several occasions, both on the record and by people who came to Tehran, for my views about what we do about the Shah, where he should live and whether he should be allowed entry into the United States.

On both occasions, on the two instances when I was asked formally by cable from Washington for my views, I responded that I felt, myself, that we had an obligation to admit the Shah into the United States, but that the timing was very significant. On both occasions—sometime in late July and again in late September—I responded that his admission was inappropriate until and unless we had demonstrated our acceptance of the change in Tehran, our acceptance of the Islamic revolution, by naming an ambassador, formally, to succeed Sullivan—who had left in March—and until we had seen in Tehran the completion in large part of the process of putting in place the institutions of government under the new regime. That involved, in particular, the election of a new *majlis* [constituent assembly], a referendum on the constitution and a number of other symbolic, but very importantly, steps that would see the revolution put in place its own institutions of government. Those two cables in which I reported those views were obviously received in Washington and considered, but a recommendation from an embassy in the field, from a chargé in the field, from an ambassador in the field, to Washington is only one of a large inflow of views affecting policy in Washington.

In 1979, at the time of the revolution and during the revolution, one of the major concerns of the revolutionaries—both nationalists and the more radical Islamic elements—was that the United States would again work behind the scenes to facilitate a return of the Shah to his throne, even after he had fled this time in the midst of that revolution. They were very apprehensive about that. There was a constant concern on the part of the revolutionaries, a greater concern in the minds of some than in others, but it was always there. It was apparent to me that that concern was very strong, and how we handled the Shah, what we did with him, the degree we seemed to be supportive of him in his ambitions, could be very decisive for our position in Tehran.

Well before I had come to Tehran in June of that year, the embassy had sought in every way possible to demonstrate to the new regime that we, despite our sense of moral obligation, not least to the Shah, had no intention to facilitate his return to Iran. It was very hard to convince them of that. It was impossible to convince them of that so long as the Shah was out there moving about. So it was for that very basic reason that I felt that anything that we did to reach out and embrace the Shah, even in humanitarian terms, could have very considerable consequences so we needed to handle it very carefully.

The Shah was sick. We didn't know how sick. There was also a humanitarian sense because the Shah had been our ally, a close friend, supportive of much of U.S. policy throughout the region and in areas well beyond the Middle East.

That was a sense of political obligation, but there was also that humanitarian sense of the guy being a good friend. Here he was bounced from his throne and trying to find a place to live, to put down his feet and his family. There was a very considerable sense of humanitarian, political, and moral obligation on the part of a good many Americans, well beyond government. I say well beyond government, because some of those were very influential in the decisions that were eventually taken.

I was not asked repeatedly in every meeting I had what we were going to do about the Shah, but I sensed it was there all the time. On several occasions, when I was instructed to convey to the Foreign Office how we handled members of his family, I said that should not be misinterpreted. Before we took the decision to admit the Shah in October, 1979, we had already admitted several of his children to attend school in the United States. Again on those occasions I was instructed, in the face of some concern expressed to me by Iranian officials, that that should be looked at in the context of our humanitarian concern for his family.

Of course, all of that culminated in the decision taken in October to admit him. I thought that was very much the wrong time to admit him because of the very sensitive political processes that were underway in Tehran, particularly the referendum on the new constitution. It was expected to occur in early December, 1979, with elections to follow that.

I warned that if we were to admit him before these other steps were taken—the completion of elections and the naming of an ambassador—there was a risk of another assault on the embassy like that of February, 1979, when the embassy was occupied and held for several hours. I did not have the prescience to predict that we would be seized and held for four-hundred and forty-four days and used in the way we were, but we at least had alerted Washington to the risk of another assault on the embassy.

It was on October 23, 1979, that at breakfast in the Residence I got a call from the Marine guard in the embassy telling me that there was a message that I had to see urgently. I asked him to bring it over to the Residence on the compound. So, a Marine brought it over to me. That was a message informing me that the Shah was about to be admitted to the United States for medical treatment and that I should inform the government at the highest level that we were taking this step for humanitarian reasons.

It came as a bit of a shock to all of us in the embassy and, of course, triggered immediately steps that we were prepared to take to strengthen our security, and these were taken. My first responsibility beyond that, was to get to the highest level of government and that was the sitting prime minister at that time, Mr.

[Mehdi] Bazargan. We got, within a couple of hours, an appointment with Mr. Bazargan, who received us in his office along with the foreign minister, Mr. Yazdi, and a number of other officials including the acting defense minister.

I communicated this information pursuant to those instructions with particular emphasis on our feeling that we had a responsibility in humanitarian terms to provide this kind of medical treatment to the Shah and that the Empress would be accompanying him. I did not receive in the instructions at that time how long we expected him to be there and I simply did not discuss with them or communicate to the prime minister any views as to how long this might entail.

I am not sure how much anybody knew about the details of his illness at that time. One of the problems in dealing with the Shah well before the revolution was that we didn't have an awareness that he had a rather serious illness. Certain French doctors with whom he had dealings were aware of it, but we were not. This always surprised me and I don't know the real answer to that. I don't recall precisely; I think I simply informed them that the condition was such as to require immediate entry and that we would be communicating to the government as soon as we had the details of the medical problem and the treatment that he was being given.

The prime minister, and even more the foreign minister, expressed their concern. The foreign minister reminded me several times during that conversation that this was a very serious step that could have some very difficult consequences and that he had warned me against this kind of thing. He, in particular, pressed for participation in the medical diagnosis by Iranian-designated doctors—that they be permitted to send a doctor to the United States to participate. I couldn't give them assurance of that, although I communicated that to Washington. In response to that, all the Department was prepared to do was to assure Yazdi and his government that we would inform them of the diagnosis by medical doctors in the United States.

I was instructed as well to get—and I obviously requested—assurances from the prime minister that the embassy would be provided adequate security in the event that there would be demonstrations on the streets stimulated by this decision on our part. After some considerable discussion of that, the prime minister said some rather fateful words that didn't seem as fateful at the time: that they would do their best to provide security. He didn't say, "We guarantee you that your embassy will be secure." He said simply, "We will do our best." And, I think, he meant that. I have no doubt that Bazargan meant what he said, that he wanted to do what he could to assure that the embassy was secure, but of course, time would demonstrate that it was not secure and that he was not able to do his best.

The immediate reaction in the streets and in the media on the part of what we dealt with as government was surprisingly moderate. Even the reaction from Khomeini, at the outset, was restrained, much less strident than I expected. He used, particularly, the expression, "Let us all hope he dies." It was almost a sense of confidence that the guy was dead anyway, politically, and that this was a way to see him die medically.

The reaction among my colleagues in the embassy varied. Some were much more concerned than others, to the point that some today say, and I think they can say with accuracy, that they were much more prescient about the consequences than I was. I thought we could manage it. Many of us—and I think this broadly defined the mission as a whole—were living on hope in some of the weeks and months leading up to that period. A sense of misplaced confidence, as things had been going rather well. The security situation—broadly in the country as we saw it and as it affected us and particularly in the city of Tehran—was gradually improving. You could move around more freely. People even traveled outside of Tehran on certain occasions. Indeed, Ann Swift [Deputy Chief of the embassy Political Section] was outside the city the weekend before the embassy was taken. We had gotten cooperation from the government in improving the security on the compound, getting rid of the resident revolutionaries there. We had opened a new consular facility and that had gone well. It certainly had gone well in terms of the number of Iranians who were seeking visas.

So, there was a sense of confidence—as it turned out, it was misplaced confidence, given the events that followed—that we could weather this. That confidence was strengthened by what I described as the first reaction on the part of the media and the Ayatollah himself, relatively restrained.

Our big concern was a very large demonstration planned for support of the revolution on November 1st, three days before the embassy was overrun. That demonstration was originally scheduled to take place around the walls of the embassy and in the immediate environs of where we were. At the last minute, indeed the night before on October 31st, the word was sent around that the Ayatollah had directed that the revolutionary demonstration take place in another area further from the embassy. The next morning, the bulk of the demonstrators did go to that other destination, but somewhere between one and two thousand demonstrators nonetheless came to the embassy compound that morning and spent the day marching back and forth around the walls. We anticipated some of that, to the point where we had added security and the Marines were on sort of battle formation that morning.

I recall, myself, going out to the gates of the embassy to look around that morning and at one point having the chief of police come rushing up in his jeep to take a look at the situation and assure me through the gates that things were under control, that I need not be concerned about any particular danger. They were noisy during the day. A lot of graffiti was put on the walls, on the outside. There were some tense moments late in the day when some of the more determined demonstrators were determined to keep it up and put some banners on the outside of our main gates denouncing us and putting up pictures of the Ayatollah. It caused us a rather difficult stretch late that evening, requiring our security officers to spend some very tense moments out there. We were finally able to resolve it.

We were demanding that the posters be taken down, that the Ayatollah's picture be taken off the gates, and that sort of thing. At one point, apparently one of the security officers or one of the Marines may have ripped one of the posters down from the inside and taken it. That caused some of the demonstrators to demand that it be returned undamaged. Eventually we did turn it back, but not before there had been a good deal of very close physical exchanges between those on the outside and those on the inside of the gate. This was on the night of November 1st, culminating a rather difficult day during which we had advised the bulk of the Americans who lived on the compound and those who lived in apartment houses immediately to the back of the compound behind the rear gates to spend the day up in the British compound in the hills of Tehran. And they did, so we were a skeleton presence that day, except for the beefed-up Marine security guard patrol on actual duty. But we weathered the day. The next day was, as I recall, a relatively quiet day in the city. We made a decision that morning that when the embassy was to be reopened on the 4th, we would keep the consular facility closed while we got the graffiti removed. Frankly, it was a gesture almost of defiance. We weren't going to let that stop our operations totally; we were going to clean it up and get on with it.

The night before the embassy was taken over was the third of November. Periodically I would have welcoming parties for new arrivals and we had scheduled one that evening in the Residence where we also showed films in the large salon for the American community. At the last minute, I was unable to host that affair because I got word from the Foreign Office that there was a command performance for the entire diplomatic corps to go to the Foreign Ministry club compound where a new documentary film on the revolution was going to be shown.

So I asked my secretary, Liz Fontaigne, to substitute for me as hostess, at least until I came back.

I saw the film, which was an interesting documentary on the revolution, not least because some important footage of the film was filmed immediately outside the embassy compound back in February showing tanks on the streets and the embassy under a state of siege at that time as well. It was rather ironic that the night before the embassy was to be overrun the second time I was at that command performance watching a film showing how we were affected by the revolution eight months before.

The next morning was our first day back at work after the events of these preceding days, the first day that the embassy was open again. The way in which we had weathered this very large demonstration on the first, three days earlier, was very much on our minds and in our senses. Here was evidence, in the way we had weathered it, that the regime meant what it said about being prepared to do its best to protect the embassy, contributing, if you will, to a further sense of confidence and wishful thinking that morning. In the country team meeting that we held that morning, I assume—I don't recall specifically—that Barry Rosen and others reported on what was in the media and what had been said in terms of the Shah. At this point I don't recall the details of that. We talked about our schedules for that day, what we intended to do. I recall particularly that we made a decision that morning to keep the flag flying around the clock and leave it on the flag pole, carefully secured and with the pole greased, as they had done before on occasions, to insure that if there was any attempt to come over the walls in any demonstration it would be difficult to get that flag down.

I recall that we agreed to keep the Marines on a state of alert, but that business would go on as usual in the embassy. I would keep a long-scheduled appointment that morning at the Foreign Ministry at ten-thirty, or whatever—I have forgotten precisely—to carry on discussions I was having with the Foreign Ministry about arranging for the future diplomatic immunity status of my reduced military liaison office.

I went to the Foreign Ministry with one of my security officers, Mike Howland, leaving the other security officer on duty, Alan Golacinski, in the embassy. The two of them had radio contact on walkie talkies, communication back and forth between Howland and the embassy and between the Foreign Ministry parking lot and the embassy.

I was scheduled also to be accompanied by the senior political officer in the political section. On the streets we passed several groups of demonstrators apparently heading for the university compound, where there were to be large demonstrations commemorating an assault on the University by the Shah's regime at an earlier time. We did not sense that they were heading towards our compound and so proceeded as planned to the Foreign Ministry.

We had a good conversation over traditional cups of tea with Iranian professional diplomats, none of whom that morning raised the issue of the Shah. Our conversation was entirely limited to the question of diplomatic immunity for the military liaison office. At the end we departed without resolving the issues, but we had not expected to. It was a reasonably productive conversation. We went down to the parking lot in the Foreign Ministry compound and there we found Mike Howland in active conversation with his counterpart in the embassy. Mike informed me that a dustup was taking place over at the compound—that there were demonstrators trying to come through the gates.

We got in the limousine and started off, followed by another Iranian security-laden car and got only a block or two when we heard the situation was getting worse at the compound and given advice by Alan Golacinski that it would be best if we not try to come there, and we agreed that we would return to the Foreign Ministry to seek what was then needed, help from the provisional government.

We turned around and got back to the Foreign Ministry and raced up the stairs. I say raced because I recall running up those stairs—the sense of urgency was that great by that time—to see the acting foreign minister because the foreign minister, Mr. Yazdi, had not yet returned that morning from Algiers where he had been with the prime minister as part of the Iranian delegation to celebrations attending the fifteenth or twentieth anniversary of the Algerian revolution.

An hour or so went by, I think, before Yazdi, the foreign minister, turned up. He had come directly from the airport to the Foreign Ministry and the conversations then continued in his office. Meanwhile the chief of protocol, who was clearly a friend and had done his best to facilitate improved security at the compound over the preceding months and had been a very good interlocutor, moved about wringing his hands, as concerned as we were. His secretary and other secretaries were milling about. Everybody was in a state of uncertainty, to some extent bewilderment, as to just what was happening because it wasn't visual to us. It was all by telephone and radio.

Eventually, [Chief Political Officer] Vic Tomseth and I ended up in the foreign minister's office, where I repeated my demands for some action to be taken to protect the embassy and to evict those who by now were coming over the walls in large numbers. Having by that time established a telephone connection with Washington with the cooperation of the Foreign Ministry, I was sitting for much of the remainder of the day at the side of the foreign minister's desk, determined not to give up that telephone connection.

It went on that way for several hours. Vic was trying to carry on to some degree normal business, while I was in conversation with a number of people in Washington from David Newsom on down. It became painfully clear in the course of the day that things weren't happening the way we had hoped they would happen. The foreign minister, Mr. Yazdi, was the man who had been the person—as the revolution had occurred in February when the embassy was over-run then—who had acted physically on the spot to restore the embassy to our control then. Now he was the foreign minister, who should have been able to act to repeat what he had done then. And I think he meant to do it, wanted to do it, actually tried to do it in the course of that day. But it became increasingly apparent as we sat there that he was no longer the locus of the kind of power that he had had been. Meanwhile, of course, the embassy had been overrun.

For the next four-hundred and forty-four days Bruce Laingen and Victor Tomseth were to remain in the Ministry of Foreign Affairs, not quite as hostages, but not able to leave the building without the real threat of being taken prisoners. Laingen was able to speak daily with the Department of State and with his family, but the effort to free the embassy hostages moved to a different stage.

ISRAELI INVASION; BOMBING OF THE EMBASSY

During the decade 1975–1985, one of the most dangerous places on earth was Lebanon. It suffered a long civil war with Christians fighting Muslims, both fighting within their own factions, and then a major invasion by Israel and near occupation by Syrian and Palestinian forces. The American ambassador was in the center of all this turmoil, beset not only by violent forces in the Middle East but by pressures from Washington and Lebanese interests in the U.S. Robert Dillon's tour in Beirut, Lebanon, was during one of the periods most costly to embassy personnel. The embassy was extensively bomb-damaged, with a large number of deaths to both Americans and Foreign Service employees.

Robert S. Dillon
Ambassador, American Embassy, Beirut, Lebanon, 1979–1983

Lebanon is a place where the American ambassador receives an enormous amount of attention. The Lebanese are flattering; many are convinced that their destiny requires them to influence foreigners, particularly the Americans. They are very good at it. They seek your advice, they listen to it. It is pretty heady stuff. People are very friendly. They entertain in great style. Unlike a lot of the rest of the Arab world, there are lots of very stylish Lebanese women at Lebanese parties, which continued even in the midst of all the horrors in that country. You eat caviar and drink expensive drinks; people are, by our standards, over-dressed, but all very stylish and charming. It is very easy for an American ambassador to overestimate his own importance and his own charm. If you believe the Lebanese, I was the most charming man in the world. Of course, there were others, like my family, who reminded me that I was not so charming and that I shouldn't take all the fawning so seriously. It is easy to believe that you are a very important man when you are in Lebanon. Of course, to some extent that is true, but you have to keep it all in perspective.

I was the ambassador to Lebanon. I dealt with all factions of Lebanese. There were fourteen or fifteen Christian sects and three Muslim groups. In Lebanon, the truth is that, as in all of the Middle East, no one reads anything. All communications are verbal; you are in a constant round of meetings. Once you have met with one individual, then you have to meet with everybody else. So, an ambassador's task is to meet all of these people. There was a major faction—the PLO [Palestinian Liberation Organization]—with whom you couldn't meet directly, but there were ways you could be in contact with them as well. I am greatly simplifying, but I would like to leave a picture of an American ambassador who was constantly out getting to know the people that inhabited Lebanon. I traveled in a long convoy, with armed bodyguards. Much of the concern for our safety stemmed from the assassination of Ambassador Frank Meloy who had been killed about five years previously by the PFLP [Popular Front for the Liberation of Palestine]. Ambassador John Gunther Dean had been fired upon several times, but never hit.

The picture in the city was very complex. There was fighting, usually about "turf." There was a Communist militia that was well organized and well armed and they had some good East German training. Sometimes, they were fighting each other; sometimes, they fought the Lebanese Forces. There were constant attempts to work out "cease-fires" that were always broken. The Christian Maronites had a pretty good artillery capability; the others tended to rely more on rockets. The conventional (clearly untrue) explanation for who supplied the Maronites was "wealthy American Lebanese." The source of the artillery was not discussed with me in Washington before I went and there may have been other sources for the artillery, which is very expensive. Resupply was difficult.

In June 1982 Israel invaded Lebanon and Ambassador Dillon found himself on the front line during much of this war.

The Israelis invaded and immediately announced that they would "drive the Palestinian artillery back from the border," where it was a threat to Israel. This rang false with us because we didn't really believe that there was artillery in southern Lebanon, although we couldn't be certain. There may have been a gun someplace. Our military attaché, who couldn't get anybody to really pay any attention to him—he would submit lots of reports, but nobody in Washington really cared about them—immediately noticed that the Israelis were using too much strength for the limited purposes they had announced. The attaché said that it was not a border foray; he predicted that there was something more than just moving a few artillery pieces back twenty-five miles. The Israelis kept coming. The Syrian air force rose to meet them and was destroyed in two days; they lost something like eighty-five airplanes. The Israelis lost one plane. Some people were, of course, delighted by the evidence that American weapons were so far better than the third-rate stuff that the Syrians had gotten from the Soviets.

The Israelis kept coming. The Palestinians chose to fight at Saida at a place called Ain El Hilweh, which was the largest refugee camp. They fought and held up the Israelis for several days. Eventually, the Israelis leveled Ain El Hilweh, then moved north and killed a lot of civilians in their advance. They used tanks and heavy weapons. My recollection is that they divided into two or three columns, one of which smashed up the coast through Ain El Hilweh and Damour. The second column moved to Beirut. One other column was in the Bekka Valley going though the mountain passes. The Syrians fought surprisingly well, but were eventually overwhelmed by superior numbers and equipment and indeed by better tactical leadership. On the tactical level, the Israelis were very good. It is at other levels that one can fault them.

In the midst of this, we were sitting in Beirut and reporting what we could see. It became clear to us that a full-scale invasion was taking place. I thought that

Beirut was the objective, even though the Israelis were still claiming that they were interested only in the forty kilometers north of their borders. But they were already well beyond that line, and not with just a few patrols. They were into mid-Lebanon in strength. It was at this time that Begin sent a reassuring message to Reagan asserting that the Israeli action was intended solely to move the artillery back. That was clearly a lie. We in Lebanon called it a lie in polite language.

As the ambassador, I didn't do a lot of traveling around. My staff did most of that; I tried to be the quarterback sitting in the center of the situation. The Israelis continued their march northward; they had entered the southern part of Beirut, still maintaining that their action was still only an "incursion" and that they would withdraw to Israel in the near future. We didn't believe them. The PLO was withdrawing into the city, setting up defenses there.

I stayed in my house, which was in the hills, not far from Babda where the Presidential Palace was. There is a road which passed my house. One day, on that road, about half a mile from my house, we could see an Israeli tank column advancing. We immediately reported that to the Operations Center of the Department. The answer was, "Well, we have assurances from Tel Aviv that the Israelis are still well south of Beirut." So, I repeated again that I could see the tanks from my house—northeast of Beirut—and they were moving towards the city. The Operations Center just wouldn't believe me. Finally I said: "Goddamn it, this is the American ambassador. Tel Aviv is lying to you. Doesn't anybody care back there?" There was a moment of silence and then a plaintive woman's voice said, "I care, Mr. Ambassador." I was touched and gratified. There was at least one person who cared. The Israelis were lying. But when you reported from Lebanon about Israeli actions, Washington called Tel Aviv to check our observations. The Israelis denied and Washington believed them, even though the American ambassador was reporting that he was seeing the tanks and the self-propelled artillery.

The Israelis had a great sense of humor. They stuck the tanks and the artillery all around my house and then proceeded to shell Beirut from there. That had two effects: one, it annoyed the American ambassador, whom they disliked in any case, and second, when the Palestinians retaliated, they had to fire in the direction of the American ambassador's house. Some Israeli officers showed up to pay a call on me; I refused to receive them. I was later told that that was very impolite of me. It wasn't; I was accredited to Lebanon and I didn't have any business receiving the officers of an invading army. What they clearly expected to do was to use my house as sort of a headquarters, which I, of course, refused.

The siege of Beirut lasted something like fifty days; it seemed forever. We were holed up in the house surrounded by Israelis. The siege was savage. Our military observers counted on some days that eight-thousand rounds of artillery were fired by the Israelis on a limited area of Beirut. Occasionally, the newspapers reported rocket and artillery "duels." Rocket and artillery "duels" consisted of Israeli rounds—a lot of one-hundred and fifty-five millimeters, which are large shells—going into the city and every once in a while some Palestinian popping out of a hole with a hand launcher, firing a rocket. The only thing that the Palestinians ever hit was the air conditioner of my house. That was not funny; there were about thirty people living in the house by that time. That was the "duel." I should also note that what thirty people do to plumbing is no joke, particularly in the middle of a hot, hot Mediterranean summer. We were living cheek-by-jowl without air conditioning. It was no lark.

Phil Habib was also living in the house. He and we were reporting at the same time. His mission got more attention than we did. There was a famous incident I should mention. A cease-fire had been declared and Habib was on the phone back to Washington reporting that the Israelis had broken it and were firing into Beirut. He got the same answer that I got. Washington said: "Ambassador Habib, we have been in touch with Tel Aviv and are assured that the cease-fire is holding. The Israelis are denying that there is any firing." Habib then stuck the phone out of the window just as two tanks fired, with a huge amount of noise. That was a famous story, which was reported in Israel, although there I was mentioned as the person on the phone. [Ariel] Sharon, the Israeli defense minister, then made a statement to the press, outraged at me, attacking me for my non-professionalism as someone who stuck a telephone out of a window believing that anyone could tell one explosion from another. He then said that if I had been one of his junior officers, he would have fired me.

There were numerous cease-fires. They were all violated by the Israelis. The Palestinians were in such a weak position that they desperately wanted the cease-fires so that they could pump water up to their shelters, carry the wounded out, etc. They wanted some respite. The Israelis didn't want cease-fires because they wanted to keep the pressure on.

After negotiations, the Palestinian fighters eventually left under the supervision of American, French, Italian, and British forces that stood between the departing Palestinians and the Israeli army. Most Palestinian families were left behind and several thousand were slaughtered by right-wing Christian militia in the Shatila-Sabra area of Beirut, with extensive Israeli complicity. Then Minister of Defense, later Prime

Minister, Arial Sharon, led the Israeli invading force. This intensified the guerrilla war in Lebanon and brought in Muslim extremists from Iran and elsewhere. There were a series of suicide bombings against the Israeli, French, and American forces in the country. Over 250 U.S. Marines were killed when their barracks near Beirut were blown up. One of the bombs also blew up the American embassy.

I was in my office on the eighth floor. It was the middle of the day on April 18, 1983. It had been a little quieter than it had been. I had resumed my jogging. I was getting ready to go to the American University in Beirut (AUB) with my security escorts, which numbered about ten by this time. They would take over the field and keep everybody at a distance, while the American ambassador would jog about three miles around the track. I was ready to go. I had just had a phone call from a German banker who worked for El Mashtek Bank, half of which was owned by Morgan Guaranty. I knew what the call was about; the issue was more a Jordanian problem than a Lebanese one. I didn't return the call because I didn't feel like discussing the matter just at that time. So, I finished what I was doing. My Lebanese social secretary had just been to see me; it was the last time I ever saw her. I started to undress and then I felt guilty about not having taken the call from the German banker. So I called him back and while talking to him, I stood in front of a window as I struggled to put on a heavy Marine tee-shirt. All of a sudden, the window blew in. I was very lucky, because I had my arm and the tee-shirt in front of my face, which protected me from the flying glass. I ended up flat on my back. I never heard the explosion. Others said that it was the loudest explosion they ever heard. It was heard from a long distance away.

As I lay on the floor on my back, the brick wall behind my desk blew out. Everything seemed to happen in slow motion. The wall fell on my legs; I could not feel them. I thought they were gone. The office filled with smoke, dust, and tear gas. What happened was that the blast first blew in the window and then traveled up an airshaft from the first floor to behind my desk. We had had tear gas canisters on the first floor. The blast set them off so that the air rush that came up through the shaft brought the tear gas with it and also collapsed the wall. I was on the floor cursing away, believing that the embassy had been hit by a rocket. We had been hit by a rocket a week earlier and I thought we had a repeat performance. I was angry as someone gets when you are attacked and you want to lash back even though you are flat on your back and helpless. I couldn't move. In a few minutes, Bob Pugh, my secretary, and Tom Barron, our administrative officer, came in. They were all covered with dust because the walls of their offices had also collapsed, but fortunately they were able to get out quickly because they had not been pinned down. They grabbed the flag staff and pried up the wall a little so I could wriggle out. I looked at my legs and to my immense pleasure, found out that they were still there and functioning. I was cut by the glass everywhere, except in the face because, as I said, my face had been protected. I had cuts and bruises and small pieces of glass in me, particularly in my arms. They itched terribly. It wasn't so much pain as itching.

So, I was in pretty good shape. The others were in good shape. We all started to cough and to wretch from the tear gas. Someone vomited, as I recall. We got out through a window and stood on a little ledge outside. A gust of wind came along and cleared the air. That made us feel much better. We didn't know what had happened. The central stairway was gone, but the building had another stairway, which we used to make our way down, picking our way through the rubble. We were astounded to see the damage below us. I didn't realize that the entire bay of the building below my office had been destroyed. I hadn't grasped that yet. I remember speculating that some people had undoubtedly been hurt. As we descended, we saw people hurt. Everybody had this funny white look because they were all covered with dust. They were staggering around.

We got to the second floor, still not fully cognizant of how bad it was, although I recognized that major damage had been done. With each second, the magnitude of the explosion became clearer. I saw Marylee MacIntyre standing; she couldn't see because her face had been cut and her eyes were full of blood. I picked her up and took her over to a window and gave her to someone. A minute later, someone came up to me and said that Bill MacIntyre was dead; he had just seen the body. That was the first time I realized that people had been killed. I didn't know how many, but I began to understand how bad the blast had been. Bill had been the chief of the AID section. I felt sick. We staggered to a window where someone had put up a ladder and we climbed down on that.

Next to our building was a large apartment house where the DCM lived and which held some temporary offices. We went there and immediately called Washington and reported what had happened. By this time, rescue workers, police, and American reporters had arrived. We found our personnel officer and put together a roster of all the people we thought would have been in the building. We then checked off those that we knew were still alive. We understood that it would be some time before the rubble could be fully searched for bodies. We wanted to report the names of survivors as quickly as possible. Pugh and the security guys were back at the embassy, supervising the rescue operations. I was on the phone to Washington. We went over our roster trying to give Washington all the information we had on our personnel. After a while, we ran out of information;

we looked at the roster and there were many, many people on whom we had no information. That really shook us.

Then I went back to the embassy, joining the mass confusion. I remember two things. One was John Reid, the PAO [Public Affairs Officer], who asked me to come to talk to the newsmen who had assembled. I didn't know what to tell them. Reid was a great man; he stuck a piece of paper in my hands and said, "Here's what you say!" That is what you need in these cases. So, I walked out in front of the TV cameras, still wearing my tee-shirt, dust in my hair, looking beaten up and stood up in front of the cameras and acted as if I had done this every day of my life. I made my statement and took a few questions. Reid tugged my elbow and pulled me away. I tell this story to illustrate why you need staff, why you need professionals like John Reid. My concern was what happened to the embassy and the finding of the survivors, but from the point of view of the United States it was important that the media be addressed with dignity and a display of courage, even if a little false. We had to give the impression that terrorism would not change our policy course. That is what I intended to convey and people later kindly said that that was what I did. Then, I returned to the building.

We were digging out. The last alive person was brought out five hours after the explosion. The last one was a Mr. Kopty, one of our Lebanese employees. He looked like a piece of hamburger; I did not recognize him. Someone had to tell me who he was; I never thought he would live. Anne Damarel, one of the AID employees, came out and I thought she would not live. In the end, there were sixty-two or sixty-three dead. We continued digging for five days, searching through the wreckage, bringing out bodies, sometimes pieces of bodies, identifying people. It was very sad. There were families of the missing Lebanese employees standing around and waiting. There were families of people who had been in the embassy on business. There were families of people who had simply disappeared. We found bodies of people who had been blown into the sea while walking past the embassy. Finally, after five days, we quit. By that time, all we were finding were scraps of people. It was very difficult to talk to the families, particularly when we couldn't find the missing member. The families were stunned. They were very quiet. There was no shrieking as you sometimes get. These families were stunned and exhausted and weeping, but on the whole surprisingly quiet. It was terrible.

I and the other Americans were busy. Somehow we were all functioning very normally, working hard. We had become so busy, so wrapped up in the mess at hand, we had shut out the enormity of the catastrophe. We acted surprisingly normal, although we were really not. A psychiatrist was sent out from the Department of State. I think it was the same doctor I saw after the terrorist attack in Kuala Lumpur. He talked to us. I remember saying to him, "I am surprised how normal I feel." He told me that was a normal and typical reaction. The defensive mechanism that we all have inside had come to the fore. If we didn't have that mechanism, we could not have functioned. That made me feel better, because I was concerned about my reaction.

I didn't break down until about ten days later. I went to the AUB chapel to talk to the families of those who had died. It was a memorial service and they were all there. John Reid had helped me to write out a brief talk. I stood there, looking at these very sad and unhappy faces and they, in turn, were looking at the American ambassador as if he would be able to say something that would make everything well. So, there I was looking at all these people, whose family members had been blown to pieces. I got most of the way though the speech. When I got to the last sentence, a sob welled up and I stopped. I couldn't say anything more. I was in tears. I felt so inadequate and sad looking at all those people. People would have liked to hear that their relatives died for some noble cause. They didn't! Within a few minutes, I recovered, but it was one of the saddest moments in my life in that chapel. I wished I could have done something for those people. To my surprise, years later the son of a man who had been killed told me how much my words had meant to him and to his mother.

The British ambassador, a good guy, immediately invited us to use his embassy. We took over the basement. He told London afterwards, which upset the Foreign Office, but it was too late by then. We were already ensconced. In general, I find that people behave well in these kinds of circumstances. We got good support from other Embassies as well; the Canadians and the British were the first, as usual, but everybody tried to help.

The AUB hospital had become so good over the years treating people like ours that we didn't feel the need to evacuate them. Eventually, we did, but their first care was at the AUB hospital.

My outrage over Lebanon has shaped my career. After that, I wanted to do things that were vaguely humanitarian or educational.

TRICKS OF THE TRADE

Not so dangerous, but still vital to U.S. interests, was Elinor Constable's term as Director of the Office of Investment Affairs in the State Department. Nowhere is a diplomat's skill in negotiating put more to the test than in the field of trade. Each country has its own strong economic interests at stake, so the diplomats have to keep in mind both the international and domestic scenes. It is particularly hard for American negotiations since the United States is a world leader and has to think in broad terms, but still has a politically powerful domestic constituency. Elinor Constable describes how she conducted negotiations and reveals some of the techniques that she used. She faced many years in trade and foreign investment negotiations with various countries and in many tense confrontations to the final moment of decision. Money and power were often the bottom line.

Elinor Constable
Director, Office of Investment Affairs, Department of State, Washington, 1978–1979

My sense on international economic policy is that the rhetoric changes more than the substance, and most changes are on the margin. A Republican administration will have a slightly different view on foreign investment, on trade, and on industrial policy. But what actually happens in the day-to-day implementation of the policy is not that dramatically different from one administration to another. Democrats tend to talk a little louder about trade retaliation. But under the Reagan administration, I can tell you, we were screaming, and pounding the table pretty hard.

There was a little more talk about industrial policy. There was a little more talk about foreign investment. But basically the positions had not changed. As the office director, I had to take over a negotiation right smack in the middle. There were negotiations in the United Nations to try and put together a code of conduct for multinational corporations. These negotiations had been going on for a few years, but they were still hot, and companies were still worried.

Developing countries had jumped on this as part of the north-south dialogue; we are going to control these big, evil, foreign companies that are coming in to rob us. And they had a few soft-headed allies, the Swedes in particular, who thought it would be just marvelous to draw up rules that would be administered by the UN about how large companies should operate. Our position: absolutely no way. Just forget the whole thing. The UN is not going to regulate American companies, thank you very much. This did not change between the Nixon and the Ford and the Carter administrations. Not one jot. The rhetoric might have softened in some quarters.

In any case, I had to take over as head of delegation. And this was a negotiation that had been going long enough so that it had become somewhat arcane in terms of its daily discussions. We had texts. We were negotiating paragraphs, and texts, and words in paragraphs, and they all had legal meanings, and ramifications, and the lawyers were playing. With a one-hour briefing from my predecessor, I had to go take it over. We had lunch and he said, okay, let me start just telling you about the issues. And I said, "I don't want to know anything about the issues." I think it wasn't quite this crisp, but this was the gist of it.

I wanted to draw a table. I got out a piece of paper, and I drew the negotiating table, and I said, "Who sits around the table? I want to know the smartest guy at the table. I want to know the dumbest guy at the table. (Actually there was one woman, but they were mostly men.) I want to know the delegation that most often supports the United States. I want to know the delegation that least often supports the United States. Then, I want you to tell me everything you can about the other delegates around the table."

I took that chart to the UN and sat down for the first session. I was scared. I thought, "How am I ever going to do this?" But you have to come into a situation like that and look supremely confident. You can't come in as the new negotiator, and go "Uh, er, uh." They'll eat you alive. These guys are pros, they can negotiate anything. A professional negotiator can negotiate anything.

I had a very good lawyer working for me. I said, "Okay, here's the deal. I will not formally agree to any changes in the text, additions or deletions, or changes, without your okay for the first couple of sessions. You can write talking points for me any way you want. But I'm going to talk. I have to talk. Okay." So, I sat and listened to the debate, and when the smart fellow said something, my flag went right up [a table flag signifying that the person behind it wanted to talk]. And I said, "You know, Mr. Chairman, that is an interesting idea. I can't formally say yes right now because I have people I have to consult. But I like that idea, that's interesting." And when the dumb guy said something, the flag went up again, and I said, "Mr. Chairman, I'm sorry, but I really don't think we should waste time on that one." And again, when the person who always supported us would say something, I would say, "Yes, I think we agree on that one." And when the guy who opposed us said his thing, the flag went up and I said, "We can't go on that."

At the end of the first morning, somebody came up to me and said, "Gee, you really know all about this, don't you?" I just smiled. Then, of course, I studied like mad, and crashed, and learned as much as I could about the issues and became progressively better informed so that by the second or third session I didn't have to rely on anybody. It's a technique that I've used ever since. I think that thing is still going on, I regret to tell you.

The negotiations just dragged on and on. It was the first multilateral negotiation that I ran for the U.S. side, where I was unambiguously in charge. I didn't have anybody looking over my shoulder and I was able to try different techniques. For two years I did it, and then I turned it over to somebody else.

We had a meeting in Mexico City where I tested a simple hypothesis: if the other fellow wants the result more than you do, then you have him under your total control. And it's something we Americans just don't do very well. We go into negotiations with the idea that there's supposed to be a nice outcome, and our focus is on the nice outcome. No. The focus is how you get there. If you want that nice outcome more than the fellow across the table, you're not going to get there.

This was a meeting of the commission. A working group did the negotiations, and then once or twice a year reported to the Commission on Transnational Corporations [a UN body]. The Mexicans wanted the Commission to meet in Mexico City. The then-Mexican delegate was a fellow by the name of Bernardo Sepulveda, who was the head of the Mexican treasury some years later. Bernardo cut quite a dashing figure, kind of the Jimmy Smits of Mexico City. He wanted to have a "Declaration of Mexico City," a document that would come out of this negotiation. He didn't really care what was in it, as long as we had a consensus document that was more than a communiqué. The meeting lasted two weeks. If you have a two-week UN meeting, you don't get down to the serious stuff until a week and five days has passed. A week and five days into this we got down to the real nitty-gritty, and did close to an all-nighter; it must have been one or two o'clock in the morning when this particular event occurred. We were almost there. We had agreed on almost the entire document, and I had enough flexibility to deal with what was left. But I was waiting for the right moment.

The then-Soviet delegate—this was before the disintegration of the Soviet Union—raised his flag, and he said, "I would like to propose some additions to this document." Bernardo, who was chairing, said, "What? All the proposals have long since been submitted, and thrashed over, and argued over, and we were down to a few brackets. And the Soviet delegate said, "I don't think...." The poor fellow, he had to speak in English because he didn't know Spanish. I don't know if we had translation in Russian or not. "I don't think there's enough about the problems associated with multinational corporations. I think we need more language in here about all the bad things they do." Everybody around the table groaned. It was late.

I raised my flag. They all looked at me. Okay, she'll take him on. And I said, I agree. What? I thought Bernardo was going to kill me. I said, I agree with my colleague. I can accept the document as it stands now. But you know, he's right we don't have enough in here about the activity of these companies. Now, I have here—and I reached in and I pulled up about a five-pound document—I have a lot of information about all the good things they do. And I think what we should do here is draft a new paragraph that has language that my Soviet colleague wants to put in, and that I would like to put in about all the constructive things that these companies do. Of course, if you'd rather not make the addition, I can live with the document the way it is.

For the next two hours the entire room ganged up on this poor Russian fellow. Every once in a while somebody would raise a flag and say, Elinor, couldn't you take some of his language? And I said, sure, I'll take as much as he wants to put in, as long as we put some extra language on our side in. Otherwise I'll accept it the way it is. And they finally beat him into submission. I don't know whatever happened to him in Moscow.

About a year later, maybe less, I was in New York negotiating a completely different set of issues. It was late, we had a document almost ready to go, and the East German delegate—there was then still an East Germany—raised his flag, and asked to make an addition. My flag went up and I said, "Mr. Chairman, I think he's absolutely right. We don't have enough in this document on this issue, and I have some stuff, and I was ready to roll again." From the gallery came this hysterical laughter from a Canadian delegate who had been with me in Mexico City, and knew exactly what I was doing. I looked at him as if to say, "Shut up." He did. Then I did exactly the same thing, and the entire room pulverized this poor fellow. Now, it's not something I could do every week. But these things were just…I sort of made them up as I went along and it was fun. I've always loved that. I had a lawyer with me in Mexico, and at one point he put his head in his hands, and I thought, oh, oh, I've done something wrong here. And when we were through, I said, "What's the problem?" And he said, "No, I was just in awe; that was just so brilliant. I've never seen anything like that before." You have to come up with different things, but it was fun.

7

Beyond the Cold War: Drug Lords and International Terrorism, End of the Cold War, and Nationalism

The last decade of the twentieth century saw the end of the ideological confrontation between the United States and the Soviet Union and of the accompanying potential for mutual nuclear destruction. As the Cold War ended, so too did Soviet leadership of the communist world. The Soviet Union disintegrated, historic Russia re-emerged, and the Soviet satellites in Eastern Europe moved to establish democracies. Except for China, a major power, only a few weak and internationally less significant communist nations remained.

The Foreign Service had reached professional maturity in fighting the Cold War, not only in Europe but in all corners of the world. From the end of World War II to the Soviet Union's collapse, it had contributed significantly to the successful outcome of the struggle between the communist and noncommunist worlds. What is more, the Foreign Service dealt with multiple forms of diplomacy around the world, some traditional, some novel, from trade wars and peace missions to careful and sophisticated interpretations of raw intelligence.

In these last fifteen years of the century, Mideast tensions continued to place American diplomats at risk from terrorist attacks. Many radical Muslim groups targeted the United States for its support of Israel. A most heinous example was the Libyan-inspired bombing of Pan Am Flight 103 over Lockerbie, Scotland, resulting in two-hundred and seventy deaths, one-hundred and eighty-nine of them American.

In Latin America, drug cartels became so powerful that they threatened the stability of certain governments, especially those of Colombia, Bolivia, and Mexico. The United States was the main consumer of their drugs. Official American efforts to curb the trade made U.S. diplomats targets of the narcotics lords, whose aim was to frighten local governments from counter-drug efforts and the United States from interfering with their profitable business.

As the Soviet Union broke apart and Russia began to decline as a world power, the Foreign Service experienced a period of euphoria. It was thought, optimistically, that perhaps the Service could go back to its pre-Cold War role of dealing with individual countries in the traditional way. This was not to be. Though the end of the superpower confrontation almost eliminated the prospect of superpower nuclear war it also rekindled previously subdued ethnic and nationalistic forces. During the Cold War, it was accepted that any split in the Balkans along ethnic lines could drag both the Soviet Union and the United States into a dangerous confrontation. Similar dangers lurked in other parts of the world as well, with local tribal and ethnic tensions and divisiveness temporarily held in check. Within the Soviet Union, itself a multi-ethnic empire formed under Russian imperialism, it had been obvious that secession from the Soviet empire would not be tolerated.

The post-war breakup of European colonial empires released historical ethnic and nationalistic tensions, especially evident in Africa and Asia. In such battlefields, the two superpowers and their allies acted out—and even encouraged—civil and bilateral wars and struggles like those in Vietnam, Congo, the Middle East, South Africa, Korea, and China.

Instead of ushering in a relaxed period of tranquility between nations, the immediate post-Cold War period found the U.S. military fighting a major war against Iraq, heavily involved in the former Yugoslavia, fighting in Somalia, and intervening in Haiti. The United States was quickly forced to redefine its foreign policy.

During this period to the end of the millennium, the Department of State and its Foreign Service made major efforts to forge relationships with the countries that emerged from the defunct Soviet empire. These were fragile entities, trained in a failed system, and susceptible to manipulation by nationalistic, religious, and commercial forces that cared little for the best interests of these small states. At times, because of this background, many of the new nations had little idea what they wanted or needed as they tried to define their new role. The United States and its diplomats often served as the most neutral and objective players in this complicated and vital nation-building effort.

Ironically, the fall of the Soviet Union coincided with the evolution of the European Union [EU], of which much was expected in developing a tidy community of nations. While full of goodwill, the EU, at least for the short term, turned out to be a "weak reed" that could not speak with one voice. It became apparent that the EU was no counter-authority to the United States. If something was to be proposed in dealing with Africa, Kuwait, Yugoslavia, or elsewhere, U.S. leadership was still called for. Consequently, the leading role of the U.S. Foreign Service was never more critical to the international process than in the closing years of the twentieth century.

UNDER THE THREAT OF COLOMBIAN DRUG LORDS

Ambassador Anthony C. Gillespie had earlier worked in the Department of State Bureau of Diplomatic Security, an ideal background for the dangerous role of chief of mission in Bogotá, Colombia. He details his preparation for the job, not only security measures for State Department and Colombian manpower, but even those of the U.S. Army's Delta Force [trained specialists in antiterrorist activities abroad]. Gillespie also sought support and advice from the State Department's medical services on psychological issues. Once at post, he and his staff—including his wife—immediately faced personal dangers from drug lords and other violent groups. Even his college-student daughter in the United States was targeted.

Anthony C. Gillespie
Ambassador, American Embassy, Bogotá, Colombia, 1985–1988

I tried to find out what the full range of U.S. interests and our operational possibilities in Colombia might be. The narcotics question was terribly important for at least two reasons: first, Colombia was a major source of narcotics flowing to the U.S.; and second, the drug trade—cocaine, in particular—was being managed by the Medellín cartel at the time. The cartel had been producing marijuana and shipping it out for a long time. In the early 1980s, the Colombian government under President Belisario Betancourt had begun to get tough with the narcotics traffickers. We needed to support him. So, that one was easy.

The Medellín cartel, named for the country's second-largest city, was headed by a man named Pablo Escobar. He had been elected an alternate member of the Colombian Congress, but he was also an outlaw with a reputation for ruthlessness. The minister of justice of Colombia had been assassinated early in 1984, and there was little doubt that the cartel and Escobar were responsible. In response, President Betancourt approved the extradition to the United States of several drug traffickers who had been indicted here. In response, the traffickers detonated a truck bomb in Bogotá near the American embassy. It did little damage to the embassy, but it did kill a Colombian passerby and damaged other buildings in the vicinity. A short time later, the traffickers let it be known that children at the American School in Bogotá, where most U.S. government employee dependents had their kids, were "at risk" of being kidnapped or hurt if there were any more extraditions. The State Department quickly ordered the evacuation of non-essential personnel and all dependent children. My predecessor, Ambassador Louis Tambs, left with his family in about December, 1984. That was the situation I faced as I prepared to go to Bogotá. I think that it's important to talk about what the department's security people and other specialized groups did in relation to that situation.

It was about this time that there was serious talk of "ambassadorial accountability" for the safety of U.S. government personnel and their families overseas. Several of our posts were considered especially dangerous. In Beirut, Lebanon, we were down to a small staff, and the ambassador was riding around in an armored personnel carrier. In El Salvador, another dangerous situation: the FMLN [*Farabundo Martí* National Liberation Movement] guerrillas were threatening official Americans. AIFLD [American Institute for Free Labor Development] people had been murdered, perhaps by rightist elements. The year 1985 was a dangerous year for many in the Foreign Service. I don't want to belittle the situation elsewhere, but the embassies in Beirut, San Salvador, and Bogotá were considered the most dangerous posts in the service.

In 1985, as I was getting ready to go to Colombia for the first time, I was briefed on security by Diplomatic Security [DS] at State, the Central Intelligence Agency [CIA], and the Defense Intelligence Agency. The briefings made it very clear that I was going into a dangerous situation where U.S. personnel were at risk of real harm. I would be "accountable" in this dangerous situation for about 100 U.S. citizen employees and about 40 or 50 adult dependents, plus about 300 Colombian Foreign Service national employees. All of them were at risk. Since my own two children were at university in California, we had no plans for either of them to come to live with us in Colombia. My wife, however, never thought of remaining in the States by herself.

I learned from the briefings that our concern in Colombia was not so much with traditional threatening letters or messages. Threat assessments were based for the most part on intercepted communications between and among traffickers or guerrillas or on reports by agents who were in or close to those groups. These were internal, private communications in which intentions or even plans to act against the U.S. embassy or the ambassador or other officials were discussed. This gives you pause, because you know the other side is serious.

DS really did a fine job briefing me on the security situation and so did CIA. At the Agency's urging and with DS's concurrence, I took CIA's week-long "crash and bang" course, consisting of some escape and evasion, firearms, and counter-surveillance familiarization and training. It turned out to be a good confidence builder. In addition, State's Office of Counter-Terrorism was beginning to look at guerrilla and narcotics-related terrorism in Colombia.

In 1985, the "M-19" (April 19th Movement), a group of relatively young, dedicated Colombian revolutionaries, was very active. That group had taken over a foreign embassy in Bogotá in 1981 and held many diplomats, including our ambassador, Diego Asencio, for many weeks before releasing them unharmed. The M-19 was active in Bogotá and other cities as well as in the countryside. The FARC (*Fuerzas Armadas Revolucionarias de Colombia*—Revolutionary Armed Forces of Colombia), the ELN (*Ejército de Liberación Nacional*—the National Liberation Army), and the EPL (*Ejército Popular de Liberación*—People's Liberation Army) were also looking at foreign diplomats as targets. All of them resented the United States and considered us an enemy. The Colombian guerrillas were in sympathy with the Sandinista government in Nicaragua and with the FMLN guerrillas in El Salvador, and we were supporting the "Contras" in Nicaragua and the government in El Salvador. Cuba, Libya, and even the Soviet Union were giving support to the Colombian rebels.

Before November, 1985, it appeared that the two lines of "threat"—one coming from the narcotics traffickers and another coming from the guerrillas—might be parallel but separate. All of this gave me a lot to think about as I got ready to go to Bogotá. I realized how serious this was and it focused my thinking. I realized that I was going to be in charge and accountable, under the microscope from Washington and, possibly, in somebody's gun sights in Colombia. I don't want to make light of this. At the time I was concerned and my wife, Vivian, was also concerned. We had serious talks about what we were getting into. It makes you stop and think.

The Department's management said there was a "support system." I started with the Director of Medical Services [MED] and asked what he could provide. He referred me and Vivian to his psychiatrists. They turned out to be fantastic and opened their doors to both of us. Over about three months, we went through at least three or four meetings separately or together. We talked openly about our concerns and our fears. The doctors developed a dialogue and we got a lot of our worries out in the open.

For both of us this included questions about how to work with the embassy staff on safety and security issues. Their suggestion was to confront the issues head on and to recognize that I was going to be accountable and responsible. That gave me a legitimate interest in what embassy personnel did or didn't do about their own security. But I could only go so far. In the doctor's view I should get "out in front" on security and stay there. It would be a serious mistake to withdraw and avoid a leadership role.

Working with MED, we made sure that the department's regional psychiatrist based in Mexico would visit post regularly. At our first meeting, he assured me that he would be in Bogotá every ninety days, "come hell or high water." He asked me to encourage everybody on the staff, Colombians as well as Americans, to meet with him. He said he wasn't there to psychoanalyze people but to help them deal with the stress of a difficult and threatening situation. He was a wonderful resource and helped all of us a lot.

So we followed that advice. It helped with the staff, especially the Americans, although not all of them took it as seriously as we did. I guess Bogotá was one of just a few "danger pay" and "hardship" differential posts at that time. This meant that most American citizen civilian employees received, in addition to their base pay, twenty-five percent of salary as "danger pay" and another twenty percent "hardship" differential. Housing was provided by the embassy. So, there was a forty-five percent "pay bonus" in effect for most American employees. That, in itself, attracted some people who were willing to take a degree of risk that others found unacceptable. There were a number of volunteers. Tours of duty were supposed to be limited to two years (the ambassador's tour was three years), although some people extended for an additional year. Even so, some people thought of Bogotá as a "velvet jail."

When I eventually arrived in Bogotá, I was met by a small army of embassy security personnel. They were at the airplane door and stationed outside on the tarmac around the airplane. Many were openly carrying submachine guns. I had been accompanied on the flight by a DS agent, Mona Moore. As I got into the ambassador's heavily armored Cadillac, she turned me over to Jim Dolan, the chief of my security detail, and we headed for the residence. We were in a motorcade that I later learned consisted of an advance car with several agents, a lead car with more, my car, and a follow car which was a Chevrolet Suburban van with even more agents. It was quite a drive through Bogotá's streets. I had ridden in security motorcades before, but it's sobering to realize that you're "it" and that you're on totally new and unknown ground.

The next morning, when I got a good look at the security around the residence in its walled compound, I began to understand that I was in a situation which, despite all of the briefings and preparation, was quite remarkable. Whenever I set foot outside the house, there were six to nine men in plain clothes, some carrying submachine guns, and uniformed guards stationed all around the house, which was ringed with floodlights that burned brightly every night. The windows in my bedroom and bath were not made of armored glass, but covered by sheets of steel about one-half inch thick. Complicating security, several high-rise apartment buildings had been built very close to the residence. Although our Security Office checked on the owners and the tenants, there were always reservations about just who might be looking out the windows down onto the ambassador's residence grounds. In fact, at one point our security confirmed that a relative of a major trafficker had an apartment on the second floor of a building just outside the residence main gate. The Bogotá residence and its grounds are very attractive, but to be there seemed a bit like being in a prison camp.

In order to be able to vary our schedules as the security officer insisted, I set up a "home office" so that I could get some work done while delaying my departure for the chancery. Working with DCM Michael Skol, my secretary Sylvester Satcher, and Mike's secretary Sue Nelson, we coordinated to be sure that either Mike or I would cover the embassy's front office whenever it was open for business. Depending a little bit on our workload, we tried to avoid having a lot of scheduled meetings within the embassy. When workload permitted, some days I would stay home and work from there. We eventually got more convenient "secure" telephones in our residences, but that was later in my tour. Even so, we could do a lot on the telephone if we needed to. I was able to do a lot of reading and writing at home, and an officer or secretary using an armored van would courier classified papers to me.

Nonetheless, I felt that it was very important that the embassy employees, and especially the Colombian staff, not get the impression that the ambassador and senior management officers were "huddled" somewhere in a bunker. I didn't stay home all that often, maybe one morning a week, or I would go in early and return to the residence at noon for the rest of that day. This was mainly because I had too many other things to do in town, closer to the chancery. Those "other things to do" were rarely handled with much advance notice. The senior regional security officer, Walter Sergeant, used to tell us that if the lead time for an event was under two or three days it was unlikely that anybody would be able to mount an operation against us. He was much more concerned about events planned well ahead of time, like lunches, dinners, and conferences. He would worry when I was an announced speaker at an event, but knew that some engagements couldn't be avoided. He was more comfortable when an event had a three-day "fuse" on it.

When I arrived in Bogotá, each shift of the ambassador's security detail was composed of an American DS officer-in-charge plus eight to ten Colombian security agents employed by the embassy. When my wife arrived in October, 1995, one Colombian agent was assigned to escort her at all times. The Colombians were all former police or military personnel. The detail was with me from early in the morning until they were sure I was in the residence for the evening and not likely to be called out again. Regrettably, our security situation kept getting "hotter" with intelligence reports that one or another group intended to kill or kidnap the American ambassador. They later included the senior DEA (Drug Enforcement Administration) agent in Colombia. DS in Washington decided to beef up my security protection. First, they sent in a special team of security officers so that my traveling detail would always have two Americans, with one in the follow car as well as one in the Cadillac. These officers were superb marksmen, specially trained to react in terrorist situations. Initially two, and later two more were assigned. The embassy leased an apartment for them on an upper floor of a building just outside the residence front gate. From their apartment, the officers could "cover" the residence day or night and they eventually had a number of technical devices there to make the job easier. I think our people also used their apartment as a base for monitoring goings-on in a lower floor unit owned by a trafficker's aunt or cousin.

Not much later, DS added even more U.S. citizen staff to the security details covering me and my wife. An American officer was assigned as head of Vivian's detail, which grew to about five agents. In addition, an American officer was assigned inside the residence for round-the-clock coverage.

Some of my predecessors had carried guns while they were in Bogotá. Even though I had carried a pistol while I was assigned as a security officer, I decided that I didn't want or need to in this job. The professional security officers carried guns, and I wasn't a security officer anymore. Vivian had never been interested in guns or shooting, but in Bogotá she decided that it would be a good idea to understand how they worked and how to use one. Some of the security detail gave her basic training, and she proved to be quite proficient on the shooting range. Regarding guns, Walt Sergeant, the embassy's chief of security, told me that everyone was impressed by Vivian's marksmanship. The guys from our security details enjoyed taking her to the range. She could shoot fast and accurately.

But they and Walt emphasized that a gun offered no protection unless you were prepared to use it, and that meant shooting at another person. Their message was that if someone's coming at you who might hurt you, you have to be mentally prepared to shoot him. Just knowing how to shoot isn't enough. You have to be able to take that serious step. We both very much "internalized" that, and it affected my thinking about whether we should permit embassy staff to carry weapons.

Our daughter Kristin came to Bogotá for Christmas, 1986, and stayed about one week. She was then twenty years old, a student at UCLA and an ardent bicycle racer. One of our Colombian security officers, also a cyclist, took her shopping a couple of times. Right after Christmas, my wife and I left with Kristin for the States. Vivian and I returned to Bogotá in late January 1987. Not long after we returned, the CIA chief reported that agents of Colombia's FBI equivalent had shot and killed three members of the M-19 whom they had been "tailing" for some time in Bogotá. It appeared as if these M-19 members had discovered that they were being "tailed" and were either going to try to get away or attack the people who were following them; I'm not sure which. When the authorities searched the guerrillas they found documents in the heel of one of their shoes. One of those documents was a report which referred to the surveillance of our daughter in Bogotá during her visit at Christmas. A paragraph in this report concluded that the U.S. ambassador and his wife were well protected and would be hard to kidnap or kill, but that the ambassador's daughter traveled with only one guard and would be much more vulnerable, proposed that the M-19 concentrate its efforts on her

You can imagine how chilling that news was. It really underscored the reality of our security situation. The incident caused us all to heighten our security. Even today I react emotionally to the incident. I didn't tell Kristin about it until well after we had left Colombia. However, just a few months after I had seen the report—I guess that was during the spring of 1987—Kristin told us that she was concerned about someone who seemed to be watching her apartment in Los Angeles, where she lived with her roommate. I immediately told Walt Sergeant and he was on the line to DS in the Department, which had its office in Los Angeles make contact with the local police. They visited Kristin and watched her apartment themselves for several days, then regularly stayed in touch with her. They took it very seriously because there were strong Colombian narcotics connections in Los Angeles.

There were other incidents that year. For example, we learned that some cartel leaders had met representatives of several of the Colombian guerrilla groups to discuss the possibility of—and the price to be paid for—the assassination of the American ambassador, the head of the DEA at the embassy, and the head of the Colombian equivalent of our FBI, the DAS [Director of Administrative Security]. The numbers were big: several millions of dollars. That was sobering, but not nearly so much so as seeing the text of the report proposing to kill or kidnap my daughter. That certainly characterized the risks that all of us at the embassy had to live with.

I've dwelt on the security aspects of living in Bogotá because they were something no one could ignore, from the ambassador to the most junior Foreign Service employee, to any Colombian member of the staff. Yet we all did the work that needed to be done in the face of this very real threat.

DEALING WITH AN AMERICAN TRAGEDY: THE AFTERMATH OF THE PAN AM 103 BOMBING

With extensive consular experience in the field, Michael M. Mahoney was ideally suited for the demanding job of directing the State Department's Citizens' Emergency Services Center. His was the principal office to ensure the appropriate protection of U.S. citizens abroad when they fell afoul of a foreign law. Americans might be jailed in the most primitive living conditions; they could be kidnapped by terrorists or common criminals; or they could be the targets of mass murder, as in the bombing of Pan Am Flight 103. Mahoney tells how the Department of State dealt with the aftermath of this terrorist attack. He spells out in great detail what was learned from errors and misunderstandings on all sides.

Michael M. Mahoney
Director, Citizens' Emergency Services Center, Bureau of Consular Affairs, Department of State, 1987–1990

The most traumatic and difficult experience of my time in running the Citizens' Emergency Services office was the bombing of Pan Am 103 in December, 1988.

A Pan American plane carrying two-hundred and fifty-nine people was blown out of the air by a bomb over Lockerbie, Scotland, on the 21st of December,

1988. About one-hundred and seventy people on the plane were Americans, many of them university students returning home for the Christmas holidays. Everybody on that plane was killed, and the wreckage of the plane, as it fell, killed eleven people on the ground, for a total of two-hundred and seventy people killed.

This event marked, certainly in my mind, if not a watershed, at least a distillation of a number of trends that had been occurring. These included the whole question of training staff how to notify people about the deaths of relatives, and defining services the State Department, specifically consular officers, must provide when things like this happen.

The Lockerbie bombing led to an intense Congressional examination of State Department procedures in these cases, a great deal of criticism of the State Department by relatives of the victims, and the introduction of a number of new, and in some ways still very controversial, approaches to this sort of terrible disaster.

What happened was something like this.

The disaster took place about three or four o'clock in the afternoon, Eastern Standard Time, about nine o'clock in the evening in the United Kingdom. It was not clear in the first day or so that what had happened was a bombing, only that the plane had somehow broken up in the air and everyone onboard had been killed. The Citizens' Emergency Center immediately relocated most of its personnel, as it had done in the case of other aircraft disasters in the past, to the Operations Center of the State Department, and a task force was convened to begin to see what we had to do and how we could do it. Initially, we ran into a major problem with the airlines, because Pan American refused to give us a passenger list.

To go back a bit, for some years the standard policy had been that when an American died abroad, a Foreign Service officer had to do one of two things. The FSO had to undertake to notify next of kin that the death had occurred, and to advise them of certain information that the FSO needed pretty quickly to work from. That is, what the local country's rules were about burial and interment, what the rules were about returning remains to the United States if the relatives so wished, how much this would cost, how quickly it could be done, what paperwork was necessary, and so forth.

Many times, however, when Americans died overseas, they died when relatives were with them. Either they lived overseas with those relatives or they might be in a tour group and the spouse was with them, and so forth. If that happened, the role of the State Department officer was usually not to make a notification—the relatives already knew that the person had died, and it would have been superflu-ous to call up and say, "By the way, I want to notify you that your relative has died"—, but to answer questions and deal with issues that the people might have had at the time. Normally, when people resided abroad, the only step that was undertaken by the State Department officer was the preparation of the death cer-tificate. So, it was not always a formal requirement that the State Department officer make a notification, only that the officer be satisfied that someone had been notified and could take appropriate action.

In the Lockerbie bombing, the airlines themselves insisted on undertaking the role of notification of relatives. In fact, for the better part of a day, they withheld the passenger list from the State Department. By the time we got the list and began to call people ourselves, to try to confirm that they knew their relative had died, everyone that we called, in fact, knew that the relative had been killed. The people who were making the calls reported to the supervisors, including me, that they were getting very negative reactions from people, saying, "Why are you call-ing us? We already know this."

It was felt that this was, in essence, counterproductive; the airline had, in fact, undertaken to do this notification, and had said that they would see to the return of all the remains to the United States at no cost to the victims. Also, they had undertaken, immediately, to fly families from the United States to Scotland, to assist and to be present as bodies were recovered and identified.

It appeared initially that the State Department's consular role in this matter was going to be fairly negligible, because the notifications had occurred and the remains were going to be returned to the United States. The State Department was certainly prepared and had people ready and on the scene in Lockerbie to prepare death certificates.

The third major issue that was raised on our side that was not initially thought of by the families was the disposition of the effects of the people who had been killed. Normally, with a death abroad, there were a couple of possibilities. If a person died abroad and there were no relatives on the scene, the consular officer became what was called the "provisional conservator of the estate of the posses-sions of a person." Normally, a tourist might have his or her wallet and some clothing and credit cards and that sort of thing. You would be immediately in touch with the relatives, the spouse or the next of kin, and they would tell you what to do with these things. You would mail them or do something else, as directed.

What happened in this case was that because the plane blew up, the effects of people were scattered over perhaps one-hundred square miles of countryside.

About two days after the bombing, it became clear that this was, in fact, a bombing and not simply an aircraft accident. The fact that it was a bombing meant that it was going to be dealt with as a criminal case by authorities in Britain. Therefore, at least initially, all of the effects of the decedents—in fact anything that was collected from the plane—were going to be held onto by the authorities, because it might have particular implications as they tried to reconstruct the nature of the blast that apparently had destroyed the plane: where did the blast take place? Was it explosives in a suitcase? Whose suitcase was it? All of these sorts of things.

As soon as this became clear, we sent officers from the United States to Scotland, and we undertook a very close collaboration with the British authorities on the question of what would become of these effects, because we felt that although the victims' families were essentially stunned by the whole event and had not raised the issue particularly, this would become a very intense issue with them later on.

But apart from that question, we did not see that we had any particular distinctive further role to play, given what we had done in the past in a number of aircraft disasters that we felt we had managed quite well. Actually, the British authorities, in conjunction with the families, were undertaking the identification of the remains, and Pan American was going to fly them back to the United States.

This was our position: we undertook to communicate to the relatives in the United States what we understood regarding the disposition of property. Many of the relatives were in the United Kingdom and received this briefing, in any case, from British and American officials who were there. Beyond that, essentially, we did nothing.

About six weeks went by after the bombing. Then we began to hear that the relatives of the victims were extremely unhappy with the U.S. government. A couple of specific issues surfaced. The first concerned the Federal Aviation Administration [FAA]. As it often did, the FAA had put out a notice supposedly only for people who worked in counter-terrorism and airline security matters: that they had received word that there was a rumor going around about the possible plan to bomb a Pan American flight sometime during the Christmas holidays. This was in December. It was not unprecedented; the FAA received, in the course of a year, dozens, if not hundreds, of rumors about planned terrorist actions against American aircraft, usually by various people with a Middle Eastern agenda, but not always.

This particular alert was sent by an unclassified cable to a number of European Foreign Service posts, but essentially was supposed to go only to the local FAA representative who would then pass it on to local police, who would take whatever security precautions they deemed appropriate. As it was discovered later, the source of this particular rumor was considered to be a person who was known to be a crank and who often called up and made these sorts of threats. This particular cable with this warning in it, for reasons that are still not clear to me, got posted on a public embassy bulletin board at the embassy in Moscow, about two weeks before the bombing of Pan Am 103.

Within about a week after the bombing, the relatives of the victims began to become aware that this warning had been posted in a public place or at least a place available to the employees of the American embassy in Moscow. Rumors began to circulate that a significant number of official Americans who were traveling back to the United States for the Christmas holidays had had reservations on various Pan Am flights coming from Europe, and had changed those reservations as the result of having seen this warning. This became transmuted by the families of the victims into a notion that the bureaucrats managed to get themselves off Pan Am planes, and their kids were killed on one because they were not given this warning and given the opportunity to remove their children from this plane.

There were extensive investigations into this in subsequent years by members of Congress and other people who were not disposed to be sympathetic to the State Department in this matter. They were unable to find any indication of anyone who had changed a booking from a Pan Am flight back to the United States. That, I think, did not mitigate the anguish of the families of the victims, who felt that in fact they had been entitled to this word and didn't get it.

Sadly, it is a fact that there were thirty employees of the U.S. Government, including military people and some State Department employees, who were on the Pan Am 103 flight and who were killed. This sequence of events—the fact that this was murder of two-hundred and seventy people, that no one was arrested for this murder or even initially identified as being the perpetrator, the view that there had been a warning about this that was not given to the American public, but was given to employees of the State Department, to the bureaucracy—began to generate, I think, a feeling of intense anger and alienation on the part of the families of these victims, particularly those who had had college-age children on this flight. This tremendous groundswell of anger began to be directed at the American government, and most particularly at the State Department.

For about six weeks after the bombing, however, we had received no feedback of any type: no congressional inquiries, no suggestions that the service that we were providing was inappropriate or incorrect or wrong or was not what people wanted. Then we began to hear that there was intense unhappiness on the part of the families with their treatment by the Department. They began making their feelings known to members of Congress. A series of Congressional hearings was going to loom on this entire subject.

The only specific request that I can remember in this entire period from the relatives of the victims was that we make available to them a list of all the other family members, so that they could form up in a group to exchange their reactions to the disaster. After some consultation about freedom of information issues, we sent a mailing to all of the relatives, saying, "A number of relatives are interested in forming a group. If you would like your name to be given to them, please let us know, or if not, not." Almost everybody agreed that their names could be given out. An organization came into being, in effect called "The Families of the Victims of Pan Am 103." This organization then began to seek ways to make its feelings felt.

For about the next year, starting from probably about March or April of 1989 until I left this job in the summer of 1990, I went through what I thought was probably the most painful experience that I've had in the State Department. A number of congressional hearings were convened, by the Foreign Affairs Committees of the House and Senate, by the Transportation Committee—because it was an aircraft—and a number of other committees, at which relatives of the victims appeared and excoriated the State Department for what they considered to be insensitivity, lack of helpful service, a whole series of things. What happened was perhaps ten or twelve experiences entered into a form of almost legendary anecdotal material. I'll give you some examples.

Traditionally, it had been the case that when people died, their passports were returned to their relatives. Someplace on the passport a canceled stamp was placed, to indicate that the passport was no longer valid. Some of the relatives received these passports. The canceled stamp, as was not unusual, was across the face of the person in the passport photograph. In retrospect, this was not a very sensitive thing to do, but it had gone on for many years. The relatives felt that this was an enormously insulting thing, as if the life of their son or daughter had been canceled by the State Department.

I think they made a valid point, and the procedure for indicating that the passports were no longer valid was changed. A punch system is now used to punch four holes at the back, or the corners are snipped off with scissors, but the word "canceled" is not used.

In one case, a woman said that she had called the State Department and kept asking people what was the precise moment that her son died. No one could give her answer to this question, because the plane had blown up in the air, and it was impossible to tell. But she felt that people were not sympathetic to her. There were a number of instances of this type.

In one case, someone was talking to an officer in the Citizens' Emergency Center, and the officer said, "Well, I know it's very difficult, but life has to continue, and you need to think about getting on with your life." This was considered to be an extremely insensitive statement, and people screamed this out at the Congressional hearings.

In another case, a woman wanted the wedding ring of her husband to be returned to her immediately. All property and artifacts of the victims were held by the British authorities for several months as part of the criminal investigation. We had to tell this woman that the wedding ring could not be immediately returned. She began to scream about this. I can still see her in the congressional hearings, screaming that the State Department would not give her back her husband's wedding ring.

Another instance: a struggle developed between the parents of one of the victims and the wife of the victim over certain effects of the victim. At the Congressional hearing, again we were excoriated by the wife for not returning the effects of the victim.

There were a number of things that frankly seemed to me to be either very minor in themselves or simply not our responsibility. This was not a case of someone saying, my relative wasn't found; my relative wasn't identified; the remains were not returned to the United States; the death certificate was improperly prepared. I think that, because of the factors I've identified, it was a murder case, and no one had been brought to judgment. A huge upsurge of anger occurred. For a year, we went from Congressional hearing to Congressional hearing. We were told by senior people in the State Department and by Congressional staff that there was no use or point in arguing or attempting in any way to rebut the specific complaints that were made about the State Department. We could not, in a public forum, appear to be disputing their version of many of these incidents that they recounted. To do so would make us appear to be more heartless and insensitive.

We finally were put in the position—a completely new phenomenon in my experience—where we had to call the relatives of the victims at least once a week, call every one of these one-hundred and eighty-nine families, every week, and ask them if there was anything that they needed from us and anything that we could do for them. They were not asking us for specific services; we were calling them only because they had said that we didn't pay enough attention to them.

This, in turn, generated a tremendous amount of tension and pressure and stress on the consular officers working in the State Department. Invariably, when the officers called these people, the people would scream at them, would yell at them, would call them murderers, all kinds of terrible things, and would bring up the business about the cable that had appeared on the wall in the embassy. Many of the consular officers who had to work on this tragedy as it involved next of kin, asked to be released from the duty and transferred to other work offices.

This led, in turn—and, I think, usefully—to an in-depth analysis of how consular officers could begin to manage stress more effectively, the need for extensive training programs that now go on, with discussions with psychiatrists and others in the State Department about how to deal with bereaved families, about how to try to handle what appear to be, initially, really unreasonable and often inappropriate demands. For example, one man had a brother killed on the plane who lived in England and was working for an American bank there. Six or eight months before, the brother had purchased a brand new and very expensive Mercedes Benz, with European specifications. One day when someone from State called him—as we had to do every week—to ask what we can do for him, he said that he wanted us to arrange for the return of his brother's Mercedes to the U.S. He said that he had initially inquired about it and was told that it could not be done without extensive modifications, because it didn't meet the requirements about emissions from the Environmental Protection Agency. He simply wished the State Department to take care of this problem for him with the Environmental Protection Agency. In fact, at very high levels, we made representations to the Environmental Protection Agency and got a waiver for the return of the car, because no one wished to confront this person, perhaps understandably, about the law concerning the importation of such vehicles to the United States.

Another man said to us that he felt that there should be a monument erected on the mall in Washington DC to the victims of terrorism. This launched an elaborate inquiry into whether or not this could be done.

Others felt that because these victims had been singled out and murdered as Americans, these civilians deserved to be awarded the same honors that were awarded to fallen military overseas. That is, their flag-draped coffins should be greeted by military bands and honor guards, and so forth, at the airport when they returned. In fact, arrangements were finally made with the National Guard around the country that in future terrorist incidents, this would be done. In my mind, a seemingly endless vista opened up of what were and were not appropriate things to be done under the heading of "American Services," particularly in disaster and potential death situations. I think the Consular Bureau, and particularly the American Services side of it, is still trying to find its way in the wake of this.

Enormous changes have taken place, many of them for the better, I think. There has not been a disaster of the Pan Am 103 type since, either terrorist or otherwise, but all kinds of mechanisms are now in place, I believe, to deal with that sort of situation, and extensive training has gone on. All new Foreign Service officers are now trained, with psychiatrists and other mental health people, in how to deal with bereaved relatives. But I worry that, in fact, this is an open-ended thing, and that it reflects, not only in disaster situations, but overall, the un-definable nature of overseas American Services. There is no real, practical definition of what the demands of our job are overseas.

The job, in essence, is to deal with whatever problem an American brings to us, as best we can. In other words, unlike a Social Security agent, who can say, "My job is Social Security, but if somebody has kidnapped your dog, that is not my job," or the IRS agent, who can say, "My job is income taxes, but if someone has cheated you out of your airline ticket, that is not my job," any demand is the job, apparently, in the mind of Americans, for the consular officer.

It is something that one can work with and manage, but, still, one should have what is called a psychological contract. I think this is really what happened with the families of the victims of Pan Am 103. They had no idea of what our job was or had traditionally been, and therefore they did not know what we were supposed to provide or not provide. The consular officers' conclusion was, in fact, that we should provide everything that they could think of as a service. And the fact that we had not provided this in the beginning, even before they asked us for the service, was something for which we were to blame. That simply led to further charges of insensitivity.

We had meetings at the State Department, very extraordinarily painful meetings, with relatives of victims, in which we asked them time and again to please list any service that they had ever asked for that they felt that they hadn't received. Secondly, they were asked to list for us what they thought the appropriate services should be. I remember one person, a brother of one of the victims, promised us that his group would give us a written summary of all the things that they were unhappy with, as well as all the things that they thought we should do in the future. No such summary was ever produced. And his only answer to us in the end was, "You have to do whatever people ask you to do."

He gave this example: one of the relatives who went over to Scotland was a smoker of French cigarettes, *Gauloises* as I remember. Not long after he arrived, he found he couldn't obtain any, so he asked the consular officer to obtain for him some *Gauloises*. He said that any request of that type should immediately be met, as a way of showing the relatives of victims that we were in sympathy with them and were anxious to do whatever it was that they needed to relieve their suffering. You can debate the particular request, the implications of it seem to me to be very complex indeed, but that was the answer that this man gave to us.

YUGOSLAVIA BREAKS UP

Robert Rackmales arrived at Belgrade as the Iron Curtain was beginning to collapse. Yugoslavia deserved its well-earned reputation as a thorn, or at least a pain, in the side of Soviet authority. Now, all was splitting apart. The Balkans remained a very rough neighborhood. Rackmales knew the players and explains how they played. Under his ambassador, Warren Zimmerman, he sent balanced reporting to Washington.

Robert Rackmales
Deputy Chief of Mission, American Embassy, Belgrade, Yugoslavia, 1989–1993

September, 1989, the time of my arrival in Belgrade, was a period of great optimism. It was the eve of the first high-profile visit to the United States by the new Yugoslav prime minister, Ante Markovic, a Croat who had been chosen earlier that year. The reason for optimism was the events elsewhere in Eastern Europe that made it clear that communism was crumbling. The Gorbachev revolution had taken hold and Communist regimes had crumbled in Hungary and Czechoslovakia. The same would happen in Romania just a few months later, in December. There was a feeling that Yugoslavia was very well poised to be a model and was in the vanguard of East European countries that were shedding communism. Markovic was already starting to allude to having multiparty elections in Yugoslavia, which already had the most open economic system in Eastern Europe. They had had a more Western orientation and more of their businessmen had been exposed to capitalism. So, there was a feeling that Yugoslavia was going to be the first East European country to join the Common Market, and to help show the way to the others. How wrong can you be?

Even before 1989, there had always been concern over the viability of the system that [Field Marshal Josip Broz] Tito [the former head of Yugoslavia] left behind, whether it could contain centrifugal forces which were obviously strong. There was growing hostility between Slovenia and Croatia on the one hand, and Serbia on the other. As it had evolved in the years since his death, Tito's system had given more and more power to the individual republics and less and less to the federal government, to the point where we all knew that the greatest threat to the optimistic scenario I just described was in the unwillingness of the republics to allow the federal government to implement coherent policies. So, our effort in '89-'90 was to try to bolster Markovic, whom we saw as the best hope, maybe the last hope, because if he failed the prospects were very gloomy. He seemed at that period, in the summer and early fall, to have the kind of leadership abilities that gave him a fighting chance to overcome the systemic problems of heading a government with very little power, with only the powers that the republics were willing to let him exercise. He went to the United States and made a good impression. He was a dynamic person and knew how to talk to Westerners. The only doubts were if he would be allowed to carry out a meaningful reform program in Yugoslavia. In the succeeding months it became clear that it probably wasn't going to happen.

In late November of 1989, the Serbs instituted an economic boycott of Slovenia, this within a country that is nominally united. In my own mind, that was the clearest evidence that Yugoslavia was probably on a rapid downward spiral in terms of unity. There were three groups of republics. On the one hand, there was Slovenia and Croatia, hellbent towards independence at the earliest possible date. The first free and open elections took place in Slovenia and Croatia in the spring of 1990. Both brought into power groups that were clearly headed in the direction of independence. Even before those elections, it was clear that that's the way things were trending, but the elections intensified that process.

Secondly, there was Serbia, which basically would have liked to have been rid of Slovenia and Croatia and felt strong enough to dominate the remainder, and so was not about to pay a price to keep the country together. Finally, there were other republics—Bosnia, Macedonia, and Montenegro—which were terrified of what a breakup would mean. Montenegro was too much in Serbia's shadow to really do much more than wring its hands. The two leaders who worked the hardest to try to keep a form of Yugoslavia together were [Alija] Izetbegovic in

Bosnia, who was elected in November of 1990, and [Kiro] Gligorov, who became the leader of Macedonia in 1991.

National unity became more difficult to maintain with the demise of the League of Communists of Yugoslavia, which formally broke up in February of 1990. The Yugoslav constitution provided for secession, but not for secession of republics—only for secession of ethnic groups, as they called it, *narodi*. The Serbian argument was if Slovenes as a nation wished to leave Yugoslavia it's in the constitution that they have that right. If Croats want to leave, essentially as Croats, that's fine. But—and this becomes now one of the root causes of the wars that sprang up—they do not have a right to take Serbs with them. The Serbs have the same right of self-determination as anyone else. That in a nutshell was the Serbian position.

Serb nationalism was really what [Slobodan] Milosevic [president of Yugoslavia] used to gain unchallenged power. In Serbia, the nationalist drive was initially focused on Kosovo. His first dramatic moment was when, in a speech in Kosovo [1987], he made a very impassioned statement about Kosovo and the Serbs and Serbian pride. It had a great resonance in Serbia. Up until that point he had been viewed as a typical apparatchik, maybe a little more professionally qualified in the area of banking than some of the others. By the way, he had had a Government IVP [International Visitor Program] grant in the field of banking back in the mid-'80s. I think he went to Chicago and other cities. But his primary focus was always political, and he pursued power in a very single-minded, ruthless way. He used nationalism as the means for this.

I think most analysts see this as opportunistic. In other words, he simply made a calculated decision that here was the right button to push. I do think there is somewhat of a messianic streak in Milosevic, that he genuinely sees himself as a kind of savior of Serbia. He is an extremely skilled, cold-blooded politician who combines that characteristic with a genuine feeling that there is no one else other than himself who can defend, protect, and promote the interests of the Serbian nation.

What we in the embassy eventually came up with was Duality: Unity and Democracy, to replace the former mantra (through the '60s, '70s and most of the '80s) of the Trinity: Independence, Unity, and Territorial Integrity. As we saw it, if either were suppressed or shattered, you couldn't have the other. In other words, in the context of a split or a destruction of the Yugoslav state, you would not—you could not—have democracy because it could not happen peacefully given the ethnic tensions, given the structure of the country. You didn't have groups neatly in areas that if you drew borders around them, they'd be more or less content to be there. In particular, the Serb and Croat population was scattered and the Muslims were intermingled, not in a well-defined separate area. Anyway, we argued forcefully that our policy should be based on support for both unity and democracy, and emphasizing the interdependence of the two. At that time, the Slovenes and the Croats were making the argument that what Milosevic wanted to do was to impose a non-democratic system. While he may talk a less communist game now—he saw the handwriting on the wall for communism in Eastern Europe—he's basically at heart a Bolshevik. Therefore, you should view Serbia as a threat to a democratic Yugoslavia. There was certainly something to be said for that argument.

But what we were promoting was the concept that you could not have a survival of democracy in a chaotic breakup of Yugoslavia. This was unlike the CIA's analysis (that got into the press), which said that a breakup of Yugoslavia was inevitable within eighteen months. They turned out to be pretty close to the mark. Our view was that a breakup of Yugoslavia was not inevitable but was a strong probability. In February, 1990, I told Ambassador Thomas in Budapest that the odds were three to one against Yugoslavia staying united at that point. The CIA, however, felt that there was a chance of getting a peaceful agreement on separation. We were very skeptical of that in the embassy. We felt it almost inevitable that we were going to have widespread violence which would, of course, undercut democracy.

As the months went by, the process of the republics taking more and more away from the Federation accelerated. Markovic badly mishandled the political process, to the point where he antagonized all major groups except for a small number of intellectuals. His leadership became faltering and uncertain. So, he was a political ghost long before he formally left office.

Some in the United States thought we were hanging on too long to a forlorn hope that Yugoslavia could stay together. We were actually the first of the major missions in Belgrade to draw attention to the seriousness of the possibility of the disintegration of the country. For example, I remember calling on my counterpart at the Soviet embassy, who was one of their most experienced Yugoslav hands. At that point, he had spent something like twelve years in the country, and was five years into his current tour as their DCM. He told me that the harsh rhetoric the various ethnic groups were using was just Balkan hot headedness, and should not be given too much weight. He was convinced the army and other federal institutions would ensure that the country stayed together. That was the basic assessment of most other missions in '89 and '90. By the end of '90 and the beginning of '91, it was becoming very clear that the country was falling apart.

Warren Zimmerman, our ambassador, and I had good relations with the heads and the deputies of all of the Western European missions, who came to see things more or less as we did. One exception was the Austrian DCM who had an animus against Yugoslavia, so he was rooting for it to fall apart, saying that it's an artificial country, it should never have existed. I think he took the assassination of Archduke Francis Ferdinand personally. He was an odd man out.

Here there were probably at least some differences of emphasis in terms of the views of our consulate general in Zagreb and the embassy in Belgrade. Although the consul general, Mike Einik, always reported professionally, there was naturally more sympathy for the emerging Croatian argument for independence. As far as the activities of [president of Croatia Franjo] Tudjman's party, what was most disturbing was the reliance on arming party members. The argument was that the Serbs were arming in their areas, and that this was just defensive. I suspect there were some areas where there had been clandestine Serbian arms shipments. Nevertheless, the scale of the Croatian action, and the fact of its having official blessing, greatly ratcheted up the tensions, and caused an increase in the arming on the other side as well. So, it represented a major shift in the direction of a violent outcome.

Both we and our consulate general in Zagreb were sending people into some of the areas which seemed to be flash-points—into the Krajina area, for example. The consulate general did an excellent report. We sent people a number of times into Bosnia. The problem with reporting wasn't that we didn't go out; it was that it was hard to really get to the areas—which were not in the larger cities—where some of the worst problems had arisen. In other words, we obviously had a pretty good take on Banja Luka, Mostar, and Sarajevo, but if I had to assess the overall performance, it's that we didn't get enough of a sense of the village-level realities. It's hard, both in terms of time and in terms of communicating with peasants who aren't used to talking to foreigners.

During his visit to Yugoslavia in June 1991, Secretary of State Jim Baker was very unhappy with the whole experience. I was on the bus with some senior NSC [National Security Council] staffers. Their attitude, I believe, reflected his as well. First of all, the Yugoslav crisis was horribly complicated. One of them called it worse than the Middle East. Secondly, there were no good guys. Baker was not happy with any of his interlocutors; he thought they were all to a greater or lesser extent—mostly greater—lying to him. He also felt that he had gotten some assurances from the Slovenes that the Slovenes later said was just a misunderstanding on his part. When a few days later the Slovenes went ahead and announced their independence, he felt personally betrayed. At that point, he was probably more angry with the Slovenes than with any others.

His basic judgment—which I remember thinking at that time, and still do think was correct—was that, boy, if the Europeans want to take this one on, let them. He saw nothing good to be gained by the United States trying to play the lead role in finding a way out of that maze. The Europeans, at that point, were trying to forge a common foreign policy. This was a period of some optimism that a more united Europe could be a positive force. I thought we should help the EC [European Community] if they came to have problems. We should be quietly supportive. But that unfortunately we didn't do, or we didn't do very effectively because there was an important conference in Ochrid [Macedonia] within a month or six weeks of Baker's visit. It was the first acid test for the Europeans, and they had hammered out a political agreement which five of the six leaders had agreed to. The holdout was Tudjman.

I remember trying to get the State Department to weigh in heavily in support of the European position, and bilaterally with the Croats to warn them that they should not walk out. And I got a wishy-washy response saying, "Well, we think the important thing is to stop Milosevic, and we think Tudjman's concerns may be justified, we don't see any reason to weigh in." And then Tudjman walked out of the meeting, the meeting broke up, and the fighting spread dramatically within the weeks after that.

Let me just wrap this up by saying one word about our coordination, or lack thereof, with our European friends. The hostility and backbiting that erupted between the Germans and the other Europeans over the issue of recognition of Slovenia and Croatia were very damaging to the European Community. I felt that one of our greatest risks was of allowing this to do the same between the Europeans and us. We feel the necessity to criticize the activity of allies who are carrying out United Nations mandates that we in many cases pressed.

The embassy had a full range of policy differences. We had the people who wanted the United States to get involved with at least air power against the Serbs; not many proponents of sending troops, never have been as far as I could see. But we had people who wanted the Air Force to start bombing. However, other embassy officers were strongly opposed to any military involvement, thinking that all it would do is expand the fighting, cause more death and misery, and still not result in a viable multiethnic state. We had the full range. One of the achievements that I am particularly proud of is that despite all this, we continued to function very effectively as a team, due to our regular discussions in country team meetings. We did not, I think, let our policy prejudices or preferences, however you want to characterize it, affect our reporting, which I think was outstanding for objectivity. Washington told us that we were far and away the most objective in reporting on the situation. I don't think anyone, whether they belong in camp A, camp B, or somewhere in between, was particularly happy with the way positions were unfolding. What we were often doing was talking as if we were going to do something that would make camp A happy, and then, in fact, behaving as if we were really in camp B. So, people were always off balance.

I remember going back to Washington at a time early in the Clinton administration when the people in camp A—the proponents of bombing the Serbs now—were saying that now it's going to happen because of what Clinton said in the campaign. He's strongly committed to this. Some of the new administration's pronouncements about "lift and strike" tended to reinforce that. When I went back to Washington in the spring of 1993, I remember a message that they sent to Milosevic reinforcing one that Bush had sent that sounded very bellicose, almost like the kind of ultimatum you send when you're really about to take action. Camp A was saying they're going to be evacuating us, and we're really going to hit the Serbs. I was skeptical and, as a result of my consultations in Washington, it became clear to me that we were no closer to a decision of that kind than we had been in the final months of the Bush administration. So, I came back and shared my impressions with my colleagues. There were some very disappointed people on the staff and others who were relieved.

I think the Pope's [John Paul II] early call for the recognition of Croatia was very short sighted, in that it turned the crisis implicitly into a religious struggle in which you side with the party who happens to share your religion. There were many contradictions and ironies. The Catholic Bishop of Sarajevo was a proponent of ethnic cooperation in Bosnia and was working to promote reconciliation. Unfortunately, he was living under a severe death threat in Sarajevo and couldn't even leave his residence. Who do you think was threatening him? Nationalist Croats. Croats whose views were like those of the Archbishop of Mostar, whom I had called on at the time of the Bosnian elections. I never met a more nationalistic Croat than the Archbishop of Mostar. He bragged about the fact that ninety-eight percent of his flock were members of Tudjman's party. He was a fire-and-brimstone nationalist.

In the case of Slovenia and Croatia, once the fighting had started, it became very difficult for us to keep in close touch. Even though Croatia did not have an embassy for a number of months, our oversight of them became a formality and an administrative fact, rather than a political fact. They became a de facto embassy and were getting some of their guidance directly from Washington, although we were always kept in the picture and could comment. With recognition, our role ended entirely. We would continue to give a bit of administrative support, because it was a very small embassy and needed help. But even that quickly shifted to Vienna and Budapest because of the practical problem: "You just couldn't get from here to there."

On the other hand, with regard to Macedonia, we had not set up any kind of an office there until almost a year after I left. So, we were still fully responsible for contacts with Macedonia. In fact, I traveled down, on average, every six to eight weeks and met with Gligorov. Within three or four months of my becoming chargé, we got an extra person to live there in a hotel in Skopje and report through us. He would either fax or come up from time to time and write reports. He was an outstanding officer; that was very useful.

From June to December 1992, the person who headed the Serbian Government, the prime minister, was a Serbian-American businessman, Milan Panic. Panic had been brought in by Milosevic. Despite that, he told Eagleburger that his plan was to get rid of Milosevic. In other words, he was going to turn Serbia around from an authoritarian communist state to a Western-oriented democratic friend of the United States. I was quite skeptical about his chances of accomplishing anything. I was also very nervous about having a United States citizen as prime minister. I was worried about freedom of information: what could I say about him in cables that he and his lawyers could access? At first, I tended to report in a very back-channel way. Later on, I got some reassurances, and I put more into the front channel, although it was always with a limited distribution. I did see Panic regularly. I don't think he ever had any chance of unseating Milosevic, even if he had been politically more savvy than he was. Milosevic is an extremely astute operator. He would not make such a dumb mistake as to bring someone all the way from the United States who is going to threaten him in any way. It was naive of Panic to think it could be otherwise. Any small chance that he theoretically might have had was undercut by his complete ignorance of the Serbian scene. He didn't know the players, or even speak the language very well. He relied on a few advisers, including a former FSO, Jack Scanlon. Jack had been ambassador before Warren, and was working for Panic in a dual capacity. One was a business capacity as Eastern European representative for Panic's chemical corporation. The other was as a foreign policy and political adviser. Unfortunately, even though Panic certainly needed advice, he didn't always listen; and when he did, the advice he got was not always sound. One of the worst mistakes he made was to try to cozy up to one or two of the senior military people who I guess he and Jack felt might help swing the army around to his side. It ended up in a humiliation for Panic, because the primary person whom they were targeting was playing a double game. Shortly before the Serbian elections in December, when Panic nominated his supposed buddy to be minister of defense, the guy responded by issuing a press release saying no self-respecting Serb would ever work for Panic. That shows what a mismatch the Milosevic-Panic contest was.

We were trying to report as fully, as accurately, and as credibly as we could, not taking at face value every initial account of an atrocity. In that part of the world, there is a long tradition to use claims of massive abuses or atrocities as a political weapon. It's a difficult subject to discuss calmly and objectively, because by its very nature an atrocity seems to call for strong emotional response. That came up with regard to the first of the mortars that fell in the Sarajevo market in '93. In the Western media, there was no initial doubt expressed that this was a Serbian atrocity. When the Serbs denied that it was their shell and accused the Bosnian Government of shelling their own people, I would say that ninety-nine percent in the West said this is absolutely outrageous and ridiculous. Here are these poor victims and now you're accusing them of murdering their own people. On the other hand, the UN personnel in Sarajevo who investigated the incident were highly suspicious of the Bosnian Government, as David Binder pointed out in an excellent *Foreign Policy* magazine article, using the cynical (but not always wrong) Italian yardstick of "who benefits from this action?" The results are straightforward. The Serbian side doesn't benefit; they get bombed and the international community comes down on them, while the Bosnian government gets more support, including military support. What worries me the most is that these atrocities, whoever is causing them, tend to drive policy. For example, the Bosnian Government called for Holbrooke not to come to Sarajevo, to stop the peace process, because of an atrocity. That is comparable to Israelis and the Palestinians not talking to each other because of bus bombings, which are also atrocities. Often, atrocities are carried out in order to disrupt the peace process. Both the media and the administration would often apply a double standard, perhaps because there were many more Serb atrocities which came earlier in the Bosnian conflict. Our embassy, for example, strongly complained following a *Washington Post* front-page story reporting that Croat forces had massacred several hundred Muslims in a town in central Bosnia. In contrast to the usual reaction to reported Serb misdeeds, the Department spokesman failed to condemn the action.

I think the main thing was the perception which the media fostered, because they were mainly seeing the war from the side of the people sitting in Sarajevo. I think they bonded emotionally with them, understandably. I might, too, if I were there, although it is interesting that many Western military in Sarajevo had an opposite reaction. Early on, people became convinced that the Serbs were the sole villains, that this was a "white hat/black hat" sort of a thing, that they precipitated it in order to form a greater Serbia, that they conquered territory that belonged to others that were a ruthless people with no respect for human life. I'm not sure that I fully understand the reasons why the public reaction to the shelling of Sarajevo was so much stronger than to the Russian shelling of Grozny, which was ten times more intense. That caused many times more casualties, mainly elderly ethnic Russians. It was also a violation of the rules of war. What the Croats did to the Serbs finally in Krajina, after what had been done elsewhere by the Serbs, people said they had coming to them.

I left in July of '93. I had been there four years and frankly felt at that point somewhat exhausted by the whole thing. I could see that what was driving policy was not the reporting or the recommendations of the embassy. Once a crisis reaches that point of political sensitivity, where the president's image and domestic political considerations are concerned, the best thing the embassy can do is simply to continue to report as honestly as they can. Before I left, I made clear to everybody in the European Bureau that I had no interest in continuing to work on that crisis. I felt after four years I needed to get away from it. In effect, I really was burned out at that point in terms of trying to come up with new suggestions.

NATION BUILDING IN KYRGYZSTAN: ESTABLISHING A U.S. PRESENCE

Edward Hurwitz, ambassador to a newly independent former Soviet republic, started from scratch. A Central Asian, moderate Islamic state, never before independent, Kyrgyzstan faced the trial of statehood with little chance for economic independence, except for in hydroelectric power. It was a new nation, with mild, gentle, nonaggressive people. In his first ambassadorial assignment, Hurwitz succeeded in encouraging the development of democratic institutions and economic openness. The Agency for International Development successfully helped in institution building, but some private undertakings were often naive or even inane. Open, democratic nation-building is slow, and it is up to each nation itself to define the route it will take. Hurwitz reminds readers what can be done in a nationalistic setting and within the realities of the country.

Edward Hurwitz
Ambassador, American Embassy, Bishkek,
Kyrgyzstan, 1992–1994

We had considerable hopes for Kyrgyzstan because it was the only or one of the only newly created ex-Soviet state that did not have the old ex-party official as the number-one guy. The president was Askar Akayev, a physicist who before assuming the presidency was president of the Kyrgyz Academy of Sciences. We had some hopes that this would be a real new leaf, and that you could have an actual democratic country arising from the ashes of the Soviet Union.

It was clear from the beginning that they would have immense economic problems. That was one thing we could not deal with immediately. What we were hoping to get—and what really evolved anyway—was a situation in which you didn't have a lot of turmoil. We were concerned at the time about the Iranians moving in. We weren't concerned about Turkish influence, but were curious about how the Turks would react to this. A big issue was how the Russians would react. Then, you had the issue of China. There was a four-hundred kilometer border with China, which was something else that concerned us. But the main issue was to try to get the Kyrgyz government and society moving on a basically democratic, stable track.

You do the basic things: you present your credentials, get to know as many people as you can, go around to the ministries, and talk to people. You hold their hands, in a certain manner of speaking. It was an incredible situation where you had all these people who understood only the trappings. They had a foreign ministry before their independence, but the Kyrgyz foreign ministry had done absolutely nothing except to arrange visits of Cuban Trade Unionists and matters like that. Kyrgyzstan had always been a distant outpost of the Soviet Union. It was perhaps the most obedient of all Soviet republics, and it was one that had prospered because of the Soviet Union. I recall in all my tours of duty in the Soviet Union, the question that used to be asked by Russians—at first in a nonpublic way because you couldn't raise questions like this—was, "Do we get more out of Central Asia or do we give it more?" By the time I went on assignment to Leningrad and *glasnost* was in full bloom, you would hear this question raised at public meetings. Why are we spending money to support these little "black" people? Well, you could argue the issue both ways, I suppose, when it came to Kazakhstan or Uzbekistan with oil, gold, and cotton. In the case of Kyrgyzstan, however, there was no question but that everything you saw: every institute, every library, every theater, every factory was there at the largesse of the Soviet Union.

The working conditions were incredibly bad. As a building, we had a structure that from every standpoint was inadequate, whether talking about security or the ability to function. It was an old, small, one-story structure that at one time had been the *Bishkek Komsomol* [Communist Youth Organization] headquarters and at one time the city tax office. I would occasionally get telephone calls concerning city taxes and had by my phone the number of the current tax office so I could direct people. Security was zilch. It was a fire trap. In my tenure there, we did have an electrical fire. Anybody who wanted to toss a note, a rock or, a bomb through the front window could have done so. We had a very small staff. People came and went, but we had about seven Americans when I was there. There were ten or twelve locals, including drivers.

It is curious, but I would say staff morale was high. You are working cheek-by—jowl here; it is not that you are not aware of problems (although very often the ambassador is less aware of problems that people might have), but I talked to everybody every day. You had that sort of hyper activity. Morale was good; you had a lot to do, a lot of challenges, and it was all new and interesting. In fact, when talking about this to personnel people in the Department, they made the point—and I think it is probably a valid one—that they were less worried about the first wave of embassy officers and staff in all these new embassies that were undergoing more or less the same problems (some had it worse than others and we had it as bad as anybody), but they were more concerned about the second wave when things were settled and when every day didn't present a new, possibly frustrating, but exciting adventure. And I think for that first wave, which I was in, and all our staff was in, that there was this feeling of excitement. The people they sent out—and this in some respects was bad—were young, a couple of first-tour officers. This hurt in terms of experience, but added something in terms of morale.

From the very beginning, Kyrgyzstan had a good reputation. I didn't know anything about Kyrgyzstan and I had spent a lot of time in the Soviet Union, as the record shows. I hadn't given much thought to Central Asia and hadn't been particularly interested in it, even though I had had a tour in Afghanistan. But Kyrgyzstan was already getting a good reputation in the Department for its seem-ingly greater interest in having a real democratic country. It was the only former Soviet republic whose president was not the last first secretary of the Communist Party. He was an academic, who was certainly able to talk up a great democracy line. Our position—the government's position and mine—was to try to see what we could do to foster this, to keep it going on a democratic track, and also to find out what they could do to overcome their economic problems, and the fact that they had so little to work with. They were indeed "running on empty," and cut off from the Soviets, and they would be facing grave economic problems. So, the major task, as I saw it, was twofold: one, to make sure they keep going politically on a democratic track and, two, economically see what they could do and use their reputation for democracy to drum up support for them among the world business community. I think we succeeded to a great extent and they succeeded, too. We have made them focus on the political atmosphere as a means of pulling themselves up by their bootstraps economically, or at least getting help so that they could begin to pull themselves up by their own bootstraps. The point I would make constantly, and which became rather a touchy thing prior to my departure, was, "Look, right now you don't have much to work with other than your reputation. Keep it going and we will do our best to get you aid and to encourage others to help out." That was more or less my function and that of the U.S. in general. We succeeded in terms of U.S. aid: at one time, Kyrgyzstan was getting more aid per capita from the U.S. than any other former Soviet republic.

There was a lot of money being thrown at the former Soviet Union. The question for the embassy was to convince the administration, and for the administration to convince Congress, that Kyrgyzstan deserved a really good share of this aid. So, we kept close track of what they were doing right and informed the Department as events progressed. There was another problem of seeing that this aid was properly used. I would have maybe fifteen people a week come through who had either already gotten AID grants or were seeking AID grants. Some of the schemes were dreams, simply off base, unrealistic, and displaying a lot of ignorance about the situation on the ground in Kyrgyzstan and about what they really needed and how they operated. My role was to tell them this wouldn't work or, if it was already on paper and beginning to take effect, to tell the Department this was a mistake. They were what I used to call "grantologists," people who had studied the whole subject of getting grants, never mind how useful these projects would actually be. For these people, it was a living.

Let me give you one example of something that had taken off and was operating. This was the farmer-to-farmer program, which to some extent was very useful, but had many aspects that were silly. Basically, the idea is that a farmer-to-farmer organization would send out delegations of American farmers or other specialists—not government officials people who had worked or were working in the field—who would visit their counterparts in the dairy industry, whatever, and advise them what they were doing wrong and what they could do better. However, in a lot of instances they come unprepared for what they were seeing. I recall a dairy delegation, actually had to do with cheese making. I had seen them once and then had nothing to do with them; they were out in the countryside. Some months later, I got a copy of their report, filled with suggestions and observations that were either totally silly or self-evident. For instance, one suggestion was that the Kyrgyz needed more modern equipment. They should have milking machines here and there. Or their barns should be air-conditioned. These were things that the Kyrgyz knew but were totally unrealistic, far beyond their means. I sent this report back to Washington and a lot of people had a good chuckle over it. The report among other things listed ways that cheese could be used in the Kyrgyz diet, and had a recipe for cheese fondue which would include taking half a pound of Swiss cheese and a glass of white wine, things that the Kyrgyz peasant never even heard of. While that was a little far out, it did typify the approach a lot of these people coming to Kyrgyzstan, looking around, dropping off their advice, and leaving.

At first the Kyrgyz were very flattered with all of this attention and they saw dollar signs floating in the air whenever one of these delegations came through. But when the delegations didn't leave behind a pile of money but instead a lot of totally irrelevant advice, the Kyrgyz began to get a little annoyed. I talked to many Kyrgyz officials who said, "Look, we really appreciate the attention, but we don?t have time to talk to all of these delegations." And you know how Americans are; you get a chairman of a small company in Ohio put on an official delegation and says, "Well, I would like to see the president and the prime minister and the minister of agriculture." For a while, we managed to get them rather high-level meetings but the Kyrgyz soon learned what the score was. But apart from that, there was a lot of useful aid. There was surplus grain that was donated. We gave very crucial advice to a key segment of Kyrgyzstan's budding industry, water power.

Water is one thing I talked endlessly about to the Kyrgyz: the whole concept of water, one of Kyrgyzstan's riches, as an exploitable resource. They had gotten used to this Soviet approach that "we are all one big happy family, so whatever Uzbekistan gets from Kyrgyzstan, that doesn't matter because we are all Soviet brothers." After the Soviet Union fell apart, however, Uzbekistan had its gold within its borders which it could extract and export at will; Kazakhstan had its oil and gas, to say nothing about enormous territory to grow wheat on; and the Kyrgyz basically had only the water. It is very rich in water resources, perhaps second only to Russia in all of the Soviet Union. But they looked on their water, which was flowing right into Uzbekistan and irrigating all of those vast cotton fields, not as a resource but as something that came from God and just flowed down. We tried to tell them that their water was a resource and they should get some *quid pro quo* for it.

To deal with the government, all I had to do was to pick up the phone. I could see anybody I wanted. Before my first year was over, the president and I had a very good relationship. I spoke very good Russian at that time. I would see him maybe once a month for lunch. He had me out to his hunting lodge three times. He would call me up and say, "Come to lunch." We would go to either his office or his home. I don't know if it did any good, though, because towards the end that changed.

The whole question of tourism was one that we talked about and listened to foreigners talk about. It was very difficult. What we told them to focus on was a sort of eco-tourism: bird watchers and people who like to go to the outer limits, like mountain climbers. However, there was a dreadful lack of facilities there. The Kyrgyz used to say Issyk Kul was a marvelous place and Europeans should come there in droves. Yet, the accommodations were disastrously bad, even by Soviet standards. It was so hard to get to, and even if you began to have reasonably good transportation, why would the average blue-haired lady, tourist type want to go there? It takes a long time to develop that sort of stuff and you have to have side interests or sights to see. You just can't come and stay in a hotel and have a lake. People come and you have to have restaurants around and other facilities, and that would just take too long. I kept telling them, "Look, your mountains aren't going away, you have time to play with this. In the meantime, put ads in the *Audubon Magazine*, put ads in other specialty magazines." They were beginning to get hunters, people who were going for various kinds of game that you don't find except in those areas. They were getting a few bird watchers and advertising for these horse tours through the mountains. Here again, it was not big scale, but it was a beginning.

Towards the end, things became more difficult. This all started up in perhaps late August or early September of 1994 and I left in October. The president simply lost patience with various segments of the press that were being very critical. There were a number of scandals about issues that had taken place pretty soon after independence: the disappearance of some gold from their reserves, and the letting of contracts for gold mining, particularly. You had the press being critical and you had the national assembly being extremely critical. The president decided that he liked being president. There was to be an election, I believe in February of 1995, as well as a national assembly election in November of 1994. The president shut down a newspaper and threatened to shut down another one and put editors in jail. Then he came out with a referendum as to whether there should be a totally different parliament system: instead of a one-house system, there should be a bicameral legislature and the election procedure would be such that, in effect, he would be in control.

We tried to talk him out of it. I went to see him constantly during the last couple of weeks. He invited me for a hunting session with him, with the head of the KGB or security services and the foreign minister, and I couldn't budge him on it. Indeed, things have developed that way now. He has lost a little of the sheen of being the only island of democracy, as they like to call themselves. I told them, "Look, you have very little going for you, except your reputation." This was the one thing that distinguished Kyrgyzstan from being just another one of these backward little third-world countries. I pointed things out to him, which he should have understood. For example, he paid a private visit to the United States in May, 1993, in connection with the Andrei Sakharov fund. Being himself a physicist, he was a close friend of Sakharov's widow, who has been living in the States and he came over to make a speech at the National Academy of Sciences in connection with Sakharov. He wanted desperately during this visit to see the president. We turned handsprings in the embassy and in the State Department—Strobe Talbot was very much in favor of this, too—to try to get him in to see the president. This was during a period of time when Clinton had not much to do with foreign policy, and didn't seem to be very interested in foreign policy. It worked out that Akayev was received in his office by Vice President Gore and during that visit, Clinton came in and they had about fifteen or twenty minutes, with lots of photos, so he could say he had been received by the president. He was in seventh heaven. I kept saying to him, "You see, when the president of Uzbekistan came here he only got as high as under secretary of state. You have gotten in to see the president. You know why? That is because you are a democratic country. You are bucking the whole trend. You are proving that something can rise out of the ashes of the Soviet Union." They ran on that and with it, and it meant a lot in terms of getting aid.

After my departure, at some time, they had their referendum and you could certify it as being rather fairly carried out, but on the other hand, votes in that part of the world, for various reasons, are not the same as in the West. I was terribly disappointed. It was a complete reversal. It happened rather suddenly. We tried very hard. There were messages that flew back and forth. Even Clinton sent messages that were very harsh. But it didn't turn him around. One element that is relevant here was brought to our attention by the most knowledgeable economic planner in Kyrgyzstan, a guy who really had some experience with the

West. He point blank said to us, "Look, you guys aren't going to be around for a long time. Your aid, despite your best intentions, is going to drop off. So, no matter how much you think we are nice guys, you are not going to do a heck of a lot for us. Besides we have the World Bank, the IMF [International Monetary Fund], the Japanese, who pay a lot less attention to these political factors. We thank you for your help and advice but it really is not crucial." And he was undoubtedly right.

ISLAND SQUABBLE

Without the unifying threat of the Soviet Union, the end of the Cold War reminded two NATO allies, Greece and Turkey, that they were potential military antagonists. Although Cyprus and other territorial issues had come up before, a nine-mile island in the Aegean Sea off the coast of Turkey brought them to loggerheads. Both claimed it as their sovereign territory. For over a year, ambassadors in both capitals, Athens and Ankara, spent endless hours on this issue.

Thomas Niles, ambassador in Athens, describes the back-and-forth discussions, including legal issues in international courts, and concludes that both countries were heartily glad the United States had interceded at the highest level. Here is one more example of the role in diplomacy today.

Thomas M.T. Niles
Ambassador, American Embassy, Athens, Greece, 1993–1997

In the fall of 1995, the Greek Parliament ratified the Law of the Sea Convention, which the Greeks claimed gave them the right to a twelve-mile territorial sea in the Aegean. The Turks were aroused about this, claiming that in many areas with a twelve-mile territorial sea the whole Aegean would have been closed off. The Turkish Grand National Assembly passed a resolution sometime in October 1995, which said that if Greece should take this step, the Government of Turkey had the right to go to war without further reference to the parliament. They used the word "war." The Greeks took the stance after this that they had no immediate plans to implement a twelve-mile territorial limit, but had the right to do so and would exercise it when it was most advantageous to them.

In the fall of 1995, before the weather in the Aegean got too bad for naval maneuvers, there were all kinds of alarms with ships going here and there. It was a very frustrating situation. There was a totally incompetent government in Turkey under Tansu Ciller, who was probably the most incompetent person recently to lead a major government. In Greece, the [Andreas] Papandreou government was totally paralyzed, in part because of his health and the inability of his ministers to act without him.

During the Cold War, you could make a case that both sides needed to keep their eyes on the ball, namely the Warsaw Pact and the Soviet threat, and to a degree they did. Once the Cold War was over, it was clear that Greece's defense effort was aimed primarily at Turkey. They also were concerned about Albania, Macedonia, and Bulgaria, but their basic defense posture was aimed at Turkey. For Turkey, however, Greece was problem number six. They were in a terrible neighborhood: they had Syria, Iraq, Iran, the former Soviet Union, Soviet troops in Armenia, the Armenians themselves, and problems with the Georgians.

This didn't mean that the Turks had a positive attitude towards Greece. They had this so-called army of the Aegean, which was stationed along the Aegean coast. I kept pointing out to the Greeks that this was a cadre army used for training and couldn't attack anybody. The cream of the Turkish army was all tied up in southeastern Turkey fighting the Kurds. It was not as big a threat to Greece as it appeared, but there was this anomaly in which two NATO [North Atlantic Treaty Organization] countries were arming against each other.

My counterparts in Ankara and I wanted not only to keep them apart but also to start a better relationship. I worked closely with Dick Barkley, who was my counterpart, and then with Marc Grossman. We always felt that we had a good interaction. I don't think either embassy had a partisan view. We felt that both sides were behaving stupidly and we needed to save them from themselves.

We also worked closely with NATO on this. The only other NATO country that was concerned about this was the United Kingdom. The Germans and the French had some interest but basically the British were our principal partners. I should add that the Dutch, during the time, were in the chair of the European Union, and were very active. I worked very closely with them. They are marvelous allies, as long as you agree with them.

The Greek-Turkish relationship continued to deteriorate. There were elections in Turkey in December of 1995. Ciller's party lost, and after the election she was removed as caretaker prime minister. Just about that time, unrelated to what was going on politically in Turkey, a strange set of incidents began around a tiny island, Imia, or Kardak, as the Turks called it. This island is about four miles off the Turkish coast in the area of Kalymnos, a Greek island in the eastern Aegean. A Turkish coastal freighter, sometime around the 10th of December, ran aground on Imia. Some Greek ships from Kalymnos came by and said, "Let us help you." The Turkish ship said, "We don't need any help from you because this is a Turkish island." The Greeks said, "No, it is not," and they pulled the freighter off the rocks.

There was then an exchange of notes between the respective embassies and foreign ministries establishing these territorial claims. It might have stayed there except that somebody in Athens leaked the notes to a right-wing Greek newspaper and they were published. The mayor of Kalymnos then proceeded to go to Imia and hoist the Greek flag. A Turkish newspaper team from one of the big newspapers flew out with a helicopter, tore down the Greek flag and put up the Turkish flag, videotaping the entire thing. Then they sent these videotapes all over the world. Everyone in Athens was in a state of outrage. Ships were sent to the Aegean. Pretty soon you had the makings of a full-blown crisis.

In the meantime, Prime Minister [Andreas] Papandreou resigned due to ill health. [Costas] Simitis had resigned as minister of industry in September 1995 over a dispute over the privatization of a bankrupt shipyard. Simitis had been working even before that with some PASO [Pan-Hellenic Socialist Movement] members who were disaffected with Papandreou. This included [Theodoros] Pangalos, the current foreign minister, Vaso Papandreou, former European Union commissioner but not related to Prime Minister Papandreou, and a guy named Averinos, who was a former minister in the PASO government of the 1980s. This was the so-called gang of four. They met from time to time and publicized their efforts. Pangalos had been alternate minister of foreign affairs from 1993 to 1995 when he resigned to run for mayor of Athens and lost. He claimed later that Papandreou had sabotaged his campaign.

When Papandreou resigned at the end of January, Simitis became prime minister on January 26, 1996. His new government included Pangalos as foreign minister and Vaso Papandreou as minister of development. There was a general turnover. This was probably a more competent government. The first thing they had to deal with, however, was the crisis around Imia. I was working with the government and warning them against taking any threatening steps. On the morning of the 29th of January, we learned that Greek forces had landed on Imia. I called the minister of defense and he confirmed that troops had landed on Imia. I told him he needed to get them out and he replied that he could not remove the troops. I called the prime minister and repeated the warning, as the Turkish response might be unpredictable.

Everyone was keyed up. Marc Grossman had replaced Dick Barkley in Ankara and was working to keep the Turks calm. One of the problems was that the Greek Chief of Staff, Admiral Lymbaris, was an ultra-nationalist and very difficult to deal with. We tried to establish contact with him and failed. Minister of Defense Arsenias had a good relationship with Secretary of Defense [William] Perry. During the day of the 29th and into the night of the 30th the crisis intensified in this narrow area around Imia. There were probably twelve to fifteen ships along with airplanes and helicopters now in this area and the weather was terrible. I was in the office throughout the night of January 30th. President Clinton had been on the phone with Simitis. Secretary Christopher had been on the phone with Pangalos. [Assistant Secretary Richard] Holbrooke had been in touch with everybody. Around two a.m. on January 30th, we learned that the Turks had placed troops on a smaller island next to Imia.

Through a concerted effort in Athens and Ankara, we were able to persuade the Turks to take their troops off the little island where they were, and the Greeks to take their troops off Imia. In the case of Imia, we are talking about nine acres of land. There is no water. The key to life in the Aegean is fresh water. There are some islands that have their water sent in by tanker. There is no water on Imia. At least no one has ever found any. Nobody lived there.

About three a.m. Athens and Ankara time, which would have been about eight p.m. Washington time, an agreement was reached that the troops would be pulled off both tiny islands. Tragically, in the process a Greek helicopter crashed and three crew members were killed. They were the only fatalities. The Greek press blamed us for the accident. When we asked them how we could have caused it, they responded that we could do anything with satellites or through other means. I went to the funeral and it was very tragic. The remarkable thing was that more people weren't killed, given the large number of ships, small boats, airplanes and helicopters, plus the terrible weather. This crisis began to wind down on the 30th. We could see a partial pullback by both sides. They took their ships out, and the number of aircraft decreased.

The problem remained, however. The Turks claimed Imia or Kardak, as they called it and so did the Greeks. We did not really have a clue, naturally. We had never heard of Imia. We set our lawyers to work to talk with the Greeks and the Turks. The Dodecanese Islands were Italian from 1911 through 1945. The Greeks took them over legally under the Treaty of Paris in 1947 and physically in 1945 when the Germans were driven out of that area. In January of 1932, the Italians and the Turks concluded a treaty that delineated that area. The Turks also accepted Italian sovereignty over the Dodecanese Islands, which they had never done before. In December of 1932, the Turks accepted a listing of the dependencies or smaller islands that were also Italian. It was clear that what they had done was to follow the three-mile limit. Anything in the Dodecanese area that was outside three miles from the Turkish coast was Italian. Imia is three-and-a-half to four miles from the Turkish coast, and Imia was mentioned in the protocol as belonging to Italy. The Turks claim that the protocol was not registered with the League of Nations and is, therefore, invalid. Turkey and Italy both registered the first treaty. These were "open" treaties that were registered with the League of Nations if you were a member. The second protocol had not been registered. Our lawyers said that was irrelevant because the basic treaty had been registered and the protocol did not need to be registered.

We took the position that we would not take a position on the sovereignty issue, but that we would encourage the states—Greece and Turkey—to work it out. We generally agreed with the Greek position that this was something that should go to the International Court of Justice. I personally think that was a big mistake. We knew by the time we took this position that the Greeks had the better position on the sovereignty argument. The Turks knew that we knew their position was very weak. When we refused to take a position, it sent a signal back to the Turks that we were not prepared to countenance or do anything about aggressive Turkish behavior toward the Greeks on the territorial issues in the Aegean. What this led to was a succession of Turkish claims and statements about the Aegean territorial issues that poisoned the relationship with Greece even further. At the time of the crisis, Mrs. Ciller talked about "thousands of islands and islets and rocks whose sovereignty was uncertain." The foreign minister in the subsequent government, Mr. [Emre] Gonensay, talked about "gray areas" in the Aegean. In May of 1996, the Turks raised an issue about a small island called Gavdos which is south of Crete. We took a strong stance and said that we thought Gavdos was a Greek island. Recently, in the fall of 1998, the Turks raised questions about several other Greek islands, including some inhabited ones. One of them is called Farmakonisi. What this does in Greece, of course, is scare people and also cause them to be very tough in any dealing with the Turks, because they see the Turks as threatening Greek sovereignty and trying to seize Greek territory.

By March 1996, John Kornblum was assistant secretary in European affairs. Dick Holbrooke retired as assistant secretary around the middle of February of 1996. John, Marc Grossman, and I worked over the next year or so to try to find some formula to deal with the Imia problem. We wanted Greece and Turkey to say in a joint statement that they would send the issue to the International Court of Justice. There was either some problem on the Greek side or, more frequently, on the Turkish side. The Turks at one point said frankly to us that they knew they would lose Imia at the Court of Justice, but they wanted to balance this with a victory. If they were to allow the issue of Imia to go to the Court of Justice, they wanted the issue of the militarization of the Dodecanese Islands also to be sent to the International Court of Justice. The Treaty of Paris of 1947, a treaty with Italy to which Greece signed but Turkey did not, ended Italy's participation in World War II. The Treaty of Paris stated that the Dodecanese Islands must be demilitarized. The Greeks claim that until the invasion of Cyprus by Turkey in 1974 they observed those provisions. I have no reason to doubt that. After 1974, using Article 51 of the United Nations Charter, which is the right to self-defense, the Greeks claim that the use of force by the Turks in Cyprus gives them the right to station forces on the Dodecanese Islands as the Turks might use force against Rhodes or one of the other islands. The real-life situation is that because of the geography of the area (the Dodecanese are right along the coast of Turkey and far from mainland Greece) it would be hard as hell for the Greeks to defend the Dodecanese. It is a little bit like the Berlin brigade defending West Berlin against the Russians. The Greeks felt they had to be there militarily, so that their people would feel secure. I didn't really buy that because the people on Rhodes knew that the garrison on Rhodes would not have been able to fend off the Turks if they really invaded.

All of our efforts to get the Imia issue to a resolution failed during my time in Athens. When I left Athens on the 27th of September 1997, the issue was unresolved. To this day it remains a problem.

The Greeks and the Turks wanted us to stop them from hostilities; in their hearts they did. Neither wanted to go to war over Imia or anything else, but the media and internal pressure on both sides prevented them from stepping back. The only reason they did so in January, 1996 was under pressure from the United States. The president down through Secretary Christopher, Assistant Secretary Holbrooke, the two ambassadors, and the chairman of the Joint Chiefs of Staff were all involved. Afterwards, Dick Holbrooke commented that we were working during the night while the Europeans slept. This was a deprecating, but largely true, comment about the European Union. The British reacted badly to this, because they were helpful, but the rest just stood around and wondered what the hell was going on. I think this is an example of the reality that if anything important is going to happen in that area, it is going to be done by the United States. We are going to have to take the lead. We can't always do it by ourselves, and shouldn't try. But, if we had not been involved with the Imia issue, Greece and Turkey would have blundered into a war.

8

Desert Storm

On August 1, 1990 the Iraqi dictator, Saddam Hussein, sent a powerful army into oil-rich Kuwait. Within a day, the Iraqis were in full control of the pocket-sized sheikdom and its oilfields. The Iraqi army was poised on the border of the Kingdom of Saudi Arabia and its immense oilfields along the Persian Gulf. The Saudis had no military force that could stop the Iraqis; neither could the oil-producing sheikdoms of the Gulf, Bahrain, Qatar, and the United Arab Emirates.

Clearly, the vital interest of the United States was at stake. If an aggressive dictator backed by a large army could control most of the oil in the Persian Gulf, he would have a stranglehold on a major source of the commodity on which the world's economy depended.

At this point, the president of the United States, George H.W. Bush, put together an impressive alliance, including several normally unfriendly Arab states, Syria and Egypt, as well as Saudi Arabia, the Gulf states, Tunisia, Morocco, and the Europeans: France, Italy, and the United Kingdom.

In order to wage a war against Iraq, it was absolutely necessary to have the full cooperation of Saudi Arabia since a huge multi-national force, mainly Christian, had to assemble and attack on Saudi territory. For a conservative, highly religious Muslim country, this was bound to put deep strains on the Saudi government and society.

At the same time, most of the Arab countries now joining the grand coalition, led by the United States, were the sworn enemies of Israel, a longtime American ally. While not bordering each other, Iraq and Israel were always at dagger points. Israel had carefully established a reputation that if attacked, it would respond massively. Yet, if Iraq were to provoke Israel, then this might upset the alliance forged by President Bush with his Arab allies.

It was the task of the American ambassador in Riyadh to see that the Saudis were able to accept the strains produced by stationing some half million foreign troops on its soil and then waging a war from that area. At the same time, it was the task of the American ambassador in Tel Aviv to keep Israel from responding in its usual tough style to the attacks of Iraq that were bound to come when the war started. In other words, the ambassadors were to keep Saudi Arabia in and Israel out.

Fortunately for the United States, our embassies in Riyadh and Tel Aviv were headed by two skilled Foreign Service officers, Charles Freeman and William Brown. A curious note is that these two men, dealing with a major crisis in the Middle East, both started their Foreign Service careers as Chinese language officers.

DESERT WAR: RIYADH

Ambassador Charles (Chas) W. Freeman Jr., served in Saudi Arabia at a time of considerable bilateral stress, but also at a time of great military activity for the United States and its allies: the Gulf War. Shortly after his arrival, he saw Washington's general lack of interest in that area—especially from Secretary James Baker—due to the earth-shattering events of the break up of Communism.

When Iraq invaded Kuwait on August 21, 1990, the day after Freeman's return to the States on home leave, he faced confusion in Washington over the next few days. But soon, a team was organized and flew to Riyadh with Freeman aboard, to brief King Fahd and receive his approval on a plan to send a large American military contingent as part of a broad alliance to attack Iraq. It was the genesis of the military operation known as Desert Storm.

Fortunately, from the outset, Freeman saw the necessity of the Forces to understand and accept the strictness of Saudi society. General Schwarzkopf, the on-the-scene military leader, understood completely (in part because of his earlier experience in Iran), and "General Order Number One," which spelled all this out explicitly (no alcohol, girly shows, etc.), was issued immediately. Freeman's personal readings in history and professional experience led him, as ambassador, to recognize the vital importance of such guidance. Frictions among the troops, with the local culture, and with authorities were kept to a minimum. Finally, in the following account, Freeman expresses dismay at Washington's failure to give instructions (especially to Schwarzkopf) on how the war should have ended, and explains how he worked with the large American civilian community to keep them from leaving their vital jobs.

Charles W. Freeman Jr
Ambassador, American Embassy, Riyadh, Saudi Arabia, 1989–1992

In February of 1990, General Norman Schwarzkopf, who had succeeded the previous summer as commander in chief of the central command (CINCCENT), turned up in my office. I had, of course, met him previously. He was stuck with a plan—approved by the joint chiefs—for the region that envisaged fighting the Soviet Union in the mountains of Iran. He and I had agreed, when we had met before, that this was probably a bit out of date, especially as it wasn't clear there was going to be a Soviet Union, and our relationship with Iran had rather changed. So, he came to my office and laid out a number of scenarios that he was exploring for exercises and focuses of battle plans.

I stopped him, and I said, "Now I think you really ought to think about three scenarios: Iraq invading Kuwait, or Iran invading Kuwait—anyway an invasion of Kuwait. The second scenario you ought to think about is Iraq invading Kuwait, and Yemen attacking Saudi Arabia from the south, by pre-arrangement. And third, you should consider the possibility of an Iranian-fomented insurrection in Saudi Arabia's eastern province among the Shi`ah, possibly beginning with intervention, through subversion, in Bahrain and/or Qatar. I think these are really more realistic scenarios than others. And while I doubt that any of them will happen, if you concentrate on these, I think you will not be wasting your time in the way that you are."

He readily agreed and indicated that he'd been thinking along much the same lines himself. We agreed that he should focus on scenario number one, an Iraqi or Iranian invasion of Kuwait.

He then went back and tried to get the joint chiefs to approve this scenario, and ran into a total lack of support. In fact, it was not until June of 1990 that Colin Powell, the chairman of the joint chiefs, personally overruled the rest of the joint chiefs and allowed Schwarzkopf to proceed to develop this scenario, which led to the command-post exercise that Schwarzkopf ran just at the very end of July, only a few days before Saddam Hussein actually did invade Kuwait; a command-post exercise that was invaluable in putting together what became known as Desert Shield. I cite this because it's an indication of the disconnection between thinking and realities in the Gulf and Washington, at all levels.

Similarly, I might say, in the spring of 1990, the Navy determined that the naval presence, which we had maintained in the Gulf since 1947, called COM-

MIDEAST Force, was no longer required in the post-Cold War era; there was no strategic interest of the United States that required defending in the Gulf; and that this force should be disbanded and withdrawn. Schwarzkopf and I and some of the other ambassadors in the region argued strenuously against this. Again, fortunately, in June of 1990, Colin Powell overruled the Navy, and we did have a naval presence in the Gulf, when Saddam went into Kuwait.

Right around this time, Saddam Hussein, in an informal talk with his officer corps and political entourage, made what was reported in the West as an unprovoked threat to rain fire on Israel. I reviewed it for my Arabic lessons, and I actually watched it. In fact, what he said was that Israel had attacked Iraq in the past, but if it did it again that he would retaliate by raining fire on Israel. He also said quite a variety of things about how Kuwaiti and Emiri—meaning United Arab Emirates—behavior on oil pricing and supplies was intolerable, and how this would have to be fixed. This threat to the Gulf was not taken seriously. The threat to Israel, however, was taken very seriously. Ironically, of course, Iraq was planning aggression against the Gulf, not against Israel.

Secretary of State Baker was totally disinterested, which was one reason that he was caught so totally by surprise by the Gulf War. That is to say, he was totally disinterested and frankly, I believe, let it be known to the bureaucracy that he did not wish extraneous distractions, like information about other areas of the Middle East, to be brought to his attention. Great things were happening elsewhere, including the fall of the Soviet Union and the reunification of Germany, which was agreed in the spring of 1990. I think he may very well have been right to concentrate on these, but we did end up paying a price in terms of not being alert to events that were occurring elsewhere.

There was no effort by Washington when, in the winter-spring of 1990, relations between Saudi Arabia and Kuwait deteriorated, in part for the same reason that Iraqi/Kuwaiti relations deteriorated; namely, Kuwait was blatantly cheating on its OPEC quota to the detriment of larger producers like Saudi Arabia and Iraq; but also, in part, because of some rather egregious Kuwaiti pokes at Saudi Arabia during a soccer match. Sports are often an instrument not of friendship, but of hostility. So, in the spring of 1990, when Saddam began to threaten to take action against Kuwait and the United Arab Emirates for cheating on their oil quotas, he had a measure of sympathy in Saudi Arabia. The Saudis, however, never imagined that he would take the sort of military action that he did.

As July went on, I was due for home leave. On July 28th, I convened a meeting of the country team to poll them as to whether I should cancel my home leave. With only one exception—the deputy chief of mission, Dave Dunford—those present, including the intelligence agency representatives, expressed considerable confidence that the worst that could happen between Iraq and Kuwait would be some sort of tussle over the Rumaila oil fields straddling the border, which Iraq conceivably might take and hold for ransom in order to obtain Kuwaiti forgiveness of debts, and which the Kuwaitis were very unwisely insisting on collecting from an essentially bankrupt Iraq. No one, including the DCM, anticipated anything beyond that. It was left that there really wasn't any reason why I shouldn't go on home leave. If something happened, I could come back. But the expectation was that if something happened, it would essentially be a limited conflict between Iraq and Kuwait, without grievous implications for Saudi Arabia.

On August 2nd, being very jet-lagged and confused about where I was physically, I awoke about four in the morning and went out and turned on the BBC, on the short-wave radio that I normally carry with me. I heard, to my astonishment, that Iraq had invaded Kuwait. I waited for the sun to rise, and when things had opened up in Washington I called David Mack, who was the deputy assistant secretary in the Bureau of Near Eastern Affairs, and was responsible for the Gulf. I asked him whether this was something with really broad implications, and whether I should plan to return to Saudi Arabia. I was told, no, it didn't look that way, it looked like a very limited action, and that I should feel free to continue with my home leave for the time being, that maybe I would have to curtail it, but I didn't have to turn right around. The same essential message was given on the 3rd of August, when I called again.

On the morning of the 4th, which was a Saturday, I called again and was told, "Well, you probably ought to come down the beginning of the week to see the president, and then plan to go back to Saudi Arabia." I had planned a family reunion for the 5th, Sunday, and there were a large number of people planning to turn up. Saturday afternoon, however, I received a call saying, "No, no, this is something very serious, it looks like Saudi Arabia is at risk, and you'd better come back tonight for meetings at the NSC [National Security Council]." So, I managed to get myself on a plane, and I got down to National Airport.

On the morning of Sunday the 5th, I found a great atmosphere of confusion surrounding what was happening. I was able to ascertain that somebody was probably going to Jeddah, which is where the king was that season, around noon. The signals kept changing. First, it was Bob Gates, the deputy national security advisor, who was to go. Then it was Brent Scowcroft, the national security advisor. Then it was Dick Cheney, the secretary of defense. Then it was General Norman Schwarzkopf, the commander in chief of the central command. When I got out to Andrews, I found Norm Schwarzkopf there, and he told me that it would be Bob Gates who was going. There was a plane standing by; I put my luggage on it. Fifteen minutes later, a call came saying, "No, that wasn't going to happen." I took my luggage off. And I said to Norm, "Look, I think I'd better go down to MacDill Air Force Base in Florida and go over there with you," because he was planning to go. Then, a call came that Dick Cheney, who had earlier been supposed to go and had been canceled, was now going. Cheney arrived; we got on the plane, and took off.

Relations with Kuwait—notwithstanding Operation Earnest Will, which had escorted Kuwaiti tankers through the Gulf during the Iran-Iraq war—were not cordial. The Kuwaitis were not asking for help. As I understand it, only a couple of hours before the actual invasion, Nat Howell, the ambassador to Kuwait, asked the Kuwaitis whether they wanted us to do anything, and was told no. In fact, at that very moment, an Iraqi sports team, which was not really a sports team, but a group of air traffic controllers, was guiding Iraqi helicopter gunships into Kuwait City, and guiding the initial assault. Furthermore, Kuwait's relations with Saudi Arabia, as I indicated, were not good; nor were they good with other members of the Gulf.

The U.S. had no defense commitment to Kuwait implicitly, and certainly not explicitly. The initial reaction was to treat this as a classic case of a quarrel in which the United States was not directly involved, where perhaps Iraq was intending to, as I said earlier, in effect conduct a bank robbery, or at least a hostage-taking, and then bargain with Kuwait for financial advantage.

When, however, the Iraqi forces began visibly to prepare for further advance into Saudi Arabia, I think people remembered that the United Arab Emirates had been as much a target of Iraqi ire as Kuwait had been. There began to be real alarm about the implications either of an Iraqi advance into Saudi Arabia or of an Iraqi position on the Saudi border, which would put it in a position to intimidate Saudi Arabia and perhaps dictate some measure of policy to Saudi Arabia.

In fact, as we proceeded on the aircraft toward Jeddah, I really found it very difficult to figure out what the Saudi reaction to all this was likely to be. King Fahd later confirmed to me that my judgment of his leadership style was correct. He said that in fifty years of public life, he had never once made a decision outside the consensus of the royal family and the Council of Ministers. In fact, the Saudi monarchy is not a Western-style monarchy. The king, in some respects, is a powerful presider over a consensus. Typically, King Fahd takes an agonizingly long time to come to a conclusion about what must be done. Therefore, I was frankly astonished, not only by the decisiveness that President Bush displayed with regard to Saudi Arabia, but also by the decisiveness of King Fahd.

The meeting with King Fahd, Secretary Cheney, General Schwarzkopf, and others, in Jeddah, has, I think, been misportrayed in the press and in much of the writing about the Gulf War. Much of the writing about the Gulf War, I might say, is really writing about Washington and the Gulf War, and tends to overlook the fact that the Gulf War took place somewhere outside the Beltway. The mission was essentially to describe the threat to King Fahd and to ascertain whether he wished assistance or not: to offer assistance, but not to cajole him into it.

I believe that, in fact, there was a great deal of effort made by Prince Bandar, who occupied a pivotal position. He was ambassador to the United States, almost a foster son, in many respects, of King Fahd, and very close to the king. He was a man of great ability and energy, with unparalleled access in both capitals. Bandar had himself flown back, just ahead of Cheney, to Riyadh to prepare the king for whomever it was that turned up, and clearly anticipated and wished to see a decisive American intervention.

But no one knew whether that would happen. So, a great deal of the discussion was: "What will the king decide?" and "How should we present the intelligence material to him?"

Accompanying the group was a CIA briefer, with a great package of what is called PHOTINT, meaning overhead satellite photography, of Iraqi dispositions in southern Kuwait and along the Saudi border. The terrain is open, with clear skies at that season of the year. We asked this briefer to run through his briefing, and it was a very good briefing, but it was very much in the peculiar style of such briefings in Washington, with: "On the one hand...." "On the other hand...." "We don't know." "Probably." "Probability of seventy percent this," and blabitty blah. It was my judgment, and I expressed it, that if King Fahd were given this sort of briefing, not being familiar with that particular style, it would simply confuse him. I suggested that the briefer come to the meeting, but that, in effect, General Schwarzkopf provide his military judgments, rather than a normal intelligence briefing. And that is what happened.

The king, as it turned out, had only two questions. One was, "Is the threat to Saudi Arabia as grave as I believe it to be?" When the king—with General Schwarzkopf on bended knee in front of him, the crown prince looking over the king's shoulder, and the foreign minister, Deputy Defense Minister, Prince 'Abd al-Rakman, and Chief of Staff, General Hamad [Bin Ali Al-Attiyah] looking on—saw these photographs, which showed Iraqi patrols inside Saudi territory, he saw his judgment confirmed. So, that answered his first question of, "Is there a serious threat?" The second question, which he put rather bluntly to us, was, "What are you prepared to do about it?" And he said, "Frankly, if your reaction is the sort of thing I had from Jimmy Carter when I was threatened by Iran..." (in which the United States persuaded Saudi Arabia to accept the deployment of a squadron of F-15's, and then, when they were in the air, en route to Saudi Arabia, announced that they were unarmed). The king said that if this was the sort of thing we had in mind, we needn't have any further discussion.

Norm Schwarzkopf then briefed the king on the plan that became known later as Desert Shield. At that point, it had no name. And when the king saw that the American response involved the deployment of two-hundred and twenty-thousand people in our armed forces to Saudi Arabia, he said, "That is a serious response, and I accept."

At this point, there was a nice reminder of the normal Saudi decision-making style. As I mentioned before, normally, in Saudi Arabia, decisions are made after lengthy discussion and the formation of consensus among the ruling group. The crown prince interrupted in Arabic—and my Arabic by that time was good enough to understand all of this—in an aside with the king, and said, "Don't you think we ought to take some more time to consider this before we make this decision and convey the request to Washington?" And the king said, "No, we don't have any time. We have to make the decision now, or what happened to Kuwait will happen to us. There is no more Kuwait." The crown prince said, "Yes, there is still a Kuwait."

And the king said, "And its territory consists solely of hotel rooms in London, Cairo, and elsewhere."

The crown prince said, "I agree with you."

And then the king went around the room, polling his other advisors present, the deputy defense minister, Prince `Abd al-Rakman; Prince Sa`d, the foreign minister; and the chief of staff, who saluted and said, "At your orders, your majesty." And that was the decision.

So, it is often made out that the United States went there determined to persuade the king to accept forces. That is not correct. The king did not require persuasion, and proved to be exceptionally decisive. He later said to me that this was in fact the only time in his many decades of public life that he had ever made a decision on his own, without waiting for consensus. And he said he felt qualified, by experience and by his understanding of the circumstances.

Secretary Cheney asked the king whether he could communicate to the president that there was a request. When he did so, the president ordered the 82nd

Airborne to deploy to Saudi Arabia, as well as Air Force units and the like. And the first phase of what became known as Desert Shield was set in motion.

Norm Schwarzkopf and I had a long chat, in which I basically made two points to him. First, was that my own readings of military history suggested that, unlike the British, who had become accustomed to operating with and among foreign forces of very different mentality, the U.S. had not really developed in the armed forces what I would call an adequate military-political function, and that liaison with Saudi forces and with local Saudi emirs, meaning governors and potentates, would be a major task. This was an opportunity for Norm to develop a system that would be a model for future operations.

Second, given the nature of Saudi society, we could anticipate a huge amount of friction between American forces and Saudi forces unless certain things were made clear. Specifically, that there could be no use of alcohol. There could be no USO shows involving scantily clad women. And there would have to be some program of orientation and indoctrination for forces, so that they understood the nature of the society they had been thrust into.

All of this discussion (which Norm, having grown up partly in Iran, understood very well, I think) paralleled his own thinking, and resulted in General Order Number One, which was a godsend, because it banned liquor, required all forces to have a one-week indoctrination in Islam and Saudi society, and it recognized the need for extreme discretion in the practice of religions other than Islam in Saudi Arabia. This, together with the exceptional discipline and remarkably high quality of the armed forces as they then existed, kept frictions to a minimum.

In parallel with this, the embassy and the consulates, most particularly Ken Stammerman, the consul general in Dhahran, established an extremely effective liaison process with the U.S. military and the local Saudi authorities, such that when incidents began to occur, they were either nipped in the bud, resolved, or, if not resolved, at least kept out of the newspapers, and therefore didn't have a snowballing effect. As time went on, the civil-affairs people in the military got awfully good at working with American consular officers on this. And the American consular officers got awfully good at working with local Saudi authorities. I think probably this element of the Gulf War experience, the fact that the relationship between the embassy and the consulates and the military was so close and cooperative, and that the two were able so effectively to manage the frictions between the Saudis and the military, was one of the great achievements.

It parallels one other, of which I'm personally very proud. Norm Schwarzkopf and I are the only war-fighting commander-in-chief and ambassador who have ever been co-located forward in a war zone. Historically, ambassadors and CINCs (commanders in chief) have had a very rocky relationship. Norm and I had an exceedingly cooperative relationship, with a great deal of mutual assistance provided. He kept me adequately informed of military plans; I kept him adequately informed of what was transpiring on the political side. I supported him, and he supported me. I think it would be worth going on at some length about that relationship, how it was managed, and why it worked, because both of us have strong personalities. Norm, in particular, unlike me, has a notorious temper and a leadership style that was very dictatorial, peremptory, and demanding. While he kept most of his subordinates in a state of fear and trepidation, the relationship that he enjoyed with me was cordial and cooperative.

These two things—that is, the good connection between the ambassador and the CINC and the excellent connections between people on the ground managing the day-to-day frictions from this large presence—played a vital role in enabling us to build up in Saudi Arabia and ultimately to liberate Kuwait.

The American community was desperately afraid of the use of chemical weapons. I was far more concerned about biological weapons being employed. Around August 10th, the embassy sent the first of twenty-seven telegrams to the Department of State, asking for support in the form of materials and guidelines for briefings of the American community that would enable us to cope with this problem. We pointed out then, and in all of the succeeding communications, that we were trying to walk a fine line between keeping essential civilian personnel at work in the kingdom and avoiding the deaths of American citizens.

The point being this (I'm really leaping ahead a bit and melding Desert Shield and Desert Storm in this regard): Saudi ARAMCO [Arabian-American Oil Company] included a vast number of expatriate personnel, some of the key ones being Americans, but many of other nationalities. The defense contractors who supported the Saudi armed forces and the military were staffed largely by Americans or British subjects, with other nationalities in a subordinate role. Altogether, at this time, there were fewer than thirty-thousand Americans in the kingdom, with the largest community in the eastern province, which was the target of Saddam's possible attack. If those Americans had left in a panic, there would have been no oil with which to fuel aircraft or tanks or to keep ships at sea. There would have been no defense contractors to maintain those weapons systems. And we would have ended up fighting to defend the two holy mosques, rather than the world's oil supplies, and doing it under gravely disadvantageous circumstances. Moreover, other communities regarded the Americans as the best informed, and an American departure would have set off a stampede of everybody, down to and including the Filipino bottle washers for the Saudi military and the Bangladeshi street sweepers. Saudi Arabia's dependence on expatriate labor therefore rested on the behavior of the American community. So, we did not want the American presence to cause attrition; we wanted the essential personnel to remain.

However, as you might guess from the figure of twenty-seven cables, the Department of State and the interagency process in Washington proved utterly unable to come to grips with this matter. First, we got instructions not to worry. Then, we got instructions not to brief the American community. Then, we got instructions, in response to our request for chemical gear that we could distribute to the American community, not to press that. I'm talking about gas masks, ponchos, that sort of thing. We were enjoined from briefing the American community at all. In the absence of briefings, panic began to rise. So, I just violated our instructions, and we provided over a hundred briefings to the American community.

The idiocy did not stop with this. In December 1990, the Department of State's Human Rights Bureau vetoed a sale of chemical gear to the Ministry of Interior in Saudi Arabia, which would have been distributed to the foreign community, including the Americans, *gratis*, on the grounds that the Ministry of Interior controlled the police, and the police in Saudi Arabia are violators of human rights. It proved impossible to overturn this decision.

There were other issues, including the avalanche of "bright lights and dim bulbs" that descended on Saudi Arabia. There were a lot of people who wanted to have their photograph taken with troops in the field: two-thousand and ten of them, to be exact, over the course of the run-up to the actual fighting in the Gulf War. Very soon we got into visitor overload. I found myself bouncing around in the kingdom, taking visitors in to see the king and the military and various other people.

Fortunately, quite early on, Norm Schwarzkopf agreed to simply make a jet plane available to me on a twenty-four-hour basis. That was a godsend. I think that over the course of the war I went to Jeddah fifty-two times on that aircraft. I remember there was one twenty-four-hour period when, because of congressional and other delegations, primarily, as well as work, I was in Jeddah three times, Dhahran three times, and Riyadh twice, all within twenty-four hours. These places are a thousand miles apart!

I did play a role, and the embassy did play a role, in holding the coalition together. We were often called upon by members of the coalition to provide ground-troop briefings. Often, I had to go to the Saudis to make requests for them to persuade a recalcitrant coalition member to do something that we thought they should do. Sometimes, this extended to the Saudis. In effect, it was buying votes in the United Nations, as they did with a series of extensions of foreign assistance to the Soviet Union. Essentially, this secured Soviet cooperation in the Security Council.

The greater role of the embassy, however, was as a sort of front for CENT-COM [Central Command] in managing the politics of the military coalition. We acted as an important channel of communication between the Saudi government and the government to concert policy, but I would say the major role there was really played by Prince Bandar, rather than by those of us in Riyadh. So, it was an extremely active time on the diplomatic front.

I found myself holding hands a great deal with the African ambassadors, as a group, reassuring them that they were not about to be obliterated in a nuclear exchange; or talking to the Filipinos, who provided a great deal of the labor supply in the kingdom; to the Bangladeshis, the Indians, and Pakistanis, to try to help them hold their workers in line and prevent panic. In other words, a major dimension of the diplomatic activity in Riyadh during the war was persuading various foreign communities, through their embassies or directly in some cases, that there was every reason to have faith in the ability of the coalition to prevail over Iraq, and that the danger to their nationals was overblown.

There were 1,600 members of the American press on Saudi territory during this time. I think I did over 700 "backgrounders" without a single leak, which testifies to the professionalism of the press. I followed a special practice, because I did not want my name in the newspaper or on the television or radio. I simply told them that my condition for giving a briefing on background was that there be no attribution at all and that, beyond that, if I saw my name in their publication under any circumstances remotely connected with the interview, they were never going to get back in to see me again. This had a sufficiently intimidating effect in that I stayed out of the public limelight, which was what I wanted. To my mind, there is no advantage for an ambassador to appear in the limelight, and I was happy to yield pride of place to those who should have it, like the secretary of state.

With Washington, I made the point that the first question you should ask yourself before launching a war is not whether your forces can prevail on the battlefield, but how you propose to end the war, on what terms, negotiated by whom, with whom, and why the other side should regard an end to the fighting, or not cheat on a truce, as preferable to fighting on. In a series of communications, I pressed for a war termination strategy and also for a statement of war aims. I got no response from Washington, for the reasons I've mentioned; namely, the potentially lethal consequences of a leak, with the result that there never was a statement of war aims. The war aims were the lowest common denominator of UN Security Council resolutions, which were the liberation of Kuwait. To that, we managed to add the reduction of the Iraqi Republican Guard and Iraqi weapons of mass destruction to a point where Iraq would not pose an intolerable threat to the region.

Schwarzkopf and I were so frustrated that on the eve of the counterattack in the air, I sent in a cable saying that, not having heard anything about war objectives, and having discussed it with General Schwarzkopf, unless instructed otherwise, these are the objectives he is going to pursue, which were what I thought the lowest common denominator was. I never had a response, and that document, in effect, was his operative statement of war objectives.

The more ludicrous development was that at the end of the fighting, at Safwan, when he met with the Iraqi generals, he had no instructions. We tried to get him instructions, he tried to get instructions, but Washington was unable to provide instructions, because they had no vision of what sort of peace they wanted to have follow the war.

Our major difficulty at the embassy was the absolute inability of Washington to respond to the danger of chemical and biological weapons. This left us essentially unprepared in many important psychological dimensions, as well as otherwise. But we had a twenty-four hour, around-the-clock, community information center that was in touch with embassy people, as well as members of the American community, and we were able, I think quite effectively, to subdue panic, or at least reduce it to acceptable dimensions.

As time went on, people began to gather on the balconies to see the nightly shrapnel show overhead—not recommended, but I'm afraid all of us did it—and the sense that these large pieces of steel falling from the sky were unlikely to fall on you personally grew to a probably dangerous level.

I had a couple of employees who, frankly, panicked and had to be sent home, because their panic was contagious. I was sorry to see that the Foreign Service was unable to deal with cases of cowardice, and took care of these people as though they had done something exemplary, rather than something that showed a weakness in their fitness to serve the United States in conditions of stress abroad.

I had only one incident that I thought was a clear case of insubordination. An intelligence agency—which had been supplied quietly by its own parent organization—distributed gas masks and the like to its own employees, while other embassy employees did not have them. I hit the ceiling and forced the recall of everything that had been handed out, on the grounds that either everybody was going to get stuff or nobody was going to get stuff, and everybody was going to get treated the same. But, with that one exception, I think people behaved, by and large, magnificently.

I was particularly proud of the Foreign Service national employees, third-country nationals in the case of Saudi Arabia, who showed a level of dedication and loyalty that was most impressive, who stayed on the job even though many of them were terribly concerned about their families. In the end, I was able to get Washington, somewhat grudgingly, to give the American employees extra R&R for all this, and to recognize the employees with a group honor award.

DESERT WAR: TEL AVIV

Ambassador William Brown was on his second tour in Israel. He had been deputy chief of mission in Tel Aviv, then moved on to other assignments, including ambassador to Thailand, before returning to Israel. The American ambassador to Israel plays a role unique to the Foreign Service. He is in the middle of an American domestic minefield; every move he makes is closely monitored by the powerful Israeli lobby, AIPAC [American Israel Public Affairs Committee], and other friends of Israel, in the United States. Nowhere in the government is the "leaking" of classified diplomatic telegrams more prevalent than those to and from Israel. It is an article of faith in the Foreign Service that the most sensitive telegram will be on the desks of certain senators and congressmen, and the Washington Post *and the* New York Times, *before it reaches the responsible officer in the Department of State. In Israel, the American ambassador is practically a member of the Israel cabinet, and is closeted with the various ministers on a daily basis.*

The normal work of the ambassador is more than hectic, but when faced with a crisis such as the Gulf War, the pressures on the embassy and its chief of mission are almost intolerable. Fortunately for the United States, William Brown was well versed in the politics and personalities of Israel before Saddam Hussein made his grab for Kuwait. His job was to keep the Israeli military from attacking Iraq. This ran completely against the spirit and doctrine of an elite, pugnacious army and air force, led by a government which included many former military leaders and a population that did not want to passively suffer enemy attack by missiles.

William Brown
Ambassador, American Embassy, Tel Aviv, Israel, 1988–1992 and 1994

The temperature of public opinion in Israel rose, particularly after August 2, 1990, when Iraq invaded Kuwait. We had meetings within the embassy with many American citizens who inquired about what was coming, what would happen, and so forth.

The Israeli gas mask distribution system was activated. The masks had not yet actually been distributed, but the word was going out that the Israeli Government had the necessary equipment on hand. Of course, we told American citizens of this announcement. Then we got into a difficult dialogue, with American citizens asking us whether Saddam Hussein would use conventional, nuclear, chemical, or biological weapons. They would ask us what we had to counter such attacks. American citizens would tell us: "You say that one of these gas masks is waiting for us in an Israeli warehouse. Will this gas mask be able to cope with VX, sarin, or mustard gas? By the way, if the attack is with mustard gas, what about the skin on the rest of me? Do you have something beyond that? Do you have rubber suits?" And on and on and on. My conversations on these questions with people in the Department of State in Washington were largely over a secure phone. The information I obtained was not very satisfactory. Ambassador Charles Freeman, in Saudi Arabia, certainly had his problems dealing with similar inquiries.

My principal contacts in the State Department were with Jock Covey as the principal deputy assistant secretary of state for Near Eastern affairs under Assistant Secretary John Kelly and, eventually, Ivan Selig, who was undersecretary of state for management. It was with one or both of these officers that I got into some pretty heated conversations when I reported that there was growing consternation among American citizens in Israel about gas masks. I learned at a meeting within the embassy that personnel in the office of the defense attaché had been issued gas masks, or at least that the officers had them, although their family members might not have had them. I was informed by these officers in the Department that this was impossible and was assured that, "We, in the State Department are the ones who authorize such distribution and we haven't authorized it." I said, "Would you like to have me read you the serial numbers on the gas masks?" This was a jolt for those people in the State Department back in Washington.

As the tension grew and we sought specific information, we sometimes got what we felt was a pretty cavalier response in these telephone conversations. I remember being told, "If we ever thought that Saddam Hussein would attack Israel with poison gas, we would have all of you out of Israel in no time." I remembered those remarks later on.

By August 2, 1990, Israeli Minister of Defense [Moshe] Arens was seeking to arrange a detailed dialogue with U.S. Secretary of Defense Cheney and the American establishment on preparations for war. Arens wasn't very happy with what he was getting. He was getting a pat on the back and was assured: "Don't worry, we're looking into this problem." It is in the nature of Israelis in such circumstances to want to have the United States speaking to their needs. You can do that at a professional, technical level: our attachés speaking with their Israeli military counterparts. However, the feeling that Minister of Defense Arens and his associates had was that they were being left behind and aside and being regarded as just another irritant by officials who were trying to manage these problems.

Iraq was viewed not only as anti-Semitic and anti-Israeli but was also viewed, over the years, as a particularly virulent threat to Israel. That is important to bear in mind. The Israelis had had a certain respect, or even anxiety, for many years about the Iraqis, much more than they felt about the Saudis. The Israelis tended to view the Saudis as weak and corrupt, and potentially dangerous because the Saudis had the money to fund Yasser Arafat and many other Arab radicals, like Assad of Syria, in the Middle Eastern region. However, the Israelis did not consider the Saudis as a fighting, expansionist threat to Israel. Iraq was a different story.

There remained—and still remains today—a strong, Israeli, strategic concern about the possibility that Iraq, under Saddam Hussein or anybody else, could easily overwhelm Jordan. From Baghdad it is an easy five-hundred kilometer distance to Amman, Jordan, and the Jordanian regime was, and remains, relatively weak. It has a nice little army, but it couldn't stand up against a massive, mechanized attack. So, the Israelis, both for political and propaganda purposes—as well as on the basis of their own strategic analyses—were, and remain, very concerned about the possibility of an Iraqi takeover of Jordan and of the possibility of the Iraqis appearing one day, in mechanized strength, at the edge of the Jordan Valley between Israel and Jordan.

On August 2, 1990, Saddam Hussein invaded Kuwait. Now the fat was really in the fire, and with it, Israeli Defense Minister Arens intensified Israeli requests for a coordinated effort to deal with the situation. When you got down to the nitty-gritty, what the Israelis wanted was better intelligence on the location of

Iraqi missiles which might be used to attack Israel. We had done some over-flights of suspected missiles in northern Iraq. On their own, as well as through intelligence exchanges with the U.S, the Israelis knew that the Iraqis had moved SCUD missiles, some of them fixed and some of them mobile, to what were called the "H2" and "H3" airfields in northern Iraq. From these positions a modified SCUD would have the range to hit Israel.

As time went on, the Israelis, by one means or another, developed the intelligence that not only there were these missiles in northern Iraq, but that the missile deployments were increasing. The missiles were pointed at Tel Aviv or Haifa. So, there was a lot of activity on the part of the Iraqis going on in northern Iraq, concurrently with other things. The Iraqis occupied Kuwait in a rather brutal way. So, Arens' requests increased, and now what he wanted was very specific. He wanted live, real-time intelligence on what was going on there. He wanted photographs of the targets, which would enable sophisticated recipients of these photographs like the Israelis to pinpoint Iraqi targets.

The U.S. was not providing this information to the Israelis. We were talking about intelligence exchanges in more generalized terms. We were saying that the Iraqi missiles were deployed in northern Iraq, but we were not providing the Israelis with specific, reconnaissance photographs of either the H2 and H3 SCUD missiles, either fixed or mobile, or anything else, out of fear that the Israelis might go overboard and resort to some preemptive action against these targets.

All of the Israeli requests for information, which we began to receive in April, 1990, intensified during the summer of that year. Secretary of Defense Cheney was polite and friendly in response to Israeli Defense Minister Arens, but he continued to "stiff arm" these requests. The arms-length approach continued, as the summer wore on.

So, Arens and company were pressing for target reconnaissance photography as part of a live, real-time intelligence exchange. Trips were being made back and forth. The administration of President Bush and Secretary of State Baker was saying, in effect: "Look, we'll manage this. We'll certainly keep Israeli interests in mind. However, don't muck things up, don't do anything preemptive. Let us go about our efforts to form a Grand Coalition against Iraq."

When President Bush committed troops to Saudi Arabia, we witnessed the extensive, continuing buildup called "Desert Shield." When the Israelis looked at this enormous buildup, they continued their efforts by proposing a direct relationship with Gen. Norman Schwarzkopf. This was turned down flat. We said that we would manage this relationship through Washington and that we would give the Israelis what was necessary. However, we made clear that we would manage it our own way.

I can remember situations when Arens was pressing me, along with Washington agencies, for a commitment to provide target photos of Iraq. As I knew what the Washington line was, I was saying, "Will you promise not to attack the Iraqis?" In other words, now that we were where we were, would the Israelis give us such a commitment? Of course, Arens wouldn't do so. I would then have to report his refusal to provide such a commitment.

Remember that the atmosphere at times was clouded by other, extraneous issues. For instance, we were upset about the Israeli relationship with South Africa, as we had been for some time. There had been developing in South Africa a missile program which progressed so far that we could anticipate the deployment of missiles in South Africa which, shall we say, had a remarkable likeness to the Israeli-developed "Jericho" missile. We were aware of big contracts involving large amounts of money. I had already previously broached this subject with Israeli Minister of Defense [Yitzhak] Rabin and, later, with Minister of Defense Arens. The Israelis do not take kindly to such approaches. They told us that they had no nuclear cooperation arrangements with the South Africans. They told us that these were well-paying contracts which had to do with conventional matters related to space exploration but not matters involving mass destruction or nuclear weapons.

Well, we were very concerned about this. From time to time, I would make strong démarches on this subject. These were not appreciated, particularly when I made them at this time, as Desert Shield was going on. Either under instructions or not under instructions, I also raised with the Israelis their technological exchanges with the People's Republic of China, because I felt so strongly on the subject. We were aware, over time, that the Israelis had been providing the People's Republic of China with fairly sophisticated technology. As an example, I might mention the Python weapons system. The Python is an air-to-air missile developed by the Israelis which gives them a BVR [beyond visual range] capability to acquire and hit an aerial target. This makes it a deadly and very important advance in aerial warfare. I told Arens that this kind of equipment could change the balance of forces over the Taiwan Straits. I told him that Israel should not be doing this. There were some spirited exchanges with Arens over that matter as well. Again, Arens was particularly irritated that we were raising this subject, given the Iraqi problem. I guess that he felt that it was inappropriate. We didn't think so. These were issues which came up concurrently, and as an old "China hand," I was particularly zeroed in on the Python air-to-air missile and let this be known.

By December 1990, the buildup was so enormous that I would say that Arens and the Israeli defense establishment had concluded that: (a) Saddam Hussein, who was so awfully stupid in so many ways, would probably not back down; and that (b) the U.S. was now so publicly committed to combat this massive, growing presence in the Middle East that we wouldn't back down, either. Indeed, we finally got a UN resolution approved which set January 15, 1991, as a deadline for an Iraqi pullout from Kuwait, "or else."

I would like to pause at this point and describe a vignette which took place in early December, 1990. This involved a very painful experience for me in highlighting the dilemma which I felt at the time. In the midst of this enormous buildup in the Gulf area and all these Iraqi actions—including the invasion of Kuwait and the butchery that Iraqi forces perpetrated and the revelations of what the Iraqis had done, one weekend in December, 1990—I received information that the Iraqis had just launched what appeared to be two or three SCUD missiles from the area around Basra in southeastern Iraq. It was expected that they would impact at a range of around five-hundred kilometers from the point at which they had been fired. Had these missiles been fired from H2 or H3, their line of flight would have taken these missiles directly to the Tel Aviv/Haifa area. This information was obviously of enormous import to us and to Israeli as a likely target.

I immediately charged my defense attaché and my CIA chief of station with getting clearance from Washington to pass this information to the Israelis. I tried to obtain clearance myself over the secure telephone available to me in the embassy in Tel Aviv. I think that this happened on a Saturday or a Sunday, I can't remember which. Certainly, it was over a weekend. We could not get any action out of Washington. We tried repeatedly, through different channels, but, over and over again, we were stonewalled. I was really pressing my CIA chief of station and my defense attaché for action. It was obvious that the necessary clearance from Washington had to come through one or both of those channels. My staff tried repeatedly to obtain clearance to pass this information but could not get it.

At this time, a Senator was visiting in Israel. Maybe it was Senator Orrin Hatch [Republican, Utah]. He was due to see Israeli Minister of Defense Arens that evening at about six p.m. local time. I was scheduled to accompany Senator Hatch on this call. I pressed all day long in anticipation of the meeting with the defense minister that evening. I hoped that I would receive authorization to pass on this vital intelligence information of deadly import to Israel. I thought of this problem in terms of our main objective of keeping the Israelis "on the reservation" and not doing anything—by commission or omission—which might prompt the Israelis to launch a preemptive strike against Iraq. That could have been disastrous at that stage to the coalition against Iraq and our more general objectives in the area. All day, this process went on of trying to obtain clearance to pass the information to the Israelis. No reply was obtained. Our defense attaché was specifically prohibited from passing this information to the Israelis until clearance was obtained from Washington.

The meeting came between Israeli Defense Minister Arens with Senator Orrin Hatch. Arens gave a very serious briefing on the overall situation and his desire for the "right kind" of help and so forth. As the meeting broke up, I asked for the opportunity to meet separately with Defense Minister Arens. We said good-bye to Senator Hatch, who left, accompanied by another embassy officer. Arens took me into his office, and we were there alone. I sat down and said, "Have you got a map of Iraq handy?" He picked up his phone and asked to arrange to have someone bring a map of Iraq. It was remarkable how long it took, at least five or ten minutes before the map was brought. This was a rather strained period. Obviously, Arens was looking at me, wondering why the American ambassador was asking him for a map of Iraq. Finally, the map appeared. The officer who brought it left Arens' office. We spread the map out on his desk. I said to him words to the following effect, "Look, my friend, I am putting my testicles in your hands. There has been, I am sure, a misunderstanding. You are going to get this information. It's just that it's a weekend, and you know how it is on a weekend in Washington, so that formal clearance hasn't come, but I'm sure that it will come. Don't jump to the wrong conclusion." I pointed to Basra on the map and said, "The fact is that the Iraqis have just launched, today, two or three missiles from about here to about there (I pointed to the two places concerned) on about a five-hundred kilometer trajectory. This was a launch within Iraqi territory on a north-westerly trajectory from here to here," I said (pointing to the map), "impacting around there." It didn't take Arens long to figure out that that was the approximate distance from H2 or H3 to Tel Aviv. I emphasized that I was sure that Arens would get this information through regular, security channels anyway, but I just wanted him to know of this development.

As I said this, internally, I was sweating bullets. I was very security conscious and very much aware of the clearances in process and all of that. However, I just felt that this had to be done if we were going to maintain a semblance of confidence and trust in achieving our main objective which, as I said, was to keep the Israelis away from launching a preemptive strike at Iraq and "keeping them on the reservation." I left Arens' office at about six-thirty or seven p.m. My defense attaché called me and said, "You're 'clean,' because the clearance has just come through."

As the crisis mounted, naturally enough, we began to develop embassy plans for reducing the size of our staff radically. In the wake of the Iranian disaster of 1979 [when the embassy in Tehran was seized by revolutionaries], I swore to myself that if I ever became a chief of mission or had any power of decision over the matter, I would devise a plan under which I could run an embassy with five people. I would reduce the embassy complement to consist of the ambassador, a communicator, a consular officer, and an administrative officer or two. I would reduce the embassy to the bone.

This situation in Israel was not the same kind of situation we had faced in Iran. However, I developed a plan for progressive, staged reductions in staff. As I tried to obtain approval for this plan from the Department, over the secure phone, I ran into a stone wall of opposition in Washington. When I pieced the various bits and pieces together, I concluded that Washington didn't want the image of Americans leaving Israel to be displayed. They didn't want it for a variety of reasons. They didn't want it in general and they certainly didn't want it as it might affect Saudi Arabia, where there was an enormous American presence working in the oilfields and in support of facilities in what was the crux of the operations, Desert Shield and Desert Storm. There were surely other political considerations as well.

You can draw all kinds of lines, including voluntary departure and the guidelines for it, the departure of non-essential people, and, in the last analysis, the directed departure of personnel. I struggled over this problem. I didn't think that at this stage it was useful to talk about the rhetoric of the matter. However, I say that we had a really, potentially serious situation in this regard. If Saddam Hussein used these weapons of terror, directed against civilian populations, and if we did not get "unnecessary" people including wives, babies, other dependents, and eventually non-essential officers out of here, we would be leaving ourselves wide open to all kinds of severe criticism. People might say, "You had all of this time. Why didn't you send some of your personnel home?"

There were differences of opinion within our official American community. My wife, Helen, being a gung-ho Foreign Service spouse, said: "I'm not going anywhere." However, a little later, after the first Iraqi SCUD missiles fell, I said to her, "You're going to Eilat" [on the Gulf of Aqaba], because we had figured out that the SCUDs couldn't reach Eilat. I said, "You're going down there. You're going to be a model and you're going to lead a bus convoy." She vigorously objected, but finally agreed. She took our cat and led a convoy of embassy dependents down to Eilat, where we had leased hotel space for the period of the conflict.

Meanwhile, many dual-citizen Israeli-Americans were swamping the airlines to get reservations to leave Israel. There were strong opinions within Israel on this score. I certainly don't want to point the finger at anybody. These were highly emotional, personal decisions, but they certainly kept our Consular Section busy as people rushed to check their visas, get their passports renewed, and leave while they could do so.

Israeli Television occasionally would cover people with long beards and black hats, going up the ramp of an aircraft and into a plane. That was unfortunate in terms of the development of a possibly critical stereotype. That is, it was thereby suggested not only that ultra-religious Jews did not fight or contribute to defending Israel, but now that they were "bugging out."

Early on the morning of January 17, 1991, the word came that the Gulf War had started. A massive bombardment of Iraq had begun. Not too long after that, I was on the telephone to Washington. I was operating out of my residence and had a very significant number of people with me, all with gas masks, and so forth. My residence was also sealed with plastic sheeting, etc. As an old artillery man, I picked up the phone and reported to Washington, "We're taking incoming fire." I heard several, loud explosions. My teams were reporting. I can't remember whether it was the first or the second report, because the response of the Operations Center in the Department was, "Yes, we're seeing it on CNN!" CNN and other networks had set up their cameras. They couldn't identify where these explosions were occurring, for security reasons. However, they could give a pretty graphic account of what was happening. Israeli TV itself was on for twenty-four hours a day. We were off to war.

We began to operate on a twenty-four hour basis. It turned out that Iraq launched, I believe, thirty-nine SCUDs throughout the period of hostilities. Most of these were launched in the direction of Tel Aviv and some to Haifa. In all cases, they were grossly inaccurate, but then they were a weapon aimed at spreading mass terror, anyway.

The SCUD explosions had a shattering effect in residential areas. Groups of apartments were damaged or destroyed. Israelis generally live in apartment houses. Most of these apartments had been built in the 1950s or '60s. They had Venetian blinds and were fairly frail and vulnerable to over-pressure waves (which exceeded atmospheric pressure). There were a lot of caved-in apartments, some of them dramatically so. When you would drive by the site of an explosion, you would see half a building sheared away, with beds and other furniture hanging out. A lot of windows were blown out. However, the number of direct casualties was miraculously low. It was said afterwards that only one person was directly killed by a SCUD missile. Some people were wounded, and then you get into the question of whether they were directly wounded or were wounded by the debris from the explosion. The anger among the people at these SCUD missile attacks, of course, rose very high. Washington felt it necessary to rush Larry Eagleburger and Paul Wolfowitz back to Israel. Israeli Minister of Defense Arens was telling Secretary of Defense Cheney, "Now we've been attacked. I propose not to sit here and 'take it.' We have developed plans to counter these attacks. We plan to use a corridor through Jordan to make these counterattacks." In reply to this, Secretary Cheney would go into a convoluted stand off and say: "Look, President Bush is trying to reach Prime Minister [Yitzhak] Shamir, so I don't have the authority to say anything. However, you know that you wouldn't want to do anything that would cause us to take extra American casualties." Arens would say, "Well, what about our casualties? We have these plans and we intend to implement them."

Although these Israeli plans were never revealed to us in detail, it didn't take a genius to figure out that the Israelis would go after the H2 and H3 airfield complexes. In Israeli style, they wouldn't necessarily rely on air attacks alone. The more common Israeli response to such a target, from which potential death and destruction were being rained on them, would be to go in with commandos. They clearly had that capability with their C-130 transport aircraft. They had their whole commando training and ethos. So, although none of these Israeli plans was ever revealed to me or, I believe, to our defense attachés, it seemed obvious that the Israelis had that sort of thing in mind.

President Bush spoke several times with Prime Minister Shamir over the secure telephone and Eagleburger and Wolfowitz came over to Israel. By this time, the Iraqi attacks on Israel, Arens had reversed course in one sense. Just before the war began, we had been training Israelis to man and operate what were called Patriot anti-missile batteries made in the U.S. These were not really anti-missile batteries. They were really anti-aircraft batteries, with the promise or hope or prayer—or all three—that the relevant software would be upgraded that they could deal with incoming missiles. Handling a high-speed jet aircraft is one thing. Handling an incoming missile traveling at missile speeds is a different matter. The Patriot missiles would go up one-hundred miles or so in the atmosphere and then come down at you. This was a different matter, as we were to find out. To the initial offer of some second-hand F-15 fighters and a couple of batteries of manned Patriot missiles. Arens initially said, "No. We defend ourselves. Nobody has ever come in here to defend us." However, his own people were still in training on Patriot missiles in the United States. With the outbreak of war and the problem of incoming SCUD missiles, Arens reversed course and said, "Okay. Send in the Patriot missiles." So, in came several batteries of U.S. manned, Patriot missiles, carried on C-5 transport aircraft and by other means.

They were a sight to behold. It was the first time in Israeli history that the Israeli Defense Forces stood aside and let the armed forces of another nation, in this case the U.S., come in and defend Israel. The Patriot crews were made up of magnificent young men and women, because Patriot batteries and the structure of our forces were such that women were also operating this weapons system. The women were mostly enlisted personnel, but I think that there were a couple of women officers as well.

As the first Patriot missile batteries were fired in Israel, they were in an automatic release mode. There were whole barrages of Patriot missiles fired up into the sky against these incoming SCUDs. Cheers went up from me and all of those present who watched them. "Hurrah," we shouted. The Patriots went up, and then you'd hear thunderous explosions. Washington was reporting a fantastic "kill" capability by the Patriot missiles. President Bush himself went to the Raytheon factory and spoke to the workers there. I received the text of President Bush's remarks at the Raytheon factory. He claimed that we had had something like a ninety-five percent "kill" rate.

Well, this turned out to be absolute rubbish! When the Gulf War was over, it didn't take long before the Israelis at the professional level turned from cheering, to very serious skepticism, to outright disillusionment. As the Israelis were taking their own photos of the interface between our outgoing Patriots and the incoming SCUDs, and then the aftermath, they determined that, at best, we might have hit one SCUD out of the thirty-nine fired at Israel. Most of the rest of the SCUDs landed in Israel. Now, fortunately, they were terribly inaccurate. Some of them landed in the Mediterranean Sea. Frantic efforts were being made at the software level to "upgrade" the upgrade of the Patriot package. We would hear rumors that the American batteries of Patriot missiles in Saudi Arabia (which did intercept some SCUDs) had better software packages than those in Israel. We had to assure the Israelis that our SCUD batteries, and the batteries assigned to Israel in particular, had the latest features. There was an awful lot of diplomacy being conducted at the political-military level. There were Israeli military personnel stationed in all of our Patriot missile fire direction centers, so that they could absorb, first hand, exactly how we were handling the missiles. We had men and women military people in the Israeli fire direction centers; as a result, there was a very warm feeling between military personnel of the two countries.

With all of this activity came an influx of people from Congress. American politicians were "oh-so-eager" to be photographed with American troops in action, defending Israel in a common effort. I had a flood of essentially pro-Israeli visitors, ranging from Senators and Congressmen to Mayor Dinkins of New York. We had to suit up each and every one of these gentlemen with gas masks and brief them, upon their arrival at Ben Gurion International Airport.

In the middle of all of this I got a call from Washington, asking me to go in and arrange for the release of a prominent Palestinian academic who had been picked up by Israeli security authorities and was behind bars. I went to a meeting with Yusip Ben Aron, the Director General of the Israeli prime minister's office, and Eli Rubenstein, the secretary of the Israeli cabinet. I said, "Washington has instructed me to ask you to release this gentleman." They were livid! In essence, they said, "Like hell!" I said, "What's the matter?" They said, "Look, this guy, with his cellular phone, was in contact with the PLO [Palestinian Liberation Organization] in Tunis, talking to a fellow Palestinian during the Gulf War." The Palestinians were already using cell phones for communicating with places abroad, including the PLO crowd in Tunis. They said that he was in conversation with a friend in Tunis, who then said, "Listen, I've got a friend here who'd like to have a word with you." That person then got on the phone and asked this Palestinian where the SCUD missiles were hitting. This person was the Iraqi ambassador in Tunis.

This academic, according to Eli Rubenstein and Yusip Ben Aron, said, "Well, they hit here and there." Eli and Yusip then indulged in some obscenities and said, "That SOB is behind bars, and that's where he belongs." I said, "Gentlemen, first of all, you know and I know that he was talking 'hot air.' He had no more idea than the man in the moon or the average person on the street as to where, specifically, this or that SCUD hit. This guy was a resident of Jerusalem, and no SCUD missiles hit up here. So, the guy was 'blowing gas,' OK? Secondly, from your viewpoint such conduct is atrocious. On the other hand, let's say that it was stupid and dumb. However, come on, I realize that this was most unfortunate behavior, but let him go." Well, the Israelis weren't about to let him go, though eventually, they did release him.

The Israeli armed forces were on a full alert. Israeli Minister of Defense Arens was making it very clear, without giving specific details, that the Israeli forces had practiced and drilled and were "rarin' to go" against the airfields at H2 and H3 in Iraq. All that Arens was waiting for was the go-ahead signal.

I spoke with an Israeli general afterwards. There were differences of view among professional Israeli military officers, let alone the division between Prime Minister Shamir and Arens. Arens was pressing Shamir to give him the green light to attack the airfields at H2 and H3, using a corridor through Jordan. This meant that, if the Jordanians tried to stand in the way, there was a strong likelihood of a conflict between the Israeli and Jordanian defense establishments.

President Bush was personally prevailing on Prime Minister Shamir not to do this. Arens and company were therefore constantly increasing the pressure on us to give them more information so that they could satisfy themselves that we were doing everything we could. With this, over time, came mounting criticism from the Israelis of our efforts against the H2 and H3 airfields. The Israelis said to us, "If you're devoting all of this effort, why isn't it working? If you can't do the job, well, we're giving you notice that we intend to do it, one way or another." However, Arens was being thwarted by his own prime minister, who was so much influenced by President Bush.

Moreover, it turns out that there were those within the Israeli Defense Forces who were saying to Arens, "Look, the Americans are doing our job. The net effect of all of this effort is to damage the Iraqi military capability. So, strategically speaking, one of our two or three mortal enemies is being pounded by the Americans. Strategically, that is happening. In that sense, the Americans are doing our overall work for us. They've been pounding Baghdad on a sustained basis, for 40 days and nights, in a way that we can't do. So why do we have to go to the second alternative? If we go through the Jordanian corridor and into H2 and H3, we will encounter a high degree of risk, as far as Israeli casualties are concerned."

Through it all, as far as my own analysis is concerned, I felt that Prime Minister Shamir's reaction, in yielding top Bush's arguments and requests, was surprising. However, had a SCUD missile hit a hospital, a school, or a major group of civilians, or a barracks like the one in Saudi Arabia, where we lost some twenty Americans killed and, perhaps, ninety wounded, if the Israelis had taken that kind of a hit, who knows? I don't think that, in such a case, Shamir could have restrained the Israeli military any longer. It was really a remarkable response by Shamir in overruling his defense minister.

After the SCUD missile attacks were over, the Israelis joined in the cheering. President George Bush and Secretary of State James Baker were regarded as heroes worldwide and in Israel as well. Together with Gen. Norman Schwarzkopf, all of them were hailed as great heroes. A great deal of camaraderie and so forth emerged from the Gulf War. Eventually, the American Patriot missiles were withdrawn from Israel, to great cheers. The Chief of Staff of the U.S. Air Force came to Israel. When he came, he delivered a grand briefing to the Israeli professional establishment. He had a surprise when he landed at Ben Gurion International Airport in his chief of staff's airplane. He arrived with a bevy of colonels, including Colonel Buster Clausson, who had been the director of the bombing effort for General Schwarzkopf. Toward the end of the list of visiting generals, colonels, lieutenant colonels, and majors, a young captain appeared before me, wearing a mustache. It took me a while to realize that it was my son! He had been a B-52 pilot and now was stationed in Saudi Arabia, flying a VIP [Very Important Person] aircraft for Ambassador Chas Freeman and General Schwarzkopf! When the Air Force Chief of Staff learned that my son was in Saudi Arabia, without my knowledge, he had him join the party in Turkey and they flew into Israel.

The Israelis were intensely interested in the professional briefing on how the air war had been conducted. I will say this: it was a magnificent effort. Colonel Clausson and company were superbly equipped by virtue of experience, training, and background to handle it. Very few, if any, air forces in the world could have done this sort of thing.

As far as our handling of Saddam Hussein and all of that is concerned, Prime Minister Shamir was quoted as saying that he almost fell off his chair when he realized that we weren't going after Saddam Hussein and Baghdad. This is not the Israeli style. The Israeli style, as I said before, is to go for the jugular vein and get a firm grasp on it, then squeeze it and bring your adversary not only to a military capitulation, but to a political settlement as well.

I would imagine that the Israelis were agog, not so much at the military portion of the Gulf War, when General Schwartzkopf dictated the terms, but rather the political aspect, where, as Ambassador Chas Freeman points out, we ended the war without any direct, political commitment by Saddam Hussein to treat with us. Ever afterwards, the decisions that followed were unilateral UN Security Council Resolutions, which were terribly important, but to which Saddam Hussein and his propaganda apparatus said, "We never agreed to this." They took the view that the war was over and that we were punishing them unilaterally on the basis of non-fulfillment of something that they never agreed to in the first place.

Imagine what would have been the situation if the Israelis had attacked H2 and H3, not only by air attacks but with ground troops consisting of a commando force! You can bet your bottom dollar that they would have had an extended stay. There would have been a tremendous commotion within the coalition, and especially in Washington, and a great deal of heartburn at the Israeli reluctance to leave the H2 and H3 area. If they had seized that area—perhaps with significant Israeli casualties—they might very well, in Israeli style, have held on unless and until the Iraqi Government came to terms with them. That could have been excruciatingly painful and highly embarrassing for us, given the way that we handled the end of the Gulf War.

9

Challenges Ahead

In 1945, following the end of World War II, the U.S. Foreign Service entered a golden age. Virtually irrelevant during the war and but a minor player prior to it, its core of professional foreign affairs officers, however, stood ready to give its expertise to help guide America in its new role as a world leader. In the words of Secretary of State Dean Acheson, they were "present at the creation." The Cold War then began with total involvement of the Foreign Service until the fall of Communism in the USSR and its allied "puppets," in 1990. The twentieth century's last decade saw the U.S. play a leading role in the expansion of democratic and capitalist philosophies and systems.

Despite this ideological victory for U.S. foreign policy, there still exist forces in the world that require careful monitoring and wise and experienced managing in the diplomatic arena. These problem areas include aspects of nationalism and religious fundamentalism at home and abroad, relatively new issues such as the environment, international crime, and narcotics use and trafficking, and more traditional questions such as protecting American commercial interests, overseeing economic responses to international crises, and fostering world health and development. Who in the U.S. Government is going to play a major role in managing these international concerns effectively, if not its Foreign Service?

TERRORISM AND INSURGENCY

On September 11, 2001, an extremist Islamic faction, al Qaeda, led by Osama bin Laden, launched murderous attacks against New York City and Washington, DC, killing almost three thousand people. There had already been attacks by the same group against two U.S. embassies in East Africa and an American destroyer off the Arabian peninsula. The rulers in Afghanistan, the Taliban, had given a home to the al Qaeda movement despite warnings from American diplomats that if they did not expel these dangerous guests they would be held responsible for whatever the terrorists might do. Following the September 11 attacks, the United States, with the support of the international community, put troops into Afghanistan. Along with anti-Taliban Afghan forces, these troops overthrew the Taliban regime and forced members of al Qaeda to flee. American diplomats were quickly on the ground in Afghanistan to help that country recover from the repressive rule of the Taliban extremists.

Immediately following the successful military campaign in Afghanistan, the civilian leaders of the Bush administration saw Iraq as a source of terrorism and threat to the United States because of its suspected possession of weapons of mass destruction. Here a serious rift opened between the professional diplomats of the State Department and the civilian leadership of the Defense Department and the White House. Those in the Foreign Service, particularly those who had served in the Middle East or dealt with it in Washington, were warning that an attack on Iraq without substantial international support could cause significant and unnecessary strains among U.S. allies in Europe and Asia and thus lower the esteem and influence of the United States in a whole series of international relationships.

In general, American FSOs also strongly questioned the optimistic planning of the civilian leaders of the Pentagon, who envisioned a quick and easy transition to democracy in the troubled, fractionalized, and war-torn country. These alerts, based on the historic realities of Iraq and its neighbors, proved accurate. A chaotic situation faced American occupation forces after a short, successful military campaign. It is noteworthy that a retired Foreign Service officer replaced a retired general as the American proconsul in Baghdad.

In Iraq and elsewhere over recent years, the professionals in the American Foreign Service and the U.S. military have grown to work together in harmony, having learned the importance of cooperation in the political/military equation from deadly experiences in Vietnam, the Balkans and Africa. Any administration learns that ignoring the advice of its professionals, diplomatic and military is done at its own peril.

More than ever, American citizens traveling and residing abroad count on services administered by consular officers. This need has sky-rocketed in the face of actions by terrorists who are aiming violence against Americans. Citizens need U.S. officials not only to renew expired passports, but to warn them of danger and help them in times of trouble.

The consuls also adjudicate visas to aliens who wish to come to America. This service follows Congressional laws nearly a century old. Other U.S. officials are ever more involved at home and abroad with this operation. The visa function has become a matter of controversy in the fight against terrorism. There is justified concern that potential terrorists will enter the United State by obtaining non-immigrant visas under false pretenses. On the other hand, too rigid and restrictive requirements for entry into the U.S. will discourage legitimate visitors from coming to America. During the decades following World War II there has been a steady flow of foreign students who have come to study at American schools and colleges. When these young men and women return to their native countries they have proved to be some of our staunchest friends. If we do not take care of this pool of support and friendship for the United States, it will dry up and the students will go elsewhere.

STRUCTURE AND POLICY

Political leaders, elected and appointed, will continue to formulate overall U.S. foreign policy; it will remain the duty of the FSOs to support and implement that policy. There are, however, fast-breaking situations which require immediate decisions or actions. Here the professionals of the Foreign Service are key players. There also are policies that seem to be perfectly sound from the vantage point of Washington, DC, but will not work in certain foreign countries or societies. Here again, the advice of those who know such countries from personal experience comes into play. For men and women who want to participate in the formulation and carrying out of American foreign policy, and who are willing to undergo the discipline and demands of the Foreign Service, the prospects are bright.

Throughout the entire post-WWII/Cold War period, the officer corps of the Foreign Service never exceeded five-thousand, and it is unlikely to expand much beyond that number in the foreseeable future. This number includes the October 1, 1999, integration of the United States Information Agency and the Arms Control and Disarmament Agency into the State Department. The Foreign Service will remain a small, elite corps with an influential role in the projection of American influence abroad. However, as a sobering balance, American diplomats abroad and at home in the Department of State and associated foreign affairs agencies will have to convince the American public, Congress, and changing administrations of their worth so that they can continue their work in promoting American interests and trying to make the world a better place.

At the beginning of the twenty-first century, diverse special interest groups in the United States have continued to emerge, each with its own foreign affairs goals and domestic political clout. Their initiatives can have a detrimental impact on a rational, unemotional American foreign policy and therefore affect the role of the Foreign Service. During the twentieth century, Irish, Jewish, Cuban and Greek ethnic lobbies, for example, developed in the United States and became powerful in influencing American interests in their respective areas of concern, sometimes not to the nation's real interest. This resulted in tilts in American foreign policy. The twenty-first century may see the rise of comparable Asian, African-American, and Hispanic lobbies in the United States.

THE FUTURE OF THE FOREIGN SERVICE

As the twenty-first century moves on, the Foreign Service faces numerous tests in regions around the world. Ethnic disputes in the Balkans, the Kurdish areas of Iraq, Iran, and Turkey, and the Caucasus and Central Asia will draw the United States in as mediators. China, with one quarter of the world's population, an energetic people, and growing participation in the world economy, could have a very fruitful relationship with the U.S. Muslim extremists in Pakistan and the Hindu nationalist movement in India have created a confrontation between the two states that requires skillful diplomacy to defuse. Many call for a policy that will bring Russia more solidly into the democratic and economically stable camp. The Israel and Palestine issue remains a problem without a solution. Water, population pressures, resource sharing, and inequities in power are some of the possible sources of further trouble between the Israelis and Palestinians.

Issues that transcend government-to-government relations also will dominate the world diplomatic scene. Among these are the environment, health, over-population, terrorism, crime/narcotics, and religious extremism. For example, AIDS [Acquired Immune Deficiency Syndrome] is a major pandemic, particularly in Africa, and will require the United States and other developed countries to make a concerted effort to curb or stop it. Diplomacy will play a key role in sensing and implementing the proper methods of assistance, cooperation, and enforcement to end this scourge. The Foreign Service is already working on these issues and training a new cadre of officers who are versed in matters that were not even dreamt of when the first generation of "cold warriors" came out of the Department of State's Foreign Service Institute in the 1940s and 1950s. Petroleum was a major issue in the last fifty years and petroleum officers were trained. Water may well be the issue of the next fifty years and the Foreign Service perhaps should start training water officers.

All of the various world issues generate well-informed, financed, and dedicated groups who work, often as private non-governmental organizations [NGOs], in all parts of the globe, with international and national bases. Many have highly qualified and experienced specialists on their staffs. The Foreign Service, in the future, will work even more closely with these organizations, despite the fact that some will be at counter-purposes with U.S. policy at any given time.

Preparing the Foreign Service officer for the twenty-first century has challenged the Department of State's Foreign Service Institute. Officers and staff are being trained in the latest developments in computers and their use; in management policy; in political, economic, consular, administrative and public diplomacy; and in foreign assistance areas. At present, dealing with terrorism has prime priority. There are courses available in negotiation, leadership, how to work in international organizations and a host of foreign languages. Today's Foreign Service has a selection of over sixty languages, including Arabic, Hebrew, Xhosa, Azerbaijani, and Swahili.

As part of the training, there are frequently scheduled war games in which senior officials of the Departments of State and Defense, CIA, and other agencies test actions-reactions of officers faced, for example, with war in a volatile area, the cutoff of vital supplies such as oil, or continuing major terrorist attacks in various countries.

The Foreign Service will continue to support and promote democracy throughout the world. It is an article of faith in American government circles that democracies do not fight each other, or at least very rarely, that democracy breeds a better life for people, and that there is less unrest in a democracy. There is traditionally an evangelical side to American foreign policy: to promote a system that benefits the greatest number. That said, the American form of democracy, which this nation knows best, does not fit all countries. It will be part of the challenges to the Foreign Service's country experts to find the proper balance.

Concurrent with the promotion of democracy throughout the world is the promotion of human rights. For the last decades of the twentieth century, various administrations and Congress have given strong priority to the cause of human rights worldwide. At first, this was seen by other countries as a bothersome peculiarity of the American people: the United States was meddling in internal affairs. The Foreign Service gathered the data from its embassies and described the human rights situation country by country in annual reports given to Congress for publication. By dint of persistence and the justice of these reports, human rights have become an accepted standard by which countries are now measured. With the growth of international media and international organizations, countries which ignore human rights criticism suffer in the international arena. The

U.S. Foreign Service will continue to be a main reporter on human rights, thus having an influence transcending that of traditional diplomats of other nations.

With the creation of a new cabinet-level department, Homeland Security, there are some not fully defined areas of interaction with foreign affairs. Immigration to the United States has been affected with the transfer to different areas of functions of the Immigration and Naturalization Service. The alien applicant screening role in the visa office of the State Department is affected. There is also impact on the definition, within the authority of the Attorney General, of who is a potential threat to U.S. security. Other nations, especially Arab, question how this activity is carried out.

While the world in which the future Foreign Service works will be one of life-endangering changes and challenges, there is one certainty. The U.S. Foreign Service will be under attack by domestic political and media leaders for not remaking the world in the ways those leaders wish. There will be constant reorganizations of the Foreign Service with the hope that, by one method or another, American diplomats can keep the peace, restructure other governments in the image of the United States, and allow Congress and the American people to bask in untroubled prosperity without having to expend financial assistance or use the military. This hope will not be realized. However, the Foreign Service will continue to do its best to bring about a better world and serve American interests as its members have done since its creation in 1924. The adventure will continue.

Biographies

Achilles, Theodore C., b. New York 1905; Stanford and Yale Universities; Foreign Service 1931; served in Cuba, Italy, the United Kingdom, France; as ambassador to Peru 1956–1960; held senior positions in Department of State, largely in the Bureau of European Affairs; retired 1954; died 1986.

Barrington, Aldene Alice, b. Grand Forks, North Dakota 1902; University of North Dakota and Barnard College; taught English in Puerto Rico; Department of Commerce Commercial Service (which was later amalgamated with the Department of State Foreign Service); Department of State tours included Colombia, Brazil, and Argentina; retired 1966; died in 2003.

Bernbaum, Maurice, b. Illinois 1910; Harvard University 1931; graduate studies University of Chicago and Northwestern University; economist, U.S. Tariff Commission; Foreign Service 1936; served in Canada, Singapore, Nicaragua, Argentina; as ambassador to Ecuador 1960–1965 and to Venezuela 1965–1969; retired 1969.

Brown, William A., b. Massachusetts 1930; undergraduate degree, 1952, Ph.D. 1963 Harvard University; U.S. Marine Corps, active duty Korean War; Foreign Service 1956; served in Hong Kong, Taiwan, Singapore, Thailand, U.S.S.R., India, Israel; return tours to Thailand as ambassador 1985–1988; and to Israel 1988–1992 and 1994; chief, American Institute on Taiwan 1979; retired 1993.

Burns, John H., b. Oklahoma 1913; University of Oklahoma; congressional staff member; Foreign Service 1941; posts in Mexico, Brazil, Haiti, Germany; ambassador to Central African Republic 1961–1963, and to Tanzania 1965–1969; director general of Foreign Service 1969–1971; retired 1971.

Butrick, Richard, b. Lockport, New York 1894; U.S. Bureau of Fisheries; U.S. Auditor's Office; Georgetown University's first School of Foreign Service class; joined Department of State Consular Service 1921, served in Valparaiso,

Chile; following creation of Foreign Service 1924, served in China 1926–1942; return tour to Chile; the Philippines Iceland; as consul general in Montreal, Canada and in Sao Paulo, Brazil; inspector; director general of the Foreign Service 1949–1952; retired 1959; died 1997.

Carlucci, Frank C. III, b. Pennsylvania 1930; Princeton University; U.S. Navy; Foreign Service 1956, assignments included South Africa, Zaire, Tanzania, and Brazil, Office of Budget and Management; as ambassador to Portugal 1974–1978; White House chief of staff; secretary of defense; retired?????; currently in private sector.

Constable, Elinor, b. California 1934; Wellesley College; Foreign Service 1955; married a fellow Foreign Service officer, was compelled to resign in accordance with then-existing regulation; accompanied spouse to Spain, Honduras, Pakistan; rejoined Foreign Service 1973; specialized in economic affairs; served in Pakistan; as ambassador to Kenya 1986–1989; inspector; retired 1993.

Crawford, William R., b. Pennsylvania 1928; Harvard University; master's University of Pennsylvania; U.S. Navy; Foreign Service 1951; Arabic language officer; served in Lebanon, Aden, Morocco, Cyprus, Italy; as ambassador to Yemen 1972–1974 and to Cyprus 1974–1978; deputy assistant secretary for Near East, Department of State; retired 1979.

Dillon, Robert S., b. Illinois 1929; Duke University; U.S. Army; Foreign Service 1956; served in Venezuela, Turkish language officer with several tours Turkey; Italy, Malaysia, Egypt; as ambassador to Lebanon 1981–1983; retired 1988; later served four years as deputy commissioner general of the U. N. Works and Relief Agency for Palestinian Refugees in Vienna, Austria.

Dunnigan, Thomas J., b. Ohio 1921; John Carroll University; U.S. Army during World War II; Foreign Service 1946; assigned to Berlin until 1950; subsequent tours included United Kingdom, Philippines, Germany, twice to the Netherlands, Denmark, Israel; Organization of American States; retired 1994.

Erickson, Eldon E. B., b. Kansas 1919; U.S. Army; Kansas State Teachers' College; Foreign Service 1947; assigned to Mukden, China, during the Civil War 1948–1950; subsequent posts included Algeria, France, Laos, twice to Japan, Lebanon, Netherlands, Canada, West Germany; retired 1979.

Freeman, Charles W. Jr., b. Washington, DC 1943; Yale University; Foreign Service 1965; assignments included India, Taiwan, China, as Chinese Language officer, Thailand; ambassador to Saudi Arabia 1989–1992 (Iraqi invasion of Kuwait, ensuing Gulf War 1991); assistant secretary for international affairs, Department of Defense; retired 1994.

Gillespie, Charles Anthony Jr., b. California 1935; UCLA; U.S. Army four years: Foreign Service 1965; posted to Philippines, Indonesia, Mexico, Belgium; assigned to Latin American policy area, Department of State, dealing with occupation of Grenada; served as ambassador to Colombia, and to Chile; National Security Council staff responsible for Latin American affairs; retired 1993.

Green, Marshall, b. Massachusetts 1916; Yale University; special to Ambassador Joseph Grew in Japan 1939–1941; U.S. Navy World War II; Foreign Service 1945; posts included New Zealand, Sweden, South Korea; assistant secretary for East Asian-Pacific Affairs; ambassador to Indonesia 1965–1969 and Australia 1973–1975; retired 1977; died 1998.

Hart, Parker T., b. Massachusetts 1910; Dartmouth College 1933: master's degree Harvard University; Foreign Service 1938; served in Austria, Brazil, Egypt, Saudi Arabia; return tour to Egypt as deputy chief of mission during the Suez crisis in 1956; was consul general Damascus, Syria; return to Saudi Arabia as ambassador 1961–1965; ambassador to Turkey 1965–1968; assistant secretary of state for the Middle East; Director of the Foreign Service Institute 1969; retired 1969; died 1998; author of *Saudi Arabia and the United States: Birth of a Security Partnership*, Indiana University Press 1998.

Harvey, Constance R., b. Buffalo, New York 1904; Smith College, and master's degree Colombia University. Foreign Service 1929; served in Ottawa, Canada; Milan, Italy; Basel and Bern, Switzerland; was transferred to the American consulate general in Lyon, France, at outbreak of World War II, awarded Medal of Freedom for wartime work; later assignments included Greece, Germany; Strasbourg, France; retired 1965; died in 1997.

Hurwitz, Edward, b. New York City 1931; Cornell and Harvard Universities; U.S. Army in Korea; Foreign Service 1956; Department of State INR/Soviet Economics; staff aide in Moscow to Ambassador Jacob Beam 1958–1960;

Korean language training at Yale University and FSI school in Korea; subsequent assignments included four years Seoul, Korea; INR; Moscow, U.S.S.R.; Kabul, Afghanistan; as consul general Leningrad, U.S.S.R.; as ambassador to Kyrgistan 1992–1994; retired 1992.

Jenkins, Kempton B, b, Florida 1926; U.S. Navy World War II; Bowling Green State University; graduate studies Harvard and George Washington Universities; Foreign Service 1950; assignments included Germany; Thailand; Soviet Union; Venezuela; Soviet Desk, USIA; and at Department of Commerce; retired 1980.

Kennedy, Charles Stuart, b. Chicago, Illinois 1928; Williams College; U.S. Army four years, including service in the Korean War; master's degree Boston University; Foreign Service 1955; posts in Germany, Saudi Arabia, Yugoslavia, South Vietnam, Greece, South Korea, Italy, and Department of State; retired 1985; Director, Foreign Affairs Oral History Program for the Association for Diplomatic Studies and Training.

Kontos, C. William, b. Chicago, Illinois 1922; University of Chicago; London School of Economics; U.S.Army World War II; Foreign Service career included posts Greece, Sri Lanka, Nigeria, Pakistan, Lebanon, Sinai Support Mission; as ambassador to Sudan 1980–1983; Department of State Policy Planning Council, and South African Advisory Commission; retired in 1987; died 2000.

Landau, George W., b. Austria 1920; George Washington University; U.S. Army World War II; Foreign Service 1957; served in Uruguay; as ambassador to Paraguay 1972–1977, to Chile 1977–1982, and to Venezuela 1982–1985; retired 1985.

Laingen, Bruce, b. Minnesota 1922; St. Olaf College; U.S. Navy during World War II; master's degree University of Minnesota; Foreign Service 1950; and served in West Germany, Iran, Pakistan, Afghanistan; as ambassador to Malta 1976–1979; sent to Iran as chargé d'affaires during 1979 crisis, detained in hostage situation, released in 1981; served as deputy commandant National Defense University in Washington, DC; retired 1987; currently, president of the American Academy of Diplomacy.

Lutkins, LaRue R. b. New York 1919; Yale University; Foreign Service 1942; assignments included Cuba, Chinese language training, Kunming, China,; Malaya, Japan, Hong Kong, Ceylon; as consul general in Johannesburg, South Africa; retired 1976.

MacArthur, Douglas II. b. Pennsylvania 1909, Yale University; U.S. Army; Foreign Service 1935; assigned to Canada, Italy, France, Belgium; as Counselor of the State Department; as ambassador to Japan 1956–1961, to Belgium 1961–1965, to Austria 1967–1969, to Iran 1969–1972; retired 1972; died 1997.

Mahoney, Michael M., b. Massachusetts 1944; St. Michaels College; University of Wyoming graduate school; Peace Corps volunteer Liberia; Foreign Service 1971; assignments included Trinidad and Tobago, Athens, Greece; Bureau of Consular Affairs; Montreal, Canada; as director, Office of Citizens' Emergency Services 1987–1990; Office of Personnel, Department of State; as consul general Rome, Italy; retired 1995.

Martens, Robert J., b. Missouri 1925; U.S. Army World War II; University of Southern California; Foreign Service 1951; posts included Italy, Austria, U.S.S.R., Indonesia, Burma, Romania, Sweden, Department of State, inspection corps; retired 1984.

McCargar, James, b. San Francisco 1920; Stanford University; Foreign Service 1941; assigned to Moscow 1942, later Vladivostok, U.S.S.R.; Dominican Republic, Hungary, Italy, France; retired 1977.

McNamara, Francis Terry, b. Troy, New York 1927; U.S. Navy submarine service World War II; Syracuse University and Russell Sage College; U.S. Navy Korean War; Foreign Service 1956; served in Southern Rhodesia, the Congo, Tanzania, Zambia, two tours in Vietnam 1967–1971 and 1974–1975, Dahomey, Quebec City, Canada; as ambassador to Gabon 1982–1984; Lebanon during the civil war 1985–1987; as ambassador to Sao Tome and Principe 1989–1992; Cape Verde; retired 1992.

Melby, John, b. Portland, Oregon 1913; Illinois Wesleyan University, graduate studies University of Chicago; Foreign Service 1937; served in Juarez, Mexico; Caracas, Venezuela, U.S.S.R., China; author of "White Paper" on "loss" of

China; targeted during McCarthy loyalty investigation, resulting in unwarranted dismissal from Department of State; died 1992.

Morgan, William D., b. Rochester, New York 1925; U.S. Army World War II; University of Rochester, master's University of Maryland for studies at University of Paris (Sorbonne) France; State Department 1950, Foreign Service 1955; assignments included U.S. Delegation to NATO (USRO) Paris, France; Birmingham, United Kingdom; served in Moscow, U.S.S.R.; Department of State Soviet desk and other areas; was consul general in Beirut, Lebanon, in Paris, France, in Montreal, Canada; retired 1987; worked as volunteer supporting programs of Association of Diplomatic Studies and Training, co-authoring with Charles Stuart Kennedy: *U.S. Consul at Work*, Greenwood press.

Niles, Thomas N. T., b. Kentucky 1939; Harvard University and University of Kentucky; Foreign Service 1963; served in Department of State, Yugoslavia, U.S.S.R., Belgium; as ambassador to Canada 1985–1989; to NATO; to Greece 1993–1997; assistant secretary for European affairs; retired 1998.

Pell, Claiborne, b. New York 1918; Princeton University; U.S. Coast Guard World War II; Foreign Service 1946; posts included Czechoslovakia, Italy; Department of State; resigned 1950; U.S. senator from Rhode Island; chairman of the Senate Foreign Relations Committee; retired from Senate in 1996.

Rackmales, Robert, b. Baltimore, Maryland, 1937; Fulbright scholar West Germany; Johns Hopkins and Harvard Universities; Foreign Service 1963; assigned to Department of State Canadian desk; New York City Passport office; Zagreb, Yugoslavia; Department of State Albanian-Bulgarian desk; Mogadishiu, Somalia; as principal officer Trieste; Rome Italy as consul general Kaduna, Nigeria; as deputy chief of mission Belgrade, Yugoslavia 1987–1989; retired 1989.

Robert Service, b. China, American missionary parents 1909; Oberlin College; Foreign Service 1933; returned to China, continued service during World War II; assigned to American Embassy Chungking 1941, and as liaison officer to General Joseph Stilwell; as liaison officer with the official American mission at Chinese Communist headquarters Yenan 1944; targeted during McCarthy "loyalty" investigations, dismissed by Department of State 1952; reinstated 1958 when U.S. Supreme Court overturned dismissal charge; then assigned to Liverpool, United Kingdom; retired 1962; died 1999.

Stabler, Wells, b. Massachusetts 1919; Harvard University; Department of State 1942; Foreign Service 1946; assigned to Jerusalem until 1950; subsequently served at the U.N. Trusteeship Council, in Italy; Department of State Bureau of European Affairs; in France; Italy; as Ambassador to Spain 1975–1978; retired 1978.

Thompson, Richard S., b. Washington state 1933; University of Washington; master's degree Oxford University; U.S. Army; Foreign Service 1960. assignments included Netherlands West Indies, Niger, Vietnamese language training, Vietnam 1968–1972; Vietnam peace talks Paris 1972–1974; return tour Vietnam; Algeria; Department of State geographic bureaus; retired 1987.

Veliotes, Nicholas L., b. California 1928; University of California; U.S. Army; Foreign Service 1955; posted in Italy, India, Laos, Israel 1973; served as ambassador to Jordan 1978–1981, to Egypt 1983–1986; assistant secretary for Near Eastern affairs; retired 1986.

Watts, William, b. New York City 1930; Yale and Syracuse Universities, master's degree Harvard's Russian Regional Studies Program; served in Korea, U.S.S.R.,; Department of State Office of Asian Communist Affairs; National Security Council staff, resigned 1970 in protest to U.S. military incursions into Cambodia.

Wendt, E. Alan, b. Illinois 1935; Yale University; advanced degrees Harvard University and *l'Institut d'Etudes Politiques* in Paris; Foreign Service 1959; served at Department of State; in West Germany, Vietnam, Belgium, Egypt; as ambassador to Slovenia 1993–1995; retired 1995.

Bibliography

The following are published personal accounts by Foreign Service officers covering the first seventy-five years of the United States Foreign Service.

Allison, John M. *Ambassador from the Prairie or Allison in Wonderland.* Boston: Houghton Mifflin, 1973.

Asencio, Diego, and Nancy Asencio, with Ron Tobias. *Our Man is Inside.* Boston: Little, Brown, 1983.

Beam, Jacob. *Multiple Exposure: An American Ambassador's Unique Perspective on East-West Issues.* New York: Macmillan, 1978.

Beaulac, Willard Leon. *Career Ambassador.* New York: Macmillan, 1951.

Benedick, Richard E. *Ozone Diplomacy: New Direction in Safeguarding the Planet.* Cambridge, MA: Harvard University Press, 1991.

Bohlen, Charles E. *Witness to History: 1929–1969.* New York: W.W. Norton, 1973.

Briggs, Ellis O. *Farewell to Foggy Bottom: The Recollections of a Career Diplomat.* New York: D. McKay Company, 1964.

———. *Proud Servant: The Memoirs of a Career Ambassador.* Kent, OH: Kent State University Press, 1998.

Brown, Winthrop G. *Postmark Asia: Letters of an American Diplomat to his Family Written from India, Laos and Korea, 1957–1966.* Published by author, no date given.

Cabot, John Moors. *First Line of Defense: Forty Years Experiences of a Career Diplomat.* Washington, DC: School of Foreign Service, Georgetown University, 1979.

Cohen, Herman J. *Intervening in Africa: Superpower Peacemaking in a Troubled Continent*. London: Macmillan, 2000.

Cooper, J. Ford. *On the Finland Watch: An American Diplomat in Finland During the Cold War*. Claremont, CA: Regina Books, 2000.

Crane, Katharine. *Mr. Carr of State: Forty-Seven Years in the Department of State*. New York: St. Martin's Press, 1960.

Cross, Charles W. *Born a Foreigner: A Memoir of the American Presence in Twentieth Century Asia*. Boulder, CO: Rowman and Littlefield, 1999.

Davis, Nathaniel. *The Last Two Years of Salvador Allende*. Ithaca, NY: Cornell University Press, 1985.

Emmerson, John K. *The Japanese Thread: Thirty Years of Foreign Service*. New York: Holt, Rinehart, and Winston, 1978.

Grew, Joseph C. *Turbulent Era: A Diplomatic Record of Forty Years, 1904–1945*. 2 vols. Walter Johnson, ed. Boston: Little, Brown, 1940.

Groth, Edward M. *To Give Room for Wandering: the Autobiography of an American Foreign Service Officer*. Los Altos, CA: Pacifica Publishing Co., 1972.

Hart, Parker T. *Saudi Arabia and the United States: Birth of a Security Partnership*. Bloomington, IN: Indiana University Press, 1998.

———. *Two NATO Allies at the Threshold of War: Cyprus: A Firsthand Account of Crisis Management, 1965–1968*. Durham, NC: Duke University Press, 1990.

Herz, Martin F. *215 Days in the Life of an American Ambassador (Diary Notes from Sofia, Bulgaria)*. Washington, DC: School of Foreign Service, Georgetown University. 1981.

Hillenbrand, Martin J. *Fragments of Our Time*. Athens, GA: University of Georgia, 1998.

Holbrooke, Richard, *To End a War*. New York: Modern Library, 1999.

Holdridge, John H. *Crossing the Divide: An Insider's Account of the Normalization of U.S.-China Relations.* Lanham, MD: Rowman & Littlefield, 1997.

Jenkins, Alfred L. *Country, Conscience and Caviar: A Diplomat's Journey in the Company of History.* Seattle, WA: BookPartners, 1993.

Johnson, U. Alexis, with Jef Olivarius McAllister. *The Right Hand of Power.* Englewood Cliffs, NJ: Prentice-Hall, 1984.

Kennen, George F. *Memoirs: 1925-50 and 1950-63.* 2 vols. Boston: Little, Brown, 1967–1972.

Kirk, Roger, and Mircea Raceanu. *Romania Versus the United States: Diplomacy of the Absurd, 1985–1989.* New York: St. Martin's Press, 1994.

Laingen, Bruce. *Yellow Ribbon: The Secret Journal of Bruce Laingen.* Washington, DC: Brassey's 1992.

Mak, Dayton and Kennedy, Charles Stuart. *American Ambassadors in a Troubled World.* Westport, CT: Greenwood, 1992.

Martin, John Bartlow. *Overtaken by Events: The Dominican Crisis from the Fall of Trujillo to the Civil War.* New York: Doubleday, 1966.

Matlock, Jack. *Autopsy on an Empire: The American Ambassador's Account of the Collapse of the Soviet Union.* New York: Random House, 1995.

McNamara, Francis Terry, with Adrian Hill. *Escape with Honor: My Last Hours in Vietnam.* Herndon, VA: Brassey's, 1997.

Melbourne, Roy M. *Conflict and Crisis: A Foreign Service Story.* Lanham, MD: University Press of America, 1993.

Meyer, Armin H. *Assignment: Tokyo: An Ambassador's Journal.* Indianapolis: Bobbs-Merrill, 1974.

Morgan, William D. and Kennedy, Charles Stuart. *The U.S. Consul at Work.* Westport, CT: Greenwood, 1991.

Murphy, Robert D. *Diplomat Among Warriors.* Garden City, NY: Doubleday, 1964. Reprint, Westport, CT: Greenwood, 1976.

Seitz, Raymond. *Over Here*. London: Weidenfeld & Nicolson, 1998.

Simpson, Howard R. *Bush Hat, Black Tie: Adventures of a Foreign Service Officer*. Herndon, VA: Brassey's, 1998.

Spain, James W. *American Diplomacy in Turkey: Memoirs of an American Ambassador Extraordinary and Plenipotentiary*. New York: Praeger, 1984.

———. *In Those Days*. Kent, Ohio: The Kent State University Press, 1998.

Steeves, John M. *Safir (Ambassador)*. Hershey, PA: By the author, 1991.

Sullivan, Joseph G., ed. *Embassies under Siege: Personal Accounts by Diplomats on the Front Line*. Washington, DC: Brassey's, 1995.

Sullivan, William H. *Mission to Iran: The Last Ambassador*. New York: W.W. Norton, 1981.

Thayer, Charles W. *Diplomat*. New York: Harper, 1959. Reprint, Westport, CT: Greenwood, 1974.

———. *Bears in the Caviar*. New York: J.B. Lippencott, 1950.

Tuthill, John Wills. *Some Things to Some Men: Serving in the Foreign Service*. London: Minerva Press, 1996.

Villard, Henry S. *Affairs at State* New York: T.Y. Crowell Co., 1965.

Weil, Martin. *A Pretty Good Club: The Founding Fathers of the U.S. Foreign Service*. New York: Norton, 1978.

Yost, Charles W. *History and Memory: A Statesman's Perceptions of the Twentieth Century*. New York: W.W. Norton, 1980.

Zimmermann, Warren. *Origins of a Catastrophe: Yugoslavia and its Destroyers*. New York: Random House, 1999.

Note: For decades, foreign affairs specialists have produced oral histories, with recent ones having been recorded by the Association for Diplomatic Studies and Training. Edited transcripts are available at Georgetown University's Lauinger Library, on CD-ROM at other university libraries, and at ADST (for information on ADST, see next page).

About ADST

The Association for Diplomatic Studies and Training (ADST) is a non-profit organization, established in 1986. Its purpose is to advance public understanding of foreign relations and the quality of American diplomacy through education.

The Association accomplishes its objectives by:

Creating the Foreign Affairs Oral History Collection, a unique first-person record of modern U.S. foreign relations that is comprehensive, candid, and up to date. Growing by some eighty histories per year, the collection conveys the experiences, analyses, wisdom, and knowledge of both career and non-career foreign affairs practitioners. (Some nine-hundred oral histories are accessible to the public on a CD-ROM.)

Supporting Department of State's National Foreign Affairs Training Center (Foreign Service Institute) seminars and policy conferences that join academics, the private sector and senior officials in discussions of critical foreign relations issues on which policy is being reviewed.

Recognizing, through prizes awarded to Foreign Service Institute instructors, excellence in teaching American civilians and military the many languages needed to carry out effective United States diplomacy.

Developing and presenting museum-quality displays that illuminate the history of American diplomacy.

Sponsoring distinguished diplomatic historians as Scholars-in-Residence at the Foreign Service Institute.

Maintaining a Research Center, producing a book series on diplomats and diplomacy, and providing advice on publishing to serving and former diplomats.

Index

0-595-32974-8

Made in the USA
Middletown, DE
07 December 2020